THOROUGH MARATHI TEACHER

New Enlarged Edition

*Novel scientific way of **making 'your own'** marāṭhī sentences.*

PRIMARY TO INTERMEDIATE MARATHI
with Transliteration

Prof. Ratnakar Narale

Ratnakar
PUSTAK BHARATI
BOOKS-INDIA

Author :

Dr. Ratnakar Narale

B.Sc. (Nagpur Univ.), M.Sc. (Pune Univ.), Ph.D. (IIT), Ph.D. (Kalidas Sanskrit Univ.);
Prof Hindi, Ryerson University, Toronto.
web : www.ratnakar-narale.com * email : ratnakaenarale@gmail.com +1 416 666 6932

Book Title :

Thorough marathi Teacher, New Enlarged Edition.

This methodical book is based on extensive **R&D**, Effective Techniques and Improved Ways beneficial to the Readers to give them proper reture for their investment of Time and Money. The book begins with simple primary steps and moves forward with **authentic examples** coupled with **Progressive Exercises** suitable to each context to bring home the topic being discussed. The Vocabulary and Illustrations are selected carefully to offer a window to the topics, as used in Real Life Situations. You will not find such contemplative work in any Maratthi learning book.

Fonts used in the Book :

Ratnakar-H for marāṭhī typing

Ratnakar-T for Transliteration Typing

Published by :

PUSTAK BHARATI (Books-India)
Division of PC Plus Ltd.,
www.ratnakar-narale.com
email : ratnakarnarale@gmail.com

FOR :

Sanskrit Hindi Research Institute, Toronto

ISBN 978-1-989416-98-3

Dedicated to

Our Loving Grandchildren

Samay, Sahas, Saanjh, Saaya, Naksh, Nyra and Navay Narale

HINDI
TEACHER
FOR
HINDU
CHILDREN
Prof. Ratnakar Narale
Sunita Narale
Ratnakar
Pustak-Bharati
Books-India

Learn Hindi
Through English Medium
IN 20 EASY STEPS
Hindi Level I
Ratnakar Narale

SANSKRIT
PRIMER
Primary to Intermediate
Prof. Ratnakar Narale
Ratnakar
Pustak-Bharati
Books-India

SANSKRIT TEACHER,
All-in-One
With transliteration
For All Levels
ALL IN ONE A-Z
Prof. Ratnakar Narale
Ratnakar
Pustak-Bharati
Books-India
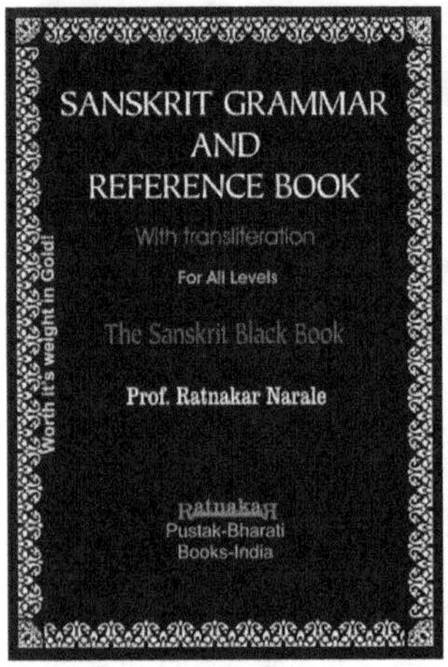
SANSKRIT GRAMMAR
AND
REFERENCE BOOK
With transliteration
For All Levels
The Sanskrit Black Book
Prof. Ratnakar Narale
Worth it's weight in Gold!
Ratnakar
Pustak-Bharati
Books-India

TAMIL
TEACHER
With Transliteration & Devanagari
Primary to Intermediate
Self-Tutor
Prof. Ratnakar Narale
Ratnakar
Pustak-Bharati
Books-India

URDU
TEACHER
With Transliteration & Devanagari
Primary to Intermediate
Self-Tutor
Prof. Ratnakar Narale
Ratnakar
Pustak-Bharati
Books-India

Learn Sanskrit
Through English Medium
Without Transliteration
Ratnakar Narale
SANSKRIT HINDI RESEARCH INSTITUTE

Learn Bengali
Through English / Hindi
With Transliteration & Devanagari
Ratnakar Narale
Self-Tutor

Learn Marathi
Through English / Hindi
With Transliteration & Devanagari
Ratnakar Narale
Self-Tutor

Learn Punjabi
Through English / Hindi
With Transliteration & Devanagari
Ratnakar Narale
Self-Tutor

Learn Gujrati
Through English / Hindi
With Transliteration & Devanagari
Ratnakar Narale
Self-Tutor

GITA AS SHE IS
In Krishna's Own Words
Volume II
(Chapters 3 - 11)
Ratnakar

Gita ka Shabdakosh
Grammatical Dictionary
of the Gita.
गीता का शब्दकोश
और अनुक्रमणी
New Edition
Prof. Ratnakar Narale
Ratnakar
Pustak-Bharati
Books-India

Yoga-Sūtras of Patañjali,
Made Easy
पातञ्जलयोगदर्शनम्
Body Mind & Soul
Prof. Ratnakar Narale

मेरे भजन
MERE BHAJAN
With English Transliteration and Meaning
VOLUME 1
Ratnakar Narale

INDEX

INTRODUCTION

Many children and adults who come from West Indies, Guyana, Suriname, Fiji, Pakistan, America, UK, Canada, Africa and Europe do want to learn marāṭhī. There are many people in India, more so in English Schools and in non-marāṭhī speaking States, who want to learn marāṭhī through English medium.

While learning marāṭhī, one must understand the grammatical aspects such as tenses, cases, gender, person, number etc. step-by-step and only then one can learn marāṭhī properly. Rather than learning pre-made pet sentences, one should understand the basics and learn to make his/her own sentences. Without this, one may speak like हम जाता है *(ham jātā hai),* हम करेगा *(ham karegā)* and मैंने करा *manė karā.* Having understood the grammar, one may still use some English vocabulary and speak like चाय का कप लीजिए *(chāya kā* cup *lījiye)* or यह मेरी कार है *(yah merī* car āhe) ... but it is quite alright for English speaking people. In fact in India it is a fashion to speak the 'Hinglish' language.

While this book is a 'Teach Yourself' manual, it also is a good tool for the teachers who teach marāṭhī to English speaking people. It starts with 'How to Write' the marāṭhī Alphabet and pronounce each character. It is unique in this book, but interesting to note that for teaching the alphabet, the characters are grouped according to their shapes, and not with their usual alphabetical order. It is seen that, with this method it is easy to recognize, relate, differentiate and remember the characters without a mix up.

In this book, the examples and exercises have been given based ONLY on what is learnt in previous steps and pages. The book is filled with virtually thousands of examples, and each dialogue is designed with the view of its practical value for the targetted people.

marāṭhī language being originated from Sanskrit language, introduction to that language becomes automatic while learning marāṭhī. In order to bring this important point to the readres' notice, the Sanskrit words that apprear in the marāṭhī writings in this book, are identified with a dotted underline.

I hope that you will follow this material step-by-step and page-by-page. In order to help new students, English transliteration of marāṭhī terms is provided. However, it is hoped that, at certain stage, you will skip the transliteration and will be comfortable reading the marāṭhī text. Follow the book with this technique and your success in learning marāṭhī will be assured.

NASALIZATION

In order to keep the Marathi Language much easier and more palatable, for the new Marathi learners, Nasal Marks (अनुस्वार) are used as less as possible in this book.

GOOD NEWS

Normally marāṭhī Learning books begin at Lesson 20 of this book, but

Even if you JUST READ **each and every** word of this book, patiently and thoughtfully, you will be able to understand marāṭhī well.

विद्या देवी वंदना

राग : खमाज

(रत्नाकर कृत सरगम सहित)

स्थायी : जै जै स्वरदा माता । देवी नमन तुला आता ।
दर्शन प्रांजळ सुंदर । आशिष पावन मंगल । मागू तुज गाता ।
जैऽ सरऽस्वती माताऽ ।।

♫ म- म- ममम- गमप- । पध निसांसां सांरेंसां निधरे- ।
पधपध नि-निध पधपध । पधपध नि-निध पधमम । पपप- धप मगरे- ।
प- प- पपपधप मगम- ।।

अंतरा-1 : जो मागे गुण तुजला । बुद्धि ज्ञानाचा । देवी ऋद्धि मानाचा ।
श्रद्धा हृदयी जयाला । वाञ्छित मिळुनी तयाला ।
ध्येय सफळ त्याला । जै० ।।

♫ पम मगपम मग पमम-। सांरेंसांनि ध-पमप-। सांसां सांरेंसांनि ध-पमप-।
पधपध नीनीनी धपधम- । पधपध निनिनि धपधम- ।
प-प पधप मगरे- । प- प- पपपधप मगम- ।।

अंतरा-2 : जो मागे सुर तुजला । सुंदर गानाचा । देवी मंजुळ तानेचा ।
संगित नृत्य शिकाया । अभिनय नाट्य शिकायाऽ ।
मार्ग सरळ त्याचा । जै० ।।

अंतरा-3 जो नर आर्त कलेचा । चित्राकारीचा । देवी वास्तुशिल्पाचा ।
चौसष्ट सगळी विद्या । अष्ट सिद्धीची लीला ।
प्राप्त सकळ त्याला । जै० ।।

अंतरा-4 : जो कवि गायक लेखक । वाङ्मय विरचेता । देवी सरगम रचयेता ।
साहित्य साधन त्याला । बुद्धि चे धन त्याला ।
हेऽतु सबळ त्याचा । जै० ।।

अंतरा-5 : जो शिक्षक नर ज्ञानी, बाण्याचा मानी । देवी विद्येचा वाणी ।
सेवा हृदयी ज्याच्या, ठेवा सात्त्विक ज्याचा,
हात सढळ त्याचा । जै० ।।

अंतरा-6 : शुभ्र वसन नथ माळा । काजळ तिळ काळा । देवी मुकुट मणी नीळा ।
केयुर कंठी चाळा । कुंदन गजरा पिवळा ।
रंग तुझा ढवळा । जै० ।।

अंतरा-7 : नारद किन्नर शंकर । तुमचे गुण गाती । देवी तुमचे ऋण ध्याती ।
शरण जो चरणी आला । भजन हे स्मरणी ज्याला ।
मोक्ष अटळ त्याला । जै० ।।

(ह्या भजनाच्या हारमोनियम सुर तालिकेकरिता लेखकाला लिहा)

HINDI
TEACHER
FOR
HINDU
CHILDREN
Prof. Ratnakar Narale
Sunita Narale
Ratnakar
Pustak-Bharati
Books-India

KNOW THIS BEFORE YOU BEGIN

हे ध्यानात असू द्या

1. marāṭhī is a Phonetic Language, while English is a Spelling Based Language. There are no spellings for the marāṭhī words, rather we write sounds represented by letters of consonants, vowels and the vowel signs. As you pronounce it, so you write it, syllable by syllable.
2. In English each letter is written capital or small. marāṭhī has only one kind of letters (अक्षर).
3. marāṭhī has 15 Vowel Sounds and 34 Consonant Sounds, arranged systematically in the Chart of Alphabet, as shown in Lesson 1, below.
4. As compared to Hindi Alphabet, marāṭhī has three extra sounds, अॅ, ऑ and ळ. Many Hindi writers have started using ऑ sound for writing words like डॉक्टर. The Devanagari letter ळ you can find in the first Sanskrit verse of the Rig Veda (अग्निमिळे पुरोहित).
5. A vowel is a letter that can be pronounced independently. A consonant is a letter which can not be pronounced without adding at least one vowel to it. A consonant without adding any vowel is called a **Half Consonant**. The consonant with added vowel is called a **Full Consonant**. Vowel अ is the Default Vowel that is added to each consonant so that each consonant in the chart of Alphabet can be read easily and comfortably.
6. In order to add Vowels to the Consonants, each vowel is symbolized by a Vowel Sign (मात्रा) which must be attached either over, below, on left side or on the right side of a consonant, depending up on that vowel sign.
7. When a vowel comes after a consonant, that vowel must be written in its vowel sign (मात्रा) form attached to that consonant. One consonant can take only one vowel sign, not more.
8. If a word begins with a vowel, that vowel must be written in its letter (अक्षर) form, not in its sign (मात्रा) form. When two vowels come in a row, the Second Vowel must be written in its letter form, not in its sign (मात्रा) form. e.g. *āī* आई (mother), *bāī* बाई (woman), etc.
9. The first 25 Consonants from k (क) to m (म) are called Class Consonants. These 25 consonants are divided in five classes. (1). k (क) class - from k (क) to ṅ (ङ); (2). ch (च) class - from ch (च) to ṅ (ञ); (3). ṭ (ट) class - from ṭ (ट) to ṇ (ण); (4). t (त) class - from t (त) to n (न); and (5). p (प) class - from p (प) to ṅ (म). In each class of 5 consonants, the first two consonants are Hard Consonants and the next three consonants are Soft Consonants.
10. The rest of the 9 consonants make up a mixed group. Please refer to the table shown below in Lesson 1, "The marāṭhī Alphabet."

LESSON 1

पहिला पाठ

मराठी वर्णमाला

THE MARATHI ALPHABET

marāṭhī Vowels :

अ	आ	इ	ई	उ	ऊ	ऋ	ए	ऐ	ओ	औ	अॅ	ऑ	अं	अः
a	ā	i	ī	u	ū	ru	e	ai	o	au	ă	ằ	ṁ	ḥ

marāṭhī Half Consonants :

क्	ख्	ग्	घ्	ङ्
k	kh	g	gh	ṅ
च्	छ्	ज्	झ्	ञ्
ch	chh	j	jh, z	ñ
ट्	ठ्	ड्	ढ्	ण्
ṭ	ṭh	ḍ	ḍh	ṇ
त्	थ्	द्	ध्	न्
t	th	d	dh	n
प्	फ्	ब्	भ्	म्
p	ph, f	b	bh	m
य्	र्	ल्	व्	
y	r	l	v, w	
श्	ष्	स्	ह्	ळ
ś́h, sh	ṣ, sḥ	s	h	ḷ

adj∘ = Adjective, adv∘ = Adverb; *conj.* = Conjunction, f∘ = Feminine gender, *ind.* = Indeclinable, m∘ = Masculine gender, n∘ = Neuter gender, pl∘ = Plural

LESSON 2

दूसरा पाठ : मराठी वर्ण

MARATHI FULL CONSONANTS

(Please see the colourful chart on the Back Cover of this book, for more details)

The Class Consonants :

क	ख	ग	घ	ङ
ka	kha	ga	gha	ṅa (nga)
च	छ	ज	झ	ञ
cha	Chha	ja	jha, za	ña
ट	ठ	ड	ढ	ण
ṭa	ṭha	ḍa	ḍha	ṇa
त	थ	द	ध	न
ta	tha	da	dha	na
प	फ	ब	भ	म
pa	pha, fa	ba	bha	ma

The non-Class Consonants :

य	र	ल	व	
ya	ra	la	va, wa	
श	ष	स	ह	ळ
śha, sha	ṣa, ṣha	sa	ha	ḷa

Special Compound Characterss :

क्ष	त्र	ज्ञ	
kṣa	tra	dnya	(Sanskrit pronounciation is *jña*)

LESSON 3

तीसरा पाठ : मराठी उच्चर

SPEAKING THE MARATHI CHARACTERS

Alphabet	marāṭhī	Sounds like, as in	
a	(अ)	a in	particular
ā	(आ)	a in	pāpā
i	(इ)	I in	pin
ī	(ई)	ee in	peel
u	(उ)	u in	pull , put
ū	(ऊ)	oo in	pool
ru	(ऋ)	ru in	ruin
e	(ए)	e, ay in	pen, pay
ai	(ऐ)	i, ai in	Spine,Saigaon
o	(ओ)	o in	pole
au	(औ)	ow, au in	powder, sauna
k	(क्)	k in	pink
kh	(ख्)	kh in	Khyber
g	(ग्)	g in	peg
gh	(घ्)	gh in	ghost
ṅ	(ङ्)	n in	packing
ch	(च्)	ch in	chop
chh	(छ्)	chh i	witch-hunt
j	(ज्)	j in	jump
jh, z	(झ्)	dgeh in	hedgehop
ñ	(ञ्)	n in	puñch
ṭ	(ट्)	t in	pet
ṭh	(ठ्)	th in	hot-house
ḍ	(ड्)	d in	pod
ḍh	(ढ्)	dh in	adhere
ṇ	(ण्)	n in	pant
t	(त्)	t in	Istanbul
th	(थ्)	th in	panther
d	(द्)	th in	other
dh	(ध्)	dh in	Buddha
n	(न्)	n in	pen
p	(प्)	p in	pup
ph,f	(फ्)	ph, f in	photo-frame
b	(ब्)	b in	pub
bh	(भ्)	bh in	abhore
m	(म्)	m in	map
y	(य्)	y in	yes, yelp
r	(र्)	r in	rip
l	(ल्, ळ्)	l in	lip
v,w	(व्)	v, w in	Volkswagon
ś́h, sh	(श्)	sh in	shop
ṣ	(ष्)	sh in	push
s	(स्)	s in	soap
h	(ह्)	h in	hop

ORGANS of PONOUNCIATION

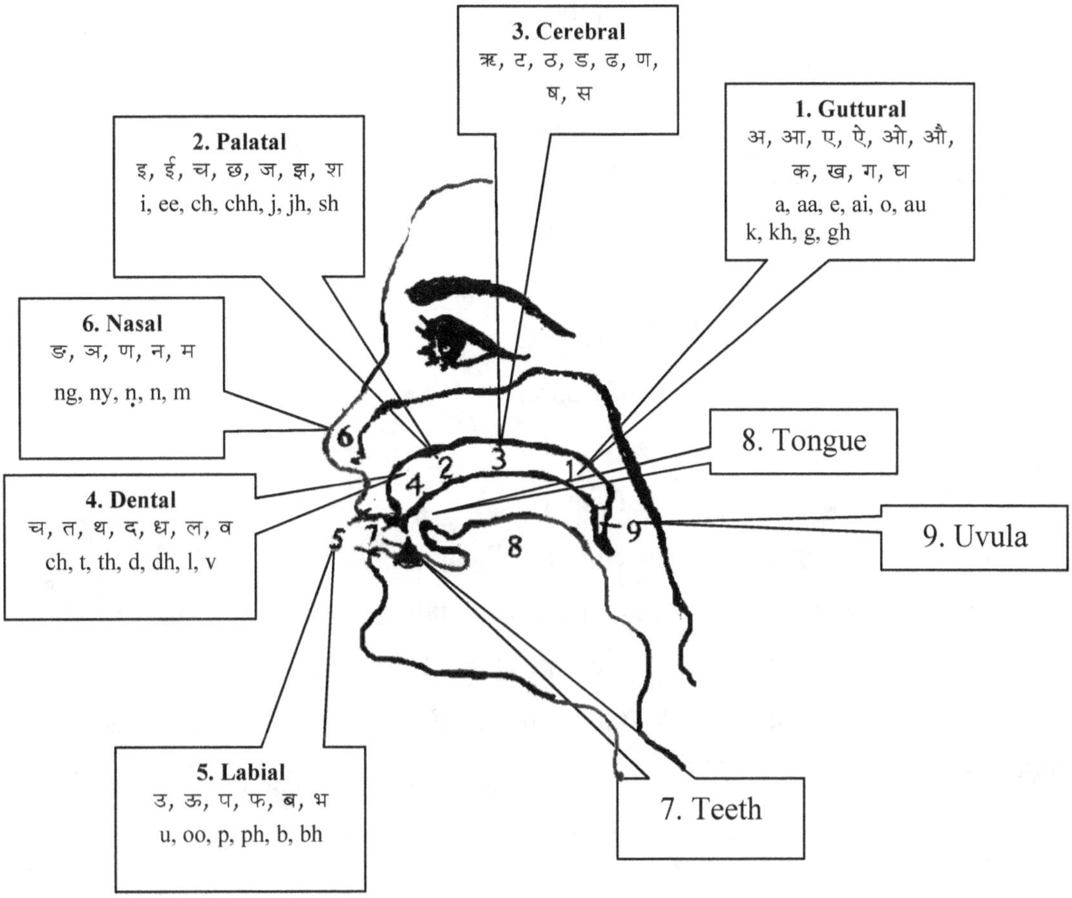

(1) Guttural	कण्ठ्य	*(kaṇṭhya)*	=	with throat
(2) Palatal	तालव्य	*(tālavya)*	=	with palate
(3) Cerebral	मूर्धन्य	*(mūrdhanya)*	=	with cerebrum
(4) Dental	दन्त्य	*(dantya)*	=	with teeth
(5) Labial	ओष्ठ्य	*(oṣhṭhya)*	=	with lips
(6) Nasal	अनुनासिक	*(anunāsik)*	=	with nose

adj∘ = Adjective, adv∘ = Adverb; *conj.* = Conjunction, f∘ = Feminine gender, *ind.* = Indeclinable, m∘ = Masculine gender, n∘ = Neuter gender, pl∘ = Plural

(1) THE VOWELS :

Vowel	Stands for	Sounds like	As in	Pronunciation
a	(अ)	A	American	Guttural
ā	(आ)	a	car	Guttural
i	(इ)	I	India	Palatal
ī	(ई)	ee	peel	Palatal
u	(उ)	u	pull	Labial
ū	(ऊ)	oo	pool	Labial
ri	(ऋ)	ri, ru	ring, crucial	Cerebral
rí	(ॠ)	rī, rū		Cerebral
lri	(ऌ)	lri, lru		Dental
lrí	(ॡ)	lrī, lrū		Dental
e	(ए)	e	grey	Guttural+Palatal
ai	(ऐ)	ai	aisle	Guttural+Palatal
o	(ओ)	o	go	Guttural+Labial
au	(औ)	au	gauge	Guttural+Labial

(2) THE SEMIVOWELS :

ḿ	(अं)	ã		nasal
:	(अः)	half-h		breath

(3) THE CONSONANTS :

Consonant	Stands for	Sounds like	As in	Pronunciation
k	(क्)	k	kit	Guttural
kh	(ख्)	kh	khyber	Guttural
g	(ग्)	g	god	Guttural
gh	(घ्)	gh	ghost	Guttural
ṅ	(ङ्)	n	ring	Guttural
ch	(च्)	ch	rich	Palatal
chh	(छ्)	chh	ch with breath	Palatal
j	(ज्)	j	jug	Palatal
jh	(झ्)	dgeh	zoo	Palatal
ñ	(ञ्)	n	hinge	Palatal

adj∘ = Adjective, adv∘ = Adverb; *conj.* = Conjunction, f∘ = Feminine gender, *ind.* = Indeclinable, m∘ = Masculine gender, n∘ = Neuter gender, pl∘ = Plural

ṭ	(ट्)	t	cuṭ	Cerebral
ṭh	(ठ्)	th	ṭ with breath	Cerebral
ḍ	(ड्)	d	red	Cerebral
ḍh	(ढ्)	dh	adhere	Cerebral
ṇ	(ण्)	n	band	Cerebral
t	(त्)	t	(soft t)	Dental
th	(थ्)	th	path	Dental
d	(द्)	th	other	Dental
dh	(ध्)	dh	Buddha	Dental
n	(न्)	n	no	Dental
p	(प्)	p	cup	Labial
ph	(फ्)	ph, f	photo	Labial
b	(ब्)	b	rub	Labial
bh	(भ्)	bh	abhore	Labial
m	(म्)	m	mug	Labial
y	(य्)	y	yes	Palatal
r	(र्)	r	rub	Cerebral
l	(ल्, ल्)	l	love	Dental
v	(व्)	v, w	wave	Dental + Labial
ś́h	(श्)	sh	shoot	Palatal
ṣh	(ष्)	sh	should	Cerebral
s	(स्)	s	sun	Dental
h	(ह्)	h	hug	Guttural
ḷ	(ळ्)	soft l		Cerebral

adj∘ = Adjective, adv∘ = Adverb; *conj.* = Conjunction, f∘ = Feminine gender, *ind.* = Indeclinable, m∘ = Masculine gender, n∘ = Neuter gender, pl∘ = Plural

Organs of Pronunciation

(1) GUTTURALS are अ, आ, क्, ख्, ग्, घ्, ङ्, ह् *(a, ā,, k, kh, g, gh, ṅ, h).*

They are pronounced from the **throat**

(2) PALATALS are इ, ई, च्, छ्, ज्, झ्, ञ्, य्, श् *i, ī, ch, chh, j, jh, ñ, y, śh.*

They are pronounced from the **palate**

(3) CEREBRALS are ऋ, ॠ, ट्, ठ्, ड्, ढ्, ण्, र्, ष् *ri rī, ṭ, ṭh, ḍ, ḍh, ṇ, r, ṣh.*

They are pronounced from the **roof of the mouth**

(4) DENTALS are ऌ, (ॡ), त्, थ्, द्, ध्, न्, ल्, स् *lri, (lrī), t, th, d, dh, n, l, s.*

They are pronounced from the **teeth**

(5) LABIALS are उ, ऊ, प्, फ्, ब्, भ्, म् *u, ū, p, ph, b, bh, m.*

They are pronounced from the **lips.** Character व *v* is dental-labial; ए, ऐ *e, ai* are guttural-palatal, ओ, औ *o, au* are guttural-labials and व *v* is dental-labial.

(6) THE **HARD** CONSONANTS

The first two consonants from each class (क्, ख्; च्, छ्; ट्, ठ्; त्, थ्; प्, फ् *k, kh, ch, chh, ṭ, ṭh, t, th, p, ph*) and three sibilants (श्, ष्, स् स्ँह, *ṣh, s*) are Hard Consonants (*kaṭhor vyañjan* कठोर व्यंजन).

(7) THE **SOFT** CONSONANTS

The rest of the consonants, namely, the last three consonants from each class (ग्, घ्, ङ्; ज्, ज्, ञ्; ड्, ढ्, ण्; द्, ध्, न्; ब्, भ्, म् *g, gh, ṅ, j, jh, ñ, ḍ, ḍh, ṇ, d, dh, n, b, bh, m*), the semi-vowels (य्, र्, ल्, व् *y, r, l, v*) and the aspirate (ह् *h*) are Soft Consonants (*mridu vyañjan* मृदु व्यंजन).

(8) THE **NASAL** CONSONANTS

The last character from each of the five classes ṅ, ñ, ṇ, n, m (ङ्, ञ्, ण्, न्, म्), are the Nasal Consonants (*anunāsik* अनुनासिक).

CHARACTERS WRITING GUIDE

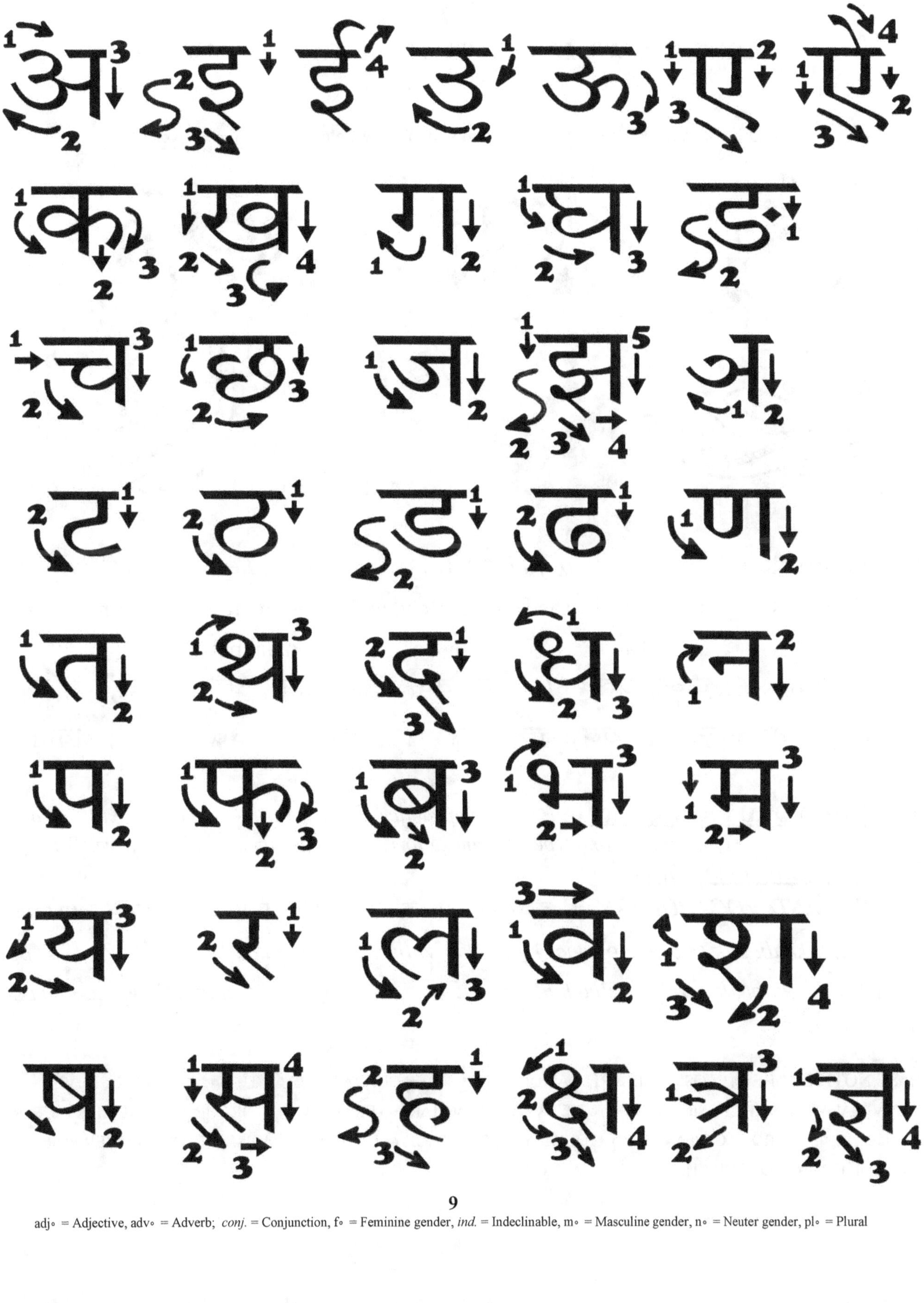

LESSON 4

चौथा पाठ

READING AND WRITING SIMPLE MARATHI CONSONANTS

(4.1) व va, ब ba, क ka (Shown with Yellow Colour on the Back Cover)

va

ba

ka

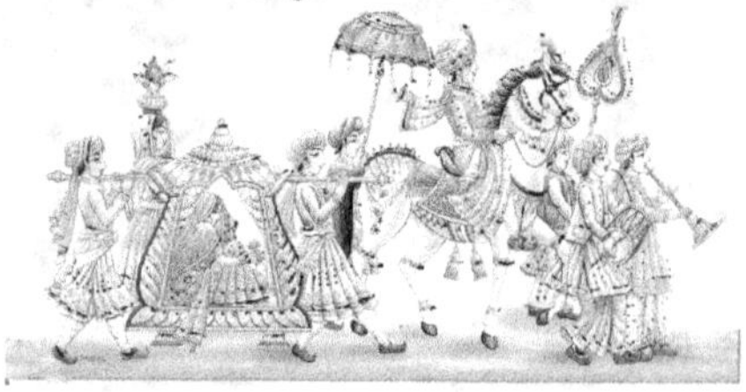

vimān (airplane) *bājā* (music) *keḷ* (banana)

EXERCISE 1 : (Only on what we learned so far) Read and Write the following in marāṭhī :

1. ka ba ka 2. ba va ka 3. va ba ka 4. kaba, baka

5. कब, बक 6. कक, वब 7. वब, वक 8. कक, बव 9. क, ब, व,

10. कक, कब, कव 11. बब, बक, वव 12. कबव, कवब, वबक, बकव

MARATHI WORD PROCESSING : *For typing practice in mara@t<h&, either use Unicode or install the Ratnakar font on your PC and type the items 5 to 12. Compare them as shown here.* ***Do it for all Exercises given in this book.***

ANSWERS AND VOCABULARY: *1. क ब क 2. ब व क 3. व ब क 4. कब, बक (a crane or duck) 5. kab, bak (a crane or duck) 6. kaka, vaba 7. vaba, vaka 8. kaka, bava 9. k, ba, va 10. kaka, kaba, kava 11. baba, baka (crane or duck), vava 12. kabava, kavaba, vabaka, bakava.*

PLEASE NOTICE : THE (i) CLOSE SIMILARITY AMONG THE THREE CHARACTERS OF THE व, ब, क GROUP GIVEN ABOVE. Also notice, (ii) CLOSE SIMILARITY BETWEEN THE CHARACTERS OF व, ब क GROUP AND THE CHARACTERS OF THE प, ष, फ GROUP GIVEN BELOW. YOU MAY DO SAME FOR ALL SHAPE GROUPS. SEE BACK COVER FOR COLOUR CODING OF THE CHARACTER SHAPE GROUPS.

adj∘ = Adjective, adv∘ = Adverb; *conj.* = Conjunction, f∘ = Feminine gender, *ind.* = Indeclinable, m∘ = Masculine gender, n∘ = Neuter gender, pl∘ = Plural

(4.2) प pa, ष ṣa, फ pha (Shown with Light Green Colour on the Back Cover)

pa

ṣa

pha, fa

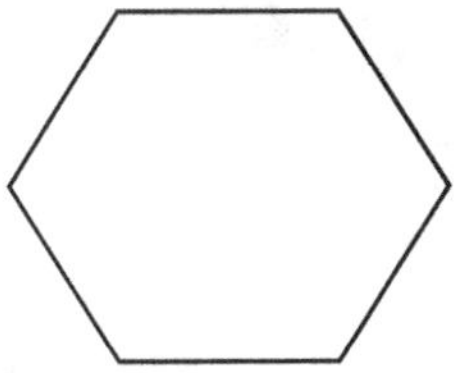

puṣhpa (flower) *ṣaṭakoṇa* (hexagon) *faṭfaṭī* (m. bike)

EXERCISE 2 : (only on what we learned so far, the 'cumulative learning')

Read and Write the following in marāṭhī :

1. kapa, ka 2. paṣa, kaṣa 3. pha, ba, ka, ṣa, pa, pava 4. bakabaka, kaba

5. पव, पफ 6. कप, कब 7. कष, पष, कफ 8. वफ, वब, पफब

ANSWERS and VOCABULARY: *1. कप, क 2. पष, कष 3. फ, ब, क, ष, प, पव 4. बकबक (chatter), कब 5. pava, papha 6. kap (cup), kab 7. kaṣa, paṣa, kaph (cough) 8. vapha, vaba, paphaba.*

(4.3) त ta, न na, ग ga, म ma, भ bha, ण ṇa (Shown with White Colour on the Back Cover)

ta

na

ga

tablā (Drum) *nāg* (cobra) *gāy* (cow)

ma

bha

ṇa

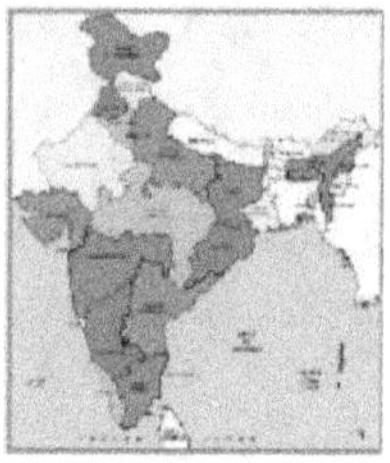

mātā-pitā (māmā-pāpā) *bhārat* (India) *bāṇa* (arrow)

EXERCISE 3 : (only on what we learned so far, the 'cumulative learning') Read and Write the following.

1. क, ब, व, ब 2. कक, कब, कव 3. बब, बक 4. वव, वक, वब 5. कबव, कवब 6. वबक, बकव 7. म, न, त 8. तत, तन 9. कक, वब 10. गबन, भव, मगन, वतन, वन, वमन, कम, नभ, नव, नमन, तब, बम, मनन 11. ष, प, फ, म, भ, न, त, वतन, भगत, गमन, मनन, पवन.

ANSWERS AND VOCABULARY: *1. ka, ba, va, ba 2. kaka, kaba, kava 3. baba, baka 4. vava, vaka, vaba 5. kabava, kavaba 6. vabaka, bakava 7. ma, na, ta 8. tata, tan (body) 9. kaka, vaba 10. gaban (embezzlement), bhava (world), magan, vatan (motherland), van (forest), vaman (vomit), kam (less), nabh (sky), nav (new), naman (salute), tab, bam, manan (meditation) 11. ṣha, pa, pha , ma, bha, na, ta, vatan (motherland), bhagat (devotee), gaman (going), manan (contemplation), pavan (wind).*

(4.4) च cha, ज ja, ञ ña, ल la (Shown with Light Orange Colour on the Back Cover)

cha *ja* *ña* *la*

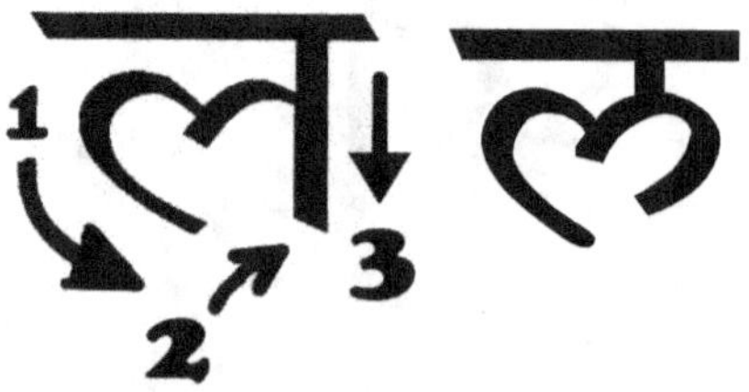

chākū (knife) *jahāj* (ship) *lasūṇ* (garlic)

NOTE : Character ñ (ञ्) is rarely used in marāṭhī. It is mostly used in Sanskrit language.

adj∘ = Adjective, adv∘ = Adverb; *conj.* = Conjunction, f∘ = Feminine gender, *ind.* = Indeclinable, m∘ = Masculine gender, n∘ = Neuter gender, pl∘ = Plural

EXERCISE 4 : (only on what we learned so far) Read and Write the following in marāṭhī :

1. कप, चमचम 2. तन, मन, गगन 3. भगत, पतन, मनन 4. भव, गण, गणक 5. नल, लगन 6. पलक, बन, पग, गम 7. जल, चल, मल 8. कण, कल, पल 9. मत, तम

ANSWERS AND VOCABULARY: *1. kap (cup), chamcham (a sweet) 2. tan (body), man (mind), gagan (sky) 3. bhagat (devotee), patan (downfall), manan (contemplation) 4. bhav (world), gaṇ (class), gaṇak (computer) 5. nal, lagan (devotion) 6. palak (wink), ban, pag, gam 7. jal (water), chal (let us go), mal (dirt) 8. kaṇ (particle), kal (inclination), pal (moment) 9. mat (voye), tam (darkness)*

IMPORTANT NOTE : In marāṭhī the letters च and ज have two sounds. **(1)** soft dental च as in the words चकली, चांगला, चटका, चढाई, चादर, चून, चाफा, चरखा, चल, चव, चळवळ; जखम, जड, जात, जरा, जवळ, जसा, जहाज, etc; and **(2)** the hard palatal च, as in the words चक्र, चणे, चिता, चंद्र, चीन, चुपचाप, चिमटा, चार, चिलखत, चिवडा, चश्मा, चहा; जग, जठर, जप, जय, जिरे, जीव, etc.

(4.5) घ gha, ध dha, छ chha (Shown with Light Blue Colour on the Back Cover)

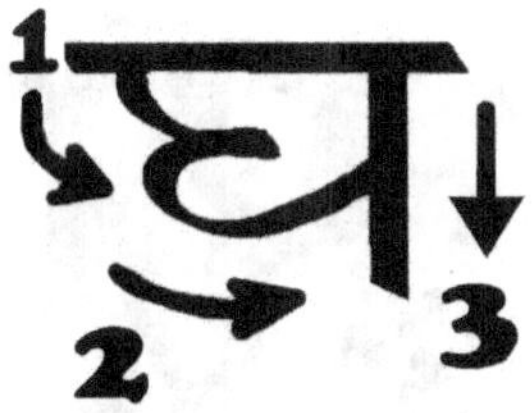

gha

dha

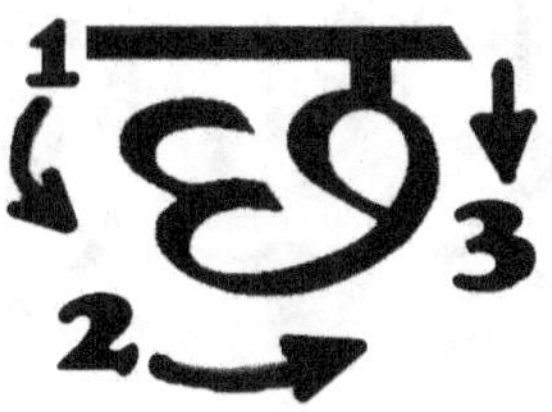

chha

ghar (house)

dhan (wealth)

chhatra (Umbrella)

adj∘ = Adjective, adv∘ = Adverb; *conj.* = Conjunction, f∘ = Feminine gender, *ind.* = Indeclinable, m∘ = Masculine gender, n∘ = Neuter gender, pl∘ = Plural

EXERCISE 5, on what is covered up to 4.6 : Read and Write the following characters.

1. ज, च, ञ 2. ल, ज, च 3. क, ल 4. गणक, जलज 5. च, ज, ल, 6. र, स, ख, श 7. रस, शर, रख, सच 8. सन, फल 9. कमल, सरल 10. शतक, फरक, परख, भरत, चमन, शकल 11. लगन, वजन, सब, सच 12. बम, बरफ, चपल 13. मगज, जल, खल, नर, पर, सम 14. चमक, चल, चख 15. जज, छल, जग, घर 16. धन, कब, वध, शक, मगज

ANSWERS AND VOCABULARY : *1. ja, ca, ña 2. la, ja, cha 3. ka, la 4. gaṇak (counter), jalaj (aquatic) 5. cha, ja, la 6. ra, sa, kha, śha 7. ras (juice), śhar (arrow), rakh, sach 8. san (year), fal (fruit) 9. kamal (lotus), saral (easy) 10. śhatak (century), farak (difference), parakh (assay), bharat, chaman, śhakal 11. lagan, vajan (weight), sab, sach (truth) 12. bam, baraf (ice), chapal (quick) 13. magaj, jal (water), khal (enemy), nar (man), par (other), sam (equal) 14. chamak (shine), chal (let us go), chakha 15. jaj (judge), chhal (deception), jag (world), ghar (house) 16. dhan (wealth), kab, vadh (murder), śhak (doubt), magaj..*

(4.6) र ra, स sa, ख kha, श śha (Shown with Grey Colour on the Back Cover)

ra

sa

kha

śha

rupayā (Rupee)

sāp (snake)

khag (bird)

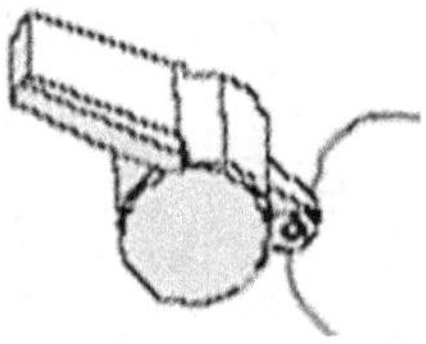

śhiṭī (whistle)

adj∘ = Adjective, adv∘ = Adverb; *conj.* = Conjunction, f∘ = Feminine gender, *ind.* = Indeclinable, m∘ = Masculine gender, n∘ = Neuter gender, pl∘ = Plural

(4.7) य ya, थ tha (Shown with Greenish Yellow Colour on the Back Cover)

y a *tha*

yadnya (ceremonial fire) *thāḷī* (plate)

EXERCISE 6 : (only on what we learned so far) Read and Write the following in marāṭhī :

1. घर, मत, रथ, धन 2. घन, फल, कल, वश, कर, सम, नरम 3. सब, जय
4. भय, शयन, चलन, रण, फसल, सरल 5. धर, जल

ANSWERS AND VOCABULARY : *1. ghar (house), mat (vote), rath (chariot), dhan (wealth) 2. ghan (dense), fal (fruit), kal (tendency), vash (in control), kar (do), sam (same), naram (soft) 3. sab (all), jay (victory) 4. bhay (fear), śhayan (sleep), chalan (behaviour), raṇ (battlefield), fasal (crop), saral (straight) 5. dhar (hold), jal (water)*

(4.8) ṭa ट, ṭha ठ, ḍha ढ, da द, ḍa ड, ṅa ड, jha झ, ha ह

(Shown with Red Colour on the Back Cover)

ṭa *ṭha* *ḍha* *da*

ṭarabūj (watermelon) *ṭhasā* (stamp) *ḍhag* (cloud) *divā* (lamp)

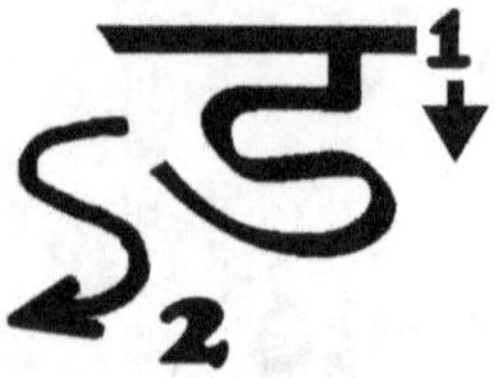

ḍa

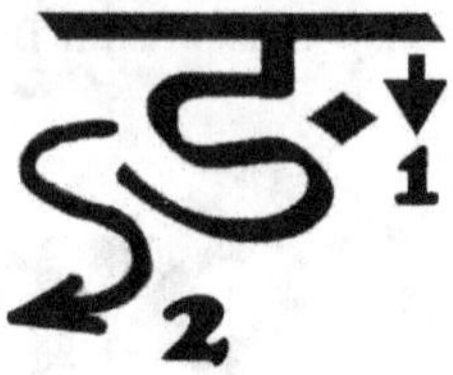

ṅa

jha

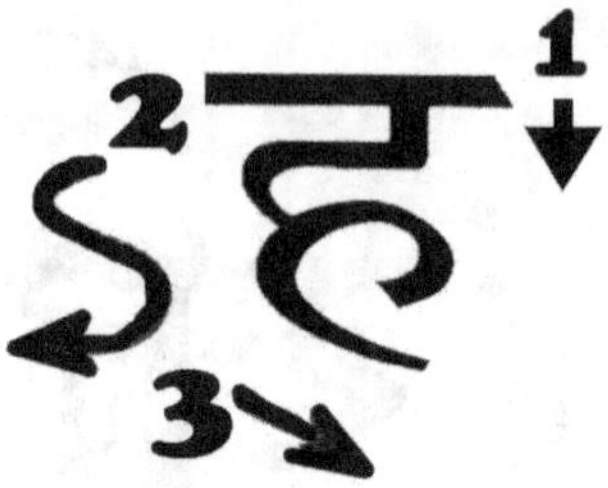

ha

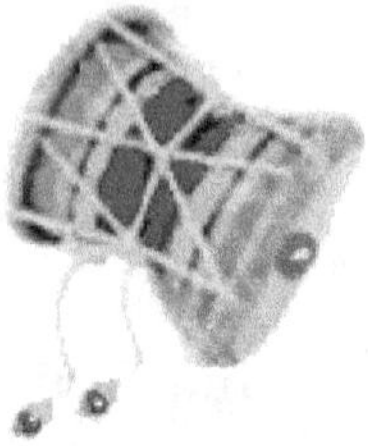

ḍamru (drum)

jhaṇḍā (flag)

hattī (elephant)

EXERCISE 7 : (only on what we learned so far, the 'cumulative learning')

Read and Write the following in marāṭhī :

1. ट, ठ, ढ, ढ, द 2. ड, ड, ङ, झ 3. झ, ह, झ 4. दल, टब, ढल, बन 5. डबल, डर 6. दहन, कदम 7. बदन, बदल, मठ 8. हठ, मत 9. कम, तट, बरगद 10. सब, हम, गम

ANSWERS AND VOCABULARY *: 1. ṭa, ṭha, ḍha, ḍha, da 2. ḍa, ḍa, ṅa, jha 3. jha, ha, jha 4. dal (group), ṭab (tub), ḍhal, ban (become) 5. ḍabal (double), ḍar (fear) 6. dahan (burning), kadam (step) 7. badan (body), badal (change) maṭh (ashram, abode) 8. haṭh, mat (vote) 9. kam (less), taṭ (rampart), baragad (Banyan tree) 10. sab (all), ham, gam.*

(4.9) The Compound Consonants : क्ष kṣa, त्र tra, ज्ञ gya (jña) (Shown with Pink Colour on the Back Cover)

kṣa

tra

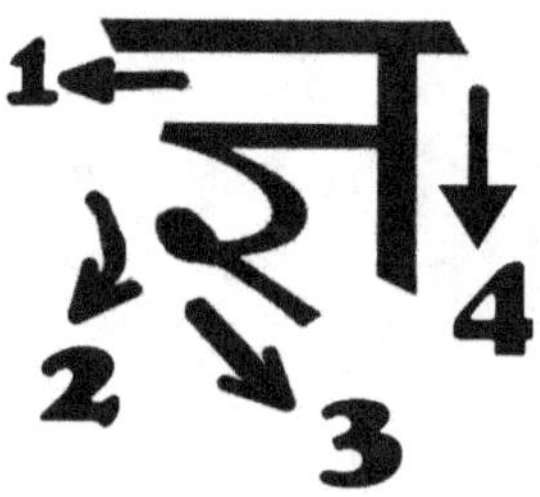

jña

NOTE : क्ष, त्र and ज्ञ *(kṣa, tra, and jña)* are compound characters, they are not alphabet.

adj◦ = Adjective, adv◦ = Adverb; *conj.* = Conjunction, f◦ = Feminine gender, *ind.* = Indeclinable, m◦ = Masculine gender, n◦ = Neuter gender, pl◦ = Plural

(4.9) Anuswāra, Chandrabindu and the Visarga - अं ṁ, अँ ṁ, अः ḥ

अं　　　　अँ　　　　अः

aṁ　　　　*ã*　　　　*aḥ*

EXERCISE 8 : Read and Write the following marāṭhī words :

1. अं (*aṁ*) अः (*aḥ*) 2. कंबल (*kambal* blanket) बंदर (*bandar* monkey) वंश (*vaṁsh* linage) पंकज (*pañkaj* lotus) 3. अंग (*aṅg* body) नंबर (*nambar* number) अनंत (*anant* endless) कंठ (*kaṇṭh* throat) 4. मंत्र (*mantra* a spell) दंड (*daṇd* stick) रंग (*raṅg* colour) 5. संग (*saṅg* union) संशय (*saṁśhay* doubt) हंस (*haṁsa* swan) लंच (*lañch* luñch) 6. अंतर (*antar* distance) स्वतः (*svataḥ* oneself) 7. चंदन (*chandan* sandlewood) कंप (*kamp* tremor) पतंग (*pataṅg* kite) खंदक (*khandak* moat) खंजर (*khañjar* dagger) मंजन (*mañjan* dentifrice) कंगन (*kaṅgan* bracelet) सः (*saḥ* he) 8. गंधक (*gandhak* sulphur) ठंडक (*ṭhandak* cold) डंठल (*ḍaṇṭhal* stem) ढंग (*ḍhaṅg* mode) तरंग (*taraṅg* wave) शंख (*śhaṅkh* coñch) संचय (*sañchay* accumulation) 9. अंब (*amb* mother) जंगल (*jaṅgal* jungle) मंच (*mañch* dias) अंबर (*ambar* sky) लंडन (*lanḍan* London) 10. बंपर (*bampar* bumper) अंदर (*andar* inside) छंद (*chand* meter) बंद (*band* closed) वंदन (*vandan* salute) मंद (*mand* slow) संघ (*sangh* group)

ँ

ã

(A) CHARACTERS WITH CHANDRABINDI :

कां (*kā̃* why?), चांद (*chā̃nd* moon), हां (*hā̃* yes), मां (*mā̃* mother).

NOTE: The ँ sign is just a slight nasal tone added to the syllable below that ँ

adj∘ = Adjective, adv∘ = Adverb; *conj.* = Conjunction, f∘ = Feminine gender, *ind.* = Indeclinable, m∘ = Masculine gender, n∘ = Neuter gender, pl∘ = Plural

DIVINITY IN THE DEVANAGARI CHARACTERS

ॐ	प्रणव, मंगल, ब्रह्म	**ट**	पृथ्वी, वीणा
अ	अमृत, ब्रह्मा, विष्णु, वैश्वानर, शिव	**ठ**	शून्य, शिव, देव, मूर्ति, आकाश मंडल
आ	महादेव, लक्ष्मी	**ड**	शिव, मृदंग, वाडवाग्नि
इ	कामदेव	**ढ**	परमेश्वर, ध्वनि, साप, ढोल, कुत्ता
ई	कामदेव	**ण**	शिव, बुद्ध, दान, ज्ञान, गहना
उ	ब्रह्मा, शिव, चंद्रबिंब	**त**	अमृत, रत्न, योद्धा, छाती, गर्भाशय
ऊ	चंद्रमा, शिव	**थ**	पर्वत, मंगल, रक्षा
ऋ	अदिति, देवमाता	**द**	दात, दाता, पर्वत, पत्नी
ॠ	दानव माता, देवमाता, भैरव	**ध**	धन, ब्रह्मा, कुबेर, धर्म
ऌ	देवमाता, पर्वत, भूमि	**न**	गणेश, मोती, धन, युद्ध
ॡ	देवमाता, नारी आत्मा, कामधेनु, शिव	**प**	वायु, पत्र, अंडा, रक्षक, राजा
ए	विष्णु, दया, स्मरण	**फ**	उष्णता, फूक, फुत्कार
ऐ	शिव	**ब**	वरुण, समुद्र, जल, योनि,
ओ	ब्रह्म	**भ**	सूर्य, राशिचक्र
औ	संकल्प	**म**	ब्रह्म, विष्णु, शिव, यम, चंद्र, जल, काल, विष, सुख
क	ब्रह्म, विष्णु, कामदेव, अग्नि, पवन, यम, सूर्य, मयूर, मेघ, मन, समय, यम, राजा, पक्षी, स्वर, हर्ष, जल, शिर	**य**	वायु, योग, त्याग, प्रकाश, कीर्ति, संयम
क्ष	विष्णु, विद्युत, क्षेत्र, किसान	**र**	देवता, अग्नि, प्रेम, स्वर्ण, वेग
ख	आकाश, स्वर्ग, सूर्य, शून्य, अनुस्वार, ज्ञान, इन्द्रिय, आनंद, अबरक, ब्राह्मण	**ल**	लघु, दस काल लकार
ग	गणेश, गंधर्व, गीत, गुरु	**व**	पवन, समुद्र, राहु, वृक्ष, मदिरा, वस्त्र
घ	घंटी	**श**	शिव, हर्ष
ङ	भैरव	**ष**	मुक्ति, मोक्ष, सर्वोत्तम
च	चंद्र	**स**	विष्णु, शिव, चंद्र, साप, पवन, पक्षी, आत्मा, ज्ञान, चिंतन
छ	स्वच्छ, अंश	**ह**	ब्रह्म, जल, आकाश, रक्त, शून्य, स्वर्ग शुभ, गर्व, वैद्य, अश्व, युद्ध, अस्त्र, आनंद पापहरण, कारण, प्रसिद्धि
ज	जनक, जन्म, विष, विष्णु, मोक्ष, कान्ति		
ज्ञ	ब्रह्मा, आत्मा, बुध, मंगल, बुद्धि		
झ	बृहस्पति, झंझावात		
ञ	शुक्र, संगीत		

LESSON 5

पाचवा पाठ : मराठी स्वर

LEARNING THE MARATHI VOWELS

(5.1) अ a, आ ā, ओ o, औ au   इ i, ई ī

अ a   आ ā   ओ o   औ au   इ i   ई ī

EXERCISE 9 : (only on what we learned so far) Read and then Write the following in marāṭhī:

1. आ, ओ, औ, आई 2. आ, अ, औ, आज 3. ओ, औ, ओढ 4. अबब, अक्षर 5. ओम्, औत, ओक 6. ओठ, ओम्, अज्ञ 7. अघ, औरस, आग, आस, आह, आज, औरत, अंबर, अज, अंश, ओघ 8. इ, ई, इख 9. काय, नवा, ईश 10. अंक, इंधन, अंदाज, चौराह।

***ANSWERS AND VOCABULARY**: 1. ā, o, au, āī (mother); 2. ā, a, au, āj (today); 3. o, au, oḍh (pull); 4. abba (Oh!), akṣhar (alphabet); 5. om (ॐ), aut (plough), ok (vomit); 6. oṭh (lip), om (ॐ) Adnyana (ignorant); 7. agha (sin), auras (legitimate), āg (fire), ās (longing), āh (sorrow), āj (today), aurat (woman), ambar (sky), aj (unborn), am̃sha (fraction), oghaḥ (flow); 8. i, ī, ikh (poison), 9. kāy (what?), navā (new), īs'h (God); 10. aṅk (number), indhan (fuel), andāj (estimate), chaurāh (intersection).*

(5.2) उ u,	ऊ ū,	ऋ ru;	ए e,	ऐ ai	(रु ru,	रू rū)
उ	ऊ	ऋ	ए	ऐ	रु	रू
u	ū	ru	e	ai	ru	rū

EXERCISE 10 : (only on what we learned so far) Read and Write the following in marāṭhī :

1. उ, ऊ, ऋ 2. उधर, उछल 3. उमर, ऊपर 4. उगम, ऊन 5. ऊंट, उठ 6. उतर, 7. ए, ऐ, ऋ 8. गए, नए 9. उकल, उकर 10. एक, ऐनक, अत: 11. रूप, तरु

ANSWERS AND VOCABULARY: 1. u, ū, ru 2. udhar (on that side), uchhal (jump) 3. umar (age), ūpar (above) 4. ugam (source), ūn (wool) 5. uṇṭ (camel), uṭh (get up) 6. utar (get down), 7. e, ai, ru 8. gae, nae 9. ukal (unwind), ukar (dig) 10. ek (one), ainak (spectacles), ataḥ (therefore). 11. rūp (form), taru (tree).

adj∘ = Adjective, adv∘ = Adverb; *conj.* = Conjunction, f∘ = Feminine gender, *ind.* = Indeclinable, m∘ = Masculine gender, n∘ = Neuter gender, pl∘ = Plural

LESSON 6

सहावा पाठ

मराठी स्वर मात्रा

6.1 WRITING MARATHI VOWEL SIGNS

Vowels	अ	आ	इ	ई	उ	ऊ	ऋ	ए	ऐ	ओ	औ
Signs		ा	ि	ी	ु	ू	ृ	े	ै	ो	ौ
Sound	a	ā	i	ī	u	ū	ru	e	ai	o	au
		aa		ee		oo	ru	é			

ा	ि	ी	ु	ू	ृ	े	ै	ो	ौ
ā	i	ī	u	ū	ru	e	ai	o	au
पा	पि	पी	पु	पू	पृ	पे	पै	पो	पौ
pā, paa	pi	pī, pee	pu	pū, poo	pru	pe	pai	po	pau

EXERCISE 11 : Read and write the marāṭhī words :

जिकडे, तिकडे, मृत, चिंता, मुळा, कोण, वापस, खंड, दिवा, दीपक, बेकार, सुखी, सुंदर, भेद, मिठाई, भिक्षा, ज्ञानी, सुंदरता, कोका कोला, महानता, सुख दु:ख, वानर, ज्ञानयोग, भारतीय, अमेरिकन, पौराणिक.

ANSWERS AND VOCABULARY : jikaḍe (where), tikḍe (there), mrut (dead), chintā (worry), muḷā (raddish), koṇ (who?), vāpas (return), khaṇḍ (part), divā (lamp), dīpak (lamp), bekār (unemployed), sukhī (happy), sundar (beautiful), bhed (difference), miṭhāī (sweets), bhikshā (alms), dnyānī (knowledgable), sundartā (beauty), kokā kolā (coke), mahānatā (greatness), sukh duhkh (happyness and sorrow), wānar (monkey), dnyānayoga (yoga of knowledge), bhāratiya (Indian), amerikan (American), paurāṇik (ancient).

6.2 CHART OF ALPHABET WITH VOWEL SIGNS

अ	आ	इ	ई	उ	ऊ	ऋ	ए	ऐ	ओ	औ	अं	अः
	ा	ि	ी	ु	ू	ृ	े	ै	ो	ौ	ं	ः
	(क्= ा)	(क्+ ि)	(क्+ ी)	(क्+ ु)	(क्+ ू)	(क्+ ृ)	(क्+ े)	(क्+ ै)	(क्+ ो)	(क्+ ौ)	(क्+ ं)	(क्+ :)
क	का	कि	की	कु	कू	कृ	के	कै	को	कौ	कं	कः
ख	खा	खि	खी	खु	खू	खृ	खे	खै	खो	खौ	खं	खः
ग	गा	गि	गी	गु	गू	गृ	गे	गै	गो	गौ	गं	गः
घ	घा	घि	घी	घु	घू	घृ	घे	घै	घो	घौ	घं	घः
ङ	ङा	ङि	ङी	ङु	ङू	–	ङे	ङै	ङो	ङौ	ङं	ङः
च	चा	चि	ची	चु	चू	चृ	चे	चै	चो	चौ	चं	चः
छ	छा	छि	छी	छु	छू	छृ	छे	छै	छो	छौ	छं	छः
ज	जा	जि	जी	जु	जू	जृ	जे	जै	जो	जौ	जं	जः
झ	झा	झि	झी	झु	झू	झृ	झे	झै	झो	झौ	झं	झः
ञ	ञा	ञि	ञी	ञु	ञू	–	ञे	ञै	ञो	ञौ	ञं	ञः
ट	टा	टि	टी	टु	टू	टृ	टे	टै	टो	टौ	टं	टः
ठ	ठा	ठि	ठी	ठु	ठू	ठृ	ठे	ठै	ठो	ठौ	ठं	ठः
ड	डा	डि	डी	डु	डू	डृ	डे	डै	डो	डौ	डं	डः
ढ	ढा	ढि	ढी	ढु	ढू	ढृ	ढे	ढै	ढो	ढौ	ढं	ढः
ण	णा	णि	णी	णु	णू	णृ	णे	णै	णो	णौ	णं	णः
त	ता	ति	ती	तु	तू	तृ	ते	तै	तो	तौ	तं	तः
थ	था	थि	थी	थु	थू	थृ	थे	थै	थो	थौ	थं	थः
द	दा	दि	दी	दु	दू	दृ	दे	दै	दो	दौ	दं	दः
ध	धा	धि	धी	धु	धू	धृ	धे	धै	धो	धौ	धं	धः
न	ना	नि	नी	नु	नू	नृ	ने	नै	नो	नौ	नं	नः
प	पा	पि	पी	पु	पू	पृ	पे	पै	पो	पौ	पं	पः
फ	फा	फि	फी	फु	फू	फृ	फे	फै	फो	फौ	फं	फः
ब	बा	बि	बी	बु	बू	बृ	बे	बै	बो	बौ	बं	बः
भ	भा	भि	भी	भु	भू	भृ	भे	भै	भो	भौ	भं	भः
म	मा	मि	मी	मु	मू	मृ	मे	मै	मो	मौ	मं	मः
य	या	यि	यी	यु	यू	यृ	ये	यै	यो	यौ	यं	यः
र	रा	रि	री	रु	रू	ऋ	रे	रै	रो	रौ	रं	रः
ल	ला	लि	ली	लु	लू	लृ	ले	लै	लो	लौ	लं	लः
व	वा	वि	वी	वु	वू	वृ	वे	वै	वो	वौ	वं	वः
श	शा	शि	शी	शु	शू	शृ	शे	शै	शो	शौ	शं	शः
ष	षा	षि	षी	षु	षू	षृ	षे	षै	षो	षौ	षं	षः
स	सा	सि	सी	सु	सू	सृ	से	सै	सो	सौ	सं	सः
ह	हा	हि	ही	हु	हू	हृ	हे	है	हो	हौ	हं	हः

EXERCISE 12 : What we learned so far, the 'cumulative learning'

6.3 A PRELIMINARY VOCABULARY OF KEY MARATHI WORDS

READ the marāṭhī words and WRITE them. Understand and remember as many as possible.

मी (*mī* I) आहे (*āhe* am, is) आम्ही (*āmhī* we)

तू (*tū* you) तुम्ही (*tumhī* you) तो - ती (*to, tī* he - she)

ते (*te* they m∘) त्या (*tyā* they f∘) त्याना (*tyānā* to them)

मला (*malā* to me) आम्हाला (*āmhālā* to us) आपण (*āpaṇ* we)

तुला (*tulā* to you) तुम्हाला (*tumhālā* to you) त्याला (*tyālā* to him)

तिला (*tilā* to her) त्याना (*tyānā* to them) आपणाला (*āpaṇālā* to tou)

माझ्याकडून (*mājhyākaḍūn* by me) तुझ्याकडून (*tujhyākaḍūn* by you)

तुमच्याकडून (*tumchyākaḍūn* by you) त्याच्याकडून (*tyāchyākaḍūn* by him)

तिच्याकडून (*tichyākaḍūn* by her) त्यांच्याकडून (*tyāñchyākaḍūn* by them)

माझ्याजवळ (*mājhyājavaḷ* with me) तुझ्याजवळ (*tujhyājavaḷ* with you)

तुमच्याजवळ (*tumchyājavaḷ* with you) त्याच्याजवळ (*tyāchyājavaḷ* with him)

तिच्याजवळ (*tichyājavaḷ* with her) त्यांच्याजवळ (*tyāñchyājavaḷ* with them)

माझा (*mājhā* my m∘) माझी (*mājhī*; my f∘) माझे (*mājhe* our pl∘)

आमचा (*āmchā* our m∘) आमची (*āmachī*; our f∘) आमचे (*āmche*; our pl∘)

तुझा (*tujhā* your m∘) तुझी (*tujhī* your f∘) आमचा (*āmchā* ourm∘)

आमची (*āmchī* our f∘) आमचे (*āmche* our pl∘)

माझ्यावर (*mājhyāvar* on me) तुझ्यावर (*tujhyāvar* on you)

तुमच्यावर (*tumchyāvar* on you) त्याच्यावर (*tyāchyāvar* on him)

तिच्यावर (*tichyāvar* on her) त्यांच्यावर (*tyāñchyāvar* on them)

माझ्याकडे (*mājhyākaḍe* at me) तुझ्याकडे (*tujhyākaḍe* at you)

तुमच्याकडे (*tumchyākaḍe* at you) त्याच्याकडे (*tyāchyākaḍe* at him)

तिच्याकडे (*tichyākaḍe* at her) त्यांच्याकडे (*tyāñchyākaḍe* at them)

काय? कोण? (*kāy? koṇ?* what? who?) ठीक (*ṭhīk*; ok, alright), आहे (*āhe* is), आहेत (*āhet* are)

नांव (*nā̃v* name), मुलगा (*mulgā* Boy), मुलगी (*mulgī* Girl),

कुत्रा (*kutrā* Dog), मांजर (*mānjar* Cat), घर (*ghar* House, home),

चहा (*chahā* Tea). पी (*pī* to Drink). गरम (*garam* Hot).

adj∘ = Adjective, adv∘ = Adverb; *conj.* = Conjunction, f∘ = Feminine gender, *ind.* = Indeclinable, m∘ = Masculine gender, n∘ = Neuter gender, pl∘ = Plural

LESSON 7

सातवा पाठ

मराठी अर्ध वर्ण

7.1 COMPOUNDING THE CONSONANTS

(Compare the following chart with the one given on page 1)

marāṭhī Half-Characters :

क्‍ (क्)	ख्‍ (ख्)	ग्‍ (ग्)	घ्‍ (घ्)	ङ्
k	kh	g	gh	ṅ
च्‍ (च्)	छ्	ज्‍ (ज्)	झ्‍ (झ्)	ञ्‍ (ञ्)
ch	chh	j	jh, z	ñ
ट्	ठ्	ड्	ढ्	ण्‍ (ण्)
ṭ	ṭh	ḍ	ḍh	ṇ
त्‍ (त्)	थ्‍ (थ्)	द्	ध्‍ (ध्)	न्‍ (न्)
t	th	d	dh	n
प्‍ (प्)	फ्‍ (फ्)	ब्‍ (ब्)	भ्‍ (भ्)	म्‍ (म्)
p	ph, f	b	bh	m
य्‍ (य्)	र्	ल्‍ (ल्)	व्‍ (व्)	
y	r	l	v,w	
श्‍ (श्)	ष्‍ (ष्)	स्‍ (स्)	ह्	ळ
śh, sh	ṣ, sh	s	h	ḷ

7.2 USE OF THE HALF CHARACTERS TO MAKE MARATHI COMPOUND LETTERS AND WORDS

*Character k (क्, क) : पक्का (k + k *pakkā* strong), क्लेष (k + l *kleṣa* distress), इतक्या (k + y *kyā* what), रक्त (k + t *rakta* blood) रुक्मिणी (k + m *rukmiṇī* Rukmiṇī)

*Character kh (ख्, ख) : सख्या (kh + y *sakhyā* O Dear!)

*Character g (ग्, ग) : ग्लास (g + l *glās* glass), दुग्ध (g + dh *dugdha* milk), अग्नि (g + n *agni* fire), भाग्य (g + y *bhāgya* fortune), ग्वाला (g + w *gwālā* milkman)

*Character gh (घ्, घ) : विघ्न विघ्न विघ्न (gh + n *vighna* obstacle), लघ्वाशी लघ्वाशी (gh + v *laghvāshī* moderate eater)

*Character ch (च्, च) : सच्चा (ch + ch *sachchā* true), अच्युत (ch + y *achyut* Krishṇa, Viṣṇu), चांगला (ch + chh *chānglā* good)

*Character j (ज्, ज) : राज्य (j + y *rājya* kingdom), सज्ज (j + j *sajja* ready), उज्ज्वल (j + j + v *ujjaval* bright), ज्वाला (j + w *jwālā* flame)

*Character ṭ (ट्) : सुट्टी, मिट्टी (ṭ + ṭ *suṭṭī* holiday) मुट्ठी (ṭ + ṭh *muṭṭhī* fist)

*Character ḍ (ड्) : चड्डी चड्डी (ḍ + ḍ *chaḍḍī* short pant)

*Character ṇ (ण्, ण) : कण्ठ (ṇ + ṭh *kaṇṭha* throat), कण्टक (ṇ + ṭh *kaṇṭak* thorn), षण्मास (ṇ + m *ṣaṇmās* six months), अण्डे (ṇ + ḍ *aṇḍe* egg)

*Character t (त्, त) : सत्कार (t + k *satkār* honour), रत्नाकर (t + n *ratnākar* ocean), आत्मा (t + m *ātmā* soul), त्याग (t + y *tyāg* sacrifice), त्रास (t + r *trās* trouble), त्वरा (t + v *tvarā* rush), सत्त्व, सत्त्व, सत्त्व (t + t + v *sattava* truth)

*Character th (थ्, थ) : तथ्य (th + y *tathya* reality)

*Character dh (ध्, ध) : ध्वज (dh + v *dhvaj* flag), दध्म (dh + m *dadhma* to blow), मध्य (dh + y *madhya* centre), ध्वनि (dh + v *dhvani* sound)

*Character n (न्, न) : आनन्द (n + d *ānand* joy), अन्न (n + n *anna* food), जन्म (n + m

adj∘ = Adjective, adv∘ = Adverb; *conj.* = Conjunction, f∘ = Feminine gender, *ind.* = Indeclinable, m∘ = Masculine gender, n∘ = Neuter gender, pl∘ = Plural

janma birth), धन्यवाद (n + y *dhanyavād* thanks), सन्त (n + t *sant* saint), आन्धार (n + dh *āndhār* darkness)

*Character p (प्, ‌ᐩ) : समाप्ति (p + t *samāpti* end), प्यादा (p + y *pyādā* pawn), स्वप्न (p + n *svapna* dream), प्लव (p + l *plava* floating)

*Character ph, f (फ्, फ) : फ्लावर (f + l *flāwar* flower), हफ्ता (f + t *haptā* week)

*Character b (ब्, ब) : धब्बा (b + b *dhabbā* spot), ब्लू (b + l *blū* blue), शब्द (b + d *shabda* sound), ब्याह (b + y *byāha* wedding), सब्जी (b + j *sabjī* vegetable)

*Character bh (भ्, भ) : अभ्यास (bh + y *abhyās* study),

*Character m (म्, म) : सम्पदा (m + p *sampadā* wealth), सम्यक् (m + y *samyak* proper), सम्मान (m + m *sammāna* honour), मुम्बई (m + b *mumbaī* Bombay), अम्ल (m + l *amla* sour), साम्य (m + y *sāmya* similarity)

*Character y (य्, य) : शय्या (y + y *shayyā* bed)

*Character r (र्) : तर्क (r + k *tarka* philosophy), वर्ग (r + g *varga* class), अर्चना (r + ch *archnā* worship), कर्ज (r + j *karja* laon), वर्ण (r + ṇ *varṇa* colour, letter, class), नर्तकी (r + t *nartakī* dancer), व्यर्थ (r + th *vyartha* unnecessary), दर्द (r + d *dard* pain), वर्धन (r + dh *vardhan* growth), सर्प (r + p *sarpa* snake), दर्भ (r + bh *darbha* grass), कर्म (r + m *karma* work, deed), कार्य (r + y *kārya* duty)

Compounds with (र) : क्रिया (k + ra *kriyā* action), ग्रीवा (g + ra *grīvā* neck), वज्र (j + ra *vajra* thunderboalt), राष्ट्र (ṣ + ṭ + ra *rāṣṭra* nation), त्रिशूल (t + ra *triśhūl* trident), भद्र (d + ra *bhadra* gentle), प्रकाश (p + ra *prakāsh* light), ब्रह्मा (b + ra *Brahmā* creator), व्रत (v + ra *vrat* austerity), श्रीमती (śh + ra *śhrīmatī* madam)

*Character l (ल्, ल) : वल्क (l + k *valka* bark), जुल्फ (l + f *julfa* hair), गुल्म (l + m *gulma* bush, a cluster of plants), कल्याण (l + y *kalyāṇ* benefit)

adj∘ = Adjective, adv∘ = Adverb; *conj.* = Conjunction, f∘ = Feminine gender, *ind.* = Indeclinable, m∘ = Masculine gender, n∘ = Neuter gender, pl∘ = Plural

LESSON 8

आठवाँ पाठ

मराठी संयुक्त वर्ण

8.1 SPECIAL COMPOUND CHARACTERS

(1) Character d (द्) forms following commonly used SEVEN compound letters :

(i). d + ga = dga writen as :	द् + ग = द्ग = द्ग	भगवद्गीता	*bhagavadgītā*
(ii) d + da = dda written as :	द् + द = द्द = द्द	उद्देश	*uddesha* (aim)
(iii) d + dha = ddha written as	द् + ध = द्ध = द्ध	बुद्ध	*buddha*
(v) d + bha = dbha written as :	द् + भ = द्भ = द्भ	श्रीमद्भगवद्गीता	*shrīmatbhagavadgītā*
(v) d + ya = dya written as :	द् + य् = द्य = द्य	विद्या	*vidyā* (knowledge)
(vi) d + ma = dma written as :	द् + म् = द्म = द्म	पद्म	*padma* (lotus)
(vii) d + va = dva written as :	द् + व् = द्व = द्व	द्वार	*dvār* (gate)

(2) Characters *ra* and *r* (र, र्) make following THREE types of marāṭhī compound letters :

(A) WHEN FULL CONSONANT *ra* (र) comes after a half consonant character, it is written as a slant line attached to that (half) consonant. (Note : Even though that half consonant apprars to be written as a full consonant, it is actually a half consonant) :

1. pr प्र   2. ṭr ट्र

(i) k (half) + ra (full) = kra	(क् + र = क्‌र = क्र)	चक्र	*chakra* (wheel)
(ii) g + ra = gra	(ग् + र = ग्‌र = ग्र)	अग्र	*agra* (tip)
(iii) t + ra = tra	(त् + र = त्‌र = त्र)	पवित्र	*pavitra* (holy)
(iv) d + ra = dra	(द् + र = द्र)	द्रव	*drava* (liquid)
(v) sh + ra =shra	(श् + र = श्र)	श्री	*shrī* (lofty)
(vi) ṭ or ḍ+ ra= tra, ḍra	(ट् + र = ट्र)	राष्ट्र	*rāṣṭra* (nation)
(vii) s + ra = sra	(स् + र = स्‌र = स्र)	सहस्र	*sahasra* (thousand)
s + t + ra = stra	(स् +त् + र = स्‌त्‌र =स्त्र)	स्त्री	*strī* (woman)

(B) WHEN THE HALF CONSONANT *r* (र्) comes before any full consonant character, the *r* (र्) is either written as (ि) over that full co nsonant or as (=) before the full consonant y (य) and h (ह).

3. ry र्य 4. ry ऱ्य

(viii) r + k (ॅ) र् + क = र्क. e.g. अर्क (*arka* extract), स्वर्ग (*svarga* heaven).

(ix) र (ऱ) + य = ऱ्य, र (ऱ) + ह = ऱ्ह. e.g. पर्याय, (option), पऱ्या (angles), तऱ्हा (manner), वऱ्हाडी (guest), आऱ्या (saws), साऱ्या (all), सर्व (all).

What is the difference between ऱ्य and र्य in the words पऱ्या and पर्याय?

The र् (ॅ) in र्य has an impact on the leter य. Thus प in पर्याय has value of two mātrā, but the र् (ऱ) in ऱ्य of पऱ्या has no impact on the leter य, Thus प now has value of only one mātrā, May be that is why it is written before the letters य and ह.

AGAIN REMEMBER :

(i) The slant line character (्) represents the full र (*ra*), it does not represent half र् (r)

e.g. प्र = प् + र प्रकाश

(ii) The curved line character (ॅ) represents half र् (*r*), it does not represent full र (*ra*)

e.g. र्प = र् + प सर्प

(3) Character ह् forms following three types of very common compound letters :

(i) h + ma = hma (ह् + म = ह्म) ब्रह्मा (*brahmā* the Creator)

(ii) h + ya = hya (ह् + य = ह्य) बाह्य (*bahya* outer)

(iii) h + ṛ = hṛ (ह् + ऋ = हृ) हृदय (*hṛday* heart)

THE SPECIAL LETTER *kta*

क्त (क्त)

(4) Character k : character k + ta = kta. *kta* can be written as क् + त = क्त, but there is a special character for this combo which is written as क् + त = क्त = क्त

e.g. रक्त (*rakta* blood), भक्ति भक्ति (*bhakti* devotion), वक्ता वक्ता (*vaktā* speaker), मुक्त मुक्त (*mukta* free), आसक्ति, आसक्ति (*āsakti* attachment), पंक्ति पंक्ति (*paṅkti* line) ...etc

adj∘ = Adjective, adv∘ = Adverb; *conj.* = Conjunction, f∘ = Feminine gender, *ind.* = Indeclinable, m∘ = Masculine gender, n∘ = Neuter gender, pl∘ = Plural

COMPOUNDING DEVANAGARI CONSONANTS

+	क	ख	ग	घ	च	छ	ज	झ	ट	ठ	ड	ढ	ण	त	थ	द
क्	क्क	क्ख	क्ग	क्घ	क्च	क्छ	क्ज	क्झ	क्ट	क्ठ	क्ड	क्ढ	ल्ण	क्त	क्थ	क्द
ख्	ख्क	ख्ख	ख्ग	ख्घ	ख्च	ख्छ	ख्ज	ख्झ	ख्ट	ख्ठ	ख्ड	डढ	ख्ण	ख्त	ख्थ	ख्द
ग्	ग्क	ग्ख	ग्ग	ग्घ	ग्च	ग्छ	ग्ज	ग्झ	ग्ट	ग्ठ	ग्ड	ग्ढ	ग्ण	ग्त	ग्थ	ग्द
घ्	घ्क	घ्ख	घ्ग	घ्घ	घ्च	घ्छ	घ्ज	घ्झ	घ्ट	घ्ठ	घ्ड	घ्ढ	घ्ण	घ्त	घ्थ	घ्द
ङ्	ङ्क	ङ्ख	ङ्ग	ङ्घ	ङ्च	ङ्छ	ङ्ज	ङ्झ	ङ्ट	ङ्ठ	ङ्ड	ङ्ढ	ङ्ण	ङ्त	ङ्थ	ङ्द
च्	च्क	च्ख	च्ग	च्घ	च्च	च्छ	च्ज	च्झ	च्ट	च्ठ	च्ड	च्ढ	च्ण	च्त	च्थ	च्द
छ्	छ्क	छ्ख	छ्ग	छ्घ	छ्च	छ्छ	छ्ज	छ्झ	छ्ट	छ्ठ	छ्ड	छ्ढ	छ्ण	छ्त	छ्थ	छ्द
ज्	ज्क	ज्ख	ज्ग	ज्घ	ज्च	ज्छ	ज्ज	ज्झ	ज्ट	ज्ठ	ज्ड	ज्ढ	ज्ण	ज्त	ज्थ	ज्द
झ्	झ्क	झ्ख	झ्ग	झ्घ	झ्च	झ्छ	झ्ज	झ्झ	झ्ट	झ्ठ	झ्ड	झ्ढ	झ्ण	झ्त	झ्थ	झ्द
ञ्	ञ्क	ञ्ख	ञ्ग	ञ्घ	ञ्च	ञ्छ	ञ्ज	ञ्झ	ञ्ट	ञ्ठ	ञ्ड	ञ्ढ	ञ्ण	ञ्त	ञ्थ	ञ्द
ट्	ट्क	ट्ख	ट्ग	ट्घ	ट्च	ट्छ	ट्ज	ट्झ	ट्ट	ट्ठ	ट्ड	ट्ढ	ट्ण	ट्त	ट्थ	ट्द
ठ्	ठ्क	ठ्ख	ठ्ग	ठ्घ	ठ्च	ठ्छ	ठ्ज	ठ्झ	ठ्ट	ठ्ठ	ठ्ड	ठ्ढ	ठ्ण	ठ्त	ठ्थ	ठ्द
ड्	ड्क	ड्ख	ड्ग	ड्घ	ड्च	ड्छ	ड्ज	ड्झ	ड्ट	ड्ठ	ड्ड	ड्ढ	ड्ण	ड्त	ड्थ	ड्द
ढ्	ढ्क	ढ्ख	ढ्ग	ढ्घ	ढ्च	ढ्छ	ढ्ज	ढ्झ	ढ्ट	ढ्ठ	ढ्ड	ढ्ढ	ढ्ण	ढ्त	ढ्थ	ढ्द
ण्	ण्क	ण्ख	ण्ग	ण्घ	ण्च	ण्छ	ण्ज	ण्झ	ण्ट	ण्ठ	ण्ड	ण्ढ	ण्ण	ण्त	ण्थ	ण्द
त्	त्क	त्ख	द्ग	द्घ	च्च	छ्छ	ज्ज	झ्झ	द्ट	द्ठ	द्ड	द्ढ	द्ण	त्त	त्थ	द्द
थ्	थ्क	थ्ख	ध्ग	ध्घ	थ्च	थ्छ	थ्ज	थ्झ	थ्ट	थ्ठ	थ्ड	थ्ढ	थ्ण	थ्त	थ्थ	ध्द
द्	द्क	द्ख	द्ग	द्घ	च्च	छ्छ	ज्ज	झ्झ	द्ट	द्ठ	द्ड	द्ढ	द्ण	त्त	त्थ	द्द
ध्	ध्क	ध्ख	ध्ग	ध्घ	ध्च	ध्छ	ध्ज	ध्झ	ध्ट	ध्ठ	ध्ड	ध्ढ	ध्ण	ध्त	ध्थ	ध्द
न्	न्क	न्ख	न्ग	न्घ	ञ्च	ञ्छ	ञ्ज	ञ्झ	ण्ट	ण्ठ	ण्ड	ण्ढ	ण्ण	न्त	न्थ	न्द
प्	प्क	प्ख	प्ग	प्घ	प्च	प्छ	प्ज	प्झ	प्ट	प्ठ	प्ड	प्ढ	प्ण	प्त	प्थ	प्द
फ्	फ्क	फ्ख	फ्ग	फ्घ	फ्च	फ्छ	फ्ज	फ्झ	फ्ट	फ्ठ	फ्ड	फ्ढ	फ्ण	फ्त	फ्थ	फ्द
ब्	ब्क	ब्ख	ब्ग	ब्घ	ब्च	ब्छ	ब्ज	ब्झ	ब्ट	ब्ठ	ब्ड	ब्ढ	ब्ण	ब्त	ब्थ	द्ब
भ्	भ्क	भ्ख	भ्ग	भ्घ	भ्च	भ्छ	भ्ज	भ्झ	भ्ट	भ्ठ	भ्ड	भ्ढ	भ्ण	भ्त	भ्थ	द्भ
म्	ङ्क	ङ्ख	ङ्ग	ङ्घ	ङ्च	ङ्छ	ङ्ज	ङ्झ	म्ट	म्ठ	म्ड	म्ढ	म्ण	म्त	म्थ	म्द
य्	य्क	य्ख	य्ग	य्घ	य्च	य्छ	य्ज	य्झ	य्ट	य्ठ	य्ड	य्ढ	य्ण	य्त	य्थ	य्द
र्	र्क	र्ख	र्ग	र्घ	र्च	र्छ	र्ज	र्झ	र्ट	र्ठ	र्ड	र्ढ	र्ण	र्त	र्थ	र्द
ल्	ल्क	ल्ख	ल्ग	ल्घ	ल्च	ल्छ	ल्ज	ल्झ	ल्ट	ल्ठ	ल्ड	ल्ढ	ल्ण	ल्त	ल्थ	ल्द
व्	व्क	व्ख	व्ग	व्घ	व्च	व्छ	व्ज	व्झ	व्ट	व्ठ	व्ड	व्ढ	व्ण	व्त	व्थ	व्द
श्	श्क	श्ख	श्ग	श्घ	श्च	श्छ	श्ज	श्झ	श्ट	श्ठ	श्ड	श्ढ	श्ण	श्त	श्थ	श्द
ष्	ष्क	ष्ख	ष्ग	ष्घ	ष्च	ष्छ	ष्ज	ष्झ	ष्ट	ष्ठ	ष्ड	ष्ढ	ष्ण	ष्त	ष्थ	ष्द
स्	स्क	स्ख	स्ग	स्घ	स्च	स्छ	स्ज	स्झ	स्ट	स्ठ	स्ड	स्ढ	स्ण	स्त	स्थ	स्द
ह्	ह्क	ह्ख	ह्ग	ह्घ	ह्च	ह्छ	ह्ज	ह्झ	ह्ट	ह्ठ	ह्ड	ह्ढ	ह्ण	ह्त	ह्थ	ह्द

+	ध	न	प	फ	ब	भ	म	य	र	ल	व	श	ष	स	ह
क्	क्ध	क्न	ग्प	ग्फ	ग्ब	ग्भ	क्म	क्य	क्र	क्ल	क्व	क्श	क्ष	क्स	ख
ख्	ख्ध	ख्न	ख्प	ख्फ	ख्ब	ख्भ	ख्म	ख्य	ख्र	ख्ल	ख्व	ख्श	ख्ष	ख्स	ख्ख
ग्	ग्ध	ग्न	ग्प	ग्फ	ग्ब	ग्भ	ग्म	ग्य	ग्र	ग्ल	ग्व	ग्श	ग्ष	ग्स	घ
घ्	घ्ध	घ्न	घ्प	घ्फ	घ्ब	घ्भ	घ्म	घ्य	घ्र	घ्ल	घ्व	घ्श	घ्ष	घ्स	घ्ह
ङ्	ङ्ध	ङ्न	ङ्प	ङ्फ	ङ्ब	ङ्भ	ङ्म	ङ्य	ङ्र	ङ्ल	ङ्व	ङ्श	ङ्क्ष	ङ्स	ङ्घ
च्	च्ध	च्न	ज्प	ज्फ	च्ब	च्भ	च्म	च्य	च्र	च्ल	च्व	च्श	च्ष	च्त	छ
छ्	छ्ध	छ्न	छ्प	छ्फ	छ्ब	छ्भ	छ्म	छ्य	छ्र	छ्ल	छ्व	छ्श	छ्ष	छ्स	छ्छ
ज्	ज्ध	ज्न	ज्प	ज्फ	ज्ब	ज्भ	ज्म	ज्य	ज्र	ज्ल	ज्व	ज्श	ज्ष	ज्स	ज्झ
झ्	झ्ध	झ्न	झ्प	झ्फ	झ्ब	झ्भ	झ्म	झ्य	झ्र	झ्ल	झ्व	झ्श	झ्ष	झ्स	झ्झ
ञ्	ञ्ध	ञ्न	ञ्प	ञ्फ	ञ्ब	ञ्भ	ञ्म	ञ्य	ञ्र	ञ्ल	ञ्व	ञ्श	ञ्ष	ञ्स	ञ्ह
ट्	ट्ध	ट्ण	ट्प	ट्फ	ट्ब	ट्भ	ट्म	ट्य	ट्र	ट्ल	ट्व	ट्श	ट्ष	ट्स	ठ
ठ्	ठ्ध	ठ्ण	ठ्प	ठ्फ	ठ्ब	ठ्भ	ठ्म	ठ्य	ठ्र	ठ्ल	ठ्व	ठ्श	ठ्ष	ठ्स	ठ्ह
ड्	ड्ध	ड्ण	ड्प	ड्फ	ड्ब	ड्भ	ड्म	ड्य	ड्र	ड्ल	ड्व	ड्श	ड्ष	ड्स	ढ
ढ्	ढ्ध	ढ्ण	ढ्प	ढ्फ	ढ्ब	ढ्भ	ढ्म	ढ्य	ढ्र	ढ्ल	ढ्व	ढ्श	ढ्ष	ढ्स	ढ्ह
ण्	ण्ध	ण्ण	ण्प	ण्फ	ण्बा	ण्भ	ण्म	ण्य	ण्र	ण्ल	ण्व	ण्श	ण्ष	ण्स	ण्ह
त्	द्ध	त्न	त्प	त्फ	द्ब	द्भ	त्म	त्य	त्र	त्ल	त्व	त्श	त्ष	त्स	थ
थ्	थ्ध	थ्न	ध्प	ध्फ	थ्ब	थ्भ	थ्म	थ्य	थ्र	थ्ल	थ्व	थ्श	थ्ष	थ्स	थ्थ
द्	द्ध	द्न	द्प	द्फ	द्ब	द्भ	द्ज	द्झ	द्र	द्ल	द्व	द्श	द्ष	द्स	ध्ह
ध्	ध्ध	ध्न	ध्प	ध्फ	ध्ब	ध्भ	ध्म	ध्य	ध्र	ध्ल	ध्व	ध्श	ध्ष	ध्स	ध्ध
न्	न्ध	न्न	न्प	न्फ	न्ब	न्भ	न्म	न्य	न्र	न्ल	न्व	ञ्श	ञ्ष	न्स	न्ह
प्	प्ध	प्न	प्प	प्फ	प्ब	प्भ	प्म	प्य	प्र	प्ल	प्व	प्श	प्ष	प्स	प्ह
फ्	फ्फ	फ्न	फ्प	फ्फ	फ्ब	फ्भ	फ्म	फ्य	फ्र	फ्ल	फ्ब	फ्श	फ्ष	फ्स	फ्ह
ब्	ब्ध	ब्न	ब्प	ब्फ	ब्ब	ब्भ	ब्म	ब्य	ब्र	ब्ल	ब्व	ब्श	ब्ष	ब्स	भ
भ्	भ्ध	भ्न	भ्प	भ्फ	भ्ब	भ्भ	भ्म	भ्य	भ्र	भ्ल	भ्ब	भ्श	भ्ष	भ्स	भ्ह
म्	म्ध	म्न	म्प	म्फ	म्ब	म्भ	म्म	म्य	म्र	म्ल	म्व	म्श	म्ष	म्स	म्ह
य्	य्ध	य्न	य्प	य्फ	य्ब	य्भ	य्म	य्य	य्र	य्ल	य्व	य्श	य्ष	य्स	य्ह
र्	र्ध	र्न	र्प	र्फ	र्ब	र्भ	र्म	र्य	र्र	र्ल	र्व	र्श	र्ष	र्स	र्ह
ल्	ल्ध	ल्न	ल्प	ल्फ	ल्ब	ल्भ	ल्म	ल्य	ल्र	ल्ल	ल्व	ल्श	ल्ष	ल्स	ल्ह
व्	व्ध	व्न	व्प	व्फ	व्ब	व्भ	व्म	व्य	व्र	व्ल	व्व	व्श	व्ष	व्स	व्ह
श्	श्ध	श्न	श्प	श्फ	श्ब	श्भ	श्म	श्य	श्र	श्ल	श्व	श्श	श्ष	श्स	श्ह
ष्	ष्क	ष्ख	ष्प	ष्फ	ष्ब	ष्भ	ष्म	ष्य	ष्र	ष्ल	ष्व	ष्श	ष्ष	ष्स	ष्थ
स्	स्ध	स्न	स्प	स्फ	स्ब	स्भ	स्म	स्य	स्र	स्ल	स्व	स्श	स्ष	स्स	स्ह
ह्	ह्ध	ह्न	ह्प	ह्फ	ह्ब	ह्भ	ह्म	ह्य	ह्र	ह्ल	ह्व	ह्श	ह्ष	ह्स	ह्ह

LESSON 9
नौवा पाठ
SANDHI
संधि

1. COMPOUNDING OF HINDI VOWELS

RATNAKAR'S CHART FOR VOWEL SANDHI RULES

When two vowels come together, they are mathematically added into a single long vowel.

	First vowel	+ Second vowel	=	Result, a long vowel
1	अ, आ	+ अ, आ	=	आ
	अ, आ	+ इ, ई	=	ए
	अ, आ	+ उ, ऊ	=	ओ
	अ, आ	+ ऋ, ॠ	=	अर्
	अ, आ	+ ए, ऐ	=	ऐ
	अ, आ	+ ओ	=	औ
2	इ, ई	+ अ, आ, उ, ऊ, ए, ऐ, ओ, औ	=	य, या, यु, यू, ये, यै, यो. यौ
	इ, ई	+ इ, ई	=	ई, ई
3	उ, ऊ	+ अ, आ, इ, ई, ए, ऐ, ओ, औ	=	व, वा, वि, वी, वे, वै, वो, वौ
4	ऋ	+ अ, आ, इ, ई, ए, ऐ, ओ, औ	=	अर् + अ, आ, इ, ई, ए, ऐ, ओ, औ
			=	अर्, अर, अरा, अरि, अरी, अरे, अरो, अरै, अरौ
5	ए	+ अ, आ, इ, ई, उ, ऊ, ए, ऐ, ओ, औ	=	अय् + अ, आ, इ, ई, उ, ऊ, ए, ऐ, ओ, औ
			=	अय्, अय, अया, अयि, अयी, अये, अयो, अयै, अयौ
	ऐ	+ अ, आ, इ, ई, उ, ऊ, ए, ऐ, ओ, औ	=	आय् + अ, आ, इ, ई, उ, ऊ, ए, ऐ, ओ, आ
			=	आय्, आय, आया, आयि, आयी, आये, आयो, आयै, आयौ
6	ओ	+ अ, आ, इ, ई, उ, ऊ, ए, ऐ, ओ, औ	=	अव् + अ, आ, इ, ई, उ, ऊ, ए, ऐ, ओ, औ
			=	अव्, अव, अवा, अवि, अवी, अवे, अवो, अवै, अवौ
	औ	+ अ, आ, इ, ई, उ, ऊ, ए, ऐ, ओ, औ	=	आव् + अ, आ, इ, ई, उ, ऊ, ए, ऐ, ओ, औ
			=	आव्, आव, आवा, आवि, आवी, आवे, आवो, आवै, आवौ

LESSON 10
दहावा पाठ

10.1 INTRODUCTION TO THE MARATHI NUMERALS
मराठी अंक

0	shūnya	0	शून्य	
1	ek	१	एक	📖 One book. *ek pustak* एक पुस्तक
2	do	२	दोन	📖 📖 Two books. *donpustake* दोन पुस्तके
3	tīn	३	तीन	📖 📖 📖 Three books. *tīn pustake* तीन पुस्तके
4	chār	४	चार	📖 📖 📖 📖
5	pāñch	५	पाच	📖 📖 📖 📖 📖
6	chhah	६	सहा	📖 📖 📖 📖 📖 📖
7	sāt	७	सात	📖 📖 📖 📖 📖 📖 📖
8	āṭh	८	आठ	📖 📖 📖 📖 📖 📖 📖 📖
9	nau	९	नऊ	📖 📖 📖 📖 📖 📖 📖 📖 📖
10	das	१0	दहा	📖 📖 📖 📖 📖 📖 📖 📖 📖 📖

EXERCISE 14 :

(1) Read the numbers in marāṭhī :
1 7 9 4 0 3 2 8 5 6

(2) Read the following marāṭhī numerals :
७ ४ १ ९ ६ 0 ५ ३ ८ २

(3) Read and Write the following marāṭhī numerals :
चार, सात, नऊ, एक, शून्य, सहा, आठ, पाच, दोन, दहा

> **ANNOUNCEMENT**
>
> With the scientific and easy to follow tools given in this book, **you can start making and speaking your own marāṭhī sentences quickly and with confidence**.

10.2

COUNTING TO ONE HUNDRED

11 akrā	अकरा	12 bārā	बारा
13 terā	तेरा	14 chaudā	चौदा
15 pandhrā	पंधरा	16 soḷā	सोळा
17 satrā	सतरा	18 aṭharā	अठरा
19 ekoṇvīs	एकोणवीस	20 vīs	वीस
21 ekvīs	एकवीस	22 bāvīs	बावीस
23 tevīs	तेवीस	24 chovīs	चोवीस
25 pachcavīs	पंचवीस	26 savvīs	सव्वीस
27 sattāvīs	सत्तावीस	28 aṭṭhāvīs	अठ्ठावीस
29 ekoṇtīs	एकोणतीस	30 tīs	तीस
31 ekatīs	एकतीस	32 battīs	बत्तीस
33 tehatīs	तेहतीस	34 chautīs	चौतीस
35 pastīs	पसतीस	36 chhattīs	छत्तीस
37 sadatīs	सदतीस	38 aḍattīs	अडतीस
39 ekoṇchāḷīs	एकोणचळीस	40 chāḷīs	चाळीस
41 ikechāḷīs	एकेचाळीस	42 bechaḷīs	बेचाळीस
43 trechāḷīs	त्रेचाळीस	44 chaurechāḷīs	चौरेचाळीस
45 pañchechāḷīs	पंचेचाळीस	46 s̀hehechāḷīs	शेहेचाळीस
47 sattechaḷīs	सत्तेचाळीस	48 aṭṭhechāḷīs	अठ्ठेचाळीस
49 ekoṇpannās	एकोणपन्नास	50 pannās	पन्नास
51 ekkāvan	एक्कावन	52 bāvan	बावन
53 trepan	त्रेपन	54 chaupan	चौपन
55 pañchāvan	पंचावन	56 chhappan	छप्पन

57 sattāvan	सत्तावन	58 aṭṭhāvan	अठ्ठावन
59 ekoṇsāṭh	एकोणसाठ	60 sāṭh	साठ
61 ekasaṣhṭa	एकसष्ट	62 bāsaṣhṭa	बासष्ट
63 tresaṢhṭa	त्रेसष्ट	64 chausaṢhṭa	चौसष्ट
65 pāsaṣhṭa	पासष्ट	66 sahāsaṣhṭa	सहासष्ट
67 sadusaṣhṭa	सदुसष्ट	68 aḍusaṣhṭa	अडुसष्ट
69 ekoṇsattar	एकोणसत्तर	70 sattar	सत्तर
71 ekāhattar	एकाहत्तर	72 bāhattar	बाहत्तर
73 tryāhattar	त्र्याहत्तर	74 chauryāhattar	चौऱ्याहत्तर
75 pañchāhattar	पंचाहत्तर	76 chhāhattar	छाहत्तर
77 sattyāhattar	सत्त्याहत्तर	78 aṭṭhyāhattar	अठ्ठ्याहत्तर
79 ekoṇans̀hī	एकोणअंशी	80 ans̀hī	अंशी
81 ekyāens̀hī	एक्याएंशी	82 byāens̀hī	ब्यांशी
83 tryāns̀hī	त्र्यांशी	84 chauryāens̀hī	चौऱ्याएंशी
85 pañchāens̀hī	पंचाएंशी	86 s̀hahāens̀hī	शहाएंशी
87 sattyāns̀hī	सत्त्यांशी	88 aṭṭhyāns̀hī	अठ्ठ्यांशी
89 ekoṇnavvad	एकोणनव्वद	90 navvad	नव्वद
91 ekyāṇṇaav	एक्याण्णव	92 byāṇṇav	ब्याण्णव
93 tryāṇṇav	त्र्याण्णव	94 chauryāṇṇav	चौऱ्यण्णव
95 pañchāṇṇav	पंचाण्णव	96 s̀hahāṇṇav	शहाण्णव
97 sattyāṇṇav	सत्त्याण्णव	98 aṭṭhyāṇṇav	अठ्ठ्याण्णव
99 navvyāṇṇav	नव्व्याण्णव	100 s̀hambhar	शंभर

MARATHI NUMERALS:

०, १, २, ३, ४, ५, ६, ७, ८, ९, १०; ११, १२, १३, १४, १५, १६, १७, १८, १९, २०; २१, २२, २३, २४, २५, २६, २७, २८, २९, ३०; ३१, ३२, ३३, ३४, ३५, ३६, ३७, ३८, ३९, ४०; ४१, ४२, ४३, ४४, ४५, ४६, ४७, ४८, ४९, ५०; ५१, ५२, ५३, ५४, ५५, ५६, ५७, ५८, ५९, ६०; ६१, ६२, ६३, ६४, ६५, ६६, ६७, ६८, ६९, ७०; ७१, ७२, ७३, ७४, ७५, ७६, ७७, ७८, ७९, ८०; ८१, ८२, ८३, ८४, ८५, ८६, ८७, ८८, ८९, ९०; ९१, ९२, ९३, ९४, ९५, ९६, ९७, ९८, ९९, १००.

NUMERALS FROM 0 TO 99

	0	1	2	3	4	5	6	7	8	9
0	૦	૧	૨	૩	૪	૫	૬	૭	૮	૯
1	૧૦	૧૧	૧૨	૧૩	૧૪	૧૫	૧૬	૧૭	૧૮	૧૯
2	૨૦	૨૧	૨૨	૨૩	૨૪	૨૫	૨૬	૨૭	૨૮	૨૯
3	૩૦	૩૧	૩૨	૩૩	૩૪	૩૫	૩૬	૩૭	૩૮	૩૯
4	૪૦	૪૧	૪૨	૪૩	૪૪	૪૫	૪૬	૪૭	૪૮	૪૯
5	૫૦	૫૧	૫૨	૫૩	૫૪	૫૫	૫૬	૫૭	૫૮	૫૯
6	૬૦	૬૧	૬૨	૬૩	૬૪	૬૫	૬૬	૬૭	૬૮	૬૯
7	૭૦	૭૧	૭૨	૭૩	૭૪	૭૫	૭૬	૭૭	૭૮	૭૯
8	૮૦	૮૧	૮૨	૮૩	૮૪	૮૫	૮૬	૮૭	૮૮	૮૯
9	૯૦	૯૧	૯૨	૯૩	૯૪	૯૫	૯૬	૯૭	૯૮	૯૯

KNOW THIS BEFORE YOU CONTINUE

GENDER :

1. Unlike Hindi words which have two genders, Masculine and Feminine, the mara@t<h& words have three genders, Masculine (m∘), Feminine (f∘) and Neuter Gender (n∘). These three genders m∘, f∘, n∘ are used for Sanskrit and English words also.

2. mara@t<h& Nouns, Pronouns, Adjectives and Verbs are Gender sensitive.

3. It is very important to clearly understand that, when we say, "this word has m∘, f∘ or n∘ gender," it is the gender assigned to that word, but not the gender, if any, of the thing represented by that word. e.g. A book itself does not have any part to show its gender, but the mara@t<h& words ग्रंथ (m∘), पोथी (f∘) and पुस्तक (n∘) are used for the "word" called "book" in English, but not the physical "thing" called book. Similarly, the English word "body" has ten mara@t<h& words namely, शरीर (m∘), विग्रह (m∘), काय (m∘), काया (f∘) अंग (n∘), कलेवर (n∘), गात्र (n∘), तन (n∘), वपु (n∘) and देह (n∘) to be used as required. It also shows that Sanskrit and the languages (like mara@t<h&) originated from Sanskrit are more opulent than the English language.

4. Same mara@t<h& words can be modified and converted from m∘ into f∘ gender. e.g. m∘ मुलगा, पोरगा (boy) to f∘ मुलगी, पोरगी (girl) and n∘ मूल, पोर (child).

NUMBER :

1. mara@t<h& Nouns are qualified in two numerical ways, Singular Number (एक वचन) for a single object and Plural Number (बहु वचन) for more than one objects, e.g. One girl (एक मुलगा), two girls (दोन मुली), etc.

2. Sanskrit words have three numbers, Singular (one object), Dual (two objects) and Plural (more than two objects), but mara@t<h& words are either Singular or Plural.

3. There are specific rules to convert a singular word into its plural form and from plural to its singular form.

4. Some words are always in plural form, e.g. क्लेश, कष्ट m∘ (suffering), रोमांच, रोंगटे m∘ (goose bump), etc.

5. In order to show respect to a person, a plural form of pronoun and verb are employed to speak about him or her. e.g. गुरुजी आले m∘, मातोश्री रागावल्या f∘, बाबा बोलले m∘, रामराव म्हणाले m∘, etc.

6. In order to talk about a group of many individuals or objects as one unit, a collective singular noun is used. e.g. आवलि f∘ (row), ओळ f∘ (row), कुळ n∘ (family), गट्ठा m∘ (bundle), गण m∘ (group), गर्दी f∘ (crowd), गुच्छ m∘ (bun~ch), घोळका m∘ (flock), चाळ f∘ (quarters), जत्था m∘ (crowd), जमावडा m∘ (crowd), जुडगा m∘ (bun~ch), ढीग m∘ (heap), ढेर f∘ (heap), दळ n∘ (group), पंक्ति f∘ (row), पंगत f∘ (row), पलटन f∘ (army), फौज f∘ (army), भीड f∘ (crowd), मंडळ n∘ (social group), मेळा m∘ (crowd), संग्रह m∘ (collection), संघ m∘ (group), संघटन n∘ (group), संचय m∘ (group), समवाय m∘ (group), समाज m∘ (group), समिति f∘ (group), समुदाय m∘ (group), सैन्य n∘ (army), etc.

adj∘ = Adjective, adv∘ = Adverb; *conj.* = Conjunction, f∘ = Feminine gender, *ind.* = Indeclinable, m∘ = Masculine gender, n∘ = Neuter gender, pl∘ = Plural

LESSON 11

अकरावा पाठ

MAKING YOUR OWN MARATHI SENTENCES : **मराठी वाक्य रचना**

PLEASE NOTE

In this book, in order to avoid making the Spoken marāṭhī Language too much nasal, unnecessary nasal dots (अनुस्वार) are avoided moderately.

11.1 MAKING SIMPLE SENTENCES - about a 'Present' event, with 'IS' (*hai* है)

NOTE: The ँ sign is just a slight nasal tone added to the syllable below that ँ sign

I	मी *(mī)*	am	आहे *(āhe)*	I am	मी आहे *mī āhe*
You	तू *(tū)*	are	आहेस *(āhes)*	You are	तुम्ही आहात *tumhī āhāt*
He, that (m∘)	तो *(to)*	is	आहे *(āhe)*	She, that is (f∘)	ती आहे *tī āhe*
This, it (n∘)	हे *(he)*	is	आहे *(āhe)*	That is (n∘)	ते आहे *te āhe*
These (m∘ pl∘)	हे *(he)*	are	आहेत *(āhet)*	Those are (m∘ pl∘)	ते आहेत *te āhet*

TABLE 1A : Speaking a Present Event, **Masculine Gender Subject**

	Subject	am	is	are
1	I मी *(mī)*	आहे *(āhe)*		
2	Weआम्ही *(āmhī)*			आहोत *(āhot)*
3	You तू *(tū)*			आहेस *(āhes)*
4	You तुम्ही *(tumhī)* respect and pl∘			आहात *(āhāt)*
5	You आपण *(tū)* formal and pl∘			आहात *(āhāt)*
6	He, that तो *(to)*		आहे *(āhe)*	
7	These हे *(he)* pl∘			आहेत *(āhet)*
8	They, those ते *(te)* pl∘			आहेत *(āhet)*

TABLE 1B : Speaking a Present Event, **Feminine Gender Subject**

	Subject	am	is	are
1	I मी *(mī)*	आहे *(āhe)*		
2	Weआम्ही *(āmhī)*			आहोत *(āhot)*

adj∘ = Adjective, adv∘ = Adverb; *conj.* = Conjunction, f∘ = Feminine gender, *ind.* = Indeclinable, m∘ = Masculine gender, n∘ = Neuter gender, pl∘ = Plural

3	You तू *(tū)*			आहेस *(āhes)*
4	You तुम्ही *(tumhī)* respect and pl∘			आहात *(āhāt)*
5	You आपण *(tū)* formal and pl∘			आहात *(āhāt)*
6	She, that ती *(tī)*		आहे *(āhe)*	
7	These ह्या *(hyā)* pl∘			आहेत *(āhet)*
8	They, those त्या *(tyā)* pl∘			आहेत *(āhet)*

TABLE 1C : Speaking a Present Event, **Neuter Gender Subject**

	Subject		is	are
1	It, this हे *(he)*		आहे *(āhe)*	
2	That ते *(te)*		आहे *(āhe)*	
3	These ही *(hī)* pl∘			आहेत *(āhet)*
4	Those ती *(tī)* pl∘			आहेत *(āhet)*

MAKING SMALL SIMPLE SENTENCES

TABLE 2A : Speaking a Present Event, **Masculine Gender Subject**

m∘ boy = मुलगा, father = वडील, President = अध्यक्ष, student= विद्यार्थी

	Subject	मराठी	*Transliteration*
1	I am a boy	मी मुलगा आहे	*mī mulgā āhe*
2	We are boys	आम्ही मुले आहोत	*āmhī mule ahot*
3	You are a boy	तू मुलगा आहेस	*tū mulgā āhes*
4	You are father (respect)	तुम्ही वडील आहात	*tumhi vaḍīl āhāt*
5	You are a President (formal)	आपण अध्यक्ष आहात	*āpaṇ adhyakśha āhāt*
6	He is a student	तो विद्यार्थी आहे	*to vidyārthī āhe*
7	These are students	हे विद्यार्थी आहेत	*he vidyārthī āhet*
8	They, those are students	ते विद्यार्थी आहेत	*te vidyārthī āhet*

TABLE 1B : Speaking a Present Event, **Feminine Gender Subject**

f∘ girl = मुलगी, father = वडील, President = अध्यक्षा, beautiful = सुंदर

	Subject	am	is
1	I am a girl	मी मुलगी आहे	*mī mulgī āhe*

2	We are girls	आम्ही मुली आहोत	*āmhī mulī ahot*
3	You are a girl	तू मुलगी आहेस	*tū mulgī āhes*
4	You are mother (respect)	तुम्ही आई आहात	*tumhi āī āhāt*
5	You are a President (formal)	आपण अध्यक्षा आहात	*āpaṇ adhyakśhā āhāt*
6	She is beautiful	ती सुंदर आहे	*tī sundar āhe*
7	These are beautiful	ह्या सुंदर आहेत	*hyā sundar āhet*
8	They, those are beautiful	त्या सुंदर आहेत	*tyā sundar āhet*

TABLE 1C : Speaking a Present Event, **Neuter Gender Subject**

n∘ flower = (adj∘ ते) फूल, flowers = (adj∘ ती) फूले, red = लाल

	Subject		
1	It, this is a flower	हे फूल आहे	*he fūl āhe*
2	That is a flower	ते फूल आहे	*te fūl āhe*
3	These are red flowers	**ही** लाल फूले आहेत	***hī** lāl fūle āhet*
4	Those are red flowers	**ती** लाल फूले आहेत	***tī** lāl fūle āhet*

NOTE : At this stage of learning, popular, difficult and unknown English nouns **may be used in marāṭhī** as if they are marāṭhī words, see below.

EXERCISE : Translate the English sentences into marāṭhī (Answers are given for help)

1. I am a man. *mī purush āhe.* मी पुरुष आहे. I am a woman. *mī strī āhe.* मी स्त्री आहे.
2. I am a dentist. *mī ḍentisṭ āhe.* मी डेंटिस्ट आहे. I am a judge. *mī jai āhe.* मी जज आहे.
3. I am a brain surgeon. *mī bren sarjan āhe.* मी ब्रेन सर्जन आहे.
4. I am truck driver. *mī ṭrak ḍrāyavar āhe.* मी ट्रक ड्रायवर आहे. It is good. *he chhān āhe.* हे छान आहे.
5. I am an engineer. *mī injīniyar āhe.* मी इंजिनियर आहे.
6. I am a laboratory inspector. *mī leboreṭorī inispekṭar āhe.* मी लेबोरेटोरी इन्स्पेक्टर आहे.
7. She is a microbiologist. *tī maykrobāyolājisṭ āhe.* ती मायक्रोबायोलाजिस्ट आहे.
8. He is a conductor. *to kanḍakṭar āhe.* तो कण्डक्टर आहे. **My name is- *māze nāँv - āhe.* माझे नांव – आहे.**
9. Rāma is a tennis player. *Rām ṭenis kheḷaḍū āhe.* राम टेनिस खेळाडू आहे.
10. You are a poet. *tū kavi āhes.* तू कवि आहेस. I am alright (ok). *mī ṭhīk āhe.* मी ठीक आहे.

adj∘ = Adjective, adv∘ = Adverb; *conj.* = Conjunction, f∘ = Feminine gender, *ind.* = Indeclinable, m∘ = Masculine gender, n∘ = Neuter gender, pl∘ = Plural

11.2 USING MARATHI PLURAL WORDS

RATNAKAR'S SEVEN NOBLE RULES

Singular to Plural

FIRST RULE: If the word is **Masculine** ending in आ then this आ changes to ए in the plural form. e.g. singular m∘ Onion कांदा *kāndā* → plural m∘ Onions कांदे *kānde*

Examples : आंबा-आंबे (mango m∘), कायदा-कायदे (law), कुत्रा-कुत्रे (dog), खडा-खडे (pebble), गुन्हा-गुन्हे (crime), घोडा-घोडे (horse), चमचा-चमचे (spoon), छकडा-छकडे (cart), जसा-जसे (as), झगा-झगे (frock), टांगा-टांगे (horse buggy), डबा-डबे (box), डोळा-डोळे (eye), ढवळा-ढवळे (white), तवा-तवे (hotplate), थवा-थवे (flock), दिवा-दिवे (lamp), धब्बा-धब्बे (spot), नारा-नारे (slogan), पत्ता-पत्ते (card), फळा-फळे (board), बेटा-बेटे (son), भाला-भाले (spear), मुका-मुके (kiss), मुद्दा-मुद्दे (issue), येवढा-येवढे (this much), रस्ता-रस्ते (road), राजा-राजे (king), लंगडा-लंगडे (lame), वारा-वारे (wind), शिक्का-शिक्के (stamp), शिंतोडा-शिंतोडे (splash), ससा-ससे (hare), हीरा-हिरे (diamond), etc.

SECOND RULE : If the word is Feminine and ends in a consonant, then आ or ई is added to make that word plural. e.g. singular singular f∘ Brick वीट *vīṭ* → plural f∘ Bricks विटा *viṭā;* f∘ Well विहिर *vihir* → plural f∘ *vihirī* विहिरी *vihirī.*

Examples : ओळख-ओळखा (introduction f∘), खंड-खिंडी (valley), गाय-गायी, गाई (cow), चूक-चुका (mistake), छट-छटा (shade), जात-जाती (cast), झुंड-झुंडी (group), झोप-झोपा (sleep), टीण-टिणा (iron sheet), ठोकर-ठोकरा (kick), डाळ-डाळी (pulse), तारीख-तारखा (date), थाप-थापा (slap), दौलत-दौलती (property), धडक-धडका (crash), नेमणूक-नेमणुका (appointment), पैज-पैजा (race), फुंका-फुका (blowing), बेरीज-बेरजा (summation), बैठक-बैठकी (meeting), भूक-भुका (hunger), माळ-माळा (necklace), म्हण-म्हणी (proverb), म्हैस-म्हशी (buffalo), येरझार-येरझारा (back and forth), रेश-रेशा (line), लाज-लाजा (shame), वेळ-वेळा (time), शिकायत-शिकायती (complaint), सडक-सडका (road), सून-सुना (daughter-in-law), सोय-सायी, सोई (facility), हाक-हाका (call), etc.

THIRD RULE : If the word is Feminine ending in ई, the ई changes to या in plural form. e.g. लेखणी-लेखण्या (pncil),

Examples : काठी-काठ्या (stick f∘), खिडकी-खिडक्या (window), गाडी-गाड्या (train), घडी-घड्या (fold), चक्की-चक्या (mill), चिमणी-चिमण्या (sparrow), छडी-छड्या (cane), जोडी-जोड्या (pair), झंडी-झंड्या (flag), टोळी-टोळ्या (group), ठिणगी-ठिणग्या (spark), डब्बी-डब्ब्या (box), ढपली-ढपल्या (drum), तिजोरी-तिजोऱ्या (safe), थैली-थैल्या (bag), दांडी-दांड्या (stem), धुनी-धुन्या (incense), नदी-नद्या (river), बी-बिया (seed), पुंगी-पुंग्या (whistle), फांदी-फांद्या (bran~ch), बंडी-बंड्या (bullock cart), भाकरी-भाकऱ्या (bread), मुंगी-मुंग्या (ant), युक्ति-युक्त्या (trick), राणी-राण्या (queen), लांबी-लांब्या (length), वडी-वड्या (slab), स्त्री-स्त्रिया (woman), हाजिरी-हाजिऱ्या (attendance).

adj∘ = Adjective, adv∘ = Adverb; *conj.* = Conjunction, f∘ = Feminine gender, *ind.* = Indeclinable, m∘ = Masculine gender, n∘ = Neuter gender, pl∘ = Plural

FOURTH RULE : If a feminine word ends in voewl ऊ, ए, ऐ ओ then vowel आ is added to that word to make it plural (Remenber : ऊ+आ= वा, ए+आ= अया, ऐ-आ=आया, ओ+आ= अवा). e.g. सासू-सासवा (mother-in-law f∘), आते-आता (gut), पै-पया (1/3 paisa)., etc.

FIFTH RULE : If a Neuter Gender word ends in vowel अ then voewl ए is added to that word and ई is added to its adjective to make them plural. e.g. ते घर - ती घरे (house n∘), etc.

Examples : किटक-किटके (insect n∘), खंदक-खंदके (moat), घड्याळ-घड्याळे (clock), चाक-चाके (wheel), छत्र-छत्रे (umbrella), जहाज-जहाजे (ship), झाड-झाडे (plant), टेकाड-टेकाडे (hill), ताट-ताटे (plate), दार-दारे (door), नाटक-नाटके (drama), पुस्तक-पुस्तके (book), फूल-फुले (flower), बेडूक-बेडके (frog), भूत-भुते (ghost), मूल-मुले (child), रहाट-रहाटे (water wheel), लिंग-लिंगे (gender), वन-वने (forest), शेत-शेते (field), संकट-संकटे (calamity), हृदय-हृदये (heart), etc.

SIXTH RULE : If a Neuter Gender word ends in vowel ई or ऊ then voewl ई or ऊ is changed to vowel ए to make that word plural. e.g. पाखरू-पाखरे (bird n∘), मिरी-मिरे (black pepper), मोती-मोते (pearl), वासरू-वासरे (calf), लिंबू-लिंबे (lemon), etc.

EIGHTH RULE : Masculine words ending in voewl अ, इ, ई, उ, ऊ, ओ stay uňchanged in plural form. Feminine word ending in vowel आ also remain same in its plural form. e.g. आज्ञा-आज्ञा (order f∘), उंदीर-उंदीर (mouse m∘), कवि-कवि (poet m∘), गहू-गहू (wheat m∘), दिशा-दिशा (direction f∘), देव-देव (God m∘), पूजा-पूजा (worship f∘), भाषा-भाषा (language f∘), लाडू-लाडू (sweet ball m∘), विद्या-विद्या (education f∘), शत्रु-शत्रु (enemy m∘), सभा-सभा (meeting f∘), हळ-हळे (water pool m∘), etc.

REVIEW

WHAT WE LEARNED SO FAR

SINGULAR					PLURAL / HONORIFIC					
I	मी *(mī)*	am	आहे	*(āhe)*	We	आम्ही	*(āmhī)*	are	आहोत	*(ahot)*
You	तू *(tū)*	are	आहेस	*(āhes)*	You	तुम्ही	*(tumhī)*	are	आहात	*(āhāt)*
He	तो *(to)*	is	आहे	*(āhe)*	They	ते	*(te)*	are	आहेत	*(āhet)*
She	ती *(tī)*	is	आहे	*(āhe)*	They	त्या	*(tyā)*	are	आहेत	*(āhet)*
It, this	हे *(he)*	is	आहे	*(āhe)*	These	हे	*(he)*	are	आहेत	*(āhet)*
That	ते *(te)*	is	आहे	*(āhe)*	They	ते	*(te)*	are	आहेत	*(āhet)*

EXERCISE : Translate the English sentences into marāṭhī (Answers are given for your help)

adj∘ = Adjective, adv∘ = Adverb; *conj.* = Conjunction, f∘ = Feminine gender, *ind.* = Indeclinable, m∘ = Masculine gender, n∘ = Neuter gender, pl∘ = Plural

1. We are men. *āmhī puruṣh āhot.* आम्ही पुरुष आहोत. We are women. *āmhī striyā āhot.* आम्ही स्त्रिया आहोत.

2. This is a house (n∘). *he ghar āhe.* हे घर आहे. Those are houses. *tī ghare āhet.* ती घरे आहेत.

3. This is a dog (m∘). *hā kutrā āhe.* हा कुत्रा आहे. Those are horses. *te ghoḍe āheta.* ते घोडे आहेत.

4. That is a cat (f∘). *hī mānjar āhe.* ही मांजर आहे. These are cats. *hyā mānjarī āhet.* ह्या मांजरी आहेत.

5. You are a painter (m∘ f∘). *tū rangārī āhes.* तू रंगारी आहेस.

6. These are maraṭhī books (n∘ pl∘)). *hī maraṭhī pustake āhet.* ही मराठी पुस्तके आहेत.

7. This is a computer (n∘). *he saṅgaṇak āhe.* हे संगणक आहे.

8. Those are red cars (f∘ pl∘). *tyā lāl gāḍyā āhet.* त्या लाल गाड्या आहेत.

9. Those cars are red (f∘ pl∘). *tyā gāḍyā lāl āhet.* त्या गाड्या लाल आहेत.

10. Rāma is a teacher (m∘). *Rāma guruji āhe.* राम गुरुजी आहे.

11. He is a Canadian (m∘). *to Kaneḍiyan āhe.* तो कनेडियन आहे.

12. She is Indian (f∘). *tī bhāratīya āhe.* ती भारतीय आहे. You are American (m∘ f∘). *tū amerikan āhes.* तू अमेरिकन आहेस. They are Chinese (m∘ f∘). *te Chīnī āheta.* ते चीनी आहेत.

11.3 SPEAKING A BOUT PAST EVENT (वर्तमान काळ)

Key words : Here = *ithe* इथे. There = *itathe* तिथे. Where? = *kuṭhe?* कुठे?

TABLE 1A : Speaking a Past Event, **Masculine Gender Subject**

	Subject	was	was	were
1	I मी *(mī)*	होतो *(hoto)*		
2	We आम्ही *(āmhī)*			होतो *(hoto)*
3	You तू *(tū)*			होतास *(hotās)*
4	You तुम्ही *(tumhī)* respect and pl∘			होता *(hotā)*
5	You आपण *(tū)* formal and pl∘			होता *(hotā)*
6	He, that तो *(to)*		होता *(hotā)*	
7	These हे *(he)* pl∘			होते *(hote)*
8	They, those ते *(te)* pl∘			होते *(hote)*

adj∘ = Adjective, adv∘ = Adverb; *conj.* = Conjunction, f∘ = Feminine gender, *ind.* = Indeclinable, m∘ = Masculine gender, n∘ = Neuter gender, pl∘ = Plural

TABLE 1B : Speaking a Past Event, **Feminine Gender Subject**

	Subject	was	was	were
1	I मी *(mī)*	होती *(hotī)*		
2	We आम्ही *(āmhī)*			होतो *(hoto)*
3	You तू *(tū)*			होतीस *(hotīs)*
4	You तुम्ही *(tumhī)* respect and pl॰			होत्या *(hotyā)*
5	You आपण *(tū)* formal and pl॰			होत्या *(hotyā)*
6	She, that ती *(tī)*		होती *(hotī)*	
7	These ह्या *(hyā)* pl॰			होत्या *(hotyā)*
8	They, those त्या *(tyā)* pl॰			होत्या *(hotyā)*

TABLE 1C : Speaking a Past Event, **Neuter Gender Subject**

	Subject		was	were
1	It, this हे *(he)*		होते *(hote)*	
2	That ते *(te)*		होते *(hote)*	
3	These ही *(hī)* pl॰			होती *(hotī)*
4	Those ती *(tī)* pl॰			होती *(hotī)*

Making small simple sentences

Masculine subject :

Singular			Plural		
I was here	मी इथे होतो	*mī ithe hoto.*	We were here	आम्ही इथे होतो.	*āmhī ithe hoto.*
You were there	तू तिथे होतास.	*tū tithe hotās.*	You were here.	तुम्ही तिथे होते.	*tumhī tithe hote.*
Where was he?	तो कुठे होता?	*to kuṭhe hotā?*	Where were they?	ते कुठे होते?	*te kuṭhe hote?*

Feminine subject :

Singular			Plural		
I was here	मी इथे होती	*mī ithe hotī.*	We were here	आम्ही इथे होतो.	*āmhī ithe hoto.*
You were there	तू तिथे होतीस.	*tū tithe hotīs.*	You were here.	तुम्ही तिथे होत्या.	*tumhī tithe hotyā.*
Where was she?	ती कुठे होती?	*tī kuṭhe hotī?*	Where were they?	त्या कुठे होत्या?	*tyā kuṭhe hotyā?*

EXERCISE 17 : Translate the English sentences into marāṭhī (Answers are given for help)

Key Words : Not = *nāhī* नाही. And = *āṇi* आणि. Or = *athavā* अथवा. Water (n॰) = *pāṇī* पाणी.

Beautiful = *sundar* सुंदर. (नाही होते = नव्हते)

adj॰ = Adjective, adv॰ = Adverb; *conj.* = Conjunction, f॰ = Feminine gender, *ind.* = Indeclinable, m॰ = Masculine gender, n॰ = Neuter gender, pl॰ = Plural

1. I was an engineer. *mī ingīniyar (abhiyantā) hoto.* मी इंजिनियर (अभियंता) होतो.
2. She was dentist. *tī ḍenṭist hotī.* ती डेंटिस्ट (दंतवैद्य) होती.
3. He was here. *to ithe hotā.* तो इथे होता. They were thieves. *te chor hote.* ते इथे होते.
4. Water is not there. *tithe pāṇī nāhī.* तिथे पाणी नाही. Water was not there. *tithe pāṇī navhate.* तिथे पाणी नव्हते. Teacher was not there. *Gurujī tithe navhate.* गुरुजी तिथे नव्हते.
5. Ramesh was sick. *rameśh ājārī hotā.* रमेश आजारी होता.
6. Sītā and Rādhā were not there. *sītā āṇi rādhā tithe navhatyā.* सीता आणि राधा तिथे नव्हत्या.
7. Rām or Shyām. *rām athvā shyām.* राम अथवा श्याम.
8. She is not here. *tī chor nāhī.* ती इथे नाही. (f∘) They were there. *tyā tithe hotyā.* त्या तिथे होत्या.
9. Rām or Shyām is there. *rām athvā shyām tithe āhe.* राम अथवा श्याम तिथे आहे.
10. Rām and Shyām are dentists. *rām āṇi shyām ḍenṭist āhet.* राम आणि श्याम डेंटिस्ट (दंतवैद्य) आहेत.
11. Nitā and Gītā are there. *nītā āṇi gītā tithe āhet.* नीता आणि गीता तिथे आहेत.
12. Sītā, Rādhā, Nītā and Gītā are beautiful. *sītā, rādhā, nītā āṇi gītā sundar āhet.* सीता, राधा, नीता आणि गीता सुंदर आहेत.

REVIEW

What we learned so far

TABLE : **SUMMARY :** The Present and Past Tenses, the 'cumulative learning'

Subject	am	is	are	was	were
1. I मी *(mī)*	आहे *(āhe)*			होतो *(hoto)*	
2. We आम्ही *(āmhī)*			आहोत *(āhot)*		होतो *(hoto)*
3. He तो *(to)*		आहे *(āhe)*		होता *(hotā)*	
4. These हे *(he)*			आहेत *(āhet)**		होते *(hote)**
5. They ते *(te)*			आहेत *(āhet)**		होते *(hote)**
6. She ती *(tī)*		आहे *(āhe)*		होती *(hotī)*	
7. These ह्या *(hyā)*			आहेत *(āhet)*		होत्या *(hotyā)*
8. They त्या *(tyā)*			आहेत *(āhet)*		होत्या *(hotyā)*
9. It हे *(he)**		आहे *(āhe)*		होते *(hote)**	
10. You तू *(tū)*			आहेस *(āhes)*		होतास *(hotās)*
11. You pl∘ तुम्ही *(tumhī)*			आहात *(āhāt)*		होते *(hote)*
12. You hon∘ आपण *(āpaṇ)*			आहात *(āhāt)*		होते *(hote)*

NOTE : * Same for : He, She, It - plural These and They.

adj∘ = Adjective, adv∘ = Adverb; *conj.* = Conjunction, f∘ = Feminine gender, *ind.* = Indeclinable, m∘ = Masculine gender, n∘ = Neuter gender, pl∘ = Plural

TABLE : **NEGATIVE** Present and Past Tenses, the 'cumulative learning'

Subject	am not	is not	are not	was not	were not
1. I मी *(mī)*	नाही *(nāhī)*			नव्हतो *(navhato)*	
2. We आम्ही *(āmhī)*			नाहीत *(nāhīt)*		नव्हतो *(navhato)*
3. He तो *(to)*		नाही *(nāhī)*		नव्हता *(navhatā)*	
4. These हे *(he)*			नाहीत *(nāhīt)**		नव्हते *(navhate)**
5. They ते *(te)*			नाहीत *(nāhīt)**		नव्हते *(navhate)**
6. She ती *(tī)*		नाही *(nāhī)*		नव्हती *(navhatī)*	
7. These ह्या *(hyā)*			नाहीत *(nāhīt)*		नव्हत्या *(navhatyā)*
8. They त्या *(tyā)*			नाहीत *(nāhīt)*		नव्हत्या *(navhatyā)*
9. It हे *(he)**		नाही *(nāhī)*		नव्हते *(navhate)**	
10. You तू *(tū)*			नाहीस *(nāhīs)*		नव्हतास *(navhatās)*
11. You pl∘ तुम्ही *(tumhī)*			नाही *(nāhī)*		नव्हते *(navhate)*
12. You hon∘ आपण *(āpaṇ)*			नाही *(nāhī)*		नव्हते *(navhate)*

NOTE : * Same for : He, She, It - plural These and They.

1. I was not there. *mī tithe navhato.* मी तिथे नव्हतो.
2. She was not sick. *tī ājārī navhatī.* ती आजारी नव्हती.
3. They were not there. *te tithe navhate.* ते तिथे नव्हते.
4. Water was not hot. *pāṇī garam navhate.* पाणी गरम नव्हते. Water was not there. *tithe pāṇī navhate.* तिथे पाणी नव्हते. Teacher was not there. *Gurujī tithe navhate.* गुरुजी तिथे नव्हते.
5. Ramesh was not crazy. *rameśh pāgal navhatā.* रमेश पागल नव्हता.
6. Sītā and Rādhā were not there. *sītā āṇi rādhā tithe navhatyā.* सीता आणि राधा तिथे नव्हत्या.
7. Rām and Shyām are not here. *rām āṇi shyām ithe nāhit.* राम आणि श्याम इथे नाहीत.
8. (f∘) They are not thieves. *tyā chor nāhīt.* त्या चोर नाहीत.
9. Rām is not there. *rām tithe nāhī.* राम तिथे नाही.
10. Where is Shyām. *shyām kuṭhe āhe?* श्याम कुठे आहे.
11. Nitā and Gītā are not there. *nītā āṇi gītā tithe nāhīt.* नीता आणि गीता तिथे नाहीत.
12. Sītā, Rādhā, Nītā and Gītā are smart. *sītā, rādhā, nītā āṇi gītā huśhār āhet.* सीता, राधा, नीता आणि गीता हुशार आहेत.

LESSON 12

MARATHI PICTORIAL DICTIONARY

f∘ Woman
nārī नारी

m∘ Child
bālak बालक

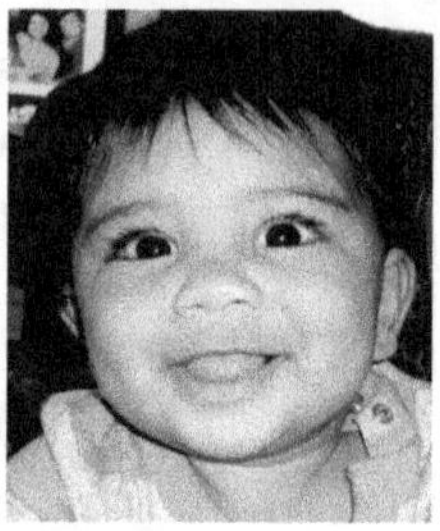

m∘ Face
cheharā चेहरा

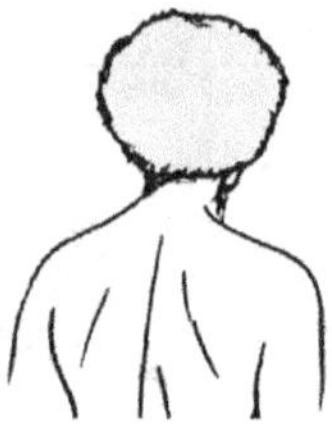

n∘ Head
ḍoke डोके

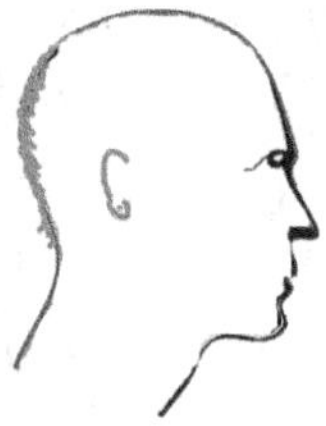

n∘ Bald
ṭakkal टक्कल

f∘ Ponytail
veṇī वेणी

m∘ Hair
kes केस

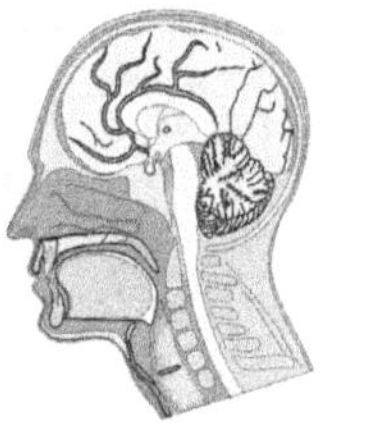

m∘ Brain
mendu मेंदु

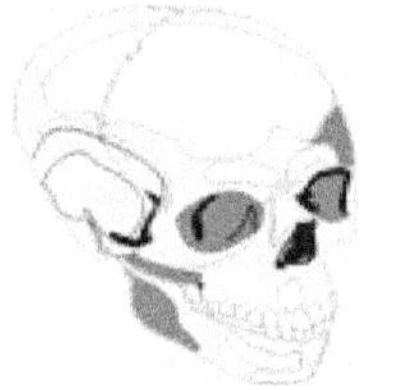

f∘ Skull
ṭakḷī टकळी

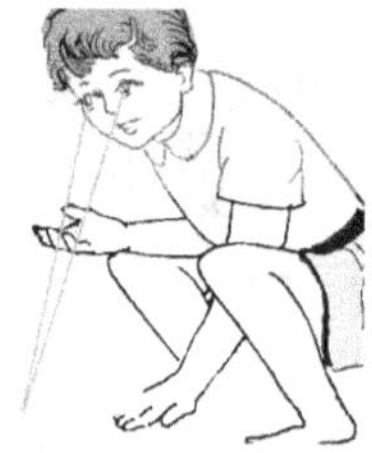

f∘ Vision
druṣhṭi दृष्टि

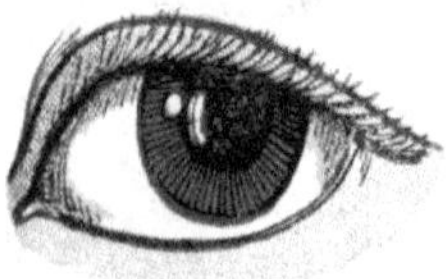

f∘ Eye
ḍoḷā डोळा

f∘ Eyebrow
bhuvaī भुवई

m∘ Tear
aśhru अश्रु

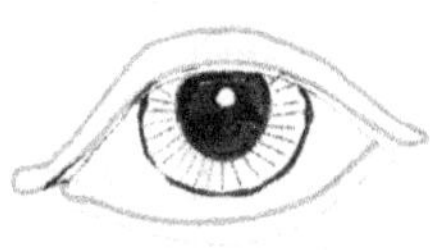

f∘ Eyeball
putaḷī पुतळी

f∘ Eyelid
pāpṇī पापणी

m∘ Cheek
gāl गाल

n∘ Forehead
kapāḷ कपाळ

m∘ Mole
tīḷ तीळ

n∘ Spilus
ṭiḷak टिळक

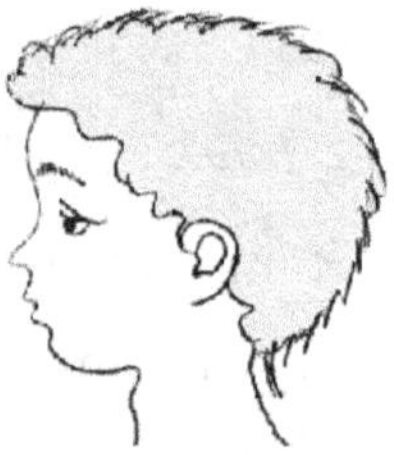

f∘ Neck
mān मान

n∘ Nose
nāk नाक

n∘ Mouth
toṇḍ तोंड

f∘ Mustache
miśhī मिशी

f∘ Beard
dāḍhī दाढी

f∘ Chin
hanuvaṭī हनुवटी

adj∘ = Adjective, adv∘ = Adverb; *conj.* = Conjunction, f∘ = Feminine gender, *ind.* = Indeclinable, m∘ = Masculine gender, n∘ = Neuter gender, pl∘ = Plural

m◦ Lip
Oṭh ओठ

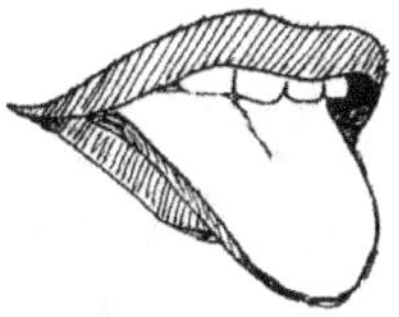

f◦ Tongue
jībh जीभ

m◦ Teeth
dāt दात

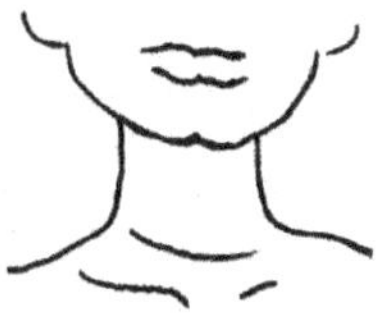

m◦ Throat
gaḷā गळा

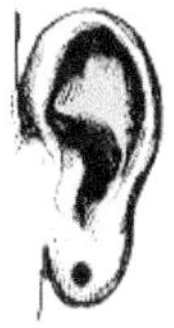

m◦ Ear
kān कान

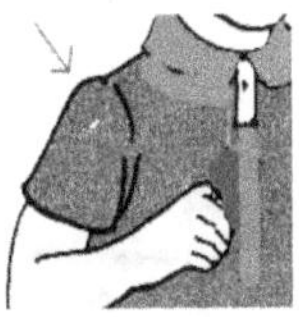

m◦ Shoulder
khāndā खांदा

m◦ Hand
hāt हात

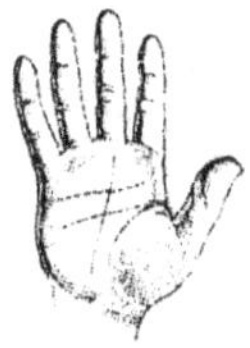

m◦ Palm
taḷhāt तळहात

m◦ Thumb
āngṭhā आंगठा

n◦ Bone
haḍ हाड

f◦ Forefinger
tarjanī तर्जनी

f◦ Middle finger
madhyamā मध्यमा

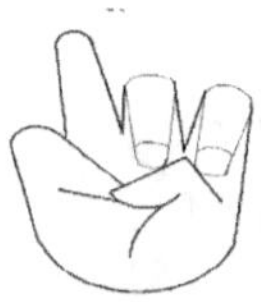

f◦ Ring finger
anāmikā अनामिका

f◦ Little finger
kanakī कनीका

n◦ Nail
nakh नख

n◦ Elbow
ḍhopar ढोपर

n◦ Wrist
mangaṭ मनगट

f◦ Fist
mūṭh मूठ

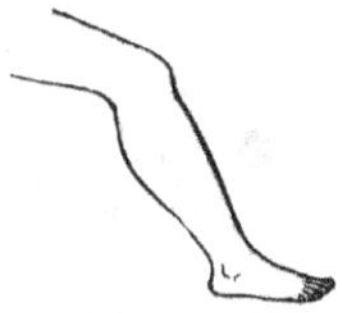

m◦ Leg
pāy पाय

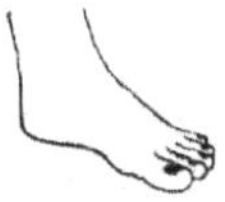

n◦ Foot
pāūl पाऊल

m◦ Sole
taḷpāy तळपाय

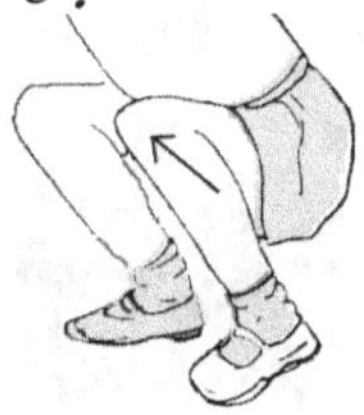

m◦ Knee
guḍhgā गुढगा

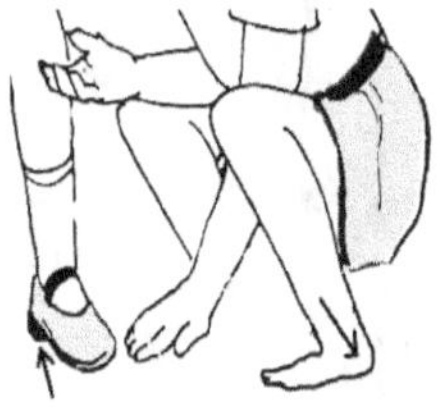

f◦ Heel
ṭāch टाच

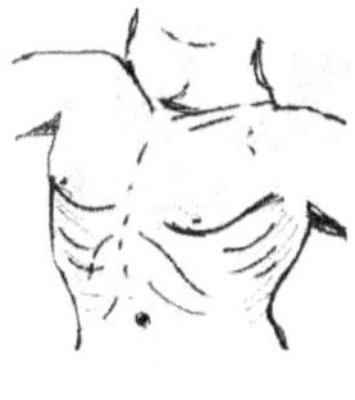

f◦ Chest
chhātī छाती

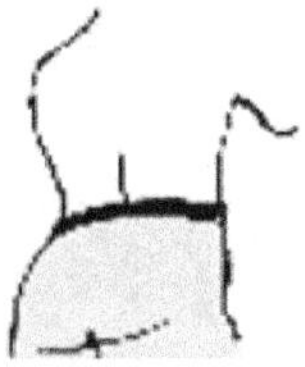

f◦ Waist
kambar कम्बर

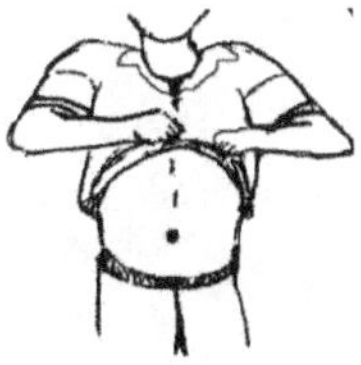

n◦ Stomach
poṭ पोट

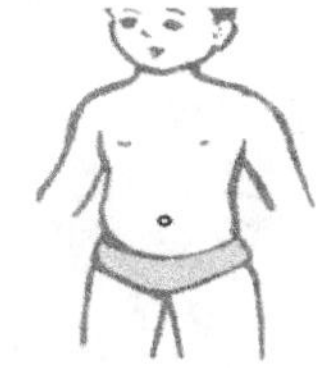

f◦ Bellybutton
nābhī नाभी

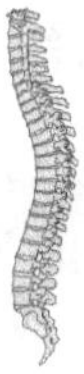

m◦ Spine
kaṇā कणा

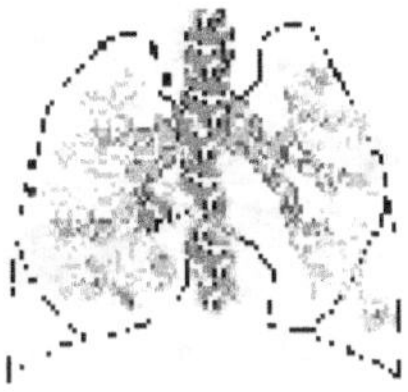

m◦ Lungs
fefade फेफडे

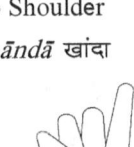

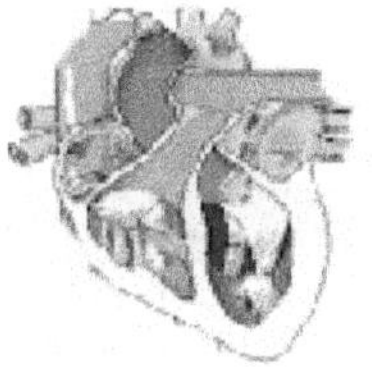

n◦ Heart
hruday हृदय

adj◦ = Adjective, adv◦ = Adverb; *conj.* = Conjunction, f◦ = Feminine gender, *ind.* = Indeclinable, m◦ = Masculine gender, n◦ = Neuter gender, pl◦ = Plural

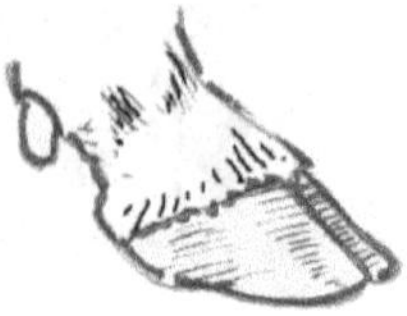

n◦ Hoof

khūr खूर

m◦ Paw

pañjā पंजा

f◦ Trunk

soṇḍ सोंड

n◦ Mane

āyāḷ आयाळ

f◦ Wool

lokar लोकर

f◦ Tail

śhepaṭī शेपटी

n◦ Horn

śhinga शिंग

f◦ Beak

choch चोच

n◦ Feather

paṅkh पंख

n◦ Egg

aṇḍe अंडे

n◦ Tree

jhāḍ झाड

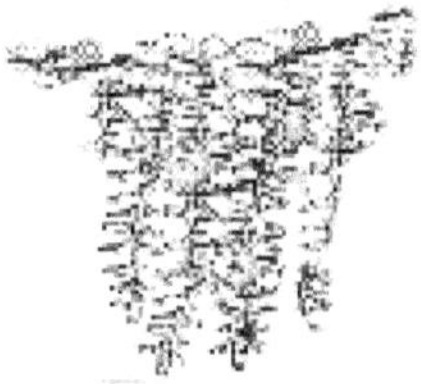

f◦ Vine

vel वेल

m◦ Banyan

vaḍ वड

m◦ Faicus

pimpaḷ पिंपळ

m◦ Mango

āmbā आंबा

m◦ Pine

devadār देवदार

m◦ Bamboo

bās बास

m◦ Palm

tāḍ ताड़

n◦ Grass

gavat गवत

n◦ wood

lākūḍ लाकूड

n◦ Leaf

pān पान

f◦ Brañch

fāndī फांदी

n◦ Root

mūḷ मूळ

n◦ Forest

Jangal जंगल

m◦ Mountain

pahāḍ पहाड़

n◦ Flower

fūl फूल

n◦ Lotus

kamaḷ कमळ

m◦ Rose

gulāb गुलाब

f◦ Jasmine

chamelī चमेली

f◦ Sunflower

sūryamukhī सूर्यमुखी

adj◦ = Adjective, adv◦ = Adverb; *conj.* = Conjunction, f◦ = Feminine gender, *ind.* = Indeclinable, m◦ = Masculine gender, n◦ = Neuter gender, pl◦ = Plural

f◦ Bud
kaḷī कळी

n◦ Fruit
faḷ फळ

n◦ Banana
keḷ केळ

n◦ Grapes
angūr अंगूर

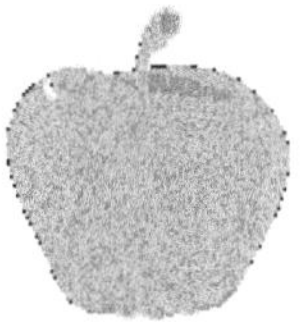

n◦ Apple
śhep शेप

n◦ Lemon
limbū लिंबू

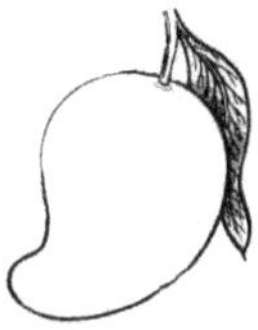

m◦ Mango
āmbā आंबा

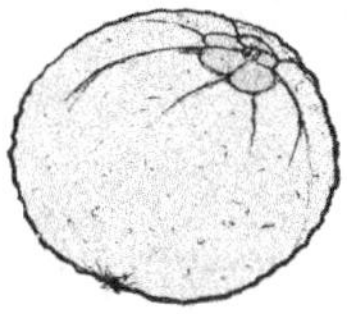

n◦ Orange
nāringa नारिंग

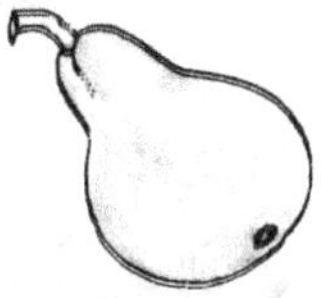

n◦ Pear
safarchand सफरचंद

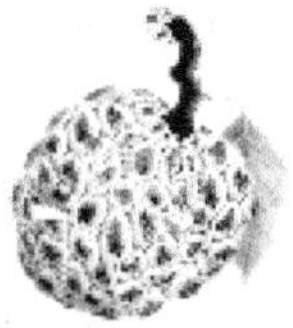

n◦ Custard apple
sītāfaḷ सीताफळ

f◦ Papaya
papaī पपई

n◦ Pineapple *ananas*
अननस

n◦ Pomegranate
ḍāḷimba डाळिंब

m◦ Sugarcane
ūs ऊस

m◦ Cashew
kājū काजू

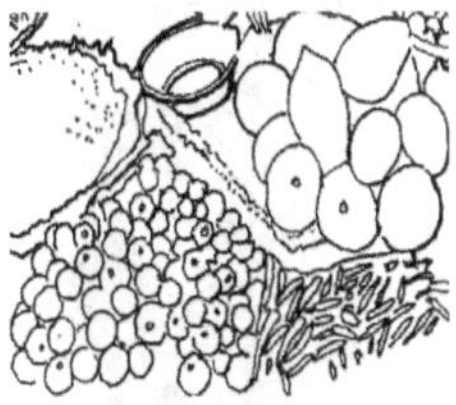

m◦ Vegetables
bhājīpālā भाजीपाला

n◦ Beet
chukandar चुकंदर

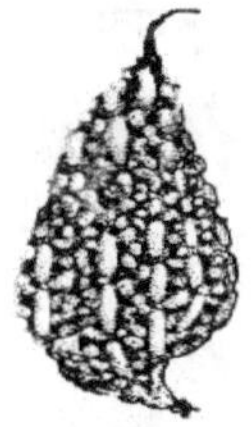

n◦ Bitter gourd
karle केरले

f◦ Cabbage
pānkobī पानकोबी

n◦ Watermelon
ṭarbūj टरबूज

n◦ Carrot
gānjar गांजर

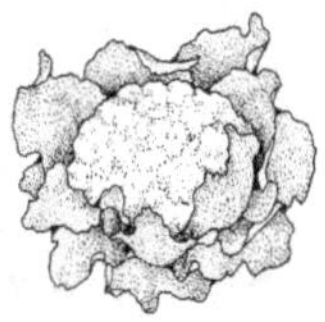

f◦ Cauliflower
fūlkobī फूलकोबी

m◦ Coriander
sāmbār सांबार

f◦ Chili
mirchī मिरची

n◦ Plum
bor बोर

n◦ Tomato
bhedur भेदुर

m◦ Mint
padinā पदिना

f◦ Beans
śheng शेंग

n◦ Zucchini
doḍke दोडके

m◦ Cocoanut
nāraḷ नारळ

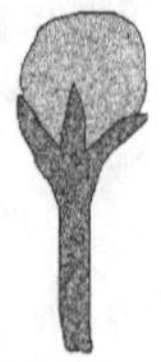

f∘ Clove
lavang लवंग

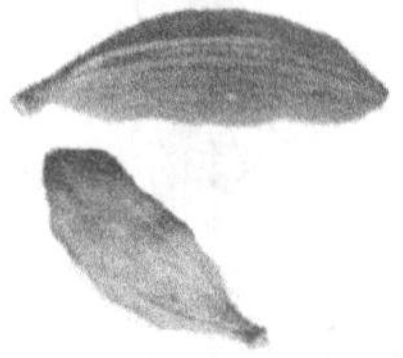

f∘ Cardamom
vilāyaychī विलायची

f∘ Almond
badām बदाम

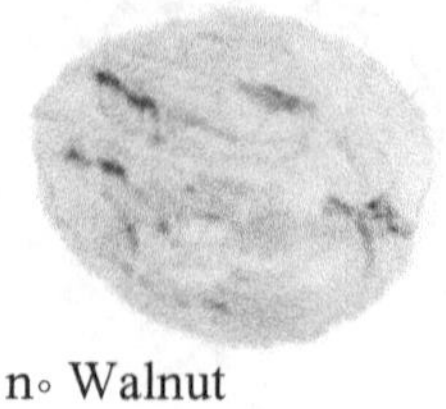

n∘ Walnut
akroḍ अक्रोड

m∘ Peanut
bhuīmūg भुईमूग

f∘ Date
khārīk खारीक

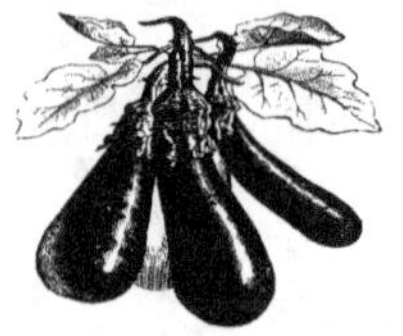

n∘ Eggplant
vānge वांगे

m∘ Garlic
lasūṇ लसूण

n∘ Ginger
āle आले

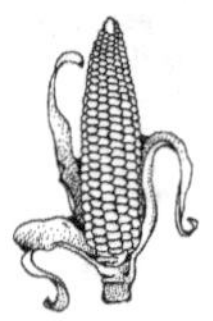

m∘ Corn
makā मका

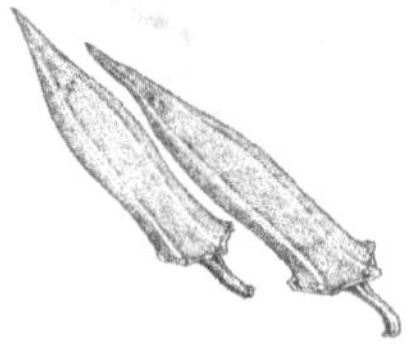

f∘ Okrā
bhenḍī भेंडी

m∘ Onion
kāndā कांदा

m∘ Potato
abaṭāṭā बटाटा

m∘ Peas
vāṭāṇe वाटाणे

f∘ Cucumber
kākḍī काकडी

n∘ Pumpkin
kohaḷe कोहळे

m∘ Radish
miḷā मुळा

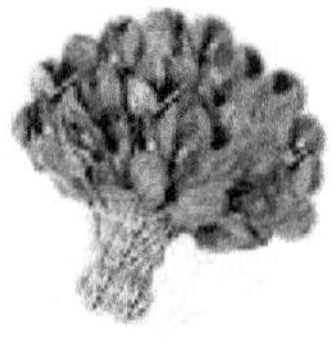

f∘ Spinach
pālak पालक

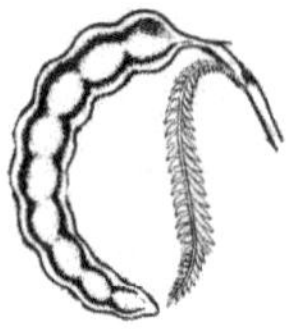

f∘ Tamarind
chiñcha चिंच

n∘ Jackfruit
syraṇ सुरण

f∘ Pulse
dāḷ दाळ

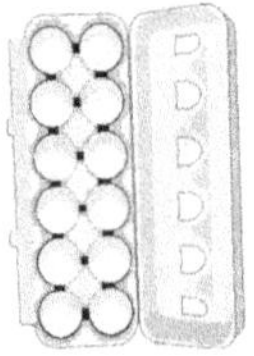

n∘ Eggs
aṇḍe अण्डे

n∘ Flour
pīṭh पीठ

n∘ Honey
sahad सहद

n∘ Oil
tel तेल

m∘ Breakfast
nāstā नास्ता

n∘ Butter
loṇī लोणी

f∘ Catsup
Chaṭṇī चटणी

m∘ Coffee
kahavā कहवा

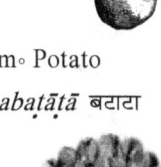

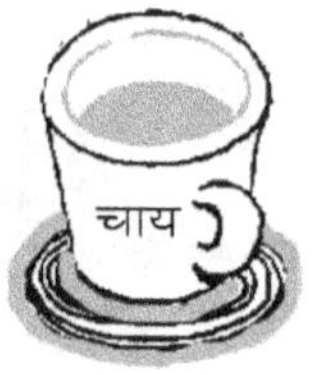

f∘ Tea
Chahā चहा

adj∘ = Adjective, adv∘ = Adverb; *conj.* = Conjunction, f∘ = Feminine gender, *ind.* = Indeclinable, m∘ = Masculine gender, n∘ = Neuter gender, pl∘ = Plural

f∘ *burfi*
बरफी

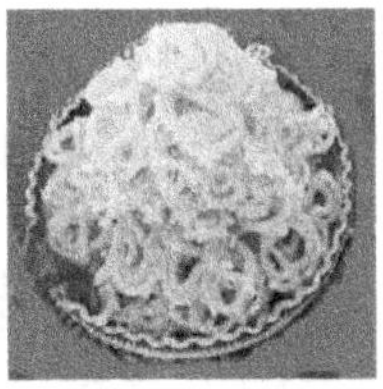

f∘ *jhilabī*
झिलबी

m∘ *lāḍū*
लाडू

n∘ Milk
dūdh दूध

n∘ Clarified-butter *tūp*
तूप

m∘ *parāṭā*
पराटा

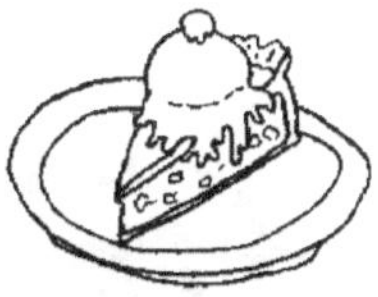

m∘ Cake
kek केक

n∘ Pickle
loṇche लोणचे

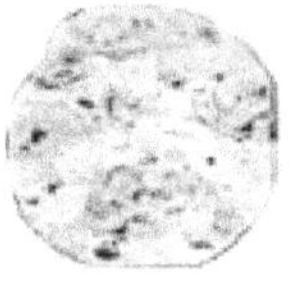

f∘ Bread
poḷī पोळी

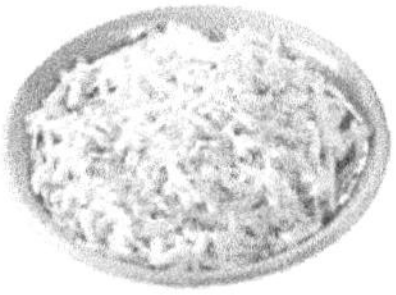

m∘ Rice
bhāt भात

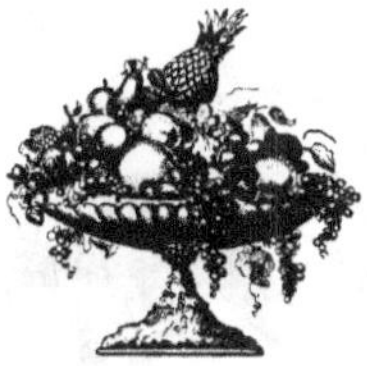

f∘ Salad
sālad सालद

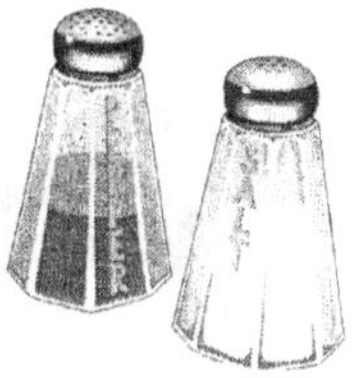

m∘ Salt
mīṭh मीठ

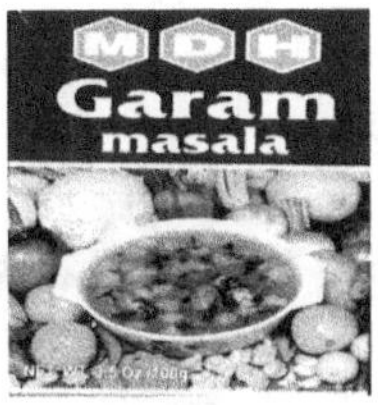

m∘ Spice
masālā मसाला

f∘ Wine
madirā मदिरा

f∘ Chicken
kombaḍī कोंबडी

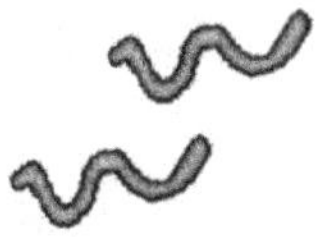

m∘ Worm
kīḍā कीडा

m∘ Animal
pashu पशु

m∘ Leopard
chitā चिता

m∘ Python
ajgar अजगर

m∘ Firefly
kājvā काजवा

f∘ Porcupine
sēḷū साळू

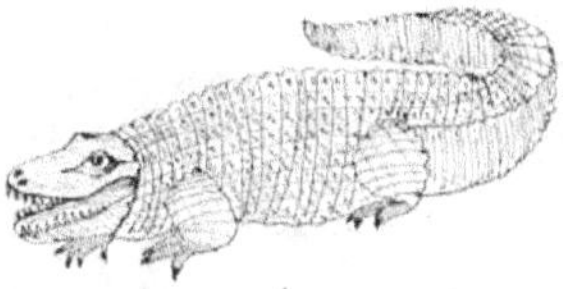

m∘ Alligator
magar मगर

f∘ Ant
mungī मुंगी

f∘ Bat
vaṭvāghuḷ वटवाघुळ

m∘ Ape
ādimāna आदिमानव

m∘ Scorpion
viñchū विंचू

f∘ Sheep
menḍhī मेंढी

m∘ Snake
sāp साप

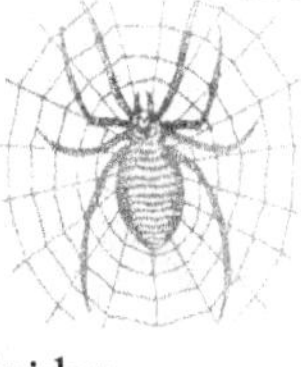

f∘ Spider
kātiṇ कातिण

n∘ Turtle
kāsav कासव

adj∘ = Adjective, adv∘ = Adverb; *conj.* = Conjunction, f∘ = Feminine gender, *ind.* = Indeclinable, m∘ = Masculine gender, n∘ = Neuter gender, pl∘ = Plural

n◦ Deer
hariṇ हरिण

m◦ Dog
kutrā कुत्रा

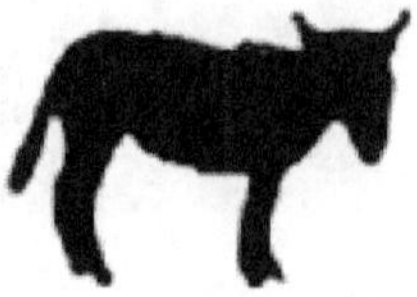

n◦ Donkey
gāḍhav गाढव

m◦ Elephant
hāttī हत्ती

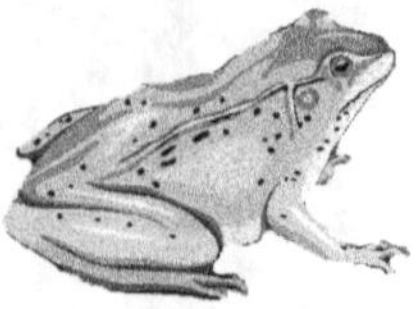

n◦ Frog
beḍuk बेडुक

n◦ Bear
aswal अस्वल

f◦ Bee
maśhī माशी

f◦ Buffalo
mhais म्हैस

n◦ Butterfly
patang पतंग

m◦ Fish
māsā मासा

m◦ Camel
uṇṭa ऊंट

f◦ Cat
mānjar मांजर

m◦ Cobra
nāg नाग

f◦ Cow
gāy गाय

m◦ Fox
kolhā कोल्हा

f◦ Goat
bakrī बकरी

m◦ Hippo
pāṇghoḍā पाणघोडा

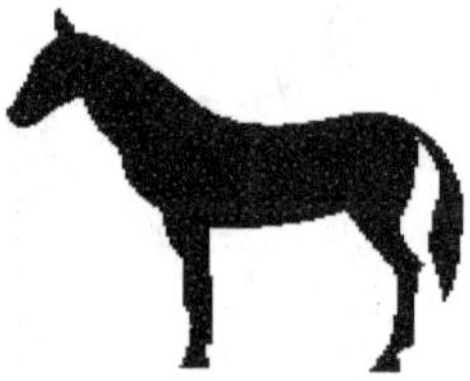

m◦ Horse
ghoḍā घोड़ा

n◦ Hyena
taras तरस

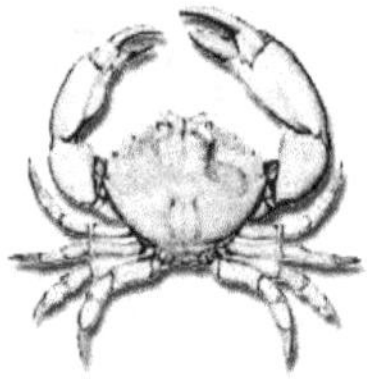

m◦ Crab
khekḍā खेकड़ा

m◦ Lion
sim̃ha सिंह

f◦ Lizard
pāl पाल

n◦ Mongoose
mungūs मुंगूस

m◦ Monkey
mākaḍ माकड

m◦ Zebra
paṭerā पटेरा

m◦ Mosquito
ḍās डास

m◦ Moth
pingāṇā पिंगाणा

m◦ Mouse
undīr उंदीर

m◦ Ox
bail बैल

f◦ Squirrel
khirāḍī खिराडी

adj◦ = Adjective, adv◦ = Adverb; *conj.* = Conjunction, f◦ = Feminine gender, *ind.* = Indeclinable, m◦ = Masculine gender, n◦ = Neuter gender, pl◦ = Plural

n◦ Pig
ḍukkar डुक्कर

m◦ Rabbit
sasā ससा

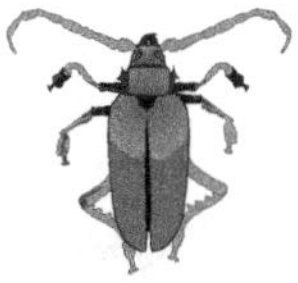

n◦ Roach
zingur झिंगुर

m◦ Rhino
geṇḍā गेंडा

m◦ Tiger
vāgh वाघ

m◦ Bird
pakṣhī पक्षी

f◦ Cuckoo
kokiḷā कोकिळा

m◦ Crow
kavḷā कावळा

n◦ Duck
badak बदक

m◦ Crane
bagaḷā बगळा

f◦ Eagle
ghār घार

f◦ Fly
māśhī माशी

f◦ Hen
kombaḍī कोंबडी

n◦ Owl
ghubaḍ घुबड

m◦ Falcon
sasāṇā ससाणा

m◦ Parrot
popaṭ पोपट

m◦ Peacock
mor मोर

m◦ Pigeon
kabūtar कबूतर

m◦ Rooster
kombḍā कोंबडा

m◦ Pheasant
titar तीतर

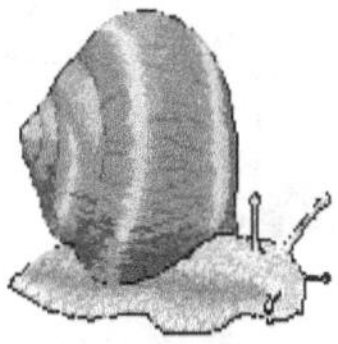

m◦ Snail
gogalgāy गोगलगाय

m◦ Swan
haṁsa हंस

n◦ Vulture
gidhāḍ गिधाड

m◦ Woodpecker
lākūḍtodyā लाकुडतोड्या

m◦ Grasshopper
nāktoḍā नाकतोडा

m◦ Ostrich
Shahāmrug शहामृग

m◦ Flamingo
marāḷ मराळ

f◦ Turkey
peru पेरु

m◦ Jay
bulbul बुलबुल

f◦ Quail
lāv लाव

adj◦ = Adjective, adv◦ = Adverb; *conj.* = Conjunction, f◦ = Feminine gender, *ind.* = Indeclinable, m◦ = Masculine gender, n◦ = Neuter gender, pl◦ = Plural

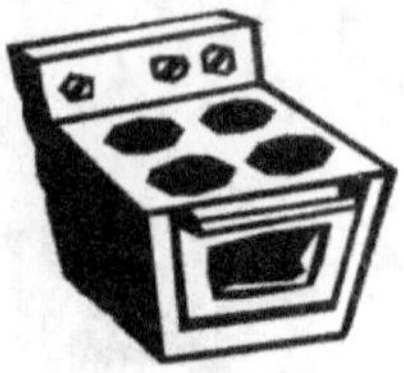

f∘ Stove

chūl चूल

m∘ Cup

chaṣhak चषक

m∘ Glass

pyālā प्याला

n∘ Plate

tāṭ ताट

f∘ Knife

sūrī सूरी

m∘ Knife

chākū चाकू

f∘ ladle

paḷī पळी

m∘ *Spoon*

chamchā चमचा

f∘ Wok

kaḍhaī कढई

f∘ Bucket

bādlī बादली

n∘ Book

pustak पुस्तक

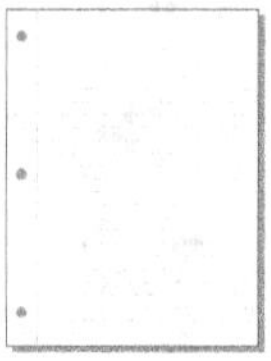

m∘ Paper

kāgad कागद

f∘ Letter

patra पत्र

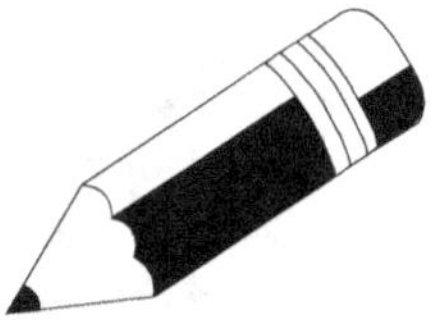

f∘ Pencil

lekhaṇī लेखणी

m∘ Pen

ṭāk टाक

n∘ Certificate

pramāṇ-patra प्रमाणपत्र

m∘ Money

paise पैसे

m∘ Ball

cheṇḍū चेंडू

n∘ Medicine

auṣhadh औषध

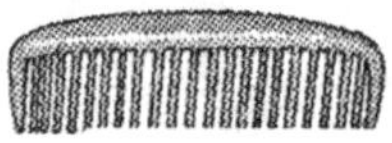

m∘ Comb

kangvā कंगवा

m∘ Shirt

sadrā सदरा

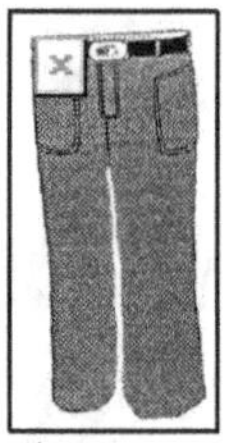

f∘ Pants

vijār विजार

m∘ Shoe

joḍā जोडा

f∘ *sāḍī*

साडी

m∘ Brush

braśh ब्रश

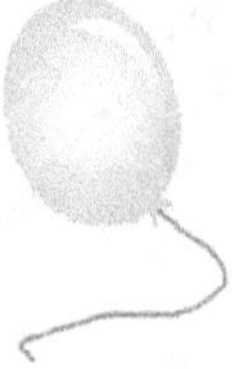

m∘ Balloon

fugā फुगा

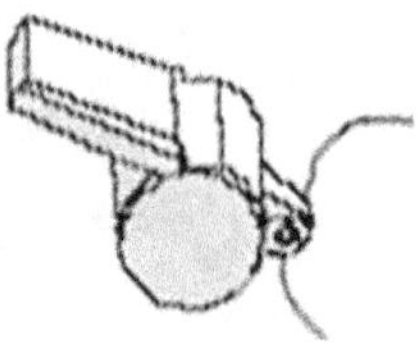

f∘ Whistle

śhiṭṭī शिट्टी

m∘ Fan

paṅkhā पंखा

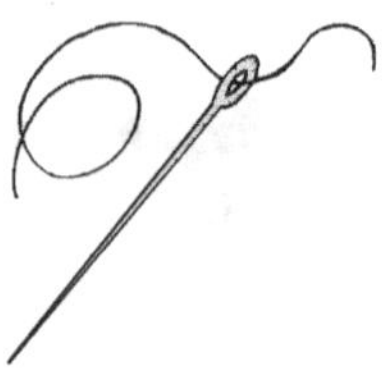

f∘ Needle

suī सुई

f∘ Stick

chhaḍī छड़ी

adj∘ = Adjective, adv∘ = Adverb; *conj.* = Conjunction, f∘ = Feminine gender, *ind.* = Indeclinable, m∘ = Masculine gender, n∘ = Neuter gender, pl∘ = Plural

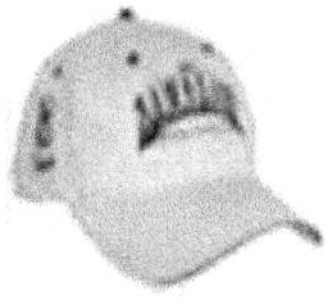

f◦ Cap
ṭopī टोपी

m◦ Bag
thailā थैला

f◦ Umbrella
chhatrī छत्री

m◦ Glasses
chaṣmā चष्मा

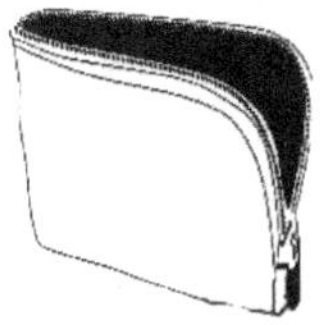

m◦ Wallet
baṭvā बटवा

n◦ House
ghar घर

f◦ Key
killī किल्ली

m◦ Lock
kulup कुलुप

m◦ Door
darwājā दरवाजा

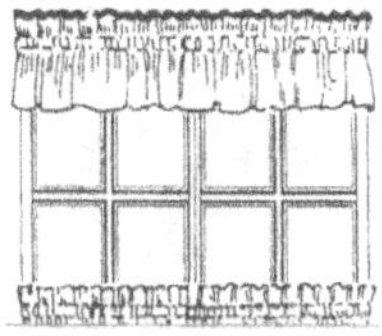

f◦ Window
khiḍakī खिड़की

f◦ Stool
chārpaī चारपाई

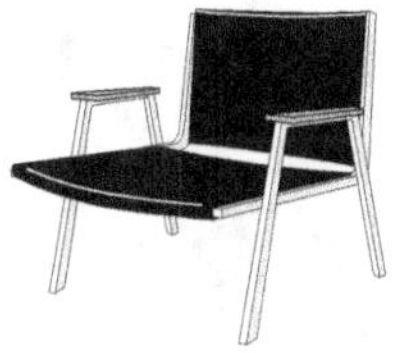

f◦ Chair
khurchī खुर्ची

m◦ Broom
jhaḍū झाडू

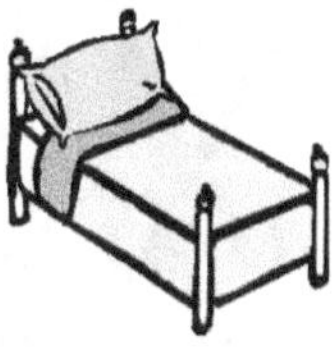

m◦ Bed
bichhānā बिछाना

f◦ Electricity
vīj वीज

f◦ Pillow
uśhī उशी

f◦ Mattress
gadī गादी

n◦ Blanket
ghongaḍe घोंगडे

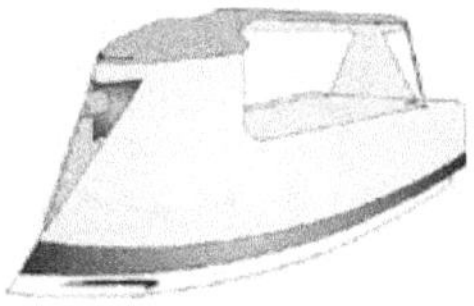

f◦ Iron
istarī इस्तरी

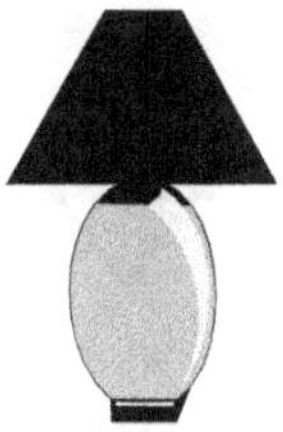

m◦ Lamp
divā दिवा

f◦ Kettle
keṭlī केटली

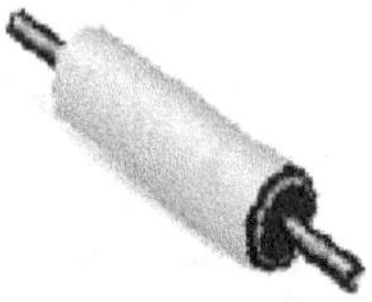

n◦ Rolling pin
laṭṇe लाटणे

f◦ Jug
suraī सुरई

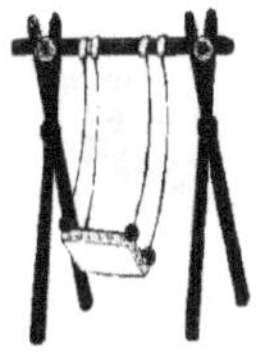

m◦ Swing
pāḷṇā पाळणा

m◦ Razor
vastarā वस्तरा

f◦ Hammer
hātoḍī हातोडी

f◦ Pliers
pakaḍ पकड

m◦ *Screwdriver*
pechkas पेचकस

f◦ Saw
ārī आरी

m◦ Wreñch
pānā पाना

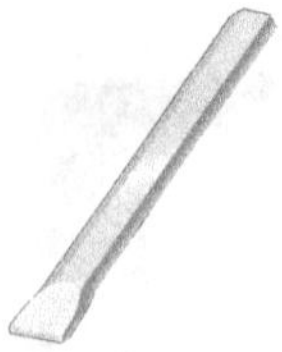

f∘ Chisel
chhannī छन्नी

f∘ Ax
kurhāḍ कुऱ्हाड

n∘ Shovel
pāvḍe पावडे

m∘ Screw
pech पेच

f∘ Nail
khiḷā खिळा

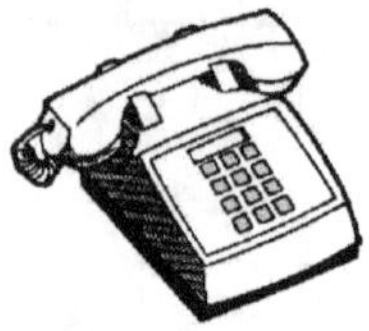

m∘ Phone
dūrabhāsh दूरभाष

f∘ Cell जंगमदूरवाणी
jangamadūravānī

f∘ Radio *ākāśavāṇī*
आकाशवाणी

n∘ TV *dūradarśan*
दूरदर्शन

n∘ Computer
saṅgaṇak संगणक

n∘ Chess
buddhibaḷ बुद्धिबळ

f∘ Scissors
kaichī कैची

m∘ Thread
dorā दोरा

m∘ Broom
jhāḍū झाडू

n∘ Watch
ghaḍyāḷ घड्याळ

m∘ Diamond
hīrā हीरा

f∘ Ring
angaṭhī आंगठी

m∘ Necklace
hār हार

m∘ Mirror
ārsā आरसा

m∘ Paper *vartaman-*
patra वर्तमानपत्र

f∘ Bicycle
sāyakal सायकल

f∘ Car
gāḍī गाड़ी

n∘ Airplane
vimān विमान

f∘ Boat
nāv नाव

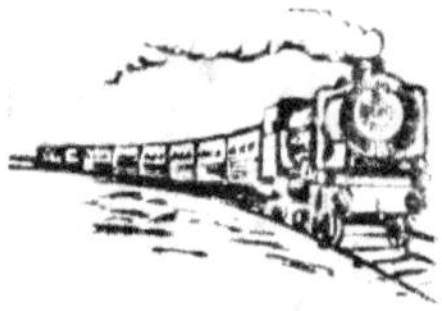

f∘ Rail
āg-gāḍī आगगाड़ी

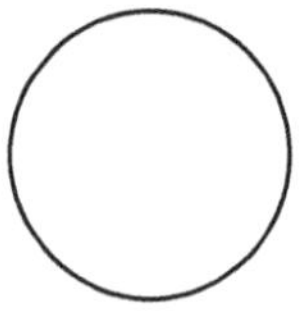

m∘ Circle
gol गोल

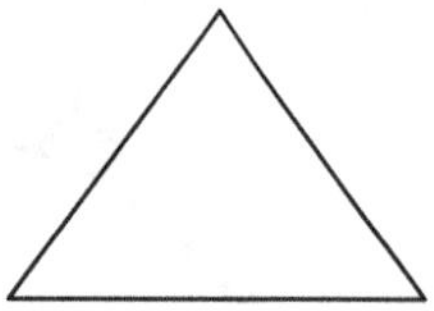

m∘ Triangle
trikoṇa त्रिकोण

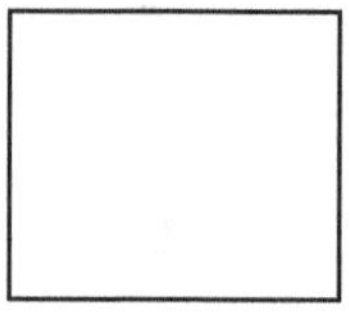

m∘ Square
chaturbhuj चतुर्भुज

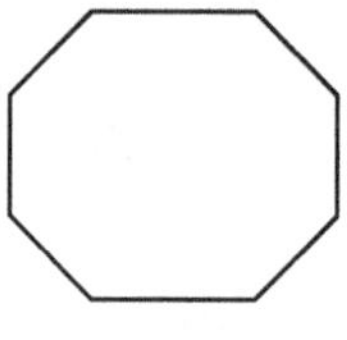

m∘ Hexagaon
shaṭkoṇa षट्कोण

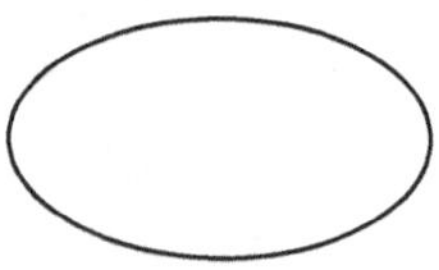

f∘ oval
aṇḍdākritī अंडाकृति

adj∘ = Adjective, adv∘ = Adverb; *conj.* = Conjunction, f∘ = Feminine gender, *ind.* = Indeclinable, m∘ = Masculine gender, n∘ = Neuter gender, pl∘ = Plural

m◦ Accountant
munīm मुनीम

m◦ Bus-wālā
bus-wālā बसवाला

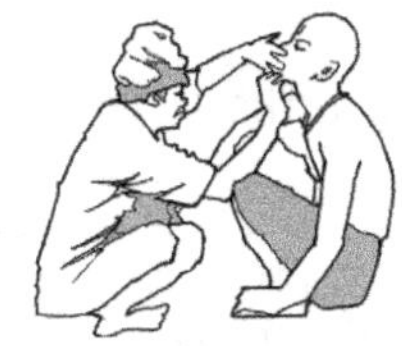

m◦ Barber
nhāvī न्हावी

m◦ Carpenter
wādhī वाढी

m◦ Boatman
nāvik नाविक

f◦ Dancer
nartakī नर्तकी

m◦ Potter
kumbhār कुम्भार

m◦ Farmer
śhetkari शेतकरी

m◦ Labourer
majūr मजूर

m◦ Lawyer
vakīl वकील

m◦ Magician
jādūgār जादूगार

m◦ Musician
sangītakār संगीतकार

m◦ Painter
rangwālā रंगवाला

m◦ Goldsmith
sonār सोनार

m◦ Police
polīs पोलीस

m◦ student
vidyārthī विद्यार्थी

m◦ Priest
pujārī पुजारी

m◦ Soldie
sainik सैनिक

m◦ Snake charmer
gāruḍī गारुडी

m◦ Tailor
śhimpī शिंपी

f◦ Teacher
māstar मास्तर

m◦ Thief
chor चोर

f◦ Typist
ṭaṅkiṇak टंकणक

m◦ Wrestler
pahelwān पहेलवान

m◦ Swimmer
pohaṇārā पोहणारा

f◦ Nurse *parichārikā* परिचारिका

m◦ Fruit vendor
bhajīwalī भाजीवाली

m◦ Ascetic
yogī योगी

m◦ Washerman
dhobī धोबी

m◦ Player
kheḷḍū खेळाडू

adj◦ = Adjective, adv◦ = Adverb; *conj.* = Conjunction, f◦ = Feminine gender, *ind.* = Indeclinable, m◦ = Masculine gender, n◦ = Neuter gender, pl◦ = Plural

COMMON MARATHI ACTION WORDS, MARATHI ROOT VERBS (* = transitive verbs)

Add णे to any Root Verb to make Infinitive, Verbal Noun or Gerund.

VERB STEMS

agree* मान *mān*
arrange* रच *rach*
become हो *ho*
become बन *ban*
bother* सताव *satāv*
break (self) तूट *tūṭ*
break* तोड *toḍ*
bring* आण *āṇ*
burn (self) जळ *jaḷ*
burn* जाळ *jāḷ*
call* बोलाव *bolāv*
can, be able शक *śhak*
come ये *ye*
cook* शिजव *śhijav*
cry रड *raḍ*
cut* काप *kāp*
die मर *mar*
dig* खोद *khod*
do* कर *kar*
drink* पी *pī*
drive* चालव *chālav*
drop* पाड *pāḍ*
eat* खा *khā*
fall पड *paḍ*
fear (self) भि *bhi*
fly (self) उड *uḍ*

VERB STEMS

fly* उडव *uḍav*
forget विसर *visar*
fry* तळ *taḷ*
get* मिळव *miḷav*
give* दे *de*
go जा *jā*
hear* ऐक *aik*
hide (self) लप *lap*
hide* लपव *lapav*
kill, hit* मार *mār*
know* जाण *jāṇ*
laugh हस *has*
learn* शिक *śhik*
live (alive) जग *jag*
loose* हरव *harav*
make* कर *kar*
meet मिळ *miḷ*
mix* मिळव *miḷav*
move (self) हाल *hāl*
move* हालव *hālav*
open (self) उघड *ughaḍ*
open* उघड *ughaḍ*
peel* छील *chhīl*
read* वाच *vāch*
rob* लुट *luṭ*
rub* मळ *maḷ*

VERB STEMS

run पळ *paḷ*
say* म्हण *mhaṇ*
show* दाखव *dākhav**
sell* विक *vik*
sew* शिव *shiv*
sing* गा *gā*
sit बस *bas*
sleep झोप *zop*
sow* पेर *per*
speak बोल *bol*
spread* पसर *pasar*
stay, live राह *rāh*
steal* चोर *chor*
stop थांब *rthāmb*
sulk रुस *rus*
take* घे *ghe*
teach* शिकव *śhikav*
tell* सांग *sāng*
walk चाल *chāl*
want, like* चाह *chāh*
wash* धु *dhu*
weigh* तोल *tol*
win* जीत *jīt*
write* लिही *lihī*

NOTE : The underlined four are most important action words required for making sentences.

adj∘ = Adjective, adv∘ = Adverb; *conj.* = Conjunction, f∘ = Feminine gender, *ind.* = Indeclinable, m∘ = Masculine gender, n∘ = Neuter gender, pl∘ = Plural

LESSON 13

क्रियापद

USING VERBS

USING THE ACTION WORDS FOR MAKING YOUR OWN SENTENCES

Let us learn **how to make our own sentences** in the following four ways

(13.1) I normally 'do' as a habit (you do; he, she, it does; we do, they do)

(13.2) I am 'doing' (you are doing; he, she, it is doing; we, they are doing)

(13.3) I 'used to do' (you used to do; he, she, it used to do; they used to do)

(13.4) I was 'doing' (you were doing; he, she, it was doing; they were doing)

PRESENT TENSE (वर्तमान काळ)

(13.1)

Habitual Present Tense

Making sentences with - I do; you do; he, she, it does; we do; they do.

	Doer of the action	drink	do, does	
Subject	marāṭhī	drink **पी** (pī)	I drink tea (**चहा** chahā)	milk (**दूध** dūdh)
1. I	मी *(mī)*	पितो *(pito)*	मी चहा पितो *(mī chahā pito)*	मी दूध पितो *(mī dūdh pito)*
2. We	आम्ही *(āmhī)*	पितो *(pito)*	आम्ही चहा पितो *(amhī chahā pito)*	आम्ही दूध पितो *(amhī dūdh pito)*
3. He	तो *(to)*	पितो *(pito)*	तो चहा पितो *(to chahā pito)*	तो दूध पितो *(to dūdh pito)*
4. These	हे *(he)*	पितात *(pitāt)*	हे चहा पितात *(he chahā pitāt)*	हे दूध पितात *(he dūdh pitāt)*
5. They	ते *(te)*	पितात *(pitāt)*	ते चहा पितात *(te chahā pitāt)*	ते दूध पितात *(te dūdh pitāt)*
6. She	ती *(tī)*	पिते *(pite)*	ती चहा पिते *(tī chahā pite)*	ती दूध पिते *(tī dūdh pite)*
7. These	ह्या *(hyā)*	पितात *(pitāt)*	ह्या चहा पितात *(hyā chahā pitāt)*	ह्या दूध पितात *(hyā dūdh pitāt)*
8. They	त्या *(tyā)*	पितात *(pitāt)*	त्या चहा पितात *(tyā chahā pitāt)*	त्या दूध पितात *(tyā dūdh pitāt)*
9. It *	हे *(he)**	पिते *(pite)*	हे चहा पिते *(he chahā pite)*	हे दूध पिते *(he dūdh pite)*
10. You	तू *(tū)*	पितोस *(pitos)*	तू चहा पितोस *(tū chahā pitos)*	तू दूध पितोस *(tū dūdh pitoa)*
11. You pl∘	तुम्ही *(tumhī)*	पिता *(pitā)*	तुम्ही चहा पिता *(tumhī chahā pitā)*	तुम्ही दूध पिता *(tumhī dūdh pitā)*
12. You hon∘	आपण *(āpaṇ)*	पिता *(pitā)*	आपण चहा पिता *(āpaṇ chahā pitā)*	आपण दूध पिता *(āpaṇ dūdh pitā)*

NOTE : * Same for : He, She, It - plural These and They.

adj∘ = Adjective, adv∘ = Adverb; *conj.* = Conjunction, f∘ = Feminine gender, *ind.* = Indeclinable, m∘ = Masculine gender, n∘ = Neuter gender, pl∘ = Plural

TABLE : Present Habitual Tense Suffixes SUMMARY

	Subject	Suffix M∘	Suffix F∘
∘	I	तो *(to)*	ते *(te)*
∘	He/she	तो *(tā)*	ते *(tī)*
*	We	तो *(to)*	तो *(to)*
*	You *(āp)*	ता *(te)*	ता *(tāt)*
*	They	तात *(te)*	तात *(tāt)*

EXERCISE 19 : Translate the English sentences into marāṭhī (Answers are given for help)

a. I drink. m∘ *mī pito (*f∘ *mī pite)* मी पीतो (मी पीते). You drink m∘ *tū pītos* तू पितोस. f∘ *tū pītes* तू पीतेस. He drinks. *to pīto* तो पीतो. She drinks *tī pite* ती पिते. We drink *āmhī pito.* आम्ही पितो. They drink. *te pitāt* ते पितात.

b. I drink tea. m∘ *mī chahā pito (*f∘ *mī chahā pite)* मी चहा पीतो (f∘ मी चहा पीते). You drink tea m∘ *tū chahā pītos* तू चहा पितोस. f∘ *tū chahā pītes* तू चहा पीतेस. He drinks tea. *to chahā pīto* तो चहा पीतो. She drinks tea *tī chahā pite* ती चहा पिते. We drink tea *āmhī chahā pito.* आम्ही चहा पितो. They drink tea *te chahā pitāt* ते चहा पितात.

c. I drink hot tea. m∘ *mī garam chahā pito (*f∘ *mī garam chahā pite)* मी गरम चहा पीतो (मी गरम चहा पीते). You drink hot tea m∘ *tū garam chahā pītos* तू गरम चहा पितोस. f∘ *tū garam chahā pītes* तू गरम चहा पीतेस. He drinks hot tea. *to garam chahā pīto* तो गरम चहा पीतो. She drinks hot tea *tī garam chahā pite* ती गरम चहा पिते. We drink hot tea *āmhī garam chahā pito.* आम्ही गरम चहा पितो. They drink hot tea. *te garam chahā pitāt* ते गरम चहा पितात.

d. I drink hot tea slowly. m∘ *mī garam chahā haḷū pito (*f∘ *mī garam chahā pite)* मी गरम चहा हळू पीतो (मी गरम चहा हळू पीते). You drink hot tea slowly.m∘ *tū garam chahā haḷū pītos* तू गरम चहा हळू पितोस. f∘ *tū garam chahā haḷū pītes* तू गरम चहा हळू पीतेस. He drinks hot tea slowly. *to garam chahā haḷū pīto* तो गरम चहा हळू पीतो. She drinks hot tea slowly. *tī garam chahā haḷū pite* ती गरम चहा हळू पिते. We drink hot teaslowly. *āmhī garam chahā haḷū pito.* आम्ही गरम चहा हळू पितो. They drink hot teaslowly. *te garam chahā haḷū pitāt* ते गरम चहा हळू पितात.

adj∘ = Adjective, adv∘ = Adverb; *conj.* = Conjunction, f∘ = Feminine gender, *ind.* = Indeclinable, m∘ = Masculine gender, n∘ = Neuter gender, pl∘ = Plural

DICTIONARY OF COMMON VERBS AND INFINITIVES

In order to form a verb from an infinitive, remove the णे ṇe suffix

In marāṭhī, the infinitives and verbal nouns end with the letter ना. e.g. (i) Root Verb "do" = √*kar* (कर) (ii) Infinitive "to do" (gerund and verbal noun) = *karaṇe* करणे.

Therefore, if you remove the suffix *ṇe* णे from any infinitive or verbal noun, you get the basic root (√) verb. Note that :-

(i) Some verbs are formed with only a single words, they are called Simple Verbs.

(ii) Some verbs are formed with two words (the second word being *karaṇe, hoṇe, jāṇe, deṇe* करणे, होणे, जाणे, देणे ...etc). The compound and transitive verbs are marked with * below.

to abandon *(√tyāga → tyāgaṇe* त्यागणे*)

to accept *(√mān → mānaṇe* मानणे*)

to answer *(√jawāb de → jawāb deṇe* जवाब देणे)*

to arrange *(√rach → rachaṇe* रचणे*)

to arrive *(√ye → yeṇe* येणे)

to ask *(√vichār → vichārṇe* विचारणे*)

to attain *(√prāpta kar → prāpta karaṇe* प्राप्त करणे)*

to attempt *(√yatna kar → yatna karaṇe* यत्न करणे)*

to bathe *(√nahā → nahāṇe* नहाणे)

to be, to become *(√ho → hoṇe* होणे)*

to beg *(√yāchanā kar → yāchanā karaṇe* याचना करणे)*

to bite *(√chāv → chāvaṇe* चावणे)

to break *(√tuṭ, toḍ → tuṭaṇe, toḍaṇe* तुटणे, तोडणे*)

to blossom *(√ful → fulṇe* फुलणे)

to boil *(√ukaḷ → ukaḷṇe* उकळणे, उकळवणे*)

to bring *(√āṇ → āṇaṇe* आणणे*)

to burn *(√jaḷ, √jāḷ → jaḷaṇe, jāḷaṇe** जळणे, जाळणे*)

to buy *(√kharīd → kharīdaṇe* खरीदणे*)

to call *(√bolāv → bolāvṇe* बोलावणे*)

to carry away *(√ne → neṇe* नेणे)*

to clean *(√sāf-kar → sāf-karṇe* साफ करणे)*

to come *(√ye → yeṇe* येणे)

to cook *(√śhij → śhijṇe* शिजणे, शिजवणे*)

to count *(√moj → mojṇe* मोजणे*)

to cover *(√jhāk → jhakṇe* झाकणे*)

to cross *(√pār kar → pār karṇe* पार करणे)*

to cry *(√raḍ → raḍṇe* रडणे)

to cut *(√kāp → kāpṇe* कापणे*)

to dance *(√nāch → nāchaṇe* नाचणे)

to desire, to want *(√chāh → chāhaṇe* चाहणे*)

to die *(√mar → maraṇe* मरणे)

to dig *(√khod → khodṇe* खोदणे*)

to do *(√kar → karṇe* करणे*)

to draw *(√kāḍh → kāḍhṇe* काढणे*)

to drink *(√pī → piṇe* पिणे*)

to dry *(√suk→ sukaṇe* सुकणे, सुकवणे*)

to dye, paint *(√rang → rangaṇe* रंगणे, रंगवणे*)

to eat *(√khā → khāṇe* खाणे*)

to enter *(√praveśh kar → praveśh karaṇe* प्रवेश करणे)

adj∘ = Adjective, adv∘ = Adverb; *conj.* = Conjunction, f∘ = Feminine gender, *ind.* = Indeclinable, m∘ = Masculine gender, n∘ = Neuter gender, pl∘ = Plural

to exist *(√rāh → rāhaṇe, asṇe, hoṇe* राहणे, असणे, होणे)

to explain *(√samajav → samajavaṇe* समजवणे*)

to fall *(√paḍ → paḍṇe* पडणे)

to fear *(√bhi → bhiṇe* भिणे)

to fight *(√laḍh → laḍhaṇe* लढणे)

to fix *(√ṭhīk kar → ṭhīk karṇe* ठीक करणे)*

to fly *(√uḍa, √uḍā → uḍṇe, uḍavaṇe* उड़णे, उडवणे*)

to forget *(√bhul → bhulṇe* भुलणे*)

to forgive *(√māf kar → māf karṇe* माफ करणे)*

to free *(√soḍ → soḍṇe* सोडणे*)

to fry *(√taḷ → taḷṇe* तळणे*)

to get *(√miḷav → miḷavṇe* मिळवणे*)

to give *(√de → deṇe* देणे*)

to glow *(√chamak → chamakṇe* चमकणे)

to glue *(√chikaṭ → chikaṭṇe* चिकटणे)

to go *(√jā → jāṇe* जाणे)

to grind *(√pis → pisṇe* पिसणे*)

to grow *(√wāḍh → wāḍhṇe* वाढ़णे)

to hang *(√laṭak → laṭakṇe,* लटकणे, लटकवणे*)

to happen, to have *(√ho → hoṇe* होणे)

to hear *(√aik → aikṇe* ऐकणे*)

to hide *(√lap → lap* लपणे, लपवणे*)

to hit *(√mār → mārṇe* मारणे*)

to hold, catch *(√pakaḍ → pakaḍaṇe* पकड़णे*)

to hum *(√guṇguṇṇe→ guṇaguṇaṇe* गुणगुणणे)

to hurt *(√dukha → dukhaṇe)* (दुखणे, दुखवणे*)

to increase *(√wāḍh → wāḍhṇe* वाढणे)

to join *(√miḷ → milāṇe* मिळणे, मिळवणे*)

to jump *(√kūd → kudaṇe* कुदणे)

to keep *(√ṭhev → ṭhevṇe* ठेवणे*)

to kill *(√mār → mārṇe* मारणे*)

to know *(√jāṇ → jāṇaṇe* जाणणे*)

to laugh *(√has → hasṇe* हसणे)

to lift *(√uchal → uchalṇe* उचलणे*)

to like *(√āvaḍ → āvaḍṇe* आवडणे*)

to live *(√jag → jagṇe* जगणे)

to lose *(√hār → hār* हारणे*)

to love *(√prem kar → prem karṇe* प्रेम करणे)*

to make *(√banvaṇe→ banavṇe* बनवणे*)

to meet *(√miḷ → miḷṇe* मिळणे, मिळवणे*)

to melt *(√pighaḷ → pighaḷṇe* पिघळणे)

to move *(√hal → halṇe* हलणे, हलवणे*)

to open *(√ughaḍ → ughaḍṇe* उघडणे*)

to pick *(√uchal → uchalṇe* उचलणे*)

to play (*√kheḷ → kheḷṇe* खेळणे*)

to press *(√dāba → dābṇe* दाबणे*)

to protect *(√rakṣā kar → rakṣā karṇe* रक्षा करणे)*

to pull *(√oḍh → oḍhṇe* ओढणे*)

to punish *(√daṇḍa de → daṇḍ deṇe* दंड देणे)*

to push *(√ḍhakal → ḍhakalṇe* ढकलणे*)

to put, keep *(√ṭhev → ṭhevṇe* ठेवणे*)

to read *(√vāch → vāchṇe* वाचणे*)

to ride, to drive *(√chālav → chālavṇe* चालवणे*)

to roam *(√fir → firṇe* फिरणे)

to rot *(√saḍ → saḍaṇe* सड़णे)

to run *(√dhāv → dhāvṇe* धावणे)

to ripen *(√pak → pakaṇe* पकणे)

to say *(√mhaṇ → mhaṇṇe)* (म्हणणे*)

to see *(√pāha → pāhṇe* पाहणे*)

to sell *(√vik → vikṇe* विकणे*)

to send *(√pāṭhav → pāṭhavṇe* पाठवणे*)

adj∘ = Adjective, adv∘ = Adverb; *conj.* = Conjunction, f∘ = Feminine gender, *ind.* = Indeclinable, m∘ = Masculine gender, n∘ = Neuter gender, pl∘ = Plural

to serve *(√sevā kar → sevā karṇe* सेवा करणे)*

to sew *(√śhiv → śhivṇe* शिवणे*)

to shine *(√chamak → chamakṇe* चमकणे)

to sing *(√gā → gāṇe* गाणे*)

to sink *(√buḍ → buḍṇe* बुडणे, बुडवणे*)

to sit *(√bas → basṇe* बसणे)

to sleep (*√zop →* zopṇe झोपणे)

to speak *(√bol → bolṇe* बोलणे*)

to stop *(√thāmb → thāmbṇe* थांबणे)

to study *(√abhyās kar → abhyāk karṇe* अभ्यास करणे*)

to take *(√ghe → gheṇe* घेणे*)

to talk *(√bol → bolaṇe* बोलणे*)

to taste *(√chākh → chākhaṇe* चाखणे*)

to tell *(√sāng → sāngṇe* सांगणे*)

to think *(√vichār kar → vichār karṇe* विचार करणे*)

to throw *(√fek → fekṇe* फेकणे*)

to tie *(√bāndh → bāndhṇe* बाँधणे*)

to travel *(√safar kar → yātrā karṇe* यात्रा करणे)*

to understand *(√samaj → samajṇe* समजणे*)

to use *(√upayog kar → upayog karaṇe* उपयोग करणे)*

to wake up *(√jāg → jāgṇe* जागणे)

to walk *(√chāl → chālṇe* चालणे)

to want *(√chah → chāhṇe* चाहणे)

to wash *(√dhu → dhuṇe* धुणे)*

to waste *(√kharāb kar → kharāb karṇe* खराब करणे)*

to wear *(√nes → nesṇe* नेसणे)*

to win *(√jink → jinkṇe* जिंकणे)*

to wish *(√ichchhā kar → ichchhā karṇe* इच्छा करणे)*

to work *(√kām kar → kām karṇe* काम करणे)*

to worship *(√pūjā kar → pūjā karṇe* पूजा करणे)*

to write *(√lihī → lihīṇe* लिहीणे) ...etc.

APPLICATION OF VERBS

Making Simple Small Sentences

1. I wish. m∘	*(mī ichchhā karto)*	मी इच्छा करतो
2. I wish. f∘	*(mī ichchhā karte)*	मी इच्छा करते
3. We worship. m∘	*(āmhī pūjā karato*	आम्ही पूजा करतो
4. We worship. f∘	*(āmhī pūjā karto*	आम्ही पूजा करतो
5. You work	*(tū kāma kartos)*	तू काम करतोस
6. You work. pl∘	*(tumhī kāma kartā)*	तुम्ही काम करता
7. He fills water.	*(to paṇī bharto)*	तो पाणी भरतो
8. They fill water. m∘	*(te paṇī bhartāt)*	ते पाणी भरतात
9. They fill water. f∘	*(tyā paṇī bhartāt)*	त्या पाणी भरतात
10. She fills water. f∘	*(tī paṇī bharte)*	ती पाणी भरते

11. It breaks (te tuṭte) ते तुटते

12. He breaks (to toḍto) तो तोडतो

13. It dries (tu sukte) ते सुकते

14. They dry (te suktāt) ते सुकतात

15. I dry clothes (mī kapḍe sukavto) मी कपडे सुकवतो

16. He dries cloths (to kapḍe sukavto) तो कपडे सुकवतो

17. We hide m∘ (āmhī lapto) आम्ही लपतो

18. We hide f∘ (āmhī lapto) आम्ही लपतो

19. We hide money (āmhī paise lapavto) आम्ही पैसे लपवतो

20. We hide monay f∘ (āmhī paise lapavto) आम्ही पैसे लपवतो

21. I speak. (mī bolto) मी बोलतो. मी बोलते

22. Rām sits. (Rām basto) राम बसतो

23. She sings. (tī gāte) ती गाते

24. They sleep. m∘ f∘ (te zoptāt) ते झोपतात

25. You sleep. m∘ f∘ (tū zoptos, tū zoptes) तू झोपतोस. तू झोपतेस

26. We write. m∘ f∘ (āmhī lihito) आम्ही लिहितो

27. You cut mango. (tū āmbā kāptos. tū āmbā kāptes. तू आंबा कापतेस. तू आंबा कापतेस

28. They smile. (te hastāt, tyā hastāt) ते हसतात, त्या हसतात.

29. Arvind paints a picture. (Arvind chitra rangavato) अरविंद चित्र रंगवतो

30. We run. m∘ f∘ (āmhī paḷto) आम्ही पळतो

We run. 5 k.m. m∘ f∘ (āmhī pāch km paḷto) आम्ही पाच कि.मि. पळतो

31. Rītā brings 10 Rupees. (Rītā dahā rupaye āṇtae) रीता दहा रुपये आणते

32. Sunil takes one book. (Sunīl ek pustak gheto) सुनील एक पुस्तक घेतो

33. He does luñch. (to bhojan karto) तो भोजन करतो. तो फराळ करतो

34. The boy cries. (mulgā raḍto) मुलगा रडतो

35. One boy cries. (ek mulgā raḍto) एक मुलगा रडतो

36. He sinks. (to buḍto) तो बुडतो

37. They put, they keep. m∘ f∘ (to ṭhevtāt) ते ठेवतात

38. We go. m∘ f∘ (āmhī jāto) आम्ही जातो

39. You sell fruits. (tū faḷe viktos. tū faḷe viktes) तू फळे विकतोस, तू फळे विकतेस

40. She sends a letter.	*(tī patra pāṭhavte)*	ती पत्र पाठवते
41. She joins hands.	*(tī hāt miḷavte)*	ती हात मिळवते (m◦ तो हात मिळवतो)
42. He throws a ball.	*(to cheṇḍū fekto)*	तो चेंडू फेकतो
43. You jump.	*(tū kudatos)*	तू कुदतोस
44. I am here.	*(mī ithe āhe)*	मी इथे आहे.
45. Where is she?	*(tī kuṭhe āhe?)*	ती कुठे आहे?
46. He is not there.	*(to tithe nāhī)*	तो तिथे नाही
47. She counts money.	*(tī paise mojte)*	ती पैसे मोजते
48. They go.	*(te jātāt)*	ते जातात
49. They come.	*(te yetāt)*	ते येतात
50. They stay	*(te rahtāt)*	ते राहतात

(11.2)

Present Continuous Tense

I am 'doing' (you are doing; he, she, it is doing; we, they are doing)

TABLE : Use of - I am doing; you are doing; he, she is doing; we are doing; they are doing

Doer of the action — drinking

Subject	marāṭhī	do drink **पी** (pī)	I am drinking hot tea (**चहा** chahā)
1. I	मी *(mī)*	पीत आहे *(pīt āhe)*	गरम चहा पीत आहे *(garam chahā pīt āhe)*
2. We	आम्ही *(āmhī)*	पीत आहो *(pīt āho)*	गरम चहा पीत आहो *(garam chahā pīt āho)*
3. He	तो *(to)*	पीत आहे *(pīt āhe)*	गरम चहा पीत आहे *(garam chahā pīt āhe)*
4. These	हे *(he)*	पीत आहे *(pīt āhe)*	गरम चहा पीत आहे *(garam chahā pīt āhe)*
5. They	ते *(te)*	पीत आहे *(pīt āhe)*	गरम चहा पीत आहे *(garam chahā pīt āhe)*
6. She	ती *(tī)*	पीत आहे *(pīt āhe)*	गरम चहा पीत आहे *(garam chahā pīt āhe)*
7. These	ह्या *(hyā)*	पीत आहेत *(pīt āhet)*	गरम चहा पीत आहेत *(garam chahā pīt āhet)*
8. They	त्या *(tyā)*	पीत आहेत *(pīt āhet)*	गरम चहा पीत आहेत *(pīt āhet)*
9. It *	हे *(he)**	पीत आहे *(pīt āhe)*	गरम चहा पीत आहे *(garam chahā pīt āhe)*
10. You	तू *(tū)*	पीत आहेस *(pīt āhes)*	गरम चहा पीत आहेस *(garam chahā pīt āhes)*
11. You pl◦	तुम्ही *(tumhī)*	पीत आहात *(pīt āhāt)*	गरम चहा पीत आहात *(garam chahā pīt āhāt)*
12. You hon◦	आपण *(āpaṇ)*	पीत आहात *(pīt āhāt)*	गरम चहा पीत आहात *(garam chahā pīt āhāt)*

NOTE : * Same for : He, She, It - plural These and They.

TABLE : Present Continuous Tense Suffixes SUMMARY (tense suffixes)

	Subject		Suffix m∘ (Root verb + suffix)	Suffix f∘ (Root verb + suffix)
∘	I	मी	(verb +) त आहे *(ta āhe)*	(verb +) त आहे *(ta āhe)*
∘	He/she	तो, ती	(verb +) त आहे *(ta āhe)*	(verb +) त आहे *(ta āhe)*
*	We	आम्ही	(verb +) त आहोत *(ta āhot)*	(verb +) त आहोत *(ta āhot)*
*	You	तू	(verb +) त आहेस *(ta āhes)*	(verb +) त आहेस *(ta āhes)*
*	They	ते, त्या	(verb +) त आहेत *(ta āhet)*	(verb +) त आहेत *(ta āhet)*

EXERCISE : Translate the English sentences into maraṭhī (Answers are given for help)

1. I am writing a letter. *mī patra lihit āhe.* मी पत्र लिहीत आहे.
2. They are singing a Marāṭhī song. *te marāṭhī gāṇe gāt āhet.* ते मराठी गाणे गात आहेत.
3. You are seeing (watching) TV. *tū TV pahāt āhes.* तू टीवी (दूरदर्शन) पहात (बघत) आहेस.
4. He is going today. *to āj jāt āhe.* तो आज जात आहे.
5. She is coming slowly. *tī haḷū-haḷū yet āhe.* ती हळू-हळू येत आहे.
6. We are playing Chess. *āmhī buddhibaḷ kheḷat āhot.* आम्ही बुद्धिबळ खेळत आहेत.
7. They are sewing shirt. *te sadrā śhivat āhet.* ते सदरा शिवत आहेत.
8. They are eating bananas. *te keḷe khāt āhet.* ते केळे खात आहेत.
9. She is sleeping. *tī zopat āhe.* ती झोपत आहे.
10. Sudhir is calling. *sudhīr bolāvat āhe.* सुधीर बोलावत आहे.
11. Sunil is playing. *sunīl kheḷat āhe.* सुनील खेळत आहे.
12. Radha and Sita are working. *rādhā āṇi sītaī kām krīt āheta.* राधा आणि सीता काम करीत आहेत.
13. Today air is hot. *āj havā garam āhe.* आज हवा गरम आहे.
14. Anil is learning the lesson. *Anil pāṭh śhikat āhe.* अनील पाठ शिकत आहे.
15. Soniya is drawing a picture. *sonīyā chitra kāḍhat āhe.* सोनीया चित्र काढत आहे.
16. Krishna is playing the flute. *kruṣhṇa bāsarī vājvat āhe.* कृष्ण बासरी वाजवत आहे.
17. Prabhakar is throwing a ball. *prabhākar cheṇḍū fekat āhe.* प्रभाकर चेंडू फेकत आहे.
18. Dada is cutting a tree. *dādā jhāḍ kāpat āhe.* दादा झाड कापत आहे.
19. Saroj is frying Papads. *saroj pāpaḍ taḷat āhe.* सरोज पापड तळत आहे.
20. Suman does not speak. *suman bolat nāhī.* सुमन बोलत नाही.

adj∘ = Adjective, adv∘ = Adverb; *conj.* = Conjunction, f∘ = Feminine gender, *ind.* = Indeclinable, m∘ = Masculine gender, n∘ = Neuter gender, pl∘ = Plural

PAST TENSE (भूतकाळ)

13.3

HABITUAL PAST TENSE

Doer of the action used to drink

Subject	marāṭhī	used to drink पी (pī), spoken in two ways
1. I	मी *(mī)*	मी प्यायचो, पीत असायचो *(pyāycho, pīt asāyachao)*
2. We	आम्ही *(āmhī)*	आम्ही पीत असू, पीत असायचो *(pīt asū, pīt asāyachao)*
3. He	तो *(to)*	तो पीत असे, पीत असायचा *(pīt ase, pīt asāyachā)*
4. These	हे *(he)*	हे पीत असत, पीत असायचे *(pīt asat, pīt asāyache)*
5. They	ते *(te)*	ते पीत असत, पीत असायचे *(pīt asat, pīt asāyache)*
6. She	ती *(tī)*	ती पीत असे, पीत असायची *(pīt ase, pīt asāyachī)*
7. These	ह्या *(hyā)*	ह्या पीत असत, पीत असायच्या *(pīt asat, pīt asāyachyā)*
8. They	त्या *(tyā)*	त्या पीत असत, पीत असायच्या *(pīt asat, pīt asāyachyā)*
9. It *	हे *(he)**	हे पीत असे, पीत असायचे *(pīt ase, pīt asāyache)*
10. You	तू *(tū)*	तू प्यायचा, पीत असायचा *(pyāychā, pīt asāyachā)*
11. You pl◦	तुम्ही *(tumhī)*	तुम्ही प्यायचे, पीत असायचे *(pyāyche, pīt asāyache)*
12. You hon◦	आपण *(āpaṇ)*	आपण प्यायचे, पीत असायचे *(pyāyche, pīt asāyache)*

NOTE : * Same for : He, She, It - plural These and They. आहे of the Present tense changes to असे, असायचा in Habitual Past Tense.

EXERCISE 20 : Translate the English sentences into marāṭhī (Answers are given for help)

1.She used to write poems. *tī kavitā lihit ase.* ती कविता लिहीत असे, लिहीत असायची, लिहायची.

2.They used to sing Marāṭhī songs. *te marāṭhī gāṇe gāt asat.* ते मराठी गाणे गात असत, गात असायचे, गायचे.

3.You used to see (watch) TV. *tū TV pahāt ase.* तू टीवी पहात असे, पहात असायचा, पहायचा.

4.He used to cry. *to raḍat ase.* तो रडत असे, रडत असायचा, रडायचा.

5.She used to come early. *tī lavkar yet ase.* ती लवकर येत असे, येत असायची, यायची.

6.We used to play Chess. *āmhī buddhibaḷ kheḷat asū.* आम्ही बुद्धिबळ खेळत असू, असायचो, खेळायचो.

7.They used to sew shirts. *te sadre śhivat asat.* ते सदरे शिवत असत, शिवत असायचे, शिवायचे.

8. They used to eat green bananas. *te hirve keḷe khāt asat.* ते हिरवे केळे खात असत, खात असायचे, खायचे.

9. She used to sleep less. *tī kamī zopat ase.* ती कमी झोपत असे, झोपत असायची, झोपायची.

10. Sharad used to stop here. *śharad ithe thāmbat ase.* शरद इथे थांबत असे, थांबत असायचा, थांबायचा.

adj◦ = Adjective, adv◦ = Adverb; *conj.* = Conjunction, f◦ = Feminine gender, *ind.* = Indeclinable, m◦ = Masculine gender, n◦ = Neuter gender, pl◦ = Plural

13.4

PAST CONTINUOUS TENSE

Doer of the action		was drinking	was drinking tea
Subject	marāṭhī	do drink **पी** (pī)	I am drinking hot tea (**चहा** chahā)
1. I	मी *(mī)*	पीत होतो *(pīt hoto)*	गरम चहा पीत होतो *(garam chahā pīt hoto)*
2. We	आम्ही *(āmhī)*	पीत होतो *(pīt hoto)*	गरम चहा पीत होतो *(garam chahā pīt hoto)*
3. He	तो *(to)*	पीत होता *(pīt hotā)*	गरम चहा पीत होता *(garam chahā pīt hotā)*
4. These	हे *(he)*	पीत होते *(pīt hote)*	गरम चहा पीत होते *(garam chahā pīt hote)*
5. They	ते *(te)*	पीत होते *(pīt hote)*	गरम चहा पीत होते *(garam chahā pīt hote)*
6. She	ती *(tī)*	पीत होती *(pīt hotī)*	गरम चहा पीत होती *(garam chahā pīt hotī)*
7. These	ह्या *(hyā)*	पीत होत्या *(pīt hotyā)*	गरम चहा पीत होत्या *(garam chahā pīt hotyā)*
8. They	त्या *(tyā)*	पीत होत्या *(pīt hotyā)*	गरम चहा पीत होत्या *(garam chahā pīt hotā)*
9. It *	हे *(he)**	पीत होते *(pīt hote)*	गरम चहा पीत होते *(garam chahā pīt hote)*
10. You	तू *(tū)*	पीत होतास *(pīt hotās)*	गरम चहा पीत होतास *(garam chahā pīt hotās)*
11. You pl∘	तुम्ही *(tumhī)*	पीत होते *(pīt hote)*	गरम चहा पीत होते *(garam chahā pīt hote)*
12. You hon∘	आपण *(āpaṇ)*	पीत होते *(pīt hote)*	गरम चहा पीत होते *(garam chahā pīt hote)*

NOTE : * Same for : He, She, It - plural These and They. आहे of the Present tense changes to होता in Past Tense.

TABLE : Past Tense Suffixes SUMMARY

Subject	मराठी	Suffix M∘	Suffix F∘
I	मी	होतो *(hoto)*	होती *(hotī)*
He/she	तो, ती	होता *(hotā)*	होती *(hotī)*
We	आम्ही	होतो *(hoto)*	होतो *(hoto)*
You	तू	होतास *(hotās)*	होतीस *(hotīs)*
They	ते, त्या	होते *(hote)*	होत्या *(hotyā)*

EXERCISE : Translate the English sentences into marāṭhī (Answers are given for help)

1. I was writing a marāṭhī poem. *mī Marāṭhī kavitā lihīt hoto.* मी मराठी कविता लिहीत होतो.
2. They were singing Hindi songs. *te Hindī gāṇe gāt hote.* ते हिंदी गाणे गात होते.
3. You were watching TV. *tū TV pahāt (baghat) hotās.* तू टीवी पहात (बघत) होतास.
4. He was crying. *to raḍat hotā.* तो रडत होता.
5. She was going slowly. *tī haḷū-haḷū jāt hotī.* ती हळू-हळू जात होती.

adj∘ = Adjective, adv∘ = Adverb; *conj.* = Conjunction, f∘ = Feminine gender, *ind.* = Indeclinable, m∘ = Masculine gender, n∘ = Neuter gender, pl∘ = Plural

6. We were playing Chess. *āmhī buddhibaḷ kheḷat hoto.* आम्ही बुद्धिबळ खेळत होतो.

7. They were sewing shirts. *te sadre śhivat hote.* ते सदरे शिवत होते.

8. The goat was eating green leaves. *bakrī hirvī pāne khāt hotī.* बकरी हिरवी पाने खात होती.

9. She was sleeping late. *tī ushirā zopat hotī.* ती उशीरा झोपत होती.

10. Sharad and Mohan were talking loudly. *śharad āṇi mohan jorāne bolat hote.* शरद आणि मोहन जोराने बोलत होते.

THE FUTURE TENSE (भविष्य काळ)

13.5

Doer of the action | will drink

Subject	marāṭhī	will drink hot tea पी (pī), two ways to say
1. I	मी *(mī)*	मी गरम चहा पिएन, पिईल, पिणार *(mī garam chahā pien, piīl, piṇār)*
2. We	आम्ही *(āmhī)*	आम्ही गरम चहा पिऊ, पिणार *(āmhī garam chahā piū, piṇār)*
3. He	तो *(to)*	तो गरम चहा पिईल, पिणार *(to garam chahā piīl, piṇār)*
4. These	हे *(he)*	हे गरम चहा पितील, पिणार *(he garam chahā pitīl, piṇār)*
5. They	ते *(te)*	ते गरम चहा पितील, पिणार *(te garam chahā pitīl, piṇār)*
6. She	ती *(tī)*	ती गरम चहा पिईल, पिणार *(tī garam chahā piīl, piṇār)*
7. These	ह्या *(hyā)*	ह्या गरम चहा पितील, पिणार *(hyā garam chahā pitīl, piṇār)*
8. They	त्या *(tyā)*	त्या गरम चहा पितील, पिणार *(tyā garam chahā pitīl, piṇār)*
9. It	हे *(he)*	हे गरम चहा पिईल, पिणार *(he garam chahā piīl, piṇār)*
10. You	तू *(tū)*	तू गरम चहा पिशील, पिणार *(tū garam chahā piśhīl, piṇār)*
11. You pl∘	तुम्ही *(tumhī)*	तुम्ही गरम चहा प्याल, पिणार *(tumhī garam chahā pyāl, piṇār)*
12. You hon∘	आपण *(āpaṇ)*	आपण गरम चहा प्याल, पिणार *(āpaṇ garam chahā pyāl, piṇār)*

TABLE : Future Tense Suffixes SUMMARY

Subject	मराठी	Suffix M∘	Suffix F∘
I	मी	एन *(en)*, ईल *(īl)*	एन *(en)*, ईल *(īl)*
He/she	तो, ती	ईल *(īl)*, एल *(īl)*	ईल *(īl*, एल *(īl)*
We	आम्ही	ऊ *(ū)*	ऊ *(ū)*
You	तू	शील *(śhīl)*	शील *(śhīl)*
They	ते, त्या	तील *(tīl)*	तील *(tīl)*

EXERCISE : Translate the English sentences into marāṭhī (Answers are given for help)

1. She will write poems. *tī kavitā lihīl.* ती कविता लिहील, लिहिणार.
2. They will sing Marāṭhī songs. *te marāṭhī gāṇe gātīl, gāṇār.* ते मराठी गाणे गातील or गाणार.
3. You will watch TV. *tū TV pahāśhīl.* तू टीवी पहाशील, पाहणार.
4. He will cry. *to raḍel.* तो रडेल, रडणार.
5. She will come early. *tī lavkar yeīl.* ती लवकर येईल, येणार.
6. We will play Chess tomorrow. *āmhī buddhibaḷ kheḷū.* आम्ही उद्या बुद्धिबळ खेळू, खेळणार.
7. They will sew shirts later. *te mag sadre śhivatīl.* ते मग सदरे शिवतील, शिवणार.
8. They will eat yellow bananas. *te pivḷe keḷe khātīl.* ते पिवळे केळे खातील, खाणार.
9. She will sleep late. *tī uśhirā zopel.* ती उशिरा झोपेल, झोपणार.
10. Sharad will stop here. *śharad ithe thāmbel.* शरद इथे थांबेल, थांबणार.

FUTURE CONTINUOUS ACTIONS

Doer of the action will be drinking

Subject	marāṭhī	will be drinking hot tea **पी** (pī), two ways to say
1. I	मी *(mī)*	मी गरम चहा पीत असेन *(mī garam chahā pīt asen)*
2. We	आम्ही *(āmhī)*	आम्ही गरम चहा पीत असू *(amhī garam chahā pīt asū)*
3. He	तो *(to)*	तो गरम चहा पीत असेल *(to garam chahā piīl asel)*
4. These	हे *(he)*	हे गरम चहा पीत असतील *(he garam chahā pīt astīl)*
5. They	ते *(te)*	ते गरम चहा पीत असतील *(he garam chahā pīt astīl)*
6. She	ती *(tī)*	ती गरम चहा पीत असेल *(tī garam chahā pīt asel)*
7. These	ह्या *(hyā)*	ह्या गरम चहा पीत असतील *(hyā garam chahā pīt astīl)*
8. They	त्या *(tyā)*	त्या गरम चहा पीत असतील *(tyā garam chahā pīt astīl)*
9. It	हे *(he)*	हे गरम चहा पीत असेल *(he garam chahā piīl asel)*
10. You	तू *(tū)*	तू गरम चहा पीत असशील *(tū garam chahā pīt asaśhīl)*
11. You pl∘	तुम्ही *(tumhī)*	तुम्ही गरम चहा पीत असाल *(tumhī garam chahā pīt asāl)*
12. You hon∘	आपण *(āpaṇ)*	आपण गरम चहा पीत असाल *(āpaṇ garam chahā pīt asāl)*

EXAMPLES :

1. She will be writing poems. *tī kavitā lihīt asel.* ती कविता लिहीत असेल.
2. They will be singing Marāṭhī songs. *te marāṭhī gāṇe gāt astīl.* ते मराठी गाणे गात असतील.

adj∘ = Adjective, adv∘ = Adverb; *conj.* = Conjunction, f∘ = Feminine gender, *ind.* = Indeclinable, m∘ = Masculine gender, n∘ = Neuter gender, pl∘ = Plural

LESSON 14
चौदावा पाठ

MAKING SENTENCES FOR **COMPLETED ACTIONS**

THE PERFECT TENSE

A perfected or completed action indicates what someone did, has done or had done.

Doer of the action I did bring = I brought

Subject	marāṭhī	I did bring or I brought a book. Bring = **आण** (āṇ)
1. I	मी *(mī)*	मी पुस्तक आणले. *(mī pustak āṇle)*
2. We	आम्ही *(āmhī)*	आम्ही पुस्तक आणले. *(āmhī pustak āṇle)*
3. He	तो *(to)*	त्याने पुस्तक आणले. *(tyāne pustak āṇle)* रामने पुस्तक आणले.
4. These	हे *(he)*	ह्याने पुस्तक आणले. *(hyāne pustak āṇle)*
5. They	ते *(te)*	त्यांनी पुस्तक आणले. *(tyānnī pustak āṇle)* मुलांनी पुस्तक आणले.
6. She	ती *(tī)*	तिने पुस्तक आणले. *(tine pustak āṇle)* सीताने पुस्तक आणले.
7. These	ह्या *(hyā)*	ह्यांनी पुस्तक आणले. *(hyannī pustak āṇle)*
8. They	त्या *(tyā)*	त्यांनी पुस्तक आणले. *(tyānnī pustak āṇle)* मुलींनी पुस्तक आणले.
9. It	हे *(he)*	ह्याने पुस्तक आणले. *(hyāne pustak āṇle)*
10. You	तू *(tū)*	तू पुस्तक आणलेस. *(tū pustak āṇles)*
11. You pl∘	तुम्ही *(tumhī)*	तुम्ही पुस्तक आणले. *(tumhī pustak āṇle)*
12. You hon∘	आपण *(āpaṇ)*	आपण पुस्तक आणले. *(āpaṇ pustak āṇle)*

The perfect (completed) actions are of four kinds

1. I did (I, we, you, he, she, it, they did)
2. I have done (I, we, you, he, she, it, they have done)
3. I had done (I, we, you, he, she, it, they had done)
4. I will have done (I, we, you, he, she, it, they will have done)

INTRANSITIVE ACTIONS
अकर्मक क्रिया

Doer of the action I did go = I went

Subject	marāṭhī	I did go, I have gone, I had gone, I will have gone.
1. I	मी *(mī)*	m∘ मी गेलो, मी गेलो आहे, मी गेलो होतो, मी गेलो असेन. f∘ मी गेली, मी गेली आहे, मी गेली होती, मी गेली असेन.

adj∘ = Adjective, adv∘ = Adverb; *conj.* = Conjunction, f∘ = Feminine gender, *ind.* = Indeclinable, m∘ = Masculine gender, n∘ = Neuter gender, pl∘ = Plural

2. We	आम्ही *(āmhī)*	आम्ही गेलो, आम्ही गेलो आहो, आम्ही गेलो होतो, आम्ही गेलो असू.
3. He	तो *(to)*	तो गेला, तो गेला आहे, तो गेला होता, तो गेला असेल.
4. These	हे *(he)*	हे गेले, हे गेले आहेत, हे गेले होते, हे गेले असतील.
5. They	ते *(te)*	ते गेले, ते गेले आहेत, ते गेले होते, ते गेले असतील.
6. She	ती *(tī)*	ती गेली, ती गेली आहे, ती गेली होती, ती गेली असेल.
7. These	ह्या *(hyā)*	ह्या गेल्या, ह्या गेल्या आहेत, ह्या गेल्या होत्या, ह्या गेल्या असतील.
8. They	त्या *(tyā)*	त्या गेल्या, त्या गेल्या आहेत, त्या गेल्या होत्या, त्या गेल्या असतील.
9. It	हे *(he)*	हे गेले, हे गेले आहेत, हे गेले होते, हे गेले असतील.
10. You	तू *(tū)*	तू गेला, तू गेला आहे, तू गेला होता, तू गेला असशील.
11. You pl∘	तुम्ही *(tumhī)*	तुम्ही गेले, तुम्ही गेले आहात, तुम्ही गेले होते, तुम्ही गेले असाल.
12. You hon∘	आपण *(āpaṇ)*	आपण गेले, आपण गेले आहात, आपण गेले होते, आपण गेले असाल.
13. Ram	राम *(Rām)* m∘	राम गेला, राम गेला आहे, राम गेला होता, राम गेला असेल.
14. Sītā	सीता *(Sītā)* f∘	सीता गेली, सीता गेली आहे, सीता गेली होती, सीता गेली असेल.
15. Boys	मुले *(mule)* n∘	मुले गेली, मुले गेली आहेत, मुले मुले गेली होती, मुले मुले गेली असतील.
15. Girls	मुली *(girls)* f∘	मुली गेल्या, मुली गेल्या आहेत, मुली गेल्या होत्या, मुली गेल्या असतील.

TRANSITIVE ACTIONS
सकर्मक क्रिया

Doer of the action I did bring = I brought

Subject	maraṭhī	I did bring, I have brought, I had brought, I will have brought.
1. I	मी *(mī)*	मी आणले, मी आणले आहे, मी आणले होते, मी आणले असेल.
2. We	आम्ही *(āmhī)*	आम्ही आणले, आम्ही आणले आहे, आम्ही आणले होते, आम्ही आणले असेल.
3. He	तो *(to)*	त्याने आणले, त्याने आणले आहे, त्याने आणले होते, त्याने आणले असेल.
4. These	हे *(he)*	ह्याने आणले, ह्याने आणले आहे, ह्याने आणले होते, ह्याने आणले असेल.
5. They	ते *(te)*	त्याने आणले, त्याने आणले आहे, त्याने आणले होते, त्याने आणले असेल.
6. She	ती *(tī)*	तिने आणले, तिने आणले आहे, तिने आणले होते, तिने आणले असेल.
7. These	ह्या *(hyā)*	ह्यांनी आणले, ह्यांनी आणले आहे, ह्यांनी आणले होते, ह्यांनी आणले असेल.
8. They	त्या *(tyā)*	त्यांनी आणले, त्यांनी आणले आहे, त्यांनी आणले होते, त्यांनी आणले असेल.
9. It	हे *(he)*	ह्यानी आणले, ह्यानी आणले आहे, ह्यानी आणले होते, ह्यानी आणले असेल.
10. You	तू *(tū)*	तू आणले, तू आणले आहे, तू आणले होते, तू आणले असेल.
11. You pl∘	तुम्ही *(tumhī)*	तुम्ही आणले, तुम्ही आणले आहे, तुम्ही आणले होते, तुम्ही आणले असेल.

adj∘ = Adjective, adv∘ = Adverb; *conj.* = Conjunction, f∘ = Feminine gender, *ind.* = Indeclinable, m∘ = Masculine gender, n∘ = Neuter gender, pl∘ = Plural

12. You hon◦	आपण *(āpaṇ)*	आपण आणले, आपण आणले आहे, आपण आणले होते, आपण आणले असेल.
13. Ram	राम *(Rām)* m◦	रामने आणले, रामने आणले आहे, रामने आणले होते, रामने आणले असेल.
14. Sītā	सीता *(Sītā)* f◦	सीताने आणले, सीताने आणले आहे, सीताने आणले होते, सीताने आणले असेल.
15. Boys	मुले *(mule)* n◦	मुलांनी आणले, मुलांनी आणले आहे, मुलांनी आणले होते, मुलांनी आणले असेल.
15. Girls	मुली *(girls)* f◦	मुलींनी आणले, मुलींनी आणले आहे, मुलींनी आणले होते, मुलींनी आणले असेल.

EXAMPLES :

(a). **Intransitive** actions m◦ f◦ , such as I came , I went, I fell, I walked :

I walked *mī chālalo, mī chālalī;* m◦ मी चाललो, f◦ मी चालली. You fell *tū paḍlās,* m◦ तू पडलास, f◦ *tū paḍlīs,* तू पडलीस. He came *to āla.* तो आला. She went *tī gelī.* ती गेली. We slept *āmhī zoplo.* आम्ही झेपलो. They sat *te basle.* m◦ ते बसले, m◦ त्या बसल्या.

(b). **Intransitive** actions m◦ f◦ : I have come, I have gone, I have fallen, I have walked :

I have walked. *mī chalalo (chalalī) āhe.* (m◦) मी चाललो (f◦ चालली) आहे. You have fallen. *tū paḍlā (paḍlī) āhes.* m◦ तू पडला (f◦ पडली) आहेस. He has come. *to ālā āhe.* तो आला आहे. She has come . *tī ālī āhe.* ती आली आहे. We have slept. *āmhI zoplo āhot.* m◦ f◦ आम्ही झोपलो आहोत. They have sat. *te basle āheta. tyā baslyā āhet.*m◦ ते बसले आहेत. f◦ त्या बसल्या आहेत.

(c). **Intransitive** actions m◦ f◦ , such as I had come, I had gone, I had fallen, I had walked :

I had walked. *mī chālalo hoto. mī chālalī hotī.* m◦ मी चाललो होतो. f◦ मी चालली होती. You had fallen. *tū paḍlā htās. tū paḍlī hotīs.*m◦ तू पड़ला होतास. f◦ तू पडली होतीस. He had come. *to ālā hotā.* तो आला होत. She had gone. *tī gelī hotī.* ती गेली होती. We had slept. *āmhī zoplo hoto.* m◦ f◦ आम्ही झोपलो होतो. They had sat. *to bolale hote. tyā bolalyā hotyā.* m◦ ते बोलले होते. f◦ त्या बोलल्या होत्या.

(d). **Transitive** actions m◦ f◦ , such as I did, I wrote, I drank, I saw :

I ate. *mī khālle.* m◦ f◦ मी खाल्ले. I ate a mango. *mī ek āmbā khāllā.* m◦ f◦ मी एक आंबा खाल्ला. I ate one guava. *mī ek perū khāllā.* m◦ f◦ मी एक पेरू खाल्ला. I ate two guavas. *mī don peru khalle.*m◦ f◦ मी दोन पेरू खाल्ले. I ate one Roṭī. *mī ek poḷī khāllī.* m◦ f◦ मी एक पोळी खाल्ली. I ate two Roṭīs. *mī don poḷyā khāllyā.* m◦ f◦ मी दोन पोळ्या खाल्या.

You drank tea. *tū chahā pilās.* m◦ तू चहा पिलास (f◦ पिलीस). Govind washed hands. *govind-ne hāt dhutle.* गोविंदने हात धुतले. Sunitā watched TV. *Sunita nī TV pāhilā.* सुनीता ने टीवी पाहिला.

adj◦ = Adjective, adv◦ = Adverb; *conj.* = Conjunction, f◦ = Feminine gender, *ind.* = Indeclinable, m◦ = Masculine gender, n◦ = Neuter gender, pl◦ = Plural

We peeled bananas. *āmhī keḷe chhilale.* m◦ f◦ आम्ही केळे छिलले. Rām and Shyām did the work. *Rām aṇi Shyām-nI kām kele.* राम आणि श्यामनी काम केले.

(e). **Transitive** actions m◦ f◦ , I have done, I have written, I have drunk, I have seen :
I have eaten. *mī khalle āhe.* m◦ f◦ मी खाल्ले आहे. I have eaten a mango. *mī ek āmbā khallā āhe.* m◦ f◦ मी एक आंबा खाल्ला आहे. I have eaten one guave. *mī ek purū khāllā āhe.* m◦ f◦ मी एक पेरू खाल्ला आहे. I have eaten two guavas. *mī don purū khālle āhet.* मी दोन पेरू खाल्ले आहेत. I have eaten one roṭī. *mī ek poḷī khāllī āhe.* m◦ f◦ मी एक पोळी खाल्ली आहे. I have eaten two roṭīs. *mī don polyā khāllyā āhet.* m◦ f◦ मी दोन पोळ्या खाल्या आहेत.

You have eaten a mango. *tū āmbā khāllā āhe.* m◦ f◦ तू एक आंबा खाल्ला आहे. Rāṇī has washed hands. *raṇī ne hāth dhutle āhet.* राणीने हात धुतले आहेत. Sunitā has watched TV. *Sunita ne TV pāhilā āhe.* सुनीताने टीवी पाहिला आहे. We have peeled potatoes. *āmhī baṭāṭe chhīlale āhet.* m◦ f◦ आम्ही बटाटे छीलले आहेत. Rām and Shyām have done the work. *Rām āṇi Shyām ne kām kele āhe.* राम आणि श्याम ने काम केले आहे.

(f). **Transitive** actions m◦ f◦ , such as - I had done, I had written, I had drunk, I had seen :
I had eaten. *mī khalle hote.* m◦ f◦ मी खाल्ले होते. I had eaten a mango. *mī āmbā khāllā hotā.* m◦ f◦ मी आंबा खाल्ला होता. I had eaten one guava. *mī ek perū khāllā hotā.* m◦ f◦ मी एक पेरू खाल्ला होता. I had eaten two guavas. *mī don perū khalle hote.* मी दोन पेरू खाल्ले होते. I had eaten one roṭī. *mī ek poḷī khallī hotī.* m◦ f◦ मी एक पोळी खाल्ली होती. I had eaten two roṭīs. *mī don polyā khallyā hotyā.* m◦ f◦ मी दोन पोळ्या खाल्या होत्या.

You had drunk tea. *tū chahā pyālā hotās.* m◦ तू चहा प्याला होतास, (f◦ प्याली होतीस). Mīnā had washed hands. *mīnā ne hāt dhutle hote.* मीनाने हात धुतले होते. Sunitā had watched TV. *Sunita ne TV pāhilā hotā.* सुनीताने टीवी पाहिला होता. We had peeled potatoes. *āmhī baṭāṭe chhīlale haote.* m◦ f◦ आम्ही बटाटे छिलले होते. Rām and Shyām had done the work. *Rām āṇi ne kām kele hote.* राम आणि श्यामने काम केले होते.

NOTE: The ँ sign is just a slight nasal tone added to the syllable below that ँ

LESSON 15
पंधरावा पाठ
THE MOODS
अर्थ

15.1
INTERROGATIVE MOOD
प्रश्नार्थ
ASKING QUESTIONS

WHAT, WHICH, WHO, WHERE, WHEN, WHY ?
HOW, HOW MUCH, HOW MANY ?

WHAT (काय)? WHICH (m◦ कोणता, f◦ कोणती, n◦ कोणते)? WHO (कोण, कोणी, कुणी)?
WHERE (कुठे, कोठे)? WHEN (केव्हा)? WHY (कां)?
HOW (m◦ कसा, f◦ कशी, n◦ कसे)? HOW MUCH (किती)? HOW MANY (किती)?

RATNAKAR'S NOBLE TRUTH : *(kyā)*

RULE : When '*kyā*' (क्या) comes at the beginning or at the end of a sentence, this *kyā* (क्या) = a question mark (?). But, when *kyā* (क्या) comes anywhere in the sentence, then this *kyā* (क्या) = what?

1. kāy काय as a Question mark?. e.g. Is it true? *kāy he khare āhe?* OR *he khare āhe kāy?* काय हे खरे आहे? हे खरे आहे काय?

   Will you drink tea? *tū chahā pis'hil kāy? kāy tū chahā pis'hil?* तू चहा पिशील काय? काय तू चहा पिशील?

2. kāy काय as an Interrogative word "what?" e.g. m◦ f◦ What will I drink? what should I drink? *mī kāy piū?* मी काय पिऊ (पिणार)? What will you drink? *tū kāy pis'hīl?* तू काय पिशील (पिणार)? What will he drink? *to kāy piel?* तो काय पिएल (पिणार)? What will she drink? *tī kāy piel?* ती काय पिएल (पिणार)? What will we drink? *āmhī kāy piū?* आम्ही काय पिऊ

(पिणार)? What will they drink? *te kāy pitīl?* ते काय पितील (पिणार)?

EXERCISE : Translate the English sentences into marāṭhī (Answers are given for help)

Time Indicating Key Words : Everyday = *roj* रोज. Never = *kadhī nāhī* कधी नाही. Always = *nehamī* नेहमी. Someone = *kuṇī koṇī* कुणी, कोणी. Sometimes = *kadhī* कधी. Anytime = *kevā hī* केव्हा ही. Some, Something = *kāhī* काही, *kāhī tarī* काही तरी. Anything, Whatever = *kāhī hī* काही ही. Where = *kuṭhe?* कुठे? Somewhere = *kuṭhe tarī* कुठे तरी. Anywhere = *kuṭhe hī* कुठे ही. Today = *āj* आज. Tomorrow = *udyā* उद्या. Yesterday = *kāl* काल. Day before yesterday, Day after yesterday = *parvā* परवा. Now = *ātā* आता. Later, After = *mag* मग. What time? = *kevhā* केव्हा? O Clock = *vājtā* वाजता.

1. Will Neil come at two O Clock. *Neil don vājta yeīl kāy? kāy Neil don vājta yeīl?* नील दोन वाजता येईल काय? काय नील दोन वाजता येईल?
2. Will Rānī not work today. *Rāṇī āj kām karṇar nahī kāy?* राणी आज काम करणार नाही काय?
3. Was Nīrā sewing the shirt yesterday? *kāl Nīrā sadarā shivat hotī kāy?* काल नीरा सदरा शिवत होती काय?
4. What will Vijay say? *Vijay kāy mhaṇel?* विजय काय म्हणेल?
5. What did Mīnā say? *Mīnā kyā mhaṇālī?* मीना काय म्हणाली?
6. Will Rājā bring a cup of tea? *Rājā ek kap chahā āṇel kāy?* राजा एक कप चहा आणेल काय?
7. When will Rīkkī go. *Rīkkī kevā jāīl?* रीक्की केव्हा जाईल?
8. Can Nīrū come now? *Nīrū ātā yeū shakel kāy?* नीरू आता येऊ शकेल काय? (शक = be able)
9. What will Dravid tell? *Dravid kyā sāngel?* द्रवीड काय सांगेल?
10. What was burning yesterday? *kāl kyā jaḷat hote?* काल काय जळत होते?
11. Did Govind wash the dishes. *Govind ne baśhyā dhutlyā kāy?* गोविंदने बश्या धुतल्या काय?
12. Will Mohan sleep here today. *Mohan āj ithe zopel kāy?* मोहन आज इथे झोपेल काय?
13. Does Vimal read something everyday? *Vimal roj kāhī tarī vāchte kāy?* विमला रोज काही तरी वाचते काय?
14. Will Sunīl be a TV star. *Sunīl TV star hoīl kāy?* सुनील टीवी स्टार होईल काय?
15. Will Vikās win tomorrow? *Vikās udyā jinkel kāy?* विकास उद्या जिंकेल काय?
16. Is it true that nobody wins always. *kuṇī hī nehamī jinkat nāhi he khare kāy?* कुणी ही नेहमी जिंकत नाही हे खरे काय?
17. Was somebody there? *kuṇī tithe hotā kāy?* कुणी तिथे होता काय?
18. Is anyone coming day after tomorrow? कुणी परवा येईल काय? कुणी परवा येणार काय? *kuṇī parvā*

adj∘ = Adjective, adv∘ = Adverb; *conj.* = Conjunction, f∘ = Feminine gender, *ind.* = Indeclinable, m∘ = Masculine gender, n∘ = Neuter gender, pl∘ = Plural

yeīl kāy? kuṇī parvā yeṇār kāy?

19. Who had come day before yesterday? परवा कोण आले होते? *parvā koṇ āle hote?*

20. May I come in? मी आंत येऊ काय? *mī ānt yeū kāy?*

15.2

MAKING A REQUEST

the Imperative Sentences

आज्ञार्थ

Making a Request, Suggestion or giving an Order, is the Imperative Mood. A Request, Suggestion or an Order is made by a person (1st person) to a person whom he is talking to (2nd person).

(A) MAKING A Respectful REQUEST :

A request is normally made in a respectful manner, using the words *tumhī* OR *āpaṇ* (तुम्ही, आपण). For making such request, only pure Root Verbs are used for Second Person तू. For तुम्ही and आपण subjects suffix आ is attached to the verb. For the use of Third Person Imperative Subjects, the suffix आवा, आवी and आवे are attached to the m◦ f◦ and n◦ Objects. Request is not applicable for First Person subjects मी and आम्ही.

MAKING A REQUEST or SUGGESTION

Doer of the action		should drink tea m◦	should drink coffee f◦	should drink milk n◦
Subject	marāṭhī	drink tea m◦ **प्यावा**	drink coffee f◦ **प्यावी**	drink milk n◦ **प्यावे**
1. He	त्याने *(tyāne)*	त्याने चहा प्यावा	त्याने कॉफी प्यावी	त्याने दूध प्यावे
2 These	ह्याने *(hyāne)*	ह्याने चहा प्यावा	ह्याने कॉफी प्यावी	ह्याने दूध प्यावे
3 They	त्यांनी *(tyānī)*	त्यांनी चहा प्यावा	त्यांनी कॉफी प्यावी	त्यांनी दूध प्यावे
4 She	तिने *(tine)*	तिने चहा प्यावा	तिने कॉफी प्यावी	तिने दूध प्यावे
5. These	ह्यांनी *(hyānī)*	ह्यांनी चहा प्यावा	ह्यांनी कॉफी प्यावी	ह्यांनी दूध प्यावे
6. They	त्यांनी *(tyānī)*	त्यांनी चहा प्यावा	त्यांनी कॉफी प्यावी	त्यांनी दूध प्यावे
7. It	ह्याने *(hyāne)*	ह्याने चहा प्यावा	ह्याने कॉफी प्यावी	ह्याने दूध प्यावे
8. You	तू *(tū)*	तू चहा पी	तू कॉफी पी	तू दूध पी
9. You pl◦	तुम्ही *(tumhī)*	तुम्ही चहा प्या	तुम्ही कॉफी प्या	तुम्ही दूध प्या
10. You hon◦	आपण *(āpaṇ)*	आपण चहा प्या	आपण कॉफी प्या	आपण दूध प्या

adj◦ = Adjective, adv◦ = Adverb; *conj.* = Conjunction, f◦ = Feminine gender, *ind.* = Indeclinable, m◦ = Masculine gender, n◦ = Neuter gender, pl◦ = Plural

IMPORTANT NOTE : The marāṭhī Learning books will tell you that the marāṭhī Verb for "sing" is gāṇe (गाणे), but it is wrong. gāṇe (गाणे) is not a Verb. It is (i) an Infinitive (to sing), or (ii) a Verbal Noun (song), or (iii) a Gerund (singing). The marāṭhī Verb (or the Verb Stem or Root Verb) is **gā** (गा) to which you add any suffix. Please remember this note in order to learn marāṭhī easily and properly.

EXAMPLES :

1. (you) please come! (come = *ye* ये; to come = *yeṇe* येणे) तू ये, तुम्ही या, आपण या. (या or यावे) *tū ye, tumhī yā, āpaṇ yā (yā or yāve)*
2. (you) Please speak! (Speak = *bol* बोल; to speak = *bolṇe* बोलणे) तू बोल, तुम्ही बोला, आपण बोला. (बोला or बोलावे) *tū bol, tumhī bolā, āpaṇ bolā (bolā or bolāve)*
3. (you) Please eat! (Eat = *khā* खा; to eat = *khāṇe* खाणे) तू खा, तुम्ही खावे, आपण खावे. (खा or खावे) *tū khā, tumhī khā, āpaṇ khā (khā or khāve)*
4. (you) Please sleep! (Sleep = *zop* झोप; to slep = *zopṇe* झोपणे) तू झोप, तुम्ही झोपा, आपण झोपा. (झोपा or झोपावे) *tū zop, tumhī zopā, āpaṇ zopā (zopā or zopāve)*
5. (you) Please walk! (let's go! = चल! to walk = *chālṇe* चालणे) तू चाल, तुम्ही चाला, आपण चाला. (चाला or चालावे). *tū chāl, tumhī chālā, āpaṇ chālā (chālā or chālāve)*
6. (you) please go! (go = *jā* ये; to go = *jāṇe* जाणे) तू जा, तुम्ही जा, आपण जा. (जा or जावे) *tū ye, tumhī jā, āpaṇ jā (jā or jāve)*

1. (He/She) should come, (He/She) may come (come = *ye* ये) त्याने यावे *tyāne yāve.* तिने यावे *tine yāve.*
2. (He/She) should speak, (He/She) may speak (Speak = *bol* बोल) त्याने बोलावे *tyāne bolāve.* तिने बोलावे *tine bolāve.*
3. (He/She) should eat, (He/She) may speak (Eat = *khā* खा) त्याने खावे *tyāne khāve.* तिने खावे *tine khāve.*
4. (He/She) should sleep, (He/She) may speak (Sleep = *zop* झोप) त्याने झोपावे *tyāne zopāve.* तिने झोपावे *tine zopāve.*
5. (He/She) should walk, (He/She) may speak (Let us go = *chal* चल) त्याने चलावे *tyāne yāve.* तिने चलावे *tine yāve.*
6. (He/She) should go, (He/She) may speak (go = त्याने जावे *tyāne jāve.* तिने जावे *ttine jāve.etc.*

NOTE: The ँ sign is just a slight nasal tone added to the syllable below that ँ

adj∘ = Adjective, adv∘ = Adverb; *conj.* = Conjunction, f∘ = Feminine gender, *ind.* = Indeclinable, m∘ = Masculine gender, n∘ = Neuter gender, pl∘ = Plural

LESSON 16
सोळावा पाठ

THE CASES
विभक्ति आणि कारक

English : **PREPOSITIONS (उपसर्ग)** become marāṭhī : **POSTPOSITIONS (प्रत्यय)**

The form of a Noun, Pronoun or Adjective (substantive) through which the Noun, Pronoun or Adjective connects or relates with the other words in a sentence, that form of a Noun, Pronoun or Adjective is called the Declension (*kārak* कारक) of that substantive. And, the suffix (*pratyay* प्रत्यय) that is attached to that Noun, Pronoun or Adjective to connect it to the other words of the sentence is called the Case Suffix (विभक्ति प्रत्यय).

There are eight such case suffixes in marāṭhī Grammar (मराठी व्याकरण). The process of forming the Declensions (कारक) of a Noun, Pronoun or Adjective is called Inflection (विभक्ति रूपांतरण) of that Noun, Pronoun or Adjective.

TABLE : The Cases विभक्ति

Form रूप	*Kārak*	कारक	Name of the Case	विभक्ति चे नांव
Subject	*karttā kārak*	कता कारक	**Nominative Case**	प्रथमा विभक्ति
Object	*karma kārak*	कर्म कारक	**Accusative Case**	द्वितीया विभक्ति
Instrument	*karaṇ kārak*	करण कारक	**Instrumental Case**	तृतीया विभक्ति
For whom, to whom	*sampradān kārak*	संप्रदान कारक	**Dative Case**	चतुर्थी विभक्ति
From where	*Apādān kārak*	अपादान कारक	**Ablative Case**	पंचमी विभक्ति
Relation	*sambamdh kārak*	संबंध कारक	**Possessive Case**	षष्ठी विभक्ति
To where	*adhikaraṇ kārak*	अधिकरण कारक	**Locative Case**	सप्तमी विभक्ति
Address	*sambodhan*	संबोधन	**Vocative**	संबोधन

The suffix (*pratyay* प्रत्यय) that is attached to a Noun, Pronoun or Adjective to connect it to the other parts of that sentence is called the Case Suffix (विभक्ति प्रत्यय).

adj∘ = Adjective, adv∘ = Adverb; *conj.* = Conjunction, f∘ = Feminine gender, *ind.* = Indeclinable, m∘ = Masculine gender, n∘ = Neuter gender, pl∘ = Plural

TABLE : The Case Suffixes विभक्ति प्रत्यय

Form रूप	Name of the Case	विभक्ति चे नांव	Singular Case Suffix		Plural Case Suffix	
Subject	**Nominative Case**	प्रथमा विभक्ति	No Case Suffix		No Case Suffix	
Object	**Accusative Case**	द्वितीया विभक्ति	स, ला	*sa, lā*	स, ला, ना	*sa, lā, nā*
Instrument	**Instrumental Case**	तृतीया विभक्ति	ने, शी	*ne, śhī*	नी, शी	*nī, śhī*
For whom, to whom	**Dative Case**	चतुर्थी विभक्ति	स, ला करिता, साठी	*sa, lā, kritā, sāṭhī*	स, ना, करिता, साठी	*sa, nā, kritā, sāṭhī*
From where	**Ablative Case**	पंचमी विभक्ति	ऊन, तून, पासून, पेक्षा	*ūn, tūn, pāsūn, pekṣhā*	हून, पासून, पेक्षा	*hūn, pāsūn, pekṣhā*
Relation	**Possessive Case**	षष्ठी विभक्ति	चा, ची, चे, झा, झी, झे	*chā, chī, che, jhā, jhī, jhe*	चा, ची, चे	*chā, chī, che*
To where	**Locative Case**	सप्तमी विभक्ति	त, आंत, वर	*ta, ā̃t, var*	त, आंत, वर	*ānt, var*
Address	**Vocative**	संबोधन	हे! अरे!	*he! are!*	हे! अहो!	*he! aho!*

CHARACTERISTICS OF THE DECLENSIONS AND CASES
कारक आणि विभक्ति चे गुण स्वभाव

(1) Nominative Case, Kartā Kārak, (कर्ता कारक, प्रथमा-विभक्ति)

The Kartā is the subject of the verb, i.e. the doer of the action. The form of the noun used for indicating the doer (*kartā* कर्ता) of the action (*kriyā* क्रिया) in a sentence is the *kartā kārak* (कर्ता कारक) of that sentence. The suffix (pratyay प्रत्यय) attached to the noun to form the *kartā Kārak* is the Nominative Case Suffix (प्रथमा विभक्ति प्रत्यय).

Scope : The noun (संज्ञा) is the doer or subject of the sentence. Normally, in Nominative Case, the Subject takes no suffix, but if the action is a Transitive Verb in any Perfect Tense then, only in that case, the subject takes *ne* (ने) suffix. As a result, now the Verb changes according to the Gender and Number of the Object the Subject has no effect on the Verb. e.g. **(1)** राम समोसा खातो, राम पोळी खातो, सीता समोसा खाते, सीता पोळी खाते, राम समोसे खातो, सीता पोळ्या खाते, etc. **(2)** रामने समोसा खल्ला. रामने समोसे खाल्ले, रामने पोळी खाल्ली, सीताने समोसा खाल्ला, सीता ने पोळी खाल्ली, राम ने पोळ्या

adj॰ = Adjective, adv॰ = Adverb; *conj.* = Conjunction, f॰ = Feminine gender, *ind.* = Indeclinable, m॰ = Masculine gender, n॰ = Neuter gender, pl॰ = Plural

खाल्या, सीताने पोळ्या खाल्या, etc.

(2) Karma Kārak, Accusative Case (कर्म कारक, द्वितीया विभक्ति) : On whom the action is performed.

The object (*karma* कर्म) on which the subject performs the verb (क्रिया) is the *karma kārak* (कर्म कारक) of that sentence. The suffix attached to the object to form the *karma kārak* is Accusative Case Suffix (द्वितीया विभक्ति प्रत्यय).

(3) Karaṇ Kārak, Instrumental Case (करण–कारक, तृतीया–विभक्ति) : The instrument or vehicle (साधन) with or by whch the (active or passive) action is performed.

The medium used for performing action on the object (कर्म) is the *karaṇ kārak* (करण कारक) of the sentence. The suffix attached to the object to form the *karaṇ kārak* is Instrumental Case Suffix (तृतीया विभक्ति प्रत्यय).

Scope : by, with, without (च्या विना), because (च्या द्वारे), along with (सह, च्या बरोबर), owing to, on account of, out of-, for the reason of (प्रयोजनार्थ), by nature (स्वभाव -ज्या मुळे), enough, enough of (बस), through (च्या माध्यमाने, च्या द्वारे), simile (च्या समान, सदृश), etc.

(4) Sampradān Kārak, Dative Case (सम्प्रदान कारक, चतुर्थी विभक्ति) : To whom or for whom the action is directed through something.

When the verb is performed for (*chyā karitā* च्या करिता) or to (*lā* ला) someone or something, that person or thing assumes *sampradān kārak* (संप्रदान कारक). The suffix attached to the noun to form the *sampradān kārak* is Dative Case Suffix (चतुर्थी विभक्ति प्रत्यय).

(5) Apādān Kārak, Ablative Case (अपादान कारक, पंचमी विभक्ति)

From where the subject is moved, or a comparison between TWO things, or group of things.

When the subject moves from (पासून) any location to (ला) other location, the location from where the subject moves is in *apādān kārak* (अपादान कारक). The suffix attached to the name of that location is Dative Case Suffix (पंचमी विभक्ति प्रत्यय).

Scope : from, than (पेक्षा), without, except (विना), far or away (दूर), outside, since, until, after, before (पूर्व), to the direction of (प्रति), motivation (अकस्मात्), in the meanings of away (अलग, पृथक्), other (अन्य), etc.

(6) Sambandh Kārak, Genitive Case (सम्बन्ध कारक, षष्ठी विभक्ति)

Also called Possessive Case is the **relation** between two things or group of things i.e. superlative degree, but not comparative.

When a noun has any relationship with the subject of the sentence, this relationship forms *sambandh kārak.* The suffix attached to this noun is called Genetive Case Suffix (षष्ठी विभक्ति प्रत्यय). e.g. कुत्र्याचा पाय तुटला, कुत्र्याची शेपटी तुटली, मांजरीचा पाय तुटला. मांजरीची शेपटी तुटली, etc. Here, the suffixes (चा, ची etc.) in the phrases कुत्र्याचा, कुत्र्याची, मांजरीचा, मांजरीची change according to the Gender and Number of the words पाय, शेपटी, etc. which are the subjects of the sentence.

Scope : of (चा, ची, चे), above (च्या वर), below (च्या खाली), in front of (च्या समोर), behind (च्या मागे), beyond (च्या पलीकडे), away (च्या दूर), in the presence of (च्या समक्ष), for the sake of (चे कारण), etc.

(7) Adhikaraṇ Kārak, Locative Case (अधिकरण कारक, सप्तमी विभक्ति) : Shows a locative relationship between two things, or a quality within a group of things.

The word that says about the location in (मध्ये) or on (वर) of the subject, that location is *adhikaraṇ kaErak* (अधिकरण कारक). The suffix attached to the name of that place or object is Locative Case Suffix (सप्तमी विभक्ति प्रत्यय). e.g. ग्लास मध्ये पाणी आहे, पुस्तक मेज वर होते, etc.

Scope : in, on, at (वर), in side (मध्ये), under (खाली), upon (वर), among (पैकी), concerning (विषयी), in the matter of (च्या बाबतीत), to express feelings for, to enter, to place, to fall, to send, to indicate time (दिवसा, प्रत:काळी, मध्याह्नात, सायङ्काळी), in occurance of the first event after which some other event takes place, with the use of expressions मध्ये, कृते, समक्ष, अन्त:, etc.

(8) Sambodhan Kārak, Vocative Case (सम्बोधन) : To call or address someone.

The words used for calling, addressing ot expressing surprise are sambandh kārak (संबंध कारक). It probably is not a separate or independent *kārak* (विभक्ति), but a modified form of the karttā *kārak* (कर्त्ता कारक)

Scope : अरे! हे! अहो! हो! भो:! हाय! हे राम! .. etc.

USE of CASE SUFFIXES

(16.1) Use of *lā* ला (to) :

1. I am giving a book to Līlā. *mī Līlālā pustak det āhe.* मी लीलाला पुस्तक देत आहे.
2. He is giving books to Mālā. *to mālālā pustake det āhe.* तो मालाला पुस्तके देत आहे.
3. She is giving keys to Mīnā. *to mīnālā kilyā det āhe.* ती मीनाला किल्या देत आहे.
4. A boy is giving a mango to a monkey. *mulgā vānrālā āmbā det āhe.* मुलगा वानराला आंबा देत आहे.
5. A boy is giving mangoes to a monkey. *mulgā vānrālā āmbe det āhe.* मुलगा वानराला आंबे देत

आहे.

6. A boy is giving mangoes to the monkeys. *mulgā vānaraṇā āmbe det āhe.* मुलगा वानरांना आंबे देत आहे.
7. The boys are giving bananas to the monkeys. *mule vānrānā āmbe det āhet.* मुले वानरांना आंबे देत आहेत.

(16.2) Use of *ne, nī* ने, नी (with, by) :

1. I go by car. *mī gāḍīne jāto (f∘ jāte),* मी गाडीने जातो (f∘ जाते). We go by car - m∘ f∘ . *āmhī gāḍīne jāto* आम्ही गाडीने जातो.
2. I cut mangoes with a knife. *mī chākūne āmbe kapto (f∘ kāpte)* मी चाकूने आंबे कपतो (f∘ कापते). Shīlā was cutting two mangoes with two knives. *Shīlā don chākūnnī don āmbe kāpat hotī.* शीला दोन चाकूंनी दोन आंबे कापत होती.
3. Jitū should go now. *Jītūne ā̃ta jāve.* जीतूने आंते जावे.

(16.3) Use of *madhye* मध्ये (in) and *var* वर (on, at) :

(i) ***madhye*** **मध्ये** = IN

1. There is no water in the glass. *glās madhye pāṇī nāhī.* ग्लास मध्ये पाणी नाही.
2. Ajay is not in the room. *Ajay kholīt nāhī.* अजय खोलीत नाही.
3. The dog is not in the house. *kutrā gharāt nāhī.* कुत्रा घरात नाही.
4. The key is in the lock. *killī kulpāt āhe.* किल्ली कुलपात आहे.

(ii) ***var*** **वर** = ON, AT

1. The cup is on the dish. *kap baśhīt āhe; kap baśhīvar āhe.* कप बशीत आहे; कप बशीवर आहे.
2. There are leaves on the tree. *jhāḍāvar pāne āhet.* झाडावर पाने आहेत.
3. Rām is at the play ground. *Rām maidānāvar āhe.* राम मैदानावर आहे.

(16.4) Use of *chā, chī* (चा, ची)

m∘ *kā* (का), f∘ *kī* (की) = of

The English preposition 'OF' becomes postposition *chā* (चा) or *chī* (ची) in marāṭhī. For showing the possessive relationship of a Masculine Object, suffix *chā* (चा) is added to the possessor, and for a Feminine Object, suffix *chī* (ची) is added. Plural चे, च्या.

adj∘ = Adjective, adv∘ = Adverb; *conj.* = Conjunction, f∘ = Feminine gender, *ind.* = Indeclinable, m∘ = Masculine gender, n∘ = Neuter gender, pl∘ = Plural

EXAMPLES :

1. Shobhā's brother. *Shobhā chā bhaū.* शोभा चा भाऊ. Gītā's sister. *Gītā chī bahiṇ.* गीता ची बहिण.
2. This is Rola's car. *hī Rolā chī cār āhe.* ही रोला ची कार आहे.
3. Those are Anītā's books. *tī Anītā chī pustake āhet.* ती अनीताची पुस्तके आहेत.
4. Where are Tarā's cats? *tārā chyā mānjarī kuṭhe āhet?* ताराच्या मांजरी कुठे आहेत?
5. That is Savitā's tea. *to savitāchā cahā āhe.* तो सविताचा चहा आहे.
6. He is Dīpak's Brother. *to dīpakchā bhāū āhe.* तो दीपकचा भाऊ आहे.
7. I eat *burfī* made of milk. *mī dudhāchī barfī khāto (f◦ khāte).* मी दुधाची बरफी खातो (f◦ खाते).
8. This is Monika's house. *he monikāche ghar āhe.* हे मोनिकाचे घर आहे.
9. This is our house. *he āmche ghar āhe.* हे आमचे n◦ घर आहे.
10. This is their house. *he tyāñche ghar āhe.* हे त्यांचे घर आहे.
11. This is his house. *he tyāche ghar āhe.* हे त्याचे घर आहे.
12. This is her house. *he tiche ghar āhe.* हे तिचे घर आहे.
13. INVITATION : (Please) come to my house. m◦ f◦ *kripayā mājhyā gharī yā.* कृपया माझ्या घरी या.
14. SUGGESTION : (Please) sit here. *kripayā ithe basā.* m◦ f◦ कृपया इथे बसा.
15. ORDER : Do not come here. *ithe yeū nakos!* m◦ f◦ इथे येऊ नकोस!
16. REQUEST : (Please) have tea. *krupayā chahā ghyā.* m◦ f◦ कृपया चहा घ्या (*chahā pyā.* m◦ f◦ कृपया चहा प्या).
17. CONSOLATION : do not cry. *raḍū nakos (raḍū nakā)* m◦ f◦ रडू नकोस (m◦ f◦ रडू नका).
18. INSTRUCTION : (Please) do work properly. *kām ṭhīk karā.* m◦ f◦ काम ठीक करा.
19. QUESTION : Sir! what is this? *he kāy āhe ho!* हे काय आहे हो!

SUMMARY :

1N◦ = **Nominative** case, the DOER of the action (the subject)
2A◦ = **Accusative** case, the OBJECT of the action, TO WHERE the action ends
3I◦ = **Instrumental** case, the INSTRUMENT with/by which action is performed
4D◦ = **Dative** case, FOR WHOM the action is performed
5A◦ = **Ablative** case, the place FROM WHERE the action starts
6P◦ = **Possessive** case, the RELATIONSHIP OF the object in a sentence
7L◦ = **Locative** case. the LOCATION of the object.

adj◦ = Adjective, adv◦ = Adverb; *conj.* = Conjunction, f◦ = Feminine gender, *ind.* = Indeclinable, m◦ = Masculine gender, n◦ = Neuter gender, pl◦ = Plural

TABLE : CHART OF SUFFIXES FOR MASCULINE NOUNS

THE marāṭhī Chart (The English Chart is on the Next Page)

NOTE : आं *(ān)* is added to all **plural** nouns m∘ f∘ and n∘, before attaching any suffix.

			(i) m∘ tiger	(ii) m∘ horse	(iii) m∘ saint	(iv) m∘ saint
Words ending in →			(i) अ (वाघ)	(ii) आ (घोडा)	(iii) ई (योगी)	(iv) उ (साधु)
1N∘		singular→	वाघ	घोडा	योगी	साधु
		plural→	वाघ	घोडे	योगी	साधू
2 A∘	to ला	singular→	वाघाला	घोड्याला	योग्याला	साधूला
	ना	plural→	वाघांना	घोड्यांना	योग्यांना	साधूंना
3 I∘	with, by ने	singular→	वाघाने	घोड्याने	योग्याने	साधूने
	नी	plural→	वाघांनी	घोड्यांनी	योग्यांनी	साधूंनी
4 D∘	for करिता	singular→	वाघाकरिता	घोड्याकरिता	योग्याकरिता	साधूकरिता
		plural→	वाघांकरिता	घोड्यांकरिता	योग्यांकरिता	साधूंकरिता
5 A∘	from पासून	singular→	वाघापासून	घोड्यापासून	योग्यापासून	साधूपासून
		plural→	वाघांपासून	घोड्यांपासून	योग्यांपासून	साधूंपासून
6 P∘	of चा	singular→	वाघाचा	घोड्याचा	योग्याचा	साधूचा
		plural→	वाघांचा	घोड्यांचा	योग्यांचा	साधूंचा
7 L∘	in त, मध्ये	singular→	वाघात	घोड्यात	योग्यात	साधूत
		plural→	वाघांत	घोड्यांत	योग्यांत	साधूंत
	on, at वर	singular→	वाघावर	घोड्यावर	योग्यावर	साधूवर
		plural→	वाघांवर	घोड्यांवर	योग्यांवर	साधूंवर

TABLE : CHART OF CASES, MASCULINE NOUNS

The English Chart (The marāṭhī Chart is on the Previous Page)

NOTE : आं *(ān)* is added to all **plural** nouns m∘ and n∘, before attaching any suffix.

		(i) m∘ tiger	(ii) m∘ horse,	(iii) m∘ saint,	(iv) m∘ saint
Word ending in →		(i) *a (wāgh)*	(ii) *ā (ghoḍā)*	(iii) *ī (yogī)*	(iv) *u (sādhu)*
1N∘	singular→	*wāgh*	*ghoḍā*	*yogī*	*sādhu*
	plural→	*wāgh*	*ghoḍe*	*yogī*	*sādhū*
2 A∘ to *lā*	singular→	*wāghālā*	*ghoḍyālā*	*yogyālā*	*sādhūlā*
nā	plural→	*wāghā̐nā*	*ghoḍyā̐nā*	*yogyā̐nā*	*sādhū̐nā*
3 I∘ with, by *ne*	singular→	*wāghāne*	*ghoḍyāne*	*yogyāne*	*sādhūne*
nī	plural→	*wāghā̐nī*	*ghoḍyā̐nī*	*yogyā̐nī*	*sādhū̐nī*
4 D∘ for *karitā*	singular→	*wāghākaritā*	*ghoḍyākritā*	*yogyākritā*	*sādhūkritā*
	plural→	*wāghā̐nkaritā*	*ghoḍyā̐kritā*	*yogyā̐kritā*	*sādhū̐kritā*
5 A∘ from	singular→	*wāghāpāsūn*	*ghoḍyāpāsūn*	*yogyāpāsūn*	*sādhūpāsūn*
pāsūn	plural→	*wāghā̐pāsūn*	*ghoḍyā̐pāsūn*	*yogyā̐pāsūn*	*sādhū̐pāsūn*
6 P∘ of *chā*	singular→	*wāghāchā*	*ghoḍyāchā*	*yogyāchā*	*sādhūchā*
	plural→	*wāghāñchā*	*ghoḍyāñchā*	*yogyāñchā*	*sādhūñchā*
7 L∘ in *ta*	singular→	*wāghāt*	*ghoḍyāt*	*yogyāt*	*sādhūt*
	plural→	*wāghā̐t*	*ghoḍyā̐t*	*yogyā̐t*	*sādhū̐t*
on, at *par*	singular→	*bālakāvar*	*ghoḍyāvar*	*yogyāvar*	*sādhūvar*
	plural→	*bālakā̐var*	*ghoḍyā̐var*	*yogyā̐var*	*sādhū̐var*

adj∘ = Adjective, adv∘ = Adverb; *conj.* = Conjunction, f∘ = Feminine gender, *ind.* = Indeclinable, m∘ = Masculine gender, n∘ = Neuter gender, pl∘ = Plural

TABLE - CHART OF CASES : FEMININE NOUNS

The marāṭhī Chart (The English Chart is on the Next Page)

NOTE : ईं *(īn)* is added to f∘ **plural** nouns ending in a or ī, before attaching any suffix.

Words ending in →		f∘ manner, (i) अ (रीत)	f∘ girl, (ii) आ (बालिका)	f∘ ant (iii) ई (मुंगी)	f∘ thing (iv) उ (वस्तु)
1N∘	singular→	रीत	बालिका	मुंगी	वस्तु
	plural→	रीती	बालिका	मुंग्या	वस्तू
2 A∘ to ला	singular→	रीतीला	बालिकेला	मुंगीला	वस्तूला
ना	plural→	रीतींना	बालिकांना	मुंग्यांना	वस्तूंना
3 I∘ with, by ने	singular→	रीतीने	बालिकेने	मुंगीने	वस्तूने
नी	plural→	रीतींनी	बालिकांनी	मुंग्यांनी	वस्तूंनी
4 D∘ for करिता	singular→	रीतीकरिता	बालिकेकरिता	मुंगीकरिता	वस्तूकरिता
	plural→	रीतींकरिता	बालिकांकरिता	मुंग्यांकरिता	वस्तूंकरिता
5 A∘ from	singular→	रीतीपासून	बालिकेपासून	मुंगीपासून	वस्तूपासून
पासून	plural→	रीतींपासून	बालिकांपासून	मुंग्यांपासून	वस्तूंपासून
6 P∘ of चा	singular→	रीतीचा	बालिकेचा	मुंगीचा	वस्तूचा
	plural→	रीतींचा	बालिकांचा	मंग्यांचा	वस्तूंचा
7 L∘ in त	singular→	रीतीत	बालिकेत	मुंगीत	वस्तूत
	plural→	रीतींत	बालिकांत	मुंग्यांत	वस्तूंत
on, at वर	singular→	रीतीवर	बालिकेवर	मुंगीवर	वस्तूवर
	plural→	रीतींवर	बालिकांवर	मुंग्यांवर	वस्तूंवर

adj∘ = Adjective, adv∘ = Adverb; *conj.* = Conjunction, f∘ = Feminine gender, *ind.* = Indeclinable, m∘ = Masculine gender, n∘ = Neuter gender, pl∘ = Plural

TABLE - CHART OF CASES : FEMININE NOUNS

The English Chart (marāṭhī Chart is on the Previous Page)

NOTE : ईं *(īn)* is added to f∘ **plural** nouns ending in a or ī, before attaching any suffix.

Word ending in →		f∘ manner, (i) *a (rīt)*	f∘ girl, (ii) *ā (bālikā)*	f∘ ant *ī (mulgī)*	f∘ thing *u (vastu)*
1N∘	singular→	*rīt*	*bālikā*	*mungī*	*vastu*
	plural→	*rītī*	*bālikā*	*mungyā*	*vastū*
2 A∘ to *lā*	singular→	*rītīlā*	*bālikelā*	*munīlā*	*vastūlā*
nā	plural→	*rītī̐nā*	*bālikā̐ā*	*mugyā̐nā*	*vastū̐nā*
3 I∘ with, by *ne*	singular→	*rītīne*	*bālikene*	*mungīne*	*vastūne*
	plural→	*rītī̐nī*	*bālikā̐nī*	*mugyā̐nī*	*vastū̐nī*
4 D∘ for *karitā*	singular→	*rītīkarītā*	*bālikekarītā*	*mungīkarītā*	*vastūkarītā*
	plural→	*rītī̐karītā*	*bālikā̐karītā*	*mugyā̐karītā*	*vastū̐karītā*
5 A∘ from *pāsūn*	singular→	*rītīpāsūn*	*bālikepāsūn*	*mungīpāsūn*	*vastūpāsūn*
	plural→	*rītī̐pāsūn*	*bālikā̐pāsūn*	*mugyā̐pāsūn*	*vastū̐pāsūn*
6 P∘ of *chā*	singular→	*rītīchā*	*bālikechā*	*mungīchā*	*vastuchā*
	plural→	*rītī̃chā*	*bālikā̃chā*	*mugyā̃chā*	*vastũchā*
7 L∘ in *ta*	singular→	*rītīt*	*bāliket*	*mungīt*	*vastūt*
	plural→	*rītī̐t*	*bālikā̐t*	*mugyā̐t*	*vastū̐t*
on, at *var*	singular→	*rītīvar*	*bālikevar*	*mulīvar*	*vastūvar*
	plural→	*rītīnvar*	*bālikānvar*	*mulīnvar*	*vastūnvar*

adj∘ = Adjective, adv∘ = Adverb; *conj.* = Conjunction, f∘ = Feminine gender, *ind.* = Indeclinable, m∘ = Masculine gender, n∘ = Neuter gender, pl∘ = Plural

USING PRONOUNS

DEFINITIONS :

(1)The word used in place of a noun (in order to avoid its repetition) is called a *Pronoun* (सर्वनाम).

(2) If a pronoun qualifies a noun, then the pronoun is called a *Pronominal or Possessive Adjective* (सार्वनामिक विशेषण).

EXPLANATION :

(i) See this sentence :

Rām is going to Rām's school to see Rām's teacher and to give Rām's teacher Rām's teacher's books. राम रामाच्या शिक्षकाला भेटायला आणि रामच्या गुरुजीची पुस्तके रामच्या गुरुजीला द्यायला रामच्या विद्यालयाला जात आहे. It sounds improper and very confusing.

(ii) Now see this one

(Same sentence can be re-written properly with the use of pronouns) :

Rām is going to his school to see his teacher and to give him his books. *(Rām āplyā gurujīlā bheṭayalā āni tyāñchī pustake tyānā dyāyalā āpalyā vidyālaylā jāt āhe)*

राम आपल्या गुरुजीला भेटायला आणि त्यांची पुस्तके त्यांना द्यायला आपल्या विद्यालयला जात आहे. It reads improper.

16.7 THE PERSONAL PRONOUNS

A word used in place of the name of a person is a Personal Pronoun (a thing, is Impersonal Pronoun) (व्यक्तिगत सर्वनाम).

e.g.	I,	we,	you,	you,	you,	he, she,	they,	it,	this,	these,	they and those.
	mī,	*āmhī,*	*tū*	*tumhī*	*āpaṇ*	*to, tī,*	*te,*	*he,*	*he,*	*he,* f∘ *hyā*	*te,* f∘ *tyā*
	मी,	आम्ही,	तू,	तुम्ही	आपण	तो, ती,	ते,	हे	हे,	हे, f∘ ह्या	ते, f∘ त्या

16.8 THE INTERROGATIVE PRONOUNS

The pronoun that is employed for asking a question is an Interrogative Pronoun (प्रश्नार्थक सर्वनाम).

(1) कोण (*koṇ?* who?) : Who sleeps here? *(ithe koṇ jhopto?)* इथे कोण झोपतो.

(2) कां? (*kān?* why?) : Why do you sleep here? *(tū ithe kān jhoptaos?)* तू इथे कां झोपतोस? (f∘ झोपतेस?)

(3) काय? (*kāy?* what?) : What are you doing here now? *(tū ātā kāy karīt āhes?)* m∘ f∘ तू आता काय करीत आहेस? What is your name? *tujhe nāv kāy āhe?* तुझे नांव काय आहे?

(4) केव्हा (*kevā?* When) : When will you come? *(tū kevhā yeśhīl?)* m∘ f∘ तू केव्हा येशील?

(5) कुठे? कोठे? (*kuṭhe? koṭhe?* where?) : Where does he live? *(to kuṭhe rāhto?)* तो कुठे राहतो? etc.

adj∘ = Adjective, adv∘ = Adverb; *conj.* = Conjunction, f∘ = Feminine gender, *ind.* = Indeclinable, m∘ = Masculine gender, n∘ = Neuter gender, pl∘ = Plural

TABLE : CHART FOR THE PRONOUNS

The marāṭhī Chart (English Chart is on the Next Page)

1st., 2nd., 3rd. Person →		**I, we, us**	**You**	**He, she, him, her, that they, them, those**	**It, these**
1st., 2nd., 3rd. Person →		मी, आम्ही	तू, तुम्ही, आपण	तो, ती, ते, त्या	हे, ही, ह्या
1N◦	singular→	मी	तू, तुम्ही, आपण	तो, ती, ते	हे
	plural→	आम्ही	तुम्ही, आपण	ते, त्या	ही, ह्या
2 A◦ to ला	singular→	मला	तुला, तुम्हाला, आपणला	त्याला, तिला	ह्याला
ना	plural→	आम्हाला	तुम्हाला, आपणला	त्याना	ह्याना
3 I◦ with, by ने	singular→	मी	तू, तुम्ही, आपण	त्याने, तिने	ह्याने
	plural→	आम्ही	तू, तुम्ही, आपण	त्यांनी	ह्यांनी
4 D◦ for करिता	singular→	माझ्याकरिता	तुझ्याकरिता, तुमच्याकरिता तुमच्याकरिता, आपणाकरिता	त्याच्याकरिता तिच्याकरिता	ह्याच्याकरिता
	plural→	आमच्याकरिता	तुमच्याकरिता, आपणाकरिता	त्यांच्याकरिता	ह्यांच्याकरिता
5 A◦ from पासून	singular→	माझ्यापासून	तुझ्यापासून, तुमच्यापासून तुमच्यापासून, आपणापासून	त्याच्यापासून तिच्यापासून	ह्याच्यापासून
	plural→	आमच्यापासून	तुमच्यापासून, आपणांपासून	त्यांच्यापासून	ह्यांच्यापासून
6 P◦ of चा, ची, चे	singular→	माझा*	तुझा, तुमचा, आपला*	त्याचा, तिचा*	ह्याचा*
	plural→	आमचा*	तुमचा, आपला*	त्यांचा*	ह्यांचा*
7 L◦ in त	singular→	माझ्यात	तुझ्यात, तुमच्यात, आपणात	त्यात	ह्यात
	plural→	आमच्यात	तुमच्यात, आपणांत	त्यांत	ह्यांत
in वर	singular→	माझ्यावर	तुझ्यावर, तुमच्यावर, आपणावर	त्यावर	ह्यावर
	plural→	आमच्यावर	तुमच्यावर, आपणांवर	त्यांवर	ह्यांवर

* Depends on the Object, not the Subject. माझा, माझी, माझे; आमचा, आमची, आमचे; तुझा, युझी, तुझे; तुमचा, तुमची, तुमचे; त्याचा, त्याची, त्याचे; त्यांचा, त्यांची, त्यांचे; आपला, आपली, आपले, ...etc.

TABLE 24 : CHART FOR THE PRONOUNS

The marāṭhī Chart (English Chart is on the Next Page)

			I, we, us	**You**	**He, she, him, her, that they, them, those**	**It, these**
1st., 2nd., 3rd. Person →			*mī, āmhī*	*tū, tumhī, āpaṇ*	*to, tī, te, tyā*	*he, hī, hyā*
1N∘		singular→	*mī*	*tū, tumhī, āpaṇ*	*to, tī, te*	*he*
		plural→	*āmhī*	*tumhī, āpaṇ*	*te, tyā*	*hī, hyā*
2 A∘	to	singular→	*malā*	*tulā, tumhālā, āpaṇālā*	*tyāla, tilā*	*hyālā*
	lā	plural→	*āmhālā*	*tumhālā, āpaṇālā*	*tyānā*	*hyānā*
3 I∘	with, by	singular→	*mī*	*tū, tumhī, āpaṇ*	*tyāne, tine*	*hyāne*
	ne	plural→	*amhī*	*tū, tumhī, āpaṇ*	*tyā̃nī*	*hyā̃nī*
4 D∘	for	singular→	*mājhyākaritā*	*tujhyāk∘, tumchyāk∘* *tumchyāk∘, āpaṇāk∘*	*tyāchyāk∘* *tichyākaritā*	*hyāchyāk∘*
	karitā	plural→	*āmchyākaritā*	*tumchyāk∘, āpṇāk∘*	*tyāñchyāk∘*	*hyāñchyāk∘*
5 A∘	from	singular→	*mājhyāpāsūn*	*tujhyāpā∘, tumchyāpā∘* *tumchyāpā∘, āpaṇāpā∘*	*tyāchyāpā∘* *tichyāpāsūn*	*hyāchyāpā∘*
	pāsūn	plural→	*āmchyāpāsūn*	*tumchyāpa∘, āpaṇāpā∘*	*tyāñchyāpa∘*	*hyāñchyāpā∘*
6 P∘	of	singular→	*mājhā**	*tujhā, tumchā, āplā **	*tyāchā, tichā**	*hyāchā**
	chā	plural→	*āmchā**	*tumchā, āplā**	*tyāñchā, tichā**	*hyāñchā**
7 L∘	in	singular→	*mājhyāt*	*tujhyāt, tumchyāt, āpṇāt*	*tyāt*	*hyāt*
	ta	plural→	*āmchyāt*	*tumchyāt, āpṇāt*	*tyā̃t*	*hyā̃t*
	on, at	singular→	*mājhyāvar*	*tujhyāvar, tumchyāvar,* *āpṇāvar*	*tyāvar*	*hyā̃var*
	var	plural→	*āpaṇāvar*	*tumchyāvar, āpanāvar,*	*tyā̃var*	*hyā̃var*

* Depends on the Object, not the Subject. माझा, माझी, माझे; आमचा, आमची, आमचे; तुझा, युझी, तुझे; तुमचा, तुमची, तुमचे; त्याचा, त्याची, त्याचे; त्यांचा, त्यांची, त्यांचे; आपला, आपली, आपले, ...etc.

USE OF PRONOUNS AND POSSESSIVE ADJECTIVES

Review of what we learned so far, the 'cumulative learning'

EXERCISE : Translate the English sentences into marāṭhī (Answers are provided for help)

1ST PERSON : I, We (m◦ f◦)

1. I, We (*mī, āmhī)* मी, आम्ही. 2. I am. *(mī āhe)* मी आहे.

3. We are friends. *(āmhī mitra āhot)* आम्ही मित्र आहोत. (Friend *mitra* मित्र)

4. Give me one Rupee. *(malā ek rupayā de)* मला एक रुपय दे. (Rupee *rupayā* रुपय)

5. Tell us one story. *(āmhalā ek kahāṇī sāng)* आम्हाला एक कहाणी सांग. (Story *kahāṇī* कहाणी)

6. It will not be done by me. *(he mājhyāne kele jānār nāhī)* हे माझ्याने केले जाणार नाही. (Do कर)

7. It will be done by us. *(he āmchyāne kele jāīl)* हे आमच्याने केले जाईल (will become होईल)

8. This is for me. *(he mājhyākaritā āhe)* हे माझ्याकरिता आहे. (for me माझ्याकरिता)

9. Bring water for us. *(āmchyākaritā pāṇī āṇ)* आमच्याकरिता पाणी आण. (Water *pāṇī* पाणी)

10. Shop is far from home. *(dukān gharāpāsūn dūr āhe)* दुकान घरापासून दूर आहे. (Far *dūr* दूर)

11. That is far from here. *(te ithūn dūr āhe)* ते इथून दूर आहे. (From here *ithūn* इथून)

12. He is my brother. *(to majhā bhāū ahe)* तो माझा भाऊ आहे. (Brother *bhāū* भाऊ)

13. Our books. *(āmchī pustake)* आमची पुस्तके. (*n*◦ Books *pustake* पुस्तके)

14. Please belive in me. *(āmchyāvar bharavsā karā)* आमच्यावर भरवसा करा (Trusr भरवसा).

15. He trusts us. *(to āmachyāvar bharavsā karto)* तो आमच्यावर भरवसा करतो.

16. My dog. *(mājhā kutrā)* माझा कुत्रा (*m*◦ Dog *kutrā* कुत्रा)

17. My dogs. *(mājhe kutre)* माझे कुत्रे.

18. Our dogs. *(āmche kutre)* आमचे कुत्रे.

19. Our dog. *(āmchā kutrā)* आमचा कुत्रा.

20. My car. *(mājhī gāḍī)* माझी गाडी.

21. My cars. *(mājhyā gāḍyā)* माझ्या गाड्या.

22. Our car. *(āmchī gāḍī)* आमची गाडी.

23. Our cars. *(āmchyā gāḍyā)* आमच्या गाड्या.

2ND PERSON : You (तू) (m◦ f◦)

1. You, *tū* तू 2. You are. *(tū āhes)* तू आहेस.

adj◦ = Adjective, adv◦ = Adverb; *conj.* = Conjunction, f◦ = Feminine gender, *ind.* = Indeclinable, m◦ = Masculine gender, n◦ = Neuter gender, pl◦ = Plural

3. You are friends. *(tumhī mitra āhāt)* तुम्ही मित्र आहात.

4. I will give you one book. *(mī tulā ek pustak deīn)* मी तुला एक पुस्तक देईन.

5. I will tell you (all) one thing. *(mī tumhālā ek goṣhṭa sāmgen.* मी तुम्हाला एक गोष्ट सांगेन.

6. It will not be done by you. *(he tujhyāne hoṇār nāhī)* हे तुझ्याने होणार नाही.

7. It will be done by you. *(he tujhyāne hoīl)* हे तुझ्याने होईल (होणार).

8. This is for you. *(he tujhyākaritā āhe)* हे तुझ्याकरिता आहे.

9. I will bring water for you. *(mī tujhyākaritā pāṇī āṇīn)* मी तुझ्याकरिता पाणी आणीन.

10. He takes money from you. *(to tujhyāpāsūn paise gheto)* तो तुझ्यापासून पैसे घेतो.

11. That is far from you. *(to tujhyāpāsūn dūr āhe)* ते तुझ्यापासून दूर आहे.

12. He is your brother. *(to tujhā bhāū āhe)* तो तुझा भाऊ आहे.

13. Your books. *(tujhī pustake)* तुझी पुस्तके.

14. I believe in you. *(mī tujhyāvar bharavsā karto)* मी तुझ्यावर भरवसा करतो.

15. He trusts on you. *(to tujhyāver bharavsā karto)* तो तुझ्यावर भरवसा (विश्वास) करतो.

16. Your dog. *(tujhā kutrā)* तुझा कुत्रा.

17. Your dogs. *(tujhe kutre)* तुझे कुत्रे.

18. Your car. *(tujhī gāḍī)* तुझी गाडी.

19. Your cars. *(tujhyā gāḍyā)* तुझ्या गाड्या.

3RD PERSON : He, she, it, they, these, those : (m∘ f∘) (book n∘, house n∘)

1. He, she, it, they, these, those *to, tī, he, te, he, te.* तो, ती, हे, ते, हे, ते.

2. He-she is. *(to-tī āhe)* तो–ती आहे. Those are friends. *(te mitra āhet)* ते मित्र आहेत.

3. They-those are friends. *(te mitra āhet)* ते मित्र आहेत. These are friends. *(he mitra āhet)* हे मित्र आहेत.

4. Give him-her one book. *(tyālā-tilā pustak de)* त्याला–तिला एक पुस्तक दे.

5. Tell them one story. *(tyānā ek kahāṇī sāng)* त्यांना एक कहाणी सांग.

6. It will not be done by him-her. *(tyāchayāne-tichyāne he hoṇār nāhī)* त्याच्याने–तिच्याने हे होणार नाही.

7. It will be there. *(he tithe asel)* हे तिथे असेल.

8. This is for her-him. *(he tyāchyākritā-tichyākaritā āhe)* हे त्याच्याकरिता–तिच्याकरिता आहे.

9. Bring water for them. *(tyāñchyā-karitā pāṇī āṇ)* त्यांच्याकरिता पाणी आण.

adj∘ = Adjective, adv∘ = Adverb; *conj.* = Conjunction, f∘ = Feminine gender, *ind.* = Indeclinable, m∘ = Masculine gender, n∘ = Neuter gender, pl∘ = Plural

10. He took it from him-her. (*tyāne he tyāchyā-tichyā pāsUn ghetle*) त्याने हे त्याच्या-तिच्या पासून घेतले.

11. She is far from them. *(tī tyāñchyā-pāsūn dūr āhe)* ती त्यांच्यापासून दूर आहे.

12. He is his-her brother. *(to tyāchā-tichā bhāū āhe)* तो त्याचा-तिचा भाऊ आहे.

13. Their books. *(tyāñchī pustake)* त्यांची पुस्तके.

14. Belive in him-her. *(tyāchyāvar-tichyāvar bharavsā kar)* त्याच्यावर-तिच्यावर भरवसा कर.

15. He trusts them. *(to tyāñchyāvar bharavsā karto)* तो त्यांच्यावर भरवसा करतो.

16. His dog. *(tyāchā kutrā)* त्याचा कुत्रा.

17. His dogs. *(tyāche kutre)* त्याचे कुत्रे.

18. Her dog. *(tichā kutrā)* तिचा कुत्रा.

19. Her dogs. *(tiche kutre)* तिचे कुत्रे.

20. Their dog. *(tyāñchā kutrā)* त्यांचा कुत्रा.

21. Their dogs. *(tyañche kutre)* त्यांचे कुत्रे.

22. His car. *(tyāchi gāḍī)* त्याची गाडी.

23. Her car. *(tichī gāḍī)* तिची गाडी.

24. His cars. *(tyāchyā gāḍyā)* त्याच्या गाड्या.

25. Her cars. *(tichyā gāḍyā)* तिच्या गाड्या.

26. Their car. *(tyāñchī gāḍī)* त्यांची गाडी.

27. Their cars. *(tyāñchyā gāḍyā)* त्यांच्या गाड्या.

28. My house (n∘) *(māhje ghar)* माझे घर. My houses *(mājhī ghare)* माझी घरे. My book (n∘) *(majhe pustak)* माझे पुस्तक. My books *(mājhī pustake)* माझी पुस्तके. My dog *(mājhā kutrā)* माझा कुत्रा. । My dogs *(mājhe kutre)* माझे कुत्रे. My car *(māhjī gādī)* माझी गाडी. My cars *(mājhyā gāḍyā)* माझ्या गाड्या.

29. Our house *(āmche ghar)* आमचे घर. Our houses *(āmchī ghare)* आमची घरे. Our book *(āmche pustak)* आमचे पुस्तक. Our books *(āmchī pustake)* आमची पुस्तके. Our dog *(āmchā kutrā)* आमचा कुत्रा. Our dogs *(āmache kutre)* आमचे कुत्रे. Our car *(āmchī gāḍī)* आमची गाडी. Our cars *(āmchyā gāḍyā)* आमच्या गाड्या. These houses *(hī ghare)* ही घरे. Those houses *(tī ghare)* ती घरे.

30. Your house *(tujhe ghar)* तुझे घर. Your houses *(tujhī ghare)* तुझी घरे. Your book *(tujhe pustak)* तुझे पुस्तक. Your books *(tujhī pustake)* तुझी पुस्तके. Your dog *(tujhā kutrā)* तुझा कुत्रा. Your dogs *(tujhe kutre)* तुझे कुत्रे. Your car *(tujhī gāḍī)* तुझी गाडी. Your cars *(tujhyā gādyā)* तुझ्या गाड्या. Your cat (f∘) *(tujhī mānjar)* तुझी मांजर., Your cats (f∘) *(tujhyā mānjarī)* तुझ्या मांजरी.

31. His-her house *(tyāche-tiche ghar)* त्याचे-तिचे घर. His-her houses *(tyāchī-tichī ghare)* त्याची-तिची घरे. His-her book *(tyāche-tiche pustak)* त्याचे-तिचे पुस्तक. His-her books *(tyāchī-tichī pustake)* त्याची-तिची पुस्तके. His-her dog *(tyāchā-tichā kutrā)* त्याचा-तिचा कुत्रा. His-her dogs

adj∘ = Adjective, adv∘ = Adverb; *conj.* = Conjunction, f∘ = Feminine gender, *ind.* = Indeclinable, m∘ = Masculine gender, n∘ = Neuter gender, pl∘ = Plural

(tyāche-tiche kutre) त्याचे-तिचे कुत्रे. His-her car *(tyāchī-tichī gaḍī)* त्याची-तिची गाडी. His-her cars *(tyāchyā-tichyā gāḍyā)* त्याच्या-तिच्या गाड्या. This car *hī gāḍī* ही गाडी. These cars *hyā gāḍyā* ह्या गाड्या.

32. Their house *(tyāñche ghar)* त्यांचे घर. Their houses *(tyāñchī ghare)* त्यांची घरे. Their book *(tyāñche pustak)* त्यांचे पुस्तक. Their books *(tyāñchī pustake)* त्यांची पुस्तके. Their dog *(tyāñchā kutrā)* त्यांचा कुत्रा. Their dogs *(tyāñche kutre)* त्यांचे कुत्रे. Their car *(tyāñchī gāḍī)* त्यांची गाडी. Their cars *(tyāñchyā gāḍyā)* त्यांच्या गाड्या. This book *(he pustak)* हे पुस्तक. That book *(te pustak)* ते पुस्तक.

33. My book *(mājhe pustak)* माझे पुस्तक. My books *(mājhī pustake)* माझी पुस्तके. Your book *(tujhe pustak)* तुझे पुस्तक. Your books *(tujhī pustake)* तुझी पुस्तके. His book *(tyāche pustak)* त्याचे पुस्तक. His books *(tyāchī pustake)* त्याची पुस्तके. Her book *(tiche pustak)* तिचे पुस्तक. Her books *(tichī pustake)* तिची पुस्तके. Their book *(tyāñche pustak)* त्यांचे पुस्तक. Their books *(tyāñchī pustake)* त्यांची पुस्तके. These books *(hī pustake)* ही पुस्तके. Those books *(tī pustake)* ती पुस्तके.

NEW ADVERBS TO LEARN :

(1) Across = *palīkḍe* (पलीकडे)
(2) After = *nantar, mag* (नंतर, मग)
(3) Again = *punhā* (पुन्हा, पुन:)
(4) Again and again = *vāramvār* (वारंवार)
(5) Although = *jarī, yadyapi* (जरी, यद्यपि)
(6) If = *jar* (जर)
(7) Then = *nantar, mag* (नंतर, मग)
(8) Before = *pahile* (पहिले)
(9) Between = *madhye* (मध्ये)
(10) Beyond = *palīkaḍe* (पलीकडे)
(11) There = *tithe* (तिथे)
(12) Here = *ithe* (इथे)
(13) On this side = *ikḍe* (इकडे)
(14) On that side = *tikḍe* (तिकडे)
(15) Where? = *kuṭhe?* (कुठे? कोठे?)
(16) On which side? = *kuṇī kaḍe?* (कुणी कडे?)
(17) Where = *jithe* (जिथे)
(18) On which side = *jikḍe* (जिकडे)
(19) Near = *javaḷ* (जवळ)
(20) With = *barobar* (बरोबर)
(21) For = *karitā* (करिता)
(22) Inside = *ā̃t* (आंत)
(23) Out side = *bāher* (बाहेर)
(24) On, Over = *var* (वर)

adj∘ = Adjective, adv∘ = Adverb; *conj.* = Conjunction, f∘ = Feminine gender, *ind.* = Indeclinable, m∘ = Masculine gender, n∘ = Neuter gender, pl∘ = Plural

SIMILARITY BETWEEN VARIOUS PRONOUNS

He	*to*	तो
She	*tī*	ती
That	*te*	ते
This	*he*	हे
This	*he*	हे
That (n∘)	*te*	ते
Who?	*koṇ*	कोण?
Who	*jo*	जो
Here	*ithe*	इथे
There	*tithe*	तिथे
Where?	*kuṭhe*	कुठे?
Where	*jithe*	जिथे
On this side	*ikḍe*	इकडे
On that side	*tikḍe*	तिकडे
On which side?	*kuṇī kaḍe?*	कुणी कडे?
On which side	*jikḍe*	जिकडे
Now	*ātā*	आता
Then (that time)	*tevā*	तेव्हा

When?	*kevā*	केव्हा?
When	*jevā*	जेव्हा
Like this	*asā*	असा
Like that	*tasā*	तसा
Like what, how?	*kasā*	कसा?
Like which, as	*jasā*	जसा
Like these	*ase*	असे
Like those	*tasae*	तसे
Like what, how?	*kise*	कसे?
Like which	*jase*	जसे
This much	*itkā*	इतका
That much	*titka*	तितका
How much?	*kiti?*	किती
As much	*jitkā*	जितका
Why?	*kān*	कां?
so, therefore	*mhaṇūn*	म्हणून
this extent	*evḍhā*	एवढा
as	*jase*	जसे

adj∘ = Adjective, adv∘ = Adverb; *conj.* = Conjunction, f∘ = Feminine gender, *ind.* = Indeclinable, m∘ = Masculine gender, n∘ = Neuter gender, pl∘ = Plural

16.9 VERB APPLICATIONS

What we have learned so far, the cumulative learning

e.g. verb stem *paḍ (पड)* - fall, verb stem *lihī* (लिही) - write

(A) INTRANSITIVE verb, fall = *paḍ* पड, verbal noun = to fall, falling *(paḍṇe)* पडणे.

(B) TRANSITIVE verb, write = *lihī* लिही, verbal noun = to write, writing *(lihīṇe)* लिहीणे.

(1) **SIMPLE PRESENT** ACTIONS : (all Even Numbered sentences are Transitive)

1. I fall, I do fall (m∘ and f∘ subject). *(m∘ mī paḍato, f∘ mī paḍte)* m∘ मी पडतो, f∘ मी पडते.
2. I write, I do write (m∘ and f∘ subject). *(mī lihīto, mī lihīte)* मी लिहीतो, मी लिहीते.
3. We fall (m∘ and f∘ subject). *(āmhī paḍto)* आम्ही पडतो.
4. We write (m∘ and f∘ subject). *(āmhī lihīto)* आम्ही लिहीतो.
5. You fall (m∘ and f∘ subject). *(tū paḍtos, tū paḍtes)* m∘ तू पडतोस, f∘ तू पडतेस.
6. You write (m∘ and f∘ subject). *(tū lihītos, tū lihīes)* m∘ तू लिहीतोस, f∘ तू लिहीतेस.
7. He falls. *(to paḍtā āhe)* तो पडतो. 8. He writes. *(to lihīto)* तो लिहीतो.
9. She falls. *(tī paḍte)* ती पडते. 10. She writes. *(tī lihīte)* ती लिहीते.
11. They fall (m∘ and f∘ subject). *(te paḍtāt)* वे पडतात.
12. They write (m∘ and f∘ subject). *(te lihītāt)* वे लिहीतात.

(2) **PRESENT CONTINUOUS** ACTIONS : (all Even Numbered sentences are Transitive)

1. I am falling (m∘ and f∘). *(mī paḍat āhe)* मी पडत आहे.
2. I am writing (m∘ and f∘). (*mī lihīt āhe)* मी लिहीत आहे.
3. We are falling (m∘ and f∘). *(āmhī paḍat āhot)* आम्ही पडत आहोत.
4. We are writing (m∘ f∘). *(āmhī lihīt āhot)* आम्ही लिहीत आहोत
5. You are falling (m∘ f∘). *(tū paḍat āhes)* तू पडत आहेस
6. You are writing (m∘ f∘). *(tū lihīt āhes)* तू लिहीत आहेस
7. He is falling. *(to paḍat āhe)* तो पडत आहे
8. He is writing. (*to lihīt āhe)* तो लिहीत आहे
9. She is falling. *(tī paḍat āhe)* ती पडत आहे
10. She is writing. (*to lihīt āhe)* ती लिहीत आहे
11. They are falling (m∘ f∘). (*te paḍat āhet, tyā paḍat āhet*) m∘ ते पडत आहेत, f∘ त्या पडत आहेत

adj∘ = Adjective, adv∘ = Adverb; *conj.* = Conjunction, f∘ = Feminine gender, *ind.* = Indeclinable, m∘ = Masculine gender, n∘ = Neuter gender, pl∘ = Plural

12. They are writing (m∘ f∘). *(te lihīt āhet, tyā lihīt āhet)* m∘ ते लिहीत आहेत, f∘ त्या लिहीत आहेत

(3) <u>**PRESENT PERFECT**</u> ACTIONS : (all Even Numbered sentences are Transitive)

1. I am fallen (m∘ f∘). *(mī paḍālo āhe, mī paḍlī āhe)* m∘ मी पडलो आहे, f∘ मी पडली आहे.
2. I have written (m∘ f∘). *(mī lihīle āhe)* मी लिहीले आहे
3. We are fallen (m∘ f∘). *(āmhī paḍlo āhot)* आम्ही पडलो आहोत.
4. We have written (m∘ f∘). *(āmhī lihīle āhe)* आम्ही लिहीले आहे.
5. You are fallen (m∘ f∘). *(tū paḍlā āhes, tū paḍlī āhes)* m∘ तू पडला आहेस, f∘ तू पडली आहेस
6. You have written (m∘ f∘). *(tū lihīle āhe)* तू लिहीले आहे
7. He is fallen. *(to paḍlā hai),* तो पडला आहे
8. He has written. *(tyāne lihīle̅ āhe)* त्याने लिहीले आहे.
9. She is fallen. *(tī paḍlī āhe)* ती पडली आहे
10. She has written. *(tine lihīle āhe)* तिने लिहीले आहे.
11. They are fallen (m∘ f∘). *(te paḍle āhet, tyā paḍlyā āhet)* m∘ ते पडले आहेत, f∘ त्या पडल्या आहेत
12. They have written (m∘ f∘). *(tyā̐nī lihīle āhe)* त्यांनी लिहीले आहे.

(4) SIMPLE PAST or <u>PAST INDEFINITE PERFECT</u> ACTIONS : (all Even ones are Transitive)

1. I fell, I did fall (m∘ f∘). *(mī paḍlo, mī paḍlī)* m∘ मी पडलो, f∘ मी पडली
2. I wrote, I did write (m∘ f∘). *(mī lihīle)* मी लिहीले.
3. We fell (m∘ f∘). *(āmhī paḍlo)* आम्ही पडलो
4. We wrote (m∘ f∘). *(āmhī lihīle)* आम्ही लिहीले
5. You fell (m∘ f∘). *(tū paḍlās, tū paḍlīs)* m∘ तू पडलास, f∘ तू पडलीस.
6. You wrote (m∘ f∘). *(tū lihīle)*तू लिहीले.
7. He fell. *(to paḍlā)* तो पडला।
8. He wrote. *(tyāne lihīle)* त्याने लिहीले.
9. She fell. *(tī paḍlī)* ती पडली
10. She wrote. *(tine lihīle)* तिने लिहीले.
11. They fell (m∘ f∘). *(te paḍie, tyā padlyā)* m∘ ते पडले, f∘ त्या पडल्या.
12. They wrote (m∘ f∘). *(tyā̐nī lihīle)* त्यांनी लिहीले.

(5) **PAST CONTINUOUS** ACTIONS : (all Even Numbered sentences are Transitive)

1. I was falling (m∘ f∘). *(mī paḍat hoto, mī paḍat hotī)* m∘ मी पडत होतो, f∘ मी पडत होती.

2. I was writing (m∘ f∘). *(mī lihīt hoto, mī lihīt hotI)* m∘ मी लिहीत होतो, f∘ मी लिहीत होती.

3. We were falling (m∘ f∘). *(āmhī paḍat hoto)* आम्ही पडत होतो.

4. We were writing (m∘ f∘). *(āmhī lihīt hoto)* आम्ही लिहीत होतो.

5. You were falling (m∘ f∘). *(tū paḍat hotās, tū paḍat hotīs)* m∘ तू पडत होतास, f∘ तू पडत होतीस.

6. You were writing (m∘ f∘). *(tū lihīt hotās, tū lihīt hotīs)* m∘ तू लिहीत होतास, f∘ तू लिहीत होतीस.

7. He was falling. *(to paḍat hotā)* तो पडत होता.

8. He was writing. *(to lihīrahā hotā)* तो लिहीत होता.

9. She was falling. *(tī paḍat hotI)* ती पडत होती.

10. She was writing. *(tī lihīt hotI)* तो लिहीत होती.

11. They were falling (m∘ f∘). *(te paḍat hote, tyā paḍat hotyā)* m∘ ते पडत होते, f∘ त्या पडत होत्या.

12. They were writing (m∘ f∘). *(te lihīt hote, yā lihīt hotyā)* m∘ ते लिहीत होते, f∘ त्या लिहीत होत्या.

(6) PAST PERFECT ACTIONS : (all Even Numbered sentences are Transitive)

1. I had fallen (m∘ f∘). *(mī paḍlo hoto, mī paḍlī hotī)* m∘ मी पडालो होतो, f∘ मी पडली होती.

2. I had written (m∘ f∘). *(mī lihīle hote)* मी लिहीले होते.

3. We had fallen (m∘ f∘). *(āmhī paḍlo hoto)* आम्ही पडलो होतो.

4. We had written (m∘ f∘). *(āmhī lihīle hote)* आम्ही लिहीले होते.

5. You had fallen (m∘ f∘). *(tū paḍlā hotās, tū paḍlī hotīs)* m∘ तू पडला होतास, f∘ तू पडली होतीस.

6. You had written (m∘ f∘). *(tū lihīle hote)* तू लिहीले होते.

7. He had fallen. *(to paḍlā hotā)* तो पडला होता.

8. He had written. *(tyāne lihīle hote)* त्याने लिहीले होते.

9. She had fallen. *(tī paḍlī hotī)* ती पडली होती.

10. She had written. *(tine lihīle hote)* तिने लिहीले होते.

11. They had fallen (m∘ f∘). *(te paḍle hote, tyā paḍlyā hotyā)* m∘ ते पडले होते, f∘ त्या पडल्या होत्या.

12. They had written (m∘ f∘). *(tyannī lihīle hote)* त्यांनी लिहीले होते.

(7) **SIMPLE FUTURE** ACTIONS : (all Even Numbered sentences are Transitive)

1. I will fall (m∘ f∘). *(mī paḍen)* मी पडेन.

2. I will write (m∘ f∘). *(mī lihen)* मी लिहेन.

adj∘ = Adjective, adv∘ = Adverb; *conj.* = Conjunction, f∘ = Feminine gender, *ind.* = Indeclinable, m∘ = Masculine gender, n∘ = Neuter gender, pl∘ = Plural

3. We will fall (m◦ f◦). *(āmhī paḍū)* आम्ही पडू.

4. We will write (m◦ f◦). *(āmhī lihū)* आम्ही लिहू.

5. You will fall (m◦ f◦). *(tū paḍashhīl)* तू पडशील.

6. You will write (m◦ f◦). *(tū lihīshīl)* तू लिहीशील.

7. He will fall. *(to paḍel)* तो पडेल.

8. He will write. *(to lihlīl)* तो लिहील.

9. She will fall. *(tī paḍel)* ती पडेल

10. She will write. *(to lihīl)* तो लिहील.

11. They will fall (m◦ f◦). *(te paḍtīl, tyā paḍtīl)* m◦ ते पडतील, f◦ त्या पडतील.

12. They will write (m◦ f◦). *(te lihītīl, tyā lihītīl)* m◦ ते लिहीतील, f◦ त्या लिहीतील.

(8) INTERROGATIVE MOOD

1. Will I fall (m◦ f◦)? *(mī paḍū kāy?)* मी पडू काय?

2. Will I write (m◦ f◦)? *(mī lihū kāy?)* मी लिहू काय?

3. Will we fall (m◦ f◦)? *(āmhī paḍū kāy?)* आम्ही पडू काय?

4. Will we write (m◦ f◦)? *(āmhī lihū kāy?)* आम्ही लिहू काय?

5. Will he fall? *(to paḍel kāy?)* तो पडेल काय?

6. Will he write? *(to lihīl kāy?)* तो लिहील काय?

7. Will she fall? *(tī paḍel kāy?)* ती पडेल काय?

8. Will she write? *(tī lihīl kāy?)* ती लिहील काये?

9. Will they fall (m◦ f◦)? *(paḍtīl kāy?)* ते पडतील काय?

10. Will they write (m◦ f◦)? *(te lihītīl kāy?)* ते लिहीतील काय? ... and so on.

adj◦ = Adjective, adv◦ = Adverb; *conj.* = Conjunction, f◦ = Feminine gender, *ind.* = Indeclinable, m◦ = Masculine gender, n◦ = Neuter gender, pl◦ = Plural

LESSON 17

सतरावा पाठ

THE ADJECTIVES and ADVERBS

17.1 THE ADJECTIVES

The word that describes, qualifies or adds something to a noun is an ADJECTIVE.

1. Good dog m∘ *(chānglā kutrā)* चांगला कुत्रा
2. Good dogs *(chāngle kutre)* चांगले कुत्रे
3. Good cat f∘ *(chānglī mānjar)* चांगली मांजर
4. Good cats *(chānglyā mānjrī)* चांगल्या मांजरी

The word that qualifies a verb or an adjective, is an ADVERB.

1. Eat slowly. *(haḷū kha)* हळू खा
2. Walk fast. *(jalad chāl)* जलद चाल
3. Very good. *(fār chhān, fār chānglā)* फार छान, फार चांगला
4. It is light. *(he halke āhe)* हे हलके आहे.

RULE : In marāṭhī, the adjectives have same gender and number as the nouns they qualify.

	Singular	Plural
MASCULINE	*mī chānglā mulgā āhe*	*āmhī chānglī mule āhot*
	tū chānglā mulgā āhes	*tumhī chānglī mule āhāt*
	to chānglā mulgā āhe	*tī chānglī mule āhet*
FEMININE	*mī chānglī mulgī āhe*	*mī chānglī mulgī āhe*
	tūp chānglī mulgī āhes	*tumhī chānglyā mulī āhāt*
	tī chānglī mulgī āhe	*tyā chānglyā mulī āhet*
MASCULINE	मी चांगला मुलगा आहे	आम्ही चांगली मुले आहोत
	तू चांगला मुलगा आहेस	तुम्ही चांगली मुले आहात
	तो चांगला मुलगा आहे	ती चांगली मुले आहेत
FEMININE	मी चांगली मुलगी आहे	आम्ही चांगल्या मुली आहेत
	तू चांगली मुलगी आहेस	तुम्ही चांगल्या मुली आहात
	ती चांगली मुलगी आहे	त्या चांगल्या मुली आहेत

NOTE : The m∘ word मुलगा and f∘ word मुलगी are indeclinable words. The m∘ word मुलगा chenges to n∘ मूल and f∘ word मुलगी changes to f∘ word मूली when you add any suffix to them or when you make them plural.

adj∘ = Adjective, adv∘ = Adverb; *conj.* = Conjunction, f∘ = Feminine gender, *ind.* = Indeclinable, m∘ = Masculine gender, n∘ = Neuter gender, pl∘ = Plural

EXERCISE 32 : Translate the English sentences into marāṭhī (Answers are given for help)

1. Rāṇī does good work. *(Rānī chānglē kām karte)* राणी चांगले काम करते.
2. The mangos are sweet. *(āmbe goḍ āhet)* आंबे गोड आहेत (Sweet = adj∘ *goḍ* गोड; n∘ संत्रे)
3. We saw a yellow rose. *(āmhī pivḷā gulāb pāhilā)* आम्ही पिवळा गुलाब पाहिला.
4. Eat with right hand. *(ujvyā hātāne khā)* उजव्या हाताने खा. (Right = m∘ *ujvā* उजवा)
5. He has one Rupee. *(tyāchyā javaḷ ek rupayā āhe)* त्याच्या जवळ एक रुपया आहे
6. Sunīl is tall boy. *(Sunīl uñch mulgā āhe)* सुनील उंच मुलगा आहे (Tall = adj∘ *uñch*)
7. The clothes are wet. *(kapaḍe ole āhet)* कपड़े ओले आहेत (Wet = m∘ *olā* ओला)
8. My shirt is blue. *(mājhā sadrā nīḷā āhe)* माझा सदरा नीळा आहे (Blue = m∘ *nīḷā* नीळा)
9. You are tired. *tū thaklā āhes.* तू थकला आहेस (Tired = m∘ *thaklā* थकला)
10. Here the water is deep. *(ithe pāṇī khol āhe)* इथे पाणी खोल आहे (deep = adj∘ *khol* खोल)
11. It is true. *(he khare āhe)* हे खरे आहे (True = *khare*)
12. The window is open. *(khiḍakī ughaḍī āhe.* खिड़की उघडी आहे (Open = f∘ *ughaḍī* उघडी)
13. This job is small. *(he kām lahān āhe)* हे काम लहान आहे (Small = adj∘ *lahān* लहान)
14. I brought fresh fruit. *(mī tāje faḷ āṇlē)* मी ताजे फळ आणले.(Fresh = n∘ *tāje* ताजे)

ADJECTIVES TO LEARN

(1) Good *chānglā* (चांगला)	(2) Bad *kharāb* (खराब)	(3) Sweet *goḍ* (गोड)
(4) Sour *āmbaṭ* (आंबट)	(5) Hot *garam* (गरम)	(6) Cold *thaṇḍa* (थंड)
(7) Heavy *bhārī* (भारी)	(8) Light *halkā* (हलका)	(9) Fat *laṭṭha* (लट्ठ)
(10) Thin *patalā* (पतला)	(11) Beautiful *sundar* (सुंदर)	(12) Dusty *maḷkā* (मळका)
(13) Young *taruṇ* (तरुण)	(14) Old *buḍḍhā* (बुड्ढा)	(15) Open *ughaḍā* (उघडा)
(16) Closed *band* (बंद)	(17) Smart *hushār* (हुशार)	(18) Lazy *āḷashī* (आळशी)
(19) Easy *sopā* (सोपा)	(20) Hard *kaḍak* (कडक)	(21) Little *chhoṭā* (छोटा)
(22) More *adhik* (अधिक)	(23) Large, big *moṭhā* (मोठा)	(24) Less *kamī* (कमी) (adv∘)
(25) True *kharā* (खरा)	(26) Tall *uñch* (उंच)	(27) False *khoṭā* (खोटा)
(28) All *sarva* (सर्व)	(29) Happy *khush* (खुश)	(30) Sad *dukhī* (दु:खी)
(31) Hard *kaṭhiṇ* (कठिण)	(32) Soft *komal* (कोमल)	(33) Wise *śhāṇā* (शहाणा)
(34) Poor *garīb* (गरीब)	(35) Foolish *mūrkha* (मूर्ख)	(36) Rich *amīr* (अमीर)
(37) Short *chhoṭā* (छोटा)	(38) Quick, *chañchal* (चंचल)	(39) Slow *mand* (मंद)
(40) Strong *balavān* (बलवान्)	(41) Weak *kamjor* (कमजोर)	(42) Dishonest *beīmān* (बेईमान)

adj∘ = Adjective, adv∘ = Adverb; *conj.* = Conjunction, f∘ = Feminine gender, *ind.* = Indeclinable, m∘ = Masculine gender, n∘ = Neuter gender, pl∘ = Plural

All names of Numerals and Colours are adjectives.

COLOURS : (m∘)

Red (*lāl*) लाल Green (*hirvā*) हिरवा Blue (*nīḷā*) नीळा Yellow (*pivḷā*) पिवळा

Black (*kāḷā*) काळा White (*pāṇḍhrā*) पांढरा Purple (*Jambhaḷā*) जांभळा Orange (*nāraṅgī*) नारंगी

Dark (*gard*) गर्द Light (*fikkā*) फिक्का

EXERCISE : Translate the English sentences into marāṭhī (Answers are given for help)

(1) Two red flowers. *(don lāl phūle)* दोन लाल फूले.

(2) This car is blue. *(hī gāḍī nīḷī āhe)* ही गाडी नीळी आहे

(3) There are yellow flowers on this tree. *(hyā jhāḍāvar pivḷī fūle āhet)* ह्या झाडावर पिवळी फूले आहेत.

(4) Please give me ten Rupees. *(malā dadā rupaye dyā)* मला दहा रुपये द्या.

(5) One sari is dark black and other sari is light green. *(ek sāḍī gard kāḷī āhe āṇi dusarī sāḍī fikkī hitvī āhe)* एक साड़ी गर्द काळी आहे आणि दुसरी साड़ी फिक्की हिरवी आहे

17.2 THE ADVERBS

DEFINITION : The word that qualifies a verb or an adjective is an Adverb.

RULE : Adverbs do not have any gender, number, person, tense or case. They do not change with the verb or adjective they qualify, therefore, they are called INDECLINABLES.

EXERCISE : Translate the English sentences into marāṭhī (Answers are given for help)

1. Rāṇī walks fast. *(rānī jalad chālte)* राणी जलद चालते.
2. He always helps. *(to nehamī madat karto)* तो नेहमी मदत करतो.
3. Please move back *(krupayā māge sarak)* कृपया मागे सरक.
4. I came before he did. *(mī tyāchyā pahile ālo)* मी त्याच्या पहिले आलो.
5. He wants money now. *(tyaala paise ātā pāhijet)* त्याला पैसे आता पाहिजेत.
6. Sunīl came here once. *(Sunīl ithe ekdā ālā)* सुनील इथे एकदा आला
7. She knows me well. *(tī malā chhān jāṇte)* ती मला छान जाणते.
8. This is better than that. *(he tyā pekshā chāngle āhe)* हे त्यापेक्षा चांगले आहे
9. Kindly give me ten dollars. *(krupayā malā dahā dālar dyā)* कृपया मला दहा डॉलर द्या
10. Otherwise I go. *(athavā mī jāto)* अथवा मी जातो.

adj∘ = Adjective, adv∘ = Adverb; *conj.* = Conjunction, f∘ = Feminine gender, *ind.* = Indeclinable, m∘ = Masculine gender, n∘ = Neuter gender, pl∘ = Plural

LESSON 18

THE CONJUNCTIONS AND INTERJECTIONS
उभयान्वयी आणि केवलप्रयोगी अव्यये

19.1 THE CONJUNCTIONS

Conjunctions are the words like : and, or, but, for, if, that, where, either, neither, nor, still, till, only, else, after, before, etc. which make a connection between two parts of a sentence.

EXERCISE : Study the following sentences.

1. Rāmū AND Sunīl are friends. *(Rāmū āṇi Sunīl mitra āhet)* रामू आणि सुनील मित्र आहेत.
2. Bring mango AND a knife. *(āmbā āṇi chākū āṇ)* आंबा आणि चाकू आण.
3. He eats rice AND dāl. *(to varaṇ va bhāt khāto)* तो वरण व भात खातो.
4. I can read AND write marāṭhī. *(mī marāṭhī vāchū evam lihū śhakto)* मी मराठी वाचू एवं लिहू शकतो.
5. She can speak AS WELL AS write Sanskrit. *(tī sanskrut bolū tathā lihū śhakte)* ती संस्कृत बोलू तथा लिहू शकते.
6. Give me an apple OR a banana. *(malā safarchane athavā keḷ de)* मला सफरचंद अथवा केळ दे.
7. Speak in marāṭhī OR in English language. *(marāṭhī kimvā ingrajī bhāṣhet bol)* मराठी किंवा इंग्रजी भाषेत बोल.
8. EITHER pay me money OR give me the book. *(malā ek tar paise de athvā pustak de)* मला एक तर पैसे दे अथवा पुस्तक दे.
9. It is NEITHER good, NOR beautiful. *(na he chāngle āhe na sundar āhe)* न हे चांगले आहे न सुंदर आहे
10. WHETHER you like it OR NOT, it will happen. *(tulā he pasant aso kimvā naso, he hoīl)* तुला हे पसंत असो किंवा नसो, हे होईल.
11. I had no idea THAT he was in America. *(malā kalpanā navtī ki to ameriket hotā)* मला कल्पना नव्हती कि तो अमेरिकेत होता.
12. He said THAT it is not right. *(to mhaṇālā ki he ṭhīk nāhī)* तो म्हणाला कि हे ठीक नाही.
13. He said THAT she would not go. *(to mhaṇālā ki tī jāṇār nāhī)* तो म्हणाला कि ती जाणार नाही.
14. He said, 'I will not go.' *(to mhaṇālā, "mī jāṇār nahī")* तो म्हणाला, "मी जाणार नाही."
15. Sit down OR ELSE go. *(khālī bas anyathā jā)* खाली बस अन्यथा जा.

16. Give me money, OTHERWISE I am going. *(malā paise de nāhī tar mī jāt āhe)* मला पैसे दे नाही तर मी जात आहे

17. We are not rich BUT our heart is big. *(āmhī amīr nāhī paṇ āmche man moṭhe āhe)* आम्ही अमीर नाही, पण आमचे मन (हृदय) मोठे आहे

18. I told to him, BUT he did not stop. *(mī tyālā sāngītle, paṇ to thāmblā nāhī)* मी त्याला सांगितले, पण तो थांबला नाही. *thāmb* थांब = stop

19. He is uneducated, BUT intelligent. *(to anpaḍh āhe, paṇ buddhimān āhe)* वह अनपढ आहे, पण बुद्धिमान् आहे

20. She is trailing, BUT will win. *(tī māge āhe, paṇ tī jinkel)* ती मागे आहे पण ती जिंकेल.

21. I have eaten, BUT I am still hungry. *(mī jevlo āhe, tarī mī bhukelā āhe)* मी जेवलो आहे, तरी मी भुकेला आहे

22. He has severe pain, YET he is quiet. *(tyālā far duhkaha āhe, tarī to shānt āhe)* त्याला फार दु:ख आहे तरी तो शांत आहे

23. ALTHOUGH he did not ask, I gave him money. *(yadyapi tyāne māgitale nāhī, tathāpi mī tyālā paise dile)* यद्यपि त्याने मागितले नाही, तथापि मी त्याला पैसे दिले.

24. THOUGH he is sick, he went out. *(jarī to ājārī āhe, tarī to bāher gelā)* जरी तो आजारी आहे, तरी तो बाहेर गेला.

25. He slept enough, STILL he is tired. *(to bharpur zoplā, tarI paṇ thaklā āhe)* तो भरपूर झोपला तरी पण तो थकला आहे

26. Notice was given IN ORDER THAT everyone may be aware. *(sūchanā dilī hotī jeṇe krūn sarvā̃na māhit aso)* सूचना दिली होती जेणे करून सर्वांना माहित असो.

27. AS SOON AS the bell rang, I went inside. *(jaśhī ghaṇṭī vājlī, tasāch mī ā̃t gelo)* जशी घंटी वाजली, तसाच मी आंत गेलो.

28. He is walking AS THOUGH he is lame. *(to asā chālat āhe jaṇū to laṅgaḍā āhe)* तो असा चालत आहे जणू तो लंगडा आहे.

29. I need ONLY five Rupees. *(malā fakta pāch rupaye pāhijet)* मला फक्त पाच रुपये पाहिजेत.

30. I do not need ONLY money. *(malā kevaḷ paise nakot)* मला केवळ पैसे नकोत.

31. Something certainly fell down, FOR I heard the noise. *(kāhī tarī avaśhya khālī paḍle, kāraṇ ki mī āwāj aiklā)* काही तरी अवश्य खाली पडले, कारण कि मी आवाज ऐकला.

32. He sat down BECAUSE he was tired. *(to khālī baslā kāraṇ ki to thaklā hotā)* तो खाली बसला कारण कि तो थकला होता.

33. AFTER rain, the sun shone AGAIN. *(pāvsā nantar sūrya punah ugavlā)* पावसा नंतर

adj∘ = Adjective, adv∘ = Adverb; *conj.* = Conjunction, f∘ = Feminine gender, *ind.* = Indeclinable, m∘ = Masculine gender, n∘ = Neuter gender, pl∘ = Plural

सूर्य पुनः उगवला.

34. WHEN I was young, I used to work very hard. *(jevhā mī taruṇ hoto tevhā mī khūp kām karit asāycho)* जेव्हा मी तरुण होतों, तेव्हा मी खूप काम करायचो.

35. His watch is WHERE he kept it. *(tyāche ghaḍyāḷ tithe āhe jithe tyāne ṭhevle hote)* त्याचे घड्याळ तिथे आहे जिथे त्याने ठेवले होते.

36. Let us give charity, WHILE we have money. *(jo paryant āpalyā javaḷ paisā āhet āpaṇ dān dyāve)* जो पर्यंत आपल्या जवळ पैसे आहेत आपण दान द्यावे.

37. WHENEVER I see him, he looks happy. *(jevā-jevhā mī tyālā pāhato, to khuśh disto)* जेव्हा-जेव्हा मी त्याला पाहतो, तो खुश दिसतो.

38. WHEREVER the rain falls, the water goes to the ocean only. *(jithe-kuṭhe pāūs paḍto, pāṇī sāgaralā jāte)* जिथे कुठे पाऊस पडतो, पाणी सागराला जाते.

39. He said yes, THEREFORE, I went there. *(to hoy mhaṇālā mhaṇūn mī tithe gelo)* तो होय म्हणाला म्हणून मी तिथे गेलो.

NOTE: The ँ sign is just a slight nasal tone added to the syllable below that ँ

GOOD NEWS

Even if you JUST READ **each and every** word of this book, patiently and thoughtfully, you will be able to understand marāṭhī.

adj∘ = Adjective, adv∘ = Adverb; *conj.* = Conjunction, f∘ = Feminine gender, *ind.* = Indeclinable, m∘ = Masculine gender, n∘ = Neuter gender, pl∘ = Plural

LESSON 19

GENERAL KNOWLEDGE

सामान्य ज्ञान

19.1 NAMES OF THE SEVEN DAYS OF THE WEEK

(1) Sunday	*ravivār*	रविवार	(2) Monday	*somavār*	सोमवार
(3) Tuesday	*mangaḷavār*	मंगळवार	(4) Wednesday	*budhavār*	बुधवार
(5) Thursday	*guruvār*	गुरुवार	(6) Friday	*shukravār*	शुक्रवार
(7) Saturday	*shanivār*	शनिवार			

19.2 NAMES OF THE TWELVE MONTHS OF THE YEAR

(1) March-April	*chaitra*	चैत्र	(2) April-May	*vaishākh*	वैशाख
(3) May-June	*jyeṣṭha*	ज्येष्ठ	(4) June-july	*āṣāḍh*	आषाढ़
(5) July-August	*śhrāvaṇ*	श्रावण	(6) August-September	*bhādrapad*	भाद्रपद
(7) September-October	*āśhvin*	आश्विन	(8) October-November	*kārtik*	कार्तिक
(9) November-December	*mārgashīrṣh*	मार्गशीर्ष	(10) December-January	*pauṣh*	पौष
(11) January-February	*māgh*	माघ	(12) February-March	*phālgun*	फाल्गुन

19.3 NAMES OF THE SIX SEASONS OF THE YEAR

(1) Spring	*vasant*	वसंत	(2) Summer	*grīṣma*	ग्रीष्म
(3) Rainy season	*varṣhā*	वर्षा	(4) Autumn	*śharad*	शरद्
(5) Winter(Nov-Jan)	*hemant*	हेमंत	(6) Winter(Jan-Mar)	*śhiśhir*	शिशिर

19.4 NAMES OF THE DIRECTIONS

East	*pūrab, pūrva*	पूर्व	West	*paśhchim*	पश्चिम
North	*uttar*	उत्तर	South	*dakṣiṇ*	दक्षिण
North east	*īshānya*	ईशान्य	South east	*vāyavya*	वायव्य
South west	*āgney*	आग्नेय	North west	*nairutya*	नैऋत्य

19.5 THE RELATIONSHIPS

Bride	*vadhū*	वधू	Brother	*bhāū*	भाऊ
Brother elder	*agraj*	अग्रज	Brother younger	*anuj*	अनुज
Brother' son	*putaṇyā*	पुतण्या	Brother's daughter	*putaṇī*	पुतणी
Brother's wife	*vahinī*	वहिनी	Child	*mūl*	मूल (n◦)
Daughter	*mulgī*	मुलगी	Daughter-in-law	*sūn*	सून
Family	*parivār*	परिवार	Father-in-law	*sāsarā*	सासरा
Father's brother	*kākā*	काका	Father's younger brother	*kākā*	काका
Father's father	*ājobā*	आजोबा	Father's mother	*ājī*	आजी
Father's sister	*ātyā*	आत्या	Friend	*mitra*	मित्र
Husband	*pati*	पति	Husband's brother	*dīr*	दीर
Husband's sister	*naṇand*	नणंद	Lover	*premī, premikā*	प्रेमी, प्रेमिका
Mother	*āī*	आई	Mother-in-law	*sāsū*	सासू
Mother's brother	*māmā*	मामा	Mother's brother's wife	*māmī*	मामी
Mother's father	*ājobā*	आजोबा	Mother's mother	*ājī*	आजी
Mother's sister	*mavśhī*	मावशी	Neighbor	*śhejārī*	शेजारी
Parents	*mātā-pitā*	माता–पिता	Relative	*bandhu*	बंधु
Sister	*bahiṇ*	बहिण	Sister, elder	*tāī*	ताई
Sister, younger	*anujā*	अनुजा	Sister's daughter	*bhāchī*	भाची
Sister's husband	*mehuṇā*	मेहुण	Sister's son	*bhachā*	भाचा
Son	*mulgā*	मुलगा	Son-in-law	*jāvāī*	जावाई
Son's daughter	*nāt*	नात	Son's son	*nātu*	नातु
Stranger	*paradeśhī*	परदेशी	Step xx	*sautelā-*	सौतेला–
Wife	*patnī*	पत्नी	Wife's brother	*sāḷā*	साळा
Wife's sister	*sāḷī*	साळी	Girl friend	*premika*	प्रेमिका
			Boy friend	*premī*	प्रेमी

adj◦ = Adjective, adv◦ = Adverb; *conj.* = Conjunction, f◦ = Feminine gender, *ind.* = Indeclinable, m◦ = Masculine gender, n◦ = Neuter gender, pl◦ = Plural

LESSON 20

GENERAL DIALOGUES

Learning through Pre-made 'Pet-Sentences'

Having learned previous 18 lessons, now you can make these and similar sentence. For you, these are not pre-made pet-sentences anymore. If you have done prevoius lessons, treat this lesson as an Exercise where the answers are provided. If this is where you are starting this book like any other marāṭhī learning book, then memorize the sentences and hope that you will be able to speak marāṭhī.

(1) Hello! *(namaste! namaskār!)* नमस्ते! नमस्कार!

(2) What is your name? *(tumche nā̃v kay? āhe?)* तुमचे नांव काय आहे?

(3) My name is *(mājhe nā̃v -------------------- āhe)* माझे नाँव -------------------- आहे

(4) How are you. How do you do? *(tumhī kase āhāt?)* तुम्ही कसे आहातं?

(5) I am fine. I am alright. *(mī ṭhīk āhe)* मी ठीक आहे

(6) Thank you. *dhanyavād!* धन्यवाद!

(7) How many brothers do you have *(tulā kitī bhāū āhet?)* तुला किती भाऊ आहेत?

(8) I have one brother *(malā ek bhāu āhe)* मला एक भाऊ आहे.

(9) How many sisters do you have? *(tulā kitī bahiṇī āhet?)* तुला किती बहिणी आहेत?

(10) I have two sisters *(malā don bahiṇī āhet)* मला दोन बहिणी आहेत.

(11) What does your brother do? *(tujhā bhāū kāy karto?)* तुझा भाऊ काय करतो.

(12) My brother is a student. *(tujhā bhāū vidyārthī āhe)* माझा भाऊ विद्यार्थी आहे.

(13) What does your father do? *(tujhe vaḍil kāy kartāt?)* तुझे वडील काय करतात.

(14) What does your sisters do? *(tujhyā bahiṇī kāy kartāt?)* तुझ्या बहिणी काय करतात.

(15) My sisters are students too. *(mājhyā bahiṇī suddhā vidyarthinī āhet)* माझ्या बहिणी सुद्धा विद्यार्थिनी आहेत.

(16) My father is a lawyer. *(mājhe vaḍīl vakīl āhet)* माझे वडील वकील आहेत.

(17) Where do you live? *(tumhī kuṭhe rahatā āhet?)* तुम्ही कुठे राहता?

(18) I live at Kanpur. *(mī Kānpurlā rahato)* मी कानपुरला रहतो

(19) Where is your Apartment? *(tumchā apartment kuṭhe āhe?)* तुमचा अपार्टमेंट कुठे आहे?

(20) What is your address? *(tumchā pattā kāy āhe?)* तुमचा पत्ता काय आहे?

(21) Who is he-she? *(hā-hī koṇ āhe?)* हा–ही कोण आहे?

(22) What is his-her name? *(hyāñche nā̃v kyā āhe?)* ह्यांचे नांव काय आहे?

(23) His-her name is *(hyāñche nā̃v -------------- ------ āhe)* ह्यांचे नांव -------------------- आहे

adj∘ = Adjective, adv∘ = Adverb; *conj.* = Conjunction, f∘ = Feminine gender, *ind.* = Indeclinable, m∘ = Masculine gender, n∘ = Neuter gender, pl∘ = Plural

(24) He-She does not speak maraṭhī. *(hā-hī marathi bolat nāhī)* हा-ही मराठी बोलत नाही.

(25) Will you take tea? *(thmhī chahā ghyāl kāy?)* तुम्ही चहा घ्याल काय?

Will you drink tea? *(thmhī chahā pyāl kāy?)* तुम्ही चहा प्याल काय?

(26) No, thanks! *(nāhī, dhanyavād!)* नाही, धन्यवाद!

(27) I do not take tea. *(mī chahā ghet nāhī)* मी चहा घेत नाही.

I do not drink tea. *(mī chahā pīt nāhī)* मी चहा पीत नाही.

(28) Do you smoke? *(tumhī dhūmrapān kartā kāy?)* तुम्ही धूम्रपान करता काय? तुम्ही सिगरेट पिता काय?

(29) No, I do not smoke. *(nāhī, mī sigareṭ pīt nāhī)* नाही, मी सिगरेट पीत नाही.

(30) Are you a vegetarian? *(thmhī shākāhārī āhāt kāy?)* तुम्ही शाकाहारी आहात काय?

(31) I have heard that Renu is sick. *(mī aikle āhe ki reṇū ājārī āhe)* मी ऐकले आहे कि रेणू आजारी आहे

(32) Is it true? *(he khare āhe kāy?)* हे खरे आहे काय?

(33) Yes, it is true. *(hoy, he khare āhe)* होय, हे खरे आहे.

(34) I did not know it. *(mī he jāṇat navhato)* मी हे जाणत नव्हतो.

(35) But, do not tell this to anyone. *(paṇ, he kuṇālā sāngū nakā)* पण, हे कुणाला सांगू नका.

(36) I promise you. *(mī tumhālā vachan deto)* मी तुम्हाला वचन देतो.

(37) Your poem is very nice. *(tumchī kavitā fār chānglī āhe)* तुमची कविता फार चांगली (छान) आहे

(38) You are making noise. *(tū āvāj karīt āhes)* तू आवाज करीत आहेस.

(39) Excuse me. Pardon me. *(malā māf-kṣamā karā)* मला माफ करा. मला क्षमा करा.

(40) She returned it. *(tine he vāpasa kele)* तिने हे वापस केले.

(41) I refused it. *(mī inkār kelā)* मी इनकार केला.

(42) I am sorry. *(mī dukhī āhe)* मी दुखी आहे

(43) That was my mistake. *(tī mājhī chūk hotī)* ती माझी चूक होती.

(44) Who was that person? *(to manuṣhya koṇ hotā?)* तो मनुष्य कोण होता?

(45) What are you doing? *(tumhī kāy karīt āhāt?)* तुम्ही काय करीत आहात?

(46) What is the matter? *(kāy goṣhṭa āhe?)* काय गोष्ट आहे?

(47) What do you have? *(tumchyā javaḷ kāy āhe?)* तुमच्या जवळ काय आहे?

(48) What does it mean? *(hyāchā arth kāy?)* ह्याचा अर्थ काय?

(49) Did you like it? *(tumhālā he āvaḍle kāy?)* तुम्हाला हे आवडले काय?

adj∘ = Adjective, adv∘ = Adverb; *conj.* = Conjunction, f∘ = Feminine gender, *ind.* = Indeclinable, m∘ = Masculine gender, n∘ = Neuter gender, pl∘ = Plural

(50) Have you done it? *(tumhī he kele kāy?)* तुम्ही हे केले काय?

(51) It is ready? *(he tayār āhe kāy?)* हे तयार आहे काय?

(52) Is it very expensive? *(he fār mahāg āhe kāy?)* हे फार महाग आहे काय?

(53) Will you come with us? *(tū āmchyā barobar yeshīl kāy?)* तू आमच्या बरोबर येशील काय?

(54) It is very nice. *(ye fār chhān āhe)* हे फार छान आहे.

(55) Should I close it? Should I open it? *(mī he band karū kāy? mī he ughaḍū kāy?)* मी हे बंद करू काय? मी हे उघडू काय?

(56) Wait for me! *(mājhyā karitā thāmbā!)* माझ्याकरिता थांबा!

(57) Do you trust her? Yes, I trust her fully *(tumhī tichyāvar bharavsā krtā kāy? hoy, mī tichyāvar pūrṇa bharavsā karto)* तुम्ही तिच्यावे भरवसा करता काय? होय, मी तिच्यावे पूर्ण भरवसा करतो. (माझा तिच्यावर पूर्ण भरवसा आहे)

(58) This is completely correct. *(he bilkul ṭhīk āhe)* हे बिलकुल ठीक आहे.

(59) I think so too. *(malā hī asech vāṭtae)* मला ही असेच वाटते.

(60) Is it possible? *(he sambhav āhe kāy?)* हे संभव आहे काय? हे शक्य आहे काय?

(61) His health is not well. *(tyāchī tabyat ṭhīk nāhī)* त्याची तब्यत ठीक नाही.

(62) Let him go. *(tyālā jāū dyā)* त्याला जाऊ द्या.

(63) I will go later. *(mī mag jāīn)* मी मग जाईन.

(64) I am in rush. *(mī ghāīt āhe)* मी घाईत आहे.

(65) You are lucky. *(tumhī bhāgyavān āhāt)* तुम्ही भाग्यवान् आहात.

(66) He met me. *(to malā bheṭlā)* तो मला भेटला.

(67) He fooled me. *(tyāne malā pāgal banavile)* त्याने मला पागल बनविले.

(68) What a surprise! *(kitī āśhcharya āhe)* किती आश्चर्य आहे.

(69) I am angry. *(mī rāgāvalo āhe)* मी रागावलो आहे

(70) What could be the reason? *(kāy kāraṇ asel?)* काय कारण असेल?

(71) Please, be patient. *(krupayā dhīr dharā)* कृपया धीर धरा.

(72) Please do not do it again. *(krupayā he punhā karū nakā)* कृपया हे पुन्हा करू नका.

(73) Try to be careful.*(sāvdhān asā)* सावधान असा.

(74) It is very hard for me. *(he mājhyā-karitā kaṭhiṇ āhe)* हे माझ्याकरिता कठिण आहे.

(75) Don't become more smart. *(adhik hushār banū nakā)* अधिक हुशार बनू नका. I remember *(malā āṭhavate)* मला आठवते.

adj∘ = Adjective, adv∘ = Adverb; *conj.* = Conjunction, f∘ = Feminine gender, *ind.* = Indeclinable, m∘ = Masculine gender, n∘ = Neuter gender, pl∘ = Plural

(76) Let us go! We will go for a walk today. *(chalā, āpaṇ firāyalā jāū)* चला! आज आपण फिरायला जाऊ.

(77) Please, walk a bit faster. *(krupayā jarā jalad chālā)* जरा जलद चाला.

(78) It is thundering. *vīj chamakat āhe.* वीज चमकत आहे.

(79) Weather is cold today. *āj vātāvaraṇ thaṇḍ āhe.* आज वातावरण (हवामान) थंड आहे.

(80) May be a storm is coming. *(kadāchit vādaḷ yeīl)* कदाचित वादळ येईल.

(81) How does it work? *(he kase kām karte?)* हे कसे काम करते?

(82) Please be careful. *(sāvadhān rahā)* सावधान रहा.

(83) I forgot to tell you one thing. *(mī tulā ek goṣhṭa sāngāyalā visarlo)* मी तुला एक गोष्ट सांगायला विसरलो (f॰ विसरली).

(84) What is the use of waiting here? *(ithe thābūn kāy lābh?)* इथे थांबून काय लाभ?

(85) The child is crying constantly. *mūl satat raḍat āhe.* मूल सतत रडत आहे

(86) Do not worry, I will take care of that. *(chintā karū nakos. mī tyāchī kāḷjī gheīn)* चिंता करू नकोस. मी त्याची काळजी घेईन.

(87) Have a safe journey! *(yātrā sukhamaya aso!)* यात्रा सुखमय असो.

(88) What is the news? *(kāy khabar āhe? kāy samaāchār āhe?)* काय खबर आहे? काय समाचार आहे?

(89) Everything is OK. *(sarva ṭhīk āhe)* सर्व ठीक आह. Be happy! *(khuśh rahā!)* खुश रहा.

(90) We will wait for you. *(āmhī taujhyā-kritā thāmbū)* आम्ही तुझ्याकरिता थांबू.

(91) Why are you sad? *(tū udās kā̃ āhes?)* तू उदास कां आहेस?

(92) Did you get my letter? *(tulā mājhe patra miḷāle kāy?)* तुला माझे पत्र मिळाले काय?

(93) Why did you go there? *(tū tithe kā̃ gelās?)* तू तिथे कां गेलास?

(94) I was impressed by his talk. *(mī tyāchyā bolṇyāne prabhāvit jhālo hoto)* मी त्याच्या बोलण्याने प्रभावित झालो होतो.

(95) How quickly time passes! *(veḷ kiti jalad jāto)* वेळ किती जलद जातो.

(96) I will return quickly. *(mī lavakr vāpasa yeīn)* मी लवकर वापस येईन.

(97) Brother! Move a bit forward. *(Bhaū sāheb! thoḍe samor sarkā)* भाऊ साहेब! थोडे समोर सरका.

(98) Could you help me? *(tumhī malā madat karāl kāy?)* तुम्ही मला मदत कराल काय?

(99) How is your health? *(tumche svāsthya kase āhe? tumcī tabyat kaśhī āhe?)* तुमचे स्वास्थ्य कसे आहे? तुमची तब्यत कशी आहे?

(100) How did your bone break? *(tumche hāḍ kase tūtle?)* तुमचे हाड कसे तुटले?

adj॰ = Adjective, adv॰ = Adverb; *conj.* = Conjunction, f॰ = Feminine gender, *ind.* = Indeclinable, m॰ = Masculine gender, n॰ = Neuter gender, pl॰ = Plural

(101) Please come in. *(kripayā ā̃t ya)* कृपया आंत या. Welcome. *susvāgatam.* सुस्वागतम्.

(102) Wish you a happy Diwālī. *(diwāḷī chī śhubh kāmā)* दिवाळी/दीपावलीची शुभ कामना।

(103) OK! We will meet again. *(ṭhik! āpaṇ punhā bheṭū yā)* ठीक! आपण पुन्हा भेटू या.

(104) Say our hello to everyone. *(sarvā̃nā āmchā namaskār sāngā)* सर्वांना आमचा नमस्कार सांगा.

(105) OK! Sir (Madam). *(ṭhīk āhe shrīmān! ṭhīk āhe shrīmatī jī!)* ठीक आहे श्रीमान्! ठीक आहे श्रीमतीजी!

(106) Hi, Hello *(namaste ji!)* नमस्ते! नमस्कार!।

(107) Happy Birthday! *(śhubha janmadivas!* शुभ जन्मदिवस! (जन्मदिन!)

(108) Good morning. *(suprabhāt)* सुप्रभात। Good night *(śhubha rātri)* शुभ रात्रि।

(109) How is your father? *(tumche vaḍīl kase āhet)* तुमचे वडील कैसे आहेत? तुमचे बाबा कैसे आहेत?

(110) He is fine. *(te kushal āhet)* ते कुशल आहेत

(110) Is everything well at home? *(gharī sarva ṭhīk āhe kāy?)* घरी सर्व ठीक आहे काय?

Yes, everything is fine. *(hoy! sarva kushal āhe)* होय, सर्व कुशल आहे

(112) Where are you coming from? *(tū kuṭhūn yet āhes?)* तू कुठून (कोठून) येत आहेस?

(113) I am coming from the shop. *(mī dukānātūn yet āhe)* मी दुकानातून येत आहे

(114) Please come in and have a seat. *(krupayā ā̃t ye āṇi bas)* कृपया आंत ये आणि बस.

(115) What was he saying? *(to kāy mhaṇat hotā?)* तो काय म्हणत होता?

(116) He said that I do not want anything. *(to mhaṇāla ki malā kāhī nako)* तो म्हणाला कि मला काही नको.

(117) What is your opinion? *(tumche mat kāy āhe?)* तुमचे मत काय आहे?

(118) Let us see what happens. *(kāy hote baghū)* काय होते बघू.

(119) I will try my best. *(mī pūrṇa prayatna karīn)* मी पूर्ण प्रयत्न करीन.

(120) It will never happen. *(he kadhī hī hoṇār nāhī).* हे कधी ही होणार नाही.

(121) It is not possible. *(he śhakya nāhī)* हे शक्य नाही.

(122) There is no doubt about it. *(hyāat saṁshay nāhī)* ह्यात संशय नाही.

(123) *active.* = I did not know it. *passive.* = It was not known to me. *(active. = mī he jānat navhato, passive. = malā he māhit navhate)* *active.* = मी हे जाणत नव्हतो. *passive.* = मला हे माहित नव्हते.

(124) How should I tell it to you? *(mī tulā he kase sāngū?)* मी तुला हे कसे सांगू?

adj∘ = Adjective, adv∘ = Adverb; *conj.* = Conjunction, f∘ = Feminine gender, *ind.* = Indeclinable, m∘ = Masculine gender, n∘ = Neuter gender, pl∘ = Plural

(125) Do you have time? *(tujhyā javaḷ veḷ āhe kāy?)* तुझ्या जवळ वेळ आहे काय?

(126) What is your program tomorrow? *(udyā tumchā kāy kāryakram āhe?)* उद्या तुमचा काय कार्यक्रम आहे?

(127) I am not sure, I do not know certainly. *(malā pakke māhit nāhī)* मला पक्के माहित नाही.

(128) I will go tomorrow again. *(mī udyā punhā jāīn)* मी उद्या पुन्हा जाईन.

(129) It happens sometimes. *(kadhī-kadhī ase hote)* कधी-कधी असे होते.

(130) Who does not want it? *(he kuṇālā nako aste?)* हे कुणाला नको असते?

(131) I have no objection. *(malā āpatti nāhī)* मला आपत्ति नाही.

(132) It is difficult. *(he kaṭhiṇ āhe)* हे कठिण आहे.

(133) Please do not worry. *(krupayā chintā karū nakā.* कृपया चिंता (काळजी) करू नका.

(134) Please listen to me. *(krupayā mājhe aikā)* कृपया माझे ऐका।

(135) What does it mean? *(hyāchā artha kāy?)* ह्याचा अर्थ काय?

(136) What is the reason for this? *(hyāche kāraṇ kāy?)* ह्याचे कारण काय?

(137) Why did it happen? *(he kā̃ jhāle?)* हे कां झाले?

(138) How did it happen? *(he kase jhāle?)* हे कसे झाले?

(139) You do not have right. *tumhālā adhikār nāhī.* तुम्हाला अधिकार नाही.

(140) Is it true? *(he khare āhe kāy?)* हे खरे आहे काय?

(141) That I also know. *(te malā suddhā māhit āhe)* ते मला सुद्धा माहित आहे

(142) Why did you not tell it before? *(he tumhī ādhī kā̃ sāngitle nāhī?)* हे तुम्ही आधी कां सांगितले नाही?

(143) Tell it again. *(he punhā sāngā)* हे पुन्हा सांगा।

(144) Where were you that time? *(tevā tumhī kuṭhe hote?)* तेव्हा तुम्ही कुठे होते?

(145) It is not my fault. *(hā mājhā doṣh nāhī)* हा माझा दोष नाही.

(146) It is my mistake. *(hī mājhī chūk āhe)* ही माझी चूक आहे

(147) I had no idea. *(malā kalpanā navhatī)* मला कल्पना नव्हती.

(148) Please do not get serious like this. *(kripaya ase gambhīr hoū nakā)* कृपया असे गंभीर होऊ नका.

(149) It is only a rumour. *(hī kevaḷ afwā āhe)* ही तो केवळ अफवा आहे I think so. *(malā ase vāṭate)* मला असे वाटते.

adj∘ = Adjective, adv∘ = Adverb; *conj.* = Conjunction, f∘ = Feminine gender, *ind.* = Indeclinable, m∘ = Masculine gender, n∘ = Neuter gender, pl∘ = Plural

(150) You are right. *(tumhi barobar āhāt)* तुम्ही बरोबर आहात

(151) At this time I can not say of anything. *(saddhyā mī kāhī bolū shakat nāhī)* सध्या मी काही बोलू शकत नाही.

(152) It should not happen. *(he hoū naye)* हे होऊ नये.

(153) I do not have your address. *(mājhyā javal tujhā pattā nāhī)* माझ्या जवळ तुझा पत्ता नाही.

(154) I was sick yesterday. *(kal mī ājārī hoto)* m∘ काल मी आजारी होतो (f∘ काल मी आजारी होते).
I am alone. m∘ *(mī ekṭā āhe,* f∘ *mī ekṭī āhe)* m∘ मी एकटा आहे, f∘ मी एकटी आहे.

(155) There was an accident on the way, that is why I came late. *(rāstyāt apghāt hotā, mhaṇūn mī us̀hirā ālo)* रस्त्यात (m∘) अपघात होता (f∘ दुर्घटना होती) म्हणून मी उशीरा आलो (f∘ आले).

(156) Have you finished your housework? *(tumhī gruha kām saṇavale kaya?)* तुम्ही गृहकार्य संपवले (पूर्ण केले) काय?

(157) I have to work now. *(ātā malā kām karāyache āhe)* आता मला काम करायचे आहे

(158) I have to go too. *(malā suddhā jāyache āhe)* मला सुद्धा (पण) जायचे आहे

(159) I will talk to you tomorrow. *(mī tumchyās̀hī udyā bolto)* मी तुमच्याशी उद्या बोलतो.

(160) Still there is plenty of time. *(ajūn hī pushkaḷ veḷ āhe)* अजून ही पुष्कळ वेळ आहे

(161) Did you come yesterday? *(tū kāl ālā hotās kāy?* तू काल आला होतास काय?

(162) Were there any calls for me. *(mājhyā karitā kāhī phon ālā hotā kāy?)* माझ्या करिता काही फोन आला होता काय?

(163) My sympothy! *(merī sahānubhuti!)* माझी सहानुभुति।

(164) See me next month. *(tumhī malā puḍhalyā mahīnyāt bhetā)* तुम्ही मला पुढच्या महीन्यात भेटा.

(165) We will sit and think about it. *(āpaṇ basūn vichār karū)* आपण बसून विचार करू.

(166) Today I am not feeling well. *(āj malā ṭhīk vāṭat nāhī)* आज मला ठीक वाटत नाही.

(167) I am sick. *(mī ājārī āhe)* मी आजारी आहे

(168) Yesterday it snowed all night. *(kāl rātra bhar barf paḍlā)* काल रात्र भर बर्फ पडला.

(169) And today it is very foggy. *(āṇī āj fār dhukaṭ āhe)* आणि आज फार धुकट आहे

(170) Drive carefully. *(sāvadhānī ne gāḍī chālavā)* सावधानीने गाड़ी चालवा.

(171) It is very cold outside. *(bāher fār thaṇḍ āhe)* बाहेर फार थंड आहे

(172) It snowed almost four iñches. *(javaḷ-javaḷ chār iñcha barf paḍlā)* जवळ-जवळ चार इंच बर्फ पडला.

adj∘ = Adjective, adv∘ = Adverb; *conj.* = Conjunction, f∘ = Feminine gender, *ind.* = Indeclinable, m∘ = Masculine gender, n∘ = Neuter gender, pl∘ = Plural

(173) Some roads are not cleared yet. *(kāhī raste ajūn sāf kelele nāhīt)* काही रस्ते अजून साफ केलले नाहीत.

(174) Tomorrow it is going to be warm. *(udyā garam hoṇar āhe)* उद्या गरम होणार आहे

(175) Tomorrow we will wash our car. *(udyā āpaṇ āplī gaḍī dhuū)* उद्या आपण आपली गाड़ी धुऊ.

(176) I organized my room. *(mī āplī kholī ṭhīk kelī)* मी आपली खोली ठीक केली.

(177) I sleep near the window. *(mī khiḍakī javaḷ zopto)* मी खिड़की जवळ झोपतो.

(178) I will keep the door open. *(mī daravājā ughaḍā ṭhevīn)* मी दरवाजा उघडा ठेवीन.

(179) I read marāṭhī magazine everyday. *(mī roj marāṭhi māsik vāchato)* मी रोज मराठी मासिक वाचतो.

(180) Our neighbor is a good person. *āmachā śhejārī chānglā manyṣhya āhe)* आमचा शेजारी चांगला मनुष्य आहे

(181) They know marāṭhī, they can speak marāṭhī. *(tyānā marāṭhī yet,,te marathi bolu śhaktāt.)* त्याना मराठी येते, ते मराठी बोलू शकतात.

(182) They will learn marāṭhī. *(te marāṭhī śhiktīl)* ते मराठी शिकतील.

(183) They were learning marāṭhī. *(te marāṭhī śhikat hote)* ते मराठी शिकत होते.

(184) Do you want to learn marāṭhī? *(tumhālā marāṭhī ṡhikāyache kāy?)* तुम्हाला मराठी शिकायचे काय?

(185) We can certainly learn marāṭhī with this book. *(hyā pustakān7 āpaṇ marāṭhī nakkī śhikū śhakto)* ह्या पुस्तकानी आपण मराठी नक्की शिकू शकतो.

(186) Can you suggest me a good restaurant? *(tumhī malā chāngle bhojanālaya sāngū śhakāl kāy?)* तुम्ही मला चांगले भोजनालय सांगू शकाल काय?

(187) Is there a vegetarian (or non-vegetarian, Chinese, Italian) restaurant near here? *(ithe javal, ekhāde śhākāhārī-māṁsāhārī-chīnī-italian- bhojanālay āhe kāy?)* इथे जवळ एखादे शाकाहारी (मांसाहारी, चीनी, इटालियन) भोजनालय आहे काय?

(188) How to go there? *(tithe kase jāve?)* तिथे कसे जावे?

(189) Thank you! *(dhanyavād!)*धन्यवाद!

(190) How far is it from the city? *(śhaharāpāsūn te kitī dūr āhe?)* शहरापासून ते किती दूर आहे?

(191) Is there a train going to Banāras from here? *(ithūn Banāras la jāṇārI gāḍī āhe kāy?)* इथून बनारसला जाणारी गाडी आहे काय?

(192) How long does it take to reach Banāras? *(Banāraslā jāṇyālā kitī veḷ lāgto?)* बनारसला

adj∘ = Adjective, adv∘ = Adverb; *conj.* = Conjunction, f∘ = Feminine gender, *ind.* = Indeclinable, m∘ = Masculine gender, n∘ = Neuter gender, pl∘ = Plural

जाण्याला किती वेळ लागतो?

(193) How much baggage can we carry? *(āmhī kitī sāmān neū śhakto)* आम्ही किती सामान नेऊ शकतो?

(194) What is the eating facility on the train? *(gāḍīt khāṇyāchī kāy vyavasthā āhe?)* गाडीत खाण्यावी काय (सोय) व्यवस्था आहे?

(195) Is the train air conditioned? *(gāḍī vātānukūlit āhe kāy?)* गाडी वातानुकूलित आहे काय?

(196) Thank you Sir! *(dhanyavād sāheb!)* धन्यवाद साहब.

(197) See you again. *(punhā bhetū)* पुन्हा भेटू.

(198) Please count the luggage. *(sāmān mujūn ghyā)* सामान मोजून घ्या, साहेब!

(199) Let us go (m◦ f◦). चला चलू. चला चलू या.

(200) Excuse me, I am late. (m◦ f◦). क्षमा करा, मला उशीर झाला.

(201) It was my mistake (m◦ f◦). ही माझी चूक होती.

(202) I feel very sorry! (m◦ f◦). मला फार वाईट वाटते

(203) I beg your pardon. (m◦ f◦). मी आपली क्षमा मागतो (मागते).

(204) Please allow me. (m◦ f◦). मला परवानगी द्यावी.

(205) Bravo! (m◦ f◦). वाहवा! or शाबास!

(206) Wonderful! Beautiful! Excellent!(m◦ f◦). फार छान! फार सुंदर! अत्युत्तम!

(207) How nice! (m◦ f◦). किती छान!

(209) Absolutely! (m◦ f◦). अगदी बरोबर!

(210) Thanks! Thank God! (m◦ f◦). आभार! देवाचे उपकार!

(211) As you like (m◦ f◦). जशी तुमची मर्जी.

(212) Anything else? (m◦ f◦). आणखी काही?

(213) That's enough (m◦ f◦). इतके पुरे.

(214) Look at me (m◦ f◦). माझेकडे बघ. माझेकडे पहा.

(215) Wait a little bit (m◦ f◦). जरा थांब. जरा थांबा

(216) Be careful! (m◦ f◦). सावध रहा. सावध असा. सावध व्हा.

(217) Go at once (m◦ f◦). ताबडतोब जा

(218) Try again (m◦ f◦). पुन: प्रयत्न कर. पुन्हा प्रयत्न करा.

(219) Did they lock the door? (m◦ f◦). त्यांनी दरवाजा बंद केला काय?

(220) Will you come tomorrow? (m◦ f◦). उद्या येशील काय? उद्या याला काय?

adj◦ = Adjective, adv◦ = Adverb; *conj.* = Conjunction, f◦ = Feminine gender, *ind.* = Indeclinable, m◦ = Masculine gender, n◦ = Neuter gender, pl◦ = Plural

(221) I shall return on Monday (m◦ f◦). मी सोमवारला परत येईन.

(222) I will come with Keshav (m◦ f◦). मी केशव बरोबर येईन.

(223) Be ready! (m◦ f◦). तयार रहा. तयार अस. तयार असा.

(224) Move aside (m◦ f◦). बाजूला हो. बाजूला व्हा. बाजूला सरक. बाजूला सरका

(225) Come soon. Return soon. (m◦ f◦). लवकर ये. लवकर या. लवकर परत. लवकर परता.

(226) Never forget it. (m◦ f◦). कधीही विसरू नकोस. कधीही विसरू नका.

(227) Always remember. (m◦ f◦). नेहमी आठवण असू दे (असू द्या).

(228) Let it be! (m◦ f◦). असू दे (असू द्या). असो!

(229) Please sign here. (m◦ f◦). इथे हस्ताक्षर करा.

(230) Please follow me. (m◦ f◦). माझ्या मागे ये (या). माझे अनुकरण कर (करा).

(231) Do not say anything (m◦ f◦). काहीही बोलू नकोस (नका).

(232) What do you want (need)? (m◦ f◦). तुला (तुम्हाला) काय पाहिजे (हवे)?

(233) I have seen the new Ram Temple. (m◦ f◦). मी नवीन राम मंदिर पाहिले (बघितले) आहे.

(234) You are fortunate (luckey) (m◦ f◦). तु भाग्यवान आहेस. तुम्ही भाग्यवान आहात.

(235) May God help you! (m◦ f◦). देव (तुझे) तुमचे भले करो! देव तुझी (तुमची) मदत करो!

(236) Which book is your most favorite? (m◦ f◦). तुझे (तुमचे) आवडते पुस्तक कोणते?

(237) Shrīmadbhagavadgītā (m◦ f◦). श्रीमद्भगवद्गीता

(238) Where is their house? (m◦ f◦). त्यांचे घर कुठे (कोठे) आहे?

(239) What happened? (m◦ f◦). काय झाले? काय घडले?

(240) Let's begin (m◦ f◦). सुरवात (आरंभ) करू या.

(241) I missed my train yesterday (m◦ f◦). काल माझी गाडी चुकली.

(242) Who is there? (m◦ f◦). तिथे कोण आहे? My brother is there (m◦ f◦). तिथे माझा भाऊ आहे.

(244) Did you call (invite) him? (m◦ f◦). तू (तुम्ही) त्याला बोलावले काय?

(245) There is not even one player on the ground. मैदानावर एकही विद्यार्थी नाही.

(246) Your both answers are correct. (m◦ f◦). तुझी (तुमची) दोन्ही उत्तरे बरोबर (ठीक) आहेत.

(247) Gangā is a holy river. गंगा एक पवित्र नदी आहे.

(248) Himalay is a tall mountain हिमालय उंच पर्वत आहे.

(249) India is a big (great) country भारत एक मोठा (महान) देश आहे.

(250) Sun is far away from here. सूर्य इथून खूप दूर आहे. Moon is bright today. आज चंद्र चकचकीत आहे.

It is an easy book (m◦ f◦). हे पुस्तक सोपे आहे. Bye! (m◦ f◦). नमस्ते! नमस्कार! भेटू या!

adj◦ = Adjective, adv◦ = Adverb; *conj.* = Conjunction, f◦ = Feminine gender, *ind.* = Indeclinable, m◦ = Masculine gender, n◦ = Neuter gender, pl◦ = Plural

STUDENTS' WORD-for-WORD, TRANSLITERATED ENGLISH-MARATHI DICTIONARY

A

bandon (v∘) *tyāgṇe, soḍṇe* त्यागणे, सोडणे*

Abbreviated (adj∘) *sankṣhipta* संक्षिप्त

Abbreviation (m∘) *sankṣhep* संक्षेप

Abdomen (n∘) *udar, poṭ* उदर, पोट

Abduction (n∘) *apaharaṇ* अपहरण

Abide (v∘) *sahan karṇe,* सहन क∘*

Ability (f∘) *kṣhamatā,* (n∘) *sāmarthya* क्षमता, सामर्थ्य

Able (adj∘) *sakṣham, samartha* सक्षम, समर्थ

Abnormal (adj∘) *asāmānya* असामान्य

Abode (n∘) *ghar* घर

Abolish (v∘) *samāpta karṇe* समाप्त क∘*

Abortion (m∘) *garbhapāt* गर्भपात

Abortive (adj∘) *niṣhphaḷ* निष्फळ

About (adv∘) *sumāre* सुमारे

Above (adv∘) *var* वर

Abroad (m∘) *pardesha* परदेश

Abrupt (adj∘) *ākasmik* आकस्मिक

Abruptly (adv∘) *ekāek, ekdam, achānak* एकाएक, एकदम, अचानक

Absence (f∘) *anupasthiti, gairhājirī* अनुपस्थिति, गैरहाजिरी

Absent (adj∘) *anupasthit, gairhājir* अनुपस्थित, गैरहाजिर

Absolutely (adv∘) *bilkul* बिलकुल

Absorption (n∘) *shoṣhaṇ* शोषण

Abstinence (n∘) *samyaman* संयमन

Absurd (adj∘) *asangat* असंगत

Abundant (adj∘) *prachur* प्रचुर

Abuse (m∘) *durupayog* दुरुपयोग

Accept (v∘) *kabūl karṇe, mānaṇe* कबूल क∘, मानणे*

Acceptance (m∘) *svīkār,* (f∘) *svikruti manjurī* स्वीकार, स्वीकृति, मंजूरी

Accident (f∘) *durghaṭṇā,* (m∘) *apaghāt* दुर्घटना, अपघात

Accidental (adj∘) *ākasmik* आकस्मिक

Accomodation, place (m∘) *āvās* आवास

Accomplishment (f∘) *safaltā, prāpti, upalabdhi* सफलता, प्राप्ति, उपलब्धि

According (prep∘) *anusāre* अनुसारे

Account (m∘) *hisheb, hishob* हिशेब, हिशोब

Accountant (m∘) *munīm* मुनीम

Accumulated (adj∘) *jamā, sañchit* जमा, संचित

Accurate (adj∘) *tantotant* तंतोतंत

Ache (f∘) *pīḍā, vedṇā,* पीडा, वेदना

Achieve (v∘) *prāpta karṇe* प्राप्त क∘*

Acid (n∘) *amla* अम्ल

Acknowledge (v∘) *mānaṇe, kabūl karṇe, svīkār karṇe* मानणे, कबूल क∘, स्वीकार क∘*

Acknowledgement (f∘) *kabūlī, svīkruti* कबूली, स्वीकृति

Acquaintance (m∘) *parichay* परिचय

Acquire (v∘) *prāpta karṇe* प्राप्त क∘*

Acronym (m∘) *sankṣhep* संक्षेप

Across (adv∘) *palīkaḍe* पलीकडे

Act (n∘) *kām, kārya, karma* काम, कार्य, कर्म

Act (v∘) *karṇe* क∘*

Acting (m∘) *abhinay* अभिनय

Action (f∘) *kriyā,* (n∘) *kām* क्रिया, काम

Active (adj∘) *sakrīya* सक्रीय

Activity (f∘) *kriyā,* (n∘) *kām* क्रिया, काम

Actor (m∘ f∘) *kalākār* कलाकार

Actual (adj∘) *aslī, khare* असली, खरे

Actuality (f∘) *satyatā* सत्यता

Acute (adj∘) *ghor, tīkṣhṇa, prakhar* घोर, तीक्ष्ण, प्रखर

Adamant (adj∘) *druḍha; jiddī, aḍiyal* दृढ; जिद्दी, अडियल

Add (v∘) *miḷavṇe, joḍṇe* मिळवणे, जोडणे*

Addict (adj∘) *vyasanī* व्यसनी

Addiction (f∘) *āsakti,* (m∘) *nashā,* (n∘) *vyasan* आसक्ति, नशा, व्यसन

Addictive (adj∘) *mādk* मादक

Address (m∘) *pattā* पत्ता

Adequate (adj∘) *purtā* पुरता

Adhere (v∘) *juḍṇe, chikaṭṇe* जुडणे, चिकटणे

Adhesive (m∘) *gond* गोंद

Adjective (n∘) *visheṣhaṇ* विशेषण

Adjoin (v∘) *joḍṇe* जोडणे*

Adjust (v∘) *anukūl hoṇe; ṭhīk karṇe** अनुकूल हो∘; ठीक क∘*

Adjustment (m∘) *sudhār* सुधार

Administration (n∘) *shāsan* शासन

Admiration (f∘) *stuti, prashansā* स्तुति, प्रशंसा

Admire (v∘) *stuti karṇe* स्तुति क∘*

Admission (m∘) *pravesh* प्रवेश

Adoration (n∘) *prem;* (f∘) *pūjā, bhakti* प्रेम, पूजा, भक्ति

Adulteration (f∘) *miḷāvaṭ* मिळावट

Advance (f∘) *peshgī* पेशगी; (adj∘) *āgāū* आगाऊ; (v∘) *puḍhe jāṇe* पुढे जाणे

Advancement (f∘) *pragati, unnati* (m∘) *vikās, utkarṣha* प्रगति, उन्नति, विकास, उत्कर्ष

Advantage (m∘) *lābh,* लाभ

Adventure (n∘) *sāhas* साहस

Adventurous (adj∘) *sāhasī* साहसी

Adverb (n∘) *kriyāvisheṣhaṇ* क्रियाविशेषण

Advertisement (f∘) *ghoṣhaṇā, jāhirāt;* (n∘) *vidnyāpan* घोषणा, जाहिरात; विज्ञापन

Advice (m∘) *upadesh* उपदेश

Advise (v∘) *upadesha deṇe* उपदेश देणे*

Affection (m∘) *lagāv,* (n∘) *prem* लगाव, प्रेम

Affluence (f∘) *amīrī, samruddhi* अमीरी, समृद्धि

Affluent (adj∘) *amīr, samruddha* अमीर, समृद्ध

Afraid (adj∘) *bhayabhīta, trast* भयभीत, त्रस्त

After (adv∘) *nantar, mag* नंतर, मग

Afternoon (f∘) *dupār* दुपार

Afterwards (adv∘) *nantar, māgūn* नंतर, मागून

Again (adv∘) *punaḥ, punhā* पुनः, पुन्हा

Again and again (adv∘) *vāramvār* वारंवार

adj∘ = Adjective, adv∘ = Adverb; *conj.* = Conjunction, f∘ = Feminine gender, *ind.* = Indeclinable, m∘ = Masculine gender, n∘ = Neuter gender, pl∘ = Plural

Against (adv∘) *pratikūl, viparīt, viruddha* प्रतिकूल, विपरीत, विरुद्ध

Age (n∘) *vay,* (f∘) *āyu* वय, आयु

Agenda (m∘) *kāryakram* कार्यक्रम

Agent (m∘) *sādhan* साधन

Aggravation (m∘) *bhaḍkāv* भडकाव

Aggressive (adj∘) *ākramak* आक्रमक

Agile (adj∘) *chapal, chañchal* चपल, चंचल

Ago (adv∘) *pahile, pūrvī* पहिले, पूर्वी

Agree (v∘) *kabūl karṇe, mānaṇe* कबूल क∘, मानणे*

Agriculture (f∘) *śhetī* शेती

Ahead (adv∘) *puḍhe* पुढे

Aid (f∘) *madat, sahāyatā* मदत, सहायता

Aim (n∘) *dhyeya, lakṣhya;* (m∘) *hetu,* ध्येय, लक्ष्य; हेतु

Air (f∘) *havā* हवा

Airconditioned (adj∘) *vātānukūlit* वातानुकूलित

Airplane (n∘) *vimān* विमान

Alarm (f∘) *sūchanā* सूचना

Albeit (conj∘) *yadyapi* यद्यपि

Alcoholic drink (f∘) *dārū* दारू

Alert (adj∘) *sāvadhān* सावधान

Algebra (n∘) *bījgaṇit* बीजगणित

Alien (adj∘) *pardeśhī* परदेशी

Alike (adj∘) *samānm, sama* समान, सम

Alive (adj∘) *sajīv, jīvita* सजीव, जीवित

All (adj∘) *pūrṇa, sārā, sarva* पूर्ण, सारा, सर्व

All along (adv∘) *nirantar, nehamī, satat, sadā* निरंतर, नेहमी, सतत, सदा

All around (adv∘) *sarvatra* सर्वत्र

All at once (adv∘) *ekadam, ekāek* एकदम, एकाएक

All of a sudden (adv∘) *akasmāt, ekadam* अकस्मात्, एकदम

All over (adv∘) *sarvatra* सर्वत्र

All right (adv∘) *ṭhīk, barobar* ठीक, बरोबर

Alley (f∘) *gallī* गल्ली

Alliance (f∘) *sandhi,* (m∘) *samjhautā* संधि, समझौता

Alligation (m∘) *ārop* आरोप

Alligator (m∘) *magar* मगर

Allocate (v∘) *vāṭṇe* वाटणे*

Allow (v∘) *anumodan deṇe* अनुमोदन देणे*

Allowance (m∘) *bhattā,* (f∘) *dalālī, sūṭ;* भत्ता, दलाली, सूट

Almighty (m∘) *sarvaśhaktimān* सर्वशक्तिमान्

Almond (f∘) *badām* बदाम

Almost (adv∘) *javaḷ-javaḷ, prāyah* जवळ-जवळ, प्राय:

Alone (adj∘) *ekṭā* एकटा

Along (adv∘) *barobar* बरोबर

Alphabet (f∘) *varṇamālā* वर्णमाला

Already (adv∘) *agodar, ādhīch* अगोदर, आधीच

Also (adv∘) *hī, dekhīl* ही, देखील

Alter (v∘) *badalṇe* बदलणे*

Alteration (m∘) *badal* बदल

Alternately (adv∘) *āḷīpāḷīne* आळीपाळीने, *yathākram* यथाक्रम

Although (adv∘) *jarī, yadyapi* जरी, यद्यपि

Altogether (adv∘) *sarvathā* सर्वथा

Always (adv∘) *sadā, satat,* सदा, सतत,

Am (v∘) *āhe* आहे

Amature (adj∘) *anipuṇ* अनिपुण

Amaze (v∘) *chakit hoṇe, chakit karṇe** चकित हो∘, चकित क∘*

Amazement (m∘) *achambā,* (n∘) *āśhcharya, vismay* अचंबा, आश्चर्य, विस्मय

Amazing (adj∘) *adbhut* अद्भुत

Ambiguous (adj∘) *aspaṣhṭa* अस्पष्ट

Ambition (f∘) *ichhā, abhilāṣhā, abhilāśhā* इच्छा, आकांक्षा, अभिलाशा

Amen (inter∘) *tathāstu, bhavatu* तथास्तु, भवतु

Amiable (adj∘) *priya, ramaṇīya* प्रिय, रमणीय

Amicable (adj∘) *mitravat, suhrud* मित्रवत्, सुहृद्

Amid (prep∘) *madhye* मध्ये

Amity (n∘) *bandhutva,* (f∘) *mitratā* बंधुत्व, मित्रता

Ammunition (f∘) *yuddha sāmagrī* युद्ध सामग्री

Amnesty (f∘) *kṣhamā,* (n∘) *dān* क्षमा दान

Among (adv∘) *madhye* मध्ये

Amoral (adj∘) *adharmī* अधर्मी

Amorous (adj∘) *rasik, kāmuk* रसिक, कामुक

Amount (f∘) *rakkam* रक्कम

Amplification (m∘) *vistār,* (f∘) *vruddhi* विस्तार, वृद्धि

Analysis (n∘) *viśhleṣhaṇ* विश्लेषण

Anarchy (f∘) *arājaktā* अराजकता

Ancestor (m∘) *pūrvaj* पूर्वज

Añchor (n∘) *naṅgar* नांगर

Ancient (adj∘) *purātan, prāchīn* पुरातन, प्राचीन

And (con∘) *āṇi* आणि

Angel (m∘) *devadūt,* (f∘) *apsarā* देवदूत, अप्सरा

Anger (m∘) *krodh, rāg* क्रोध, राग

Angle (m∘) *koṇ* कोण

Angry (adj∘) *kruddha* क्रुद्ध

Anguish (m∘) *duhkh, santāp;* (f∘) *vedṇā* दु:ख, संताप; वेदना

Animal (n∘) *janāvar,* (m∘) *paśhu, jantu* जनावर, पशु, जंतु

Animosity (f∘) *śhatrutā* शत्रुता

Annihilate (v∘) *miṭavṇe* मिटवणे*

Anniversary (f∘) *varṣhagāṭh* वर्षगाठ

Announcement (f∘) *ghoṣhaṇa, jāhirāt, sūchanā,* (n∘) *vidnyāpan* घोषणा, जाहिरात, सूचना, विज्ञापन

Annoy (v∘) *dukhavṇe* दुखवणे*

Annoyance (m∘) *chhaḷ, trās, upadrav* छळ, त्रास, उपद्रव

Annual (adj∘) *vārṣhik* वार्षिक

Anonymous (adj∘) *anāmak* अनामक

Another (adj∘) *dusrā, nirāḷā* दुसरा, निराळा

Answer (n∘) *uttar* उत्तर; (v∘) *uttar deṇe* उत्तर देणे*

Ant (f∘) *mungī* मुंगी

Anthem (n∘) *stutigān* स्तुतिगान

Anticipate (v∘) *āśhā karṇe* आशा क∘*

Antique (adj∘) *purātan, prāchīn, junā* पुरातन, प्राचीन, जुना

Antonym (m∘) *viruddhārthī bda* विरुद्धार्थी शब्द

Any (adv∘) *kuṇīhi, konṭāhi* कुणीहि, कोणताहि

Anybody (pr∘) *kuṇīhī* कुणीही

Anyhow (adv∘) *kzsehī* कसेही

adj∘ = Adjective, adv∘ = Adverb; *conj.* = Conjunction, f∘ = Feminine gender, *ind.* = Indeclinable, m∘ = Masculine gender, n∘ = Neuter gender, pl∘ = Plural

Anything (adv∘) *kāhlhī* काहीही

Anywhere (adv∘) *kuṭhehi* कुठेहि

Apart (adv∘) *alag, pruthak, bhinna* अलग, पृथक्, भिन्न

Apex (n∘) *s'hikhar,* (m∘) *kaḷas* शिखर, कळस

Apology (f∘) *kṣhamā yāchanā* क्षमा याचना

Apparent (adj∘) *prakaṭ, spaṣhṭa* प्रकट, स्पष्ट

Appear (v∘) *disṇe* दिसणे

Append (v∘) *joḍṇe, miḷavṇe* जोडणे, मिळवणे*

Appetite (f∘) *bhūk* भूक

Applaud (v∘) *ṭāḷī bajāvṇe* टाळी बजावणे*

Applause (f∘) *stuti* स्तुति

Apple (n∘) *s'hep* शेप

Application (f∘) *prārthanāpatra* प्रार्थनापत्र

Appoint (v∘) *niyukta karṇe* नियुक्त क∘*

Appointment (f∘) *niyukti* नियुक्ति

Appreciation (n∘) *mūlyāṅkan* मूल्यांकन

Approach (n∘) *āgaman,* (m∘) *shirkāv* आगमन, शिरकाव

Approval (n∘) *Anumodn* (f∘) *svīkṛti* अनुमोदन, स्वीकृति

Approximately (adv∘) *andāje* अंदाजे

Approximation (m∘) *andāj* अंदाज

Aquatic (adj∘) *jalchar* जलचर

Arch (f∘) *kamān* कमान

Archaeology (n∘) *purātattva* पुरातत्त्व

Architect (m∘) *s'hilpakār* शिल्पकार

Architecture (f∘) *s'hilpavidyā* शिल्पविद्या

Ardent (adj∘) *prakhar* प्रखर

Are (v∘) *āhet* आहेत

Arguement (m∘) *vivād, tark* विवाद, तर्क

Aristocrat (adj∘) *kulīn* कुलीन

Arithmatic (n∘) *gaṇit, aṅkgaṇit* गणित, अंकगणित

Arm (m∘) *hāt,* (f∘) *bāhu, bhujā* हात, बाहु, भुजा

Aroma (m∘) *sugandh* सुगंध

Around (adv∘) *sabhovatī* सभोवती

Arrange (v∘) *rachaṇe* रचणे*

Arrangement (f∘) *rachaṇā* रचना

Arrival (n∘) *yeṇe, pohachaṇe* येणे, पोहचणे

Arrive (v∘) *yeṇe, pohachaṇe* येणे, पोहचणे

Arrogant (adj∘) *haṭṭī, ahamkārī* हट्टी, अहंकारी

Arrow (m∘) *bāṇ* बाण

Art (f∘) *kalā* कला

Artful (adj∘) *chatur* चतुर

Artificial (adj∘) *krutrim, banāvaṭī* कृत्रिम, बनावटी

Artisan (m∘) *kārāgīr* कारागीर

As (adv∘) *yathā, jase* यथा, जसे

As if (adv∘) *jase, jaṇu* जसे, जणु

As though (adv∘) *jase* जसे

Ascetic (m∘) *yogī, tapasvī* योगी, तपस्वी

Ash (f∘) *rakṣhā, rākh* रक्षा, राख

Ashamed (adj∘) *lajjit* लज्जित

Aside (adv∘) *ekīkaḍe* एकीकडे

Ask (v∘) *vicharṇe* विचारणे*

Asleep (adj∘) *nidrit, supta* निद्रित, सुप्त

Assassin (m∘) *mārak, ghātak* मारक, घातक

Assembly (f∘) *sabhā, manḍaḷī* सभा, मंडळी

Assention (f∘) *anumati, svīkruti* अनुमति, स्वीकृति

Assets (f∘) *sampatti* संपत्ति

Assignment (f∘) *niyukti* नियुक्ति

Assistance (m∘) *sahārā* (f∘) *madat* सहारा, मदत

Association (f∘) *sabhā, pariṣhad* सभा, परिषद्

Assult (m∘) *dhāvā* (f∘) *chaḍhāī* धावा, चढाई

Assumption (f∘) *kalpaṇā* कल्पना

Assurance (m∘) *vis'hvās* विश्वास

Asthmā (m∘) *damā* दमा

Astonishment (n∘) *ās'hcharya,* (m∘) *achambā* आश्चर्य, अचंबा

Astrology (n∘) *jyotiṣhya* ज्योतिष्य

Astronomy (f∘) *khagol vidyā* खगोल विद्या

Asylum (m∘) *ās'hraya,* (f∘) *s'haraṇ* आश्रय, शरण

At (prep∘) *kaḍe* कडे

At any time (adv∘) *kevhāhī* केव्हाही

At last (adv∘) *s'hevaṭī* शेवटी

At least (adv∘) *kamītkamī* कमीतकमी

At night *(adv∘) rātrī* रात्री

At once (adv∘) *jalad, ekadam* जलद, एकदम

At one time (adv∘) *ekadā,* एकदा

At present (adv∘) *saddhyā, hallī* सध्या, हल्ली

At this time (adv∘) *saddhyā, hallī* सध्या, हल्ली

At what time (adv∘) *kevā* केव्हा

Atheist (adj∘) *nāstik* नास्तिक

Atmosphere (n∘) *vātāvaraṇ* वातावरण

Atom (m∘) *aṇu, paramāṇu* अणु, परमाणु

Attach (v∘) *bāndhṇe, joḍṇe* बांधणे, जोडणे*

Attain (v∘) *prāpta karaṇe* प्राप्त क∘*

Attempt (m∘) *prayatna* प्रयत्न, *yatna* यत्न; (v∘) *prayatna karaṇe* प्रयत्न क∘*

Attention (n∘) *dhyān* ध्यान

Attentive (adj∘) *sāvadhān, sāvadh* सावधान, सावध

Attitude (f∘) *vṛtti* वृत्ति

Attraction (n∘) *ākarṣhaṇ,* (m∘) *moha* आकर्षण, मोह

Attractive (adj∘) *ākarṣhak, mohak* आकर्षक, मोहक

Attribute (m∘) *guṇa, dharma* गुण, धर्म

Auction (m∘) *lilāv* लिलाव

Audience (m∘) *hrotāgaṇa* श्रोतागण

Auspicious (adj∘) *s'hubha, maṅgal* शुभ, मंगल

Authentic (adj∘) *kharā, assal* खरा, अस्सल

Author (m∘) *lekhak* लेखक

Authority (m∘) *adhikār* अधिकार

Autobiography (n∘) *ātmacharitra* आत्मचरित्र

Autumn (m∘) *s'harad rutu* शरद् ऋतु

Available (adj∘) *sulabh, sugam* सुलभ, सुगम

Avarage (f∘) *sarāsarī* सरासरी

Awake (v∘) *jāgaṇe* जागणे

Award (n∘) *Pāritoshak* पारितोषक

Aware (adj∘) *sachet, sajag* सचेत, सजग

Away (adv∘) *dūr* दूर

Aweful (adj∘) *bhayaṅkar* भयंकर

Ax (f∘) *kurhāḍ* कुऱ्हाड

B

Babble (f∘) *bakbak. gappā* बकबक, गप्पा; (v∘) *baḍbaḍṇe* बडबडणे

adj∘ = Adjective, adv∘ = Adverb; *conj.* = Conjunction, f∘ = Feminine gender, *ind.* = Indeclinable, m∘ = Masculine gender, n∘ = Neuter gender, pl∘ = Plural

Baboon (n◦) *langūr* लंगूर

Bachelor (adj◦) 1. (single) *avivāhit,* अविवाहित; 2. (graduate) *snātak* स्नातक

Back (f◦) body: *pāṭh* पाठ

Backbone (m◦) *kaṇā* कणा

Background (f◦) *pārśhvabhūmi* पार्श्वभूमी

Backing (m◦) *āśhray, pāṭhimbā, sahārā,* (n◦) *samarthan, anumodan* आश्रय, पाठिंबा, सहारा, समर्थन, अनुमोदन

Backward (adj◦) *māgāslā* मागासला

Backwards (adj◦) *māghārā* माघारा

Bad (adj◦) *kharāb, wāīṭ* खराब, वाईट

Badly (adv◦) *nikadīne* निकडीने

Baffle (v◦) *ghābarṇe* घाबरणे

Bag (f◦) *thailī, piśhvī* थैली, पिशवी

Balance (m◦) *tarājū* तराजू; (v◦) *tolṇe, mojṇe* तोलणे, मोजणे*

Bald (adj◦) *boḍkā, ṭaklā* बोडका, टकला

Ball (m◦) *cheṇḍū* चेंडू

Balloon (m◦) *fugā* फुगा

Balm (m◦) *malam* मलम

Bamboo (m◦) *bās* बास

Banana (n◦) *keḷ* केळ

Band (n◦) *bandhan,* (m◦) *paṭṭā,* बंधन, पट्टा

Bangle (f◦) *bāngaḍī* बांगडी

Banyan (m◦) *vaḍ, vaṭ* वड, वट

Bar (m◦) *daṇḍā,* (f◦) *chhaḍī* दंडा, छडी

Barbaric (adj◦) *janglī, asabhya* जंगली, असभ्य

Barber (m◦) *nhāvī* न्हावी

Bare (adj◦) *nagnā, ughaḍā* नग्न, उघडा.

Bark (v◦) *bhunkṇe* भुंकणे

Barn (n◦) *koṭhār* कोठार

Barrel (m◦) *pipa* पिपा

Base, foundation (n◦) *mūḷ* मूळ; lowly (adj◦) *nīch* नीच

Basil (f◦) *tuḷas* तुळस

Basis (m◦) *ādhār* आधार

Basket (f◦) *ṭoplī, karaṇḍī* टोपली, करंडी

Bat (n◦) *vāghūḷ* वाघूळ; sport (f◦) *faḷī* फळी

Bathe (v◦) *nahāṇe* नहाणे

Battle (n◦) *yuddha,* (f◦) *laḍhāī* युद्ध, लढाई

Battlefield (f◦) *raṇabhūmi* रणभूमि

Be (v◦) *rāhaṇe, asṇe; hoṇe* राहणे, असणे; हो◦*

Be born (v◦) *janma gheṇe* जन्म घेणे

Bead (m◦) *maṇī* मणी

Beak (f◦) *choch* चोच

Bean (f◦) *śheng* शेंग

Bear (n◦) *aswal* अस्वल

Bear (v◦) *saham karṇe* सहन क◦*

Beard (f◦) *dāḍhī* दाढी

Beast (m◦) *paśhu* पशु

Beat (v◦) *pīṭṇe, mārṇe* पीटणे, मारणे*

Beautiful (adj◦) *sundar, suśhobhit* सुंदर, सुशोभित

Beautify (v◦) *sajavaṇe* सजवणे*

Beauty (f◦) *sundartā, śhobhā* सूंदरता, शोभा

Because (adv◦) *kāraṇ ki* कारण कि

Bed (m◦) *bichhānā* बिछाना

Bedroom (n◦) *śhayanāgār* शयनागार

Bee (f◦) *māshī;* (m◦) *bhramar* माशी; भ्रमर

Before (adv◦) *samor, pahile* सामोर, पहिले

Before, time-place (adv◦) *pūrva* पूर्व

Beg (v◦) *yāchaṇe karaṇe* याचना क◦*

Beggar (m◦) *bhikārī* भिकारी

Behaviour (n◦) *ācharaṇ* आचरण

Behead (v◦) *kattal karṇe* कत्तल क◦*

Behind (adv◦) *māge* मागे

Behold (v◦) *pāhaṇe* पाहणे*

Being (m◦) *jīv, prāṇī* जीव, प्राणी

Belch (v◦) *ḍakārṇe, okṇe* डकारणे, ओकणे

Believe (v◦) *viśhvās karṇe* विश्वास क◦*

Bell (f◦) *ghaṇṭī* घंटी

Bellybutton (f◦) *nābhi, nābhī* नाभि, नाभी

Beloved (adj◦) *priya* प्रिय

Below *(adv◦) khālī* खाली

Belt (m◦) *paṭṭā* पट्टा

Bend (v◦) *vākaṇe, vākavṇe, jhukṇe, jhukavne** वाकणे, वाकवणे,* झुकणे; झुकवणे*

Beneath (adv◦) *khālī* खाली

Benediction (m◦) *āśhīrvād* आशीर्वाद

Benefactor (m◦) *dātā, hitkārī* दाता, हितकारी

Benefit (m◦) *lābh,* (n◦)*hit* लाभ, हित

Benevolence (f◦) *dayā, krupā* दया, कृपा

Bent (adj◦) *jhuklelā* झुकलेला

Beside (prep◦) *nikaṭ, pās* निकट, पास

Besides (adv◦) *śhivāy* शिवाय

Best (adj◦) *uttam, śhreṣhtha* उत्तम, श्रेष्ठ

Bet (m◦) *ḍāv, paṇ,* (f◦) *bājī* डाव, पण, बाजी

Better (adj◦) *yodnyatar, uttamtar* योग्यतर, उत्तमतर

Between (prep◦) *madhye* मध्ये

Beverage (n◦) *peya* पेय

Beyond (prep◦) *pār, palīkaḍe* पार, पलीकडे

Bias (m◦) *pakṣhapāt* पक्षपात

Bibliography (f◦) *grantha-sūchī* ग्रंथ-सूची

Bicycle (f◦) *sāykal* सायकल

Big (adj◦) *moṭhā* मोठा

Bill (f◦) *pāvtī* पावती

Billingual (adj◦) *dubhāṣhī* दुभाषी

Bin (f◦) *ṭoplī* टोपली

Bind (v◦) *bāndhaṇe* बाँधणे*

Binding (n◦) *bandhan* बंधन

Binocular (f◦) *dūrbīṇ* दूरबीण

Biography (n◦) *charitra* चरित्र

Biology (n◦) *prāṇīśhāstra* प्राणीशास्त्र

Bird (m◦) *pakṣhi* पक्षी

Birth (m◦) *janma* जन्म

Bite, cut (v◦) *chavṇe* चावणे*

Bitter (adj◦) *kaḍū* कडू

Bittergourd (n◦) *kārle* कारले

Black (adj◦) *kāḷā* काळा

Blacksmith (m◦) *lohār* लोहार

Blame (v◦) *doṣh lāvṇe* दोष लावणे*

Blank (adj◦) *korā, śhūnya* कोरा, शून्य

Blanket (n◦) *kambḷe, ghongḍe* कांबळे, घोंगडे

Blast (m◦) *visphot* विस्फोट

Blaze (v◦) *bhaḍakṇe, jaḷṇe* भडकणे, जळणे

Bleed (v◦) *rakta vāhaṇe* रक्त वाहणे

Blemish (m◦) *dhabbā, ḍāg* धब्बा, डाग

Blessing (n◦) *vardān,* (f◦) *krupā* वरदान, कृपा

Blind (adj◦) *andhaḷā* अंधळा

Blink (v◦) *ṭimṭimaṇe* टिमटिमणे

adj◦ = Adjective, adv◦ = Adverb; *conj.* = Conjunction, f◦ = Feminine gender, *ind.* = Indeclinable, m◦ = Masculine gender, n◦ = Neuter gender, pl◦ = Plural

Bliss (f∘) *krupā* कृपा

Blister (m∘) *ghoglā* घोगला

Blizzard (n∘) *vādaḷ* वादळ

Block (m∘) *avarodh, pratirodh* अवरोध, प्रतिरोध

Blockade (f∘) *nākabandī,* (m∘) *gherāv* नाकाबंदी, घेराव

Blood (m∘) *rakta* रक्त

Bloom (f∘) *bahār* बहार

Blossom (v∘) *khilaṇe* खिलणे

Blot (m∘) *dhabbā, ḍāg* धब्बा, डाग

Blotch (m∘) *dhabbā, dāg* धब्बा, डाग

Blow (m∘) *āghāt, dhakkā, vār, prahār* आघात, धक्का, वार, प्रहार

Blow (v∘) *funkṇe* फुंकणे*

Blue (adj∘) *nīḷā* नीळा

Blunder (f∘) *ghoḍchūk* घोडचूक

Blunt (adj∘) *bothaṭ, atīkṣhṇa* बोथट, अतीक्ष्ण

Blur (adj∘) *aspaṣhṭa* अस्पष्ट

Blush (v∘) *lājṇe* लाजणे

Board (m∘) *taktā* तक्ता

Boast (v∘) *ḍīng mārṇe* डींग मारणे*

Boat (f∘) *nāv, naukā, jahāj* नाव, नौका, जहाज

Body (n∘) *śharīr,* (m∘) *deh* शरीर, देह

Boil (v∘) *ukaḍṇe* उकडणे*

Bold (adj∘) *nidar, sāhasī* निडर, साहसी

Bombay (f∘) *Mumbaī* मुंबई

Bondage (f∘) *dāsatā, gulāmī* दासता, गुलामी

Bone (n∘) *hāḍ* हाड

Book (n∘) *paustak* पुस्तक

Boon (n∘) *vardāb* वरदान

Boost (m∘) *baḍhāvā* बढावा

Boot (m∘) *joḍā* जोडा

Booze (f∘) *dārū* दारू

Bore (adj∘) *kaṇṭāḷvāṇā* कंटाळवाणा

Borrow (v∘) *udhār gheṇe* उधार घेणे*

Borrowed (adj∘) *udhār* उधार

Bosom (f∘) *chhātī* छाती

Boss (m∘) *mālak* मालक

Botany (n∘) *vanaspati śhastra* वनस्पति शास्त्र

Both (adj∘) *donnhī* दोन्ही

Bother (v∘) *satāvaṇe, bhanḍāvṇe* सतावणे, भंडावणे*

Bottle (f∘) *śhiśhī* शिशी

Bottom (m∘) *taḷ* तळ

Bounce (v∘) *usaḷṇe* उसळणे

Boundry (f∘) *sīmā, sarhad* सीमा, सरहद

Bow (n∘) *dhanuṣhya* धनुष्य; (v∘) *jhukṇe* झुकणे

Bowl (m∘) *kaṭorā* कटोरा

Box (m∘) *ḍabā, sandūk* डबा, संदूक

Boy (m∘) *mulgā,* (n∘) *bālak* मुलगा, बालक

Boycott (m∘) *bahiṣhkār* बहिष्कार

Brag (v∘) *ḍīng mārṇe, śhekhī baghārṇe* डींग मारणे, शेखी बघारणे*

Brain (m∘) *mendū* मेंदू

Brañch (f∘) *śhakhā, fāndī* शाखा, फांदी

Brave (adj∘) *bahādur, vīr* बहादुर, वीर

Bread (f∘) *roṭī* रोटी

Break (v∘) *tūṭṇe, toḍaṇe* टूटणे, तोडणे*

Breakfast (m∘) *nāstā* नास्ता

Breath (m∘) *śhvās* श्वास

Breathless (adj∘) *bedam* बेदम

Breeze (f∘) *mand havā* मंद हवा

Bribe (f∘) *lāch* लाच

Brick (f∘) *vīṭ* वीट

Bride (f∘) *vadhū* वधू

Bridge (m∘) *pul, setu* पुल, सेतु

Brief (adj∘) *alpa, saṅkṣhipta* अल्प, संक्षिप्त

Bright (adj∘) *chamkdār* चमकदार

Brilliant (adj∘) *prakhar, prabhāvī* प्रखर, प्रभावी

Brim (m∘) *kāṭh, kinārā* काठ, किनारा

Bring (v∘) *āṇaṇe* आणणे*

Brink (m∘) *kinārā* किनारा

Brisk (adj∘) *chapaḷ* चपळ

Brittle (adj∘) *kurkurā, ṭhisūḷ* कुरकुरा, ठिसूळ

Broad (adj∘) *rund* रुंद

Broke (adj∘) *kaṅgāl; tūṭkā* कंगाल, तुटका

Broker (m∘) *dalāl* दलाल

Brokerage (f∘) *dalālī* दलाली

Bronze (n∘) *kāsē* कासे

Broom (f∘) *jhaḍṇī,* (m∘) *faḍā* झाडणी, फडा

Brother (m∘) *bhāū* भाऊ

Brother-in-law (m∘) *sāḷā, dīr* साळा, दीर

Brown (adj∘) *karḍā* करडा

Brush (m∘) *kūñchalā* कुंचला

Bucket (f∘) *bādlī* बादली

Bud (f∘) *kaḷī* कळी

Buffalo (f∘) *mhais* म्हैस

Bug (m∘) *kīḍā* कीडा

Building (f∘) *imārat,* (n∘) *bhavan* इमारत, भवन

Buñch (m∘) *guchha* गुच्छ

Bundle (m∘) *gaṭṭhā* गट्ठा

Bungalow (m∘) *baṅglā* बंगला

Burden (m∘) *bhār* भार

Bureaucracy (f∘) *daptarśhāhī, naukarśhāhī* दप्तरशाही, नौकरशाही

Burglar (m∘) *gharfodyā* घरफोड्या

Burglary (f∘) *gharfoḍī* घरफोडी

Burial (n∘) *purṇe* पुरणे

Burn (v∘) *jaḷṇe, jāḷṇe** जळणे, जाळणे*

Burp (m∘) *ḍhekar* ढेकर

Burrow (n∘) *bīḷ* बीळ

Burst (m∘) *visphoṭ* विस्फोट

Bury (adv∘) *gāḍṇe* गाडणे

Bush (f∘) *jhāḍī* झाडी

Busy (adj∘) *vyasta* व्यस्त

But (adv∘) *kintu, parantu* किंतु, परंतु

Butter (n∘) *loṇī* लोणी

Butterfly (f∘) *patang* पतंग

Buy (v∘) *vikat gheṇe* विकत घेणे*

Buzz (f∘) *gunguṇ* गुणगुण

By (prep∘) *pās, samīp* पास, समीप

By day (adv∘) *divsā* दिवसा

By night (adv∘) *rātrī* रात्री

Bypass (m∘) *upa-mārg* उपमार्ग

C

Cabbage (f∘) *pān-kobī* पानकोबी

Cable (f∘) *tār* तार

Cafe (n∘) *jalpāṅgruha* जलपानगृह

Cage (m∘) *piñjarā* पिंजरा

Cajole (v∘) *fuslāvaṇe* फुसलावणे*

Calamity (n∘) *saṅkaṭ* (f∘) *vipatti* संकट, विपत्ति

adj∘ = Adjective, adv∘ = Adverb; *conj.* = Conjunction, f∘ = Feminine gender, *ind.* = Indeclinable, m∘ = Masculine gender, n∘ = Neuter gender, pl∘ = Plural

Calcium (m∘) *chunā* चुना

Calculation (m∘) *his'heb* हिशेब

Calcutta (m∘) *kolkātā* कोलकाता

Calf (m∘) *bachhaḍā* बछडा

Call (v∘) *bolāvṇe* बोलावणे*

Calm (adj∘) *s'hānt* शांत; (f∘) *s'hānti* शांति

Camel (m∘) *unṭ* उंट

Camp (n∘) *s'hibir*, (f∘) *chhāvaṇī* शिबिर, छावणी

Campaign (n∘) *abhiyān* अभियान

Can (m∘) *dabā* डबा

Canal (m∘) *nahar* नहर

Cancel (v∘) *radda karṇe* रद्द क∘*

Candid (adj∘) *spashṭa* स्पष्ट

Candidate (m∘) *umedvār* उमेदवार

Candle (f∘) *meṇbattī* मेणबत्ती

Cane (f∘) *chhaḍī* छडी

Cannon (f∘) *tof* तोफ

Canoe (f∘) *hoḍī* होडी

Cap (f∘) *ṭopī* टोपी

Capability (f∘) *kshamatā* क्षमता

Capacity (f∘) *kshamatā* क्षमता

Capital (f∘) *rājdhānī* राजधानी

Capitalism (f∘) *bhānḍvals'hāhī* भांडवलशाही

Capsize (v∘) *buḍṇe* बुडणे

Captivated (adj∘) *mugdha, mohit* मुग्ध, मोहित

Capture (v∘) *pakaḍṇe* पकडणे*

Car (f∘) *gāḍī* गाडी

Cardamom (f∘) *vilāyachī* विलायची

Care (f∘) *kāḷjī* काळजी

Career (m∘) *dhandā* धंदा

Careful (adj∘) *sāvadhān* सावधान

Careless (adj∘) *nishkāḷjī* निष्काळजी

Caretaker (m∘) *rakhavāldār* रखवालदार

Carpenter (m∘) *vāḍhī* वाढी

Carpet (f∘) *satranjī* सतरंजी

Carrot (n∘) *gānjar* गांजर

Carry (v∘) *vāhṇe* वाहणे*

Case (f∘) *vishay, samasyā* विषय, समस्या

Cash (adj∘) *nagad, rokaḍ* नगद, रोकड

Cashew (m∘) *kājū* काजू

Cast (v∘) *fekṇe* फेकणे*

Caste (f∘) *jāti* जाति

Castle (m∘) *killā, durg* किल्ला, दुर्ग

Casual (adj∘) *anaupachārik* अनौपचारिक

Cat (f∘) *mānjar* मांजर

Catch (v∘) *pakaḍṇe* पकडणे*

Catsup (f∘) *chaṭṇī* चटणी

Cattle (n∘) *ḍhor* ढोर

Caugh (m∘) *khoklā* खोकला

Cauliflower (f∘) *fūlkobī* फूलकोबी

Cause (m∘) *kāraṇ* कारण

Caustic (adj∘) *dāhak, tikhaṭ* दाहक, तिखट

Caution (f∘) *sāvadhānī* सावधानी

Cautious (adj∘) *sāvadhān* सावधान

Cave (f∘) *guhā* गुहा

Celebrate (v∘) *manavṇe* मनवणे*

Cell-phone जंगम-दूरवाणी (f∘) *jaṅgama-dūravāṇī*

Centenary (f∘) *s'hatābdī* शताब्दी

Central (adj∘) *kendrīya, madhya* केन्द्रीय, मध्य

Century (n∘) *s'hatak* शतक

Ceremony (m∘) *samārambha* समारंभ

Certainly (adv∘) *avas'hya, nis'hchit* अवश्य, निश्चित

Certainty (m∘) *nis'hchay* निश्चय

Certificate (n∘) *pramāṇ-patra* प्रमाण-पत्र

Chain (f∘) *sākhaḷī* साखळी

Chair (f∘) *khuchī* खुर्ची

Chairman (m∘) *sabhāpati, adhyaksha* सभापति, अध्यक्ष

Chalk (m∘) *khaḍū* खडू

Challange (f∘) *āhvān* आह्वान

Chamber (m∘) *kaksha* कक्ष

Chance (f∘) *sambhāvanā* संभावना

Change (m∘) *badal*, (n∘) *parivartan* बदल, परिवर्तन; (v∘) *badalṇe* बदलणे

Chaos (m∘) *gondhaḷ* गोंधळ

Chapter (m∘) *pāṭh, adhyāy* पाठ, अध्याय

Chariot (m∘) *rath* रथ

Charm (n∘) *ākarshaṇ*, (f∘) *jādū*, (m∘) *moha* आकर्षण, जादू, मोह

Chat (f∘) *gappā* गप्पा

Chatter (f∘) *vaṭvaṭ, baḍbaḍ, kiṭkiṭ* वटवट, बडबड, किटकिट

Cheap (adj∘) *svast* स्वस्त

Cheat (v∘) *ṭhagavṇe* ठगवणे*

Check (n∘) *niyantraṇ* नियंत्रण

Cheek (m∘) *gāl* गाल

Cheer (m∘) *jayghosh*, (f∘) *vāhvā* जयघोष, वाहवा

Cheerful (adj∘) *prasanna* प्रसन्न

Cheerless (adj∘) *khinna, udās* खिन्न, उदास

Cheese (n∘) *panīr* पनीर

Cheetah (m∘) *chittā* चित्ता

Chemical (n∘) *rasāyan* रसायन

Chemistry (n∘) *rasāyan-s'hāstra* रसायनशास्त्र

Chess (n∘) *buddhibaḷ* बुद्धिबळ

Chest (f∘) *chhātī* छाती

Chew (v∘) *chāvṇe* चावणे*

Chicken (f∘) *kombaḍī* कोंबडी

Chief (m∘) *mukhya* मुख्य

Child (n∘) *bālak* बालक

Chill (f∘) *siharan* सिहरन

Chilly (f∘) *mirchī* मिरची

Chin (f∘) *hanuvaṭī* हनुवटी

Chisel (f∘) *chhannī* छन्नी

Choice (f∘) *pasantī* पसंती

Choke (v∘) *gudmarṇe* गुदमरणे

Choose (v∘) *nivaḍṇe* निवडणे*

Chop (v∘) *kāpṇe* कापणे*

Chronicle (m∘) *itihās* इतिहास

Chronology (m∘) *kāḷkram* काळक्रम

Chubby (adj∘) *gabdul* गबदुल

Chum (m∘) *dosta, kitra* दोस्त, मित्र

Chunk (m∘) *tukḍā* तुकडा

Church (m∘) *girjāghar* गिरजाघर

Churn (v∘) *ghusaḷṇe* घुसळणे*

Churner (f∘) *ravī* रवी

Cinamon (f∘) *kalmī* कलमी

Circle (m∘) *gol, vrutta* गोल, वृत्त

Circumference (m∘) *parigh, gherā, veḍhā* परिघ, घेरा, वेढा

Circumstance (f∘) *paristhiti* परिस्थिति

Citizen (m∘) *nāgarik* नागरिक

adj∘ = Adjective, adv∘ = Adverb; *conj.* = Conjunction, f∘ = Feminine gender, *ind.* = Indeclinable, m∘ = Masculine gender, n∘ = Neuter gender, pl∘ = Plural

City (m∘) *nagar, ś́hahar* नगर, शहर

Civilization (f∘) *sabhyatā* सभ्यता

Claim (m∘) *adhikār* अधिकार; (v∘) *dāvā karṇe* दावा क∘*

Clamour (m∘) *gongāṭ, hallā* गोंगाट, हल्ला

Clamp (f∘) *pakaḍ* पकड

Clap (f∘) *ṭāḷī* टाळी

Clarified-butter (n∘) *tūp* तूप

Clarify (v∘) *spashṭa karṇe* स्पष्ट क∘*

Clarity (f∘) *spashṭtā* स्पष्टता

Clash (f∘) *ṭakkar,* (m∘) *virodh* टक्कर, विरोध

Class (m∘) *varga* वर्ग

Classification (n∘) *vargīkaraṇ* वर्गीकरण

Claw (m∘) *pañjā* पंजा

Clean (adj∘) *sāf, svachha, nirmaḷ* साफ़, स्वच्छ, निर्मळ; (v∘) *-karaṇe* ∘क∘*

Cleanliness (f∘) *svachhatā* स्वच्छता

Clear (adj∘) *spashṭa* स्पष्ट

Clearly (adv∘) *sāf-sāf* साफ़–साफ़

Clerk (m∘) *kārkun* कारकुन

Client (m∘) *girhāik, grāhak pakshakār* गिऱ्हाइक, ग्राहक, पक्षकार

Cliff (m∘) *kaḍā, suḷkā* कडा, सुळका

Climate (n∘) *vātāvaraṇ* वातावरण

Climax (f∘) *parākāshṭhā* पराकाष्ठा

Climb (v∘) *chaḍhaṇe* चढणे

Cling (v∘) *chiṭakṇe, lipaṭṇe* चिटकणे, लिपटणे

Clock (n∘) *ghaḍyāḷ* घड्याळ

Close (adj∘) *javaḷ, samīp* जवळ, समीप; (v∘) *band karṇe* बंद क∘*

Closed (adj∘) *band* बंद

Clot (f∘) *guṭhaḷī* गुठळी

Cloth (n∘) *kāpaḍ,* (m∘) *kāpḍā* कापड, कपडा

Cloud (m∘) *ḍhag* ढग

Clove (f∘) *lavang* लवंग

Clown (m∘) *vidushak* विदुषक

Club (m∘) *mudgal* मुदगल

Clue (m∘) *sanket* संकेत

Clumsy (adj∘) *beḍaul, beḍhab* बेडौल, बेढब

Cluster (m∘) *guchha* गुच्छ

Clutch (f∘) *pakaḍ* पकड

Clutter (f∘) *astavyastatā, aḍgaḷ* अस्तव्यस्तता, अडगळ

Coagulate (v∘) *jamaṇe, goṭhaṇe* जमणे, गोठणे

Coal (m∘) *koḷsā* कोळसा

Coarse (adj∘) *jāḍābharḍā* जाडाभरडा

Coast (m∘) *samudrataṭ* समुद्रतट

Coax (v∘) *fusalāvaṇe* फुसलावणे*

Cob (n∘) *kaṇīs* कणीस

Cobra (m∘) *nāg* नाग

Cock (m∘) *kombḍā* कोंबडा

Cockroach (n∘) *jhuraḷ* झुरळ

Coconut (n∘) *nāraḷ* नारळ

Coffee (m∘) *kahavā* कहवा

Coin (n∘) *nāṇe* नाणे

Coincidence (m∘) *sañyog* संयोग

Cold (adj∘) *thanḍ, ś́hītal* थंड, शीतल

Cold (f∘) *sardī, thanḍī* सर्दी, थंडी

Collapse (v∘) *paḍṇe* पडणे

Colleague (m∘) *sahayogī* सहयोगी

Collection (m∘) *sangraha* संग्रह

College (n∘) *vidyālay* विद्यालय

Collide (v∘) *ṭakrāvaṇe* टकरावणे

Collision (f∘) *ṭakkar* टक्कर

Colour (m∘) *rang* रंग; (v∘) *rangavṇe* रंगवणे*

Column (m∘) *khambā, stambh* खंबा, स्तंभ

Comb (m∘) *kangvā,* (f∘) *faṇī* कंगवा, फणी

Combat (f∘) *laḍhāī* लढाई

Combat (v∘) *laḍhaṇe* लढणे

Combine (v∘) *miḷavṇe* मिळवणे*

Come (v∘) *yeṇe* येणे

Comfort (m∘) *ārām,* (f∘) *chain* आराम, चैन

Comfortable (adj∘) *sukhdāyak* सुखदायक

Comical (adj∘) *hāsyamay* हास्यमय

Command (m∘) *adhikār; ādeś́h, hukum* अधिकार; आदेश, हुकुम

Comment (f∘) *ṭīkā* टीका

Commentary (f∘) *ṭīkā* टीका

Commerce (n∘) *vāṇijja* वाणिज्य

Commission (m∘) *baṭṭā* (f∘) *dalālī* बट्टा, दलाली

Committee (f∘) *samiti* समिति

Common (adj∘) *sādhāraṇ* साधारण

Commonwealth (m∘) *rājyasangha* राज्यसंघ

Commotion (m∘) *gondhaḷ* गोंधळ

Communal (adj∘) *sāmudāyik* सामुदायिक

Communication (n∘) *sañcharaṇ* संचरण

Communism (m∘) *sāmyavād* साम्यवाद

Community (m∘) *samāj* समाज

Companion (m∘) *sahachar* सहचर

Comparable (adj∘) *tulya, samān* तुल्य, समान

Compare (v∘) *tulṇā karṇe* तुलना क∘*

Comparison (f∘) *tulnā* तुलना

Compassion (f∘) *dayā* दया

Compatible (adj∘) *anukūl* अनुकूल

Compel (v∘) *bādhya karṇe* बाध्य क∘*

Compete (v∘) *spardhā karṇe* स्पर्धा क∘*

Competition (f∘) *spardhā, hoḍ* स्पर्धा, होड

Competitor (m∘) *pratiyogī* प्रतियोगी

Compilation (n∘) *sankalan* संकलन

Complain (v∘) *takrār karṇe* तक्रार क∘*

Complaint (f∘) *takrār* तक्रार

Complementary (adj∘) *pūrak* पूरक

Complete (adj∘) *purṇa* पूर्ण

Complete (v∘) *purṇa karṇe* पूर्ण क∘*

Complex (adj∘) *bikaṭ* बिकट

Complexion (m∘) *rang-rūp* रंग-रूप

Complicated (adj∘) *bikaṭ* बिकट

Component (m∘) *avayava, ghaṭak* अवयव, घटक

Compose (v∘) *rachaṇe* रचणे*

Composition (f∘) *rachanā* रचना

Compound (n∘) *miś́hraṇ* मिश्रण

Compress (v∘) *ṭhūsaṇe* ठूसणे*

Compromise (f∘) *taḍjaḍ* तडजोड

Compulsion (m∘) *dabāv,* (f∘) *sakti* दबाव, सक्ति

Compulsory (adj∘) *āvaś́hyak, anivārya* आवश्यक, अनिवार्य

Computer (n∘) *sanganak* संगणक

Comred (m∘) *sahachar* सहचर

Con (v∘) *ṭhagṇe* ठगणे*

Concede (v∘) *kabūl karṇe* कबूल क∘*

Conceit (f∘) *ghamenḍ,* (m∘) *ahamkār* घमेंड, अहंकार

adj∘ = Adjective, adv∘ = Adverb; *conj.* = Conjunction, f∘ = Feminine gender, *ind.* = Indeclinable, m∘ = Masculine gender, n∘ = Neuter gender, pl∘ = Plural

Concentration (f∘) *ekāgratā* एकाग्रता
Conception (f∘) *dhāraṇā* धारणा
Concern (f∘) *chintā* चिंता
Concerted (adj∘) *saṅgaṭhit* संगठित
Concession (f∘) *sūṭ* सूट
Concise (adj∘) *saṅkṣhipta* संक्षिप्त
Conclude (v∘) *nirṇay gheṇe* निर्णय घेणे*
Conclusion (m∘) *niṣkarṣha* निष्कर्ष
Condemn (v∘) *nindā karṇe* निंदा क∘*
Condensed (adj∘) *ghana* घन
Condiment (m∘) *masālā* मसाला
Condition (f∘) *sthiti, avasthā* स्थिति, अवस्था
Condolence (m∘) *śhok* शोक
Conduct (n∘) *ācharaṇ* आचरण
Conduction (m∘) *pravāh* प्रवाह
Conductive (adj∘) *sahāyak* सहायक
Conductor (m∘) *sañchālak* संचालक
Cone (m∘) *śhaṅku* शंकु
Confederation (m∘) *mahāsaṅgha* महासंघ
Confer (v∘) *pradān karṇe* प्रदान क∘*
Confess (m∘) *kabūl karṇe* कबूल क∘*
Confession (m∘) *svīkār,* (f∘) *kabuīlī* स्वीकार, कबूली
Confidence (m∘) *bharavsā, viśhvās* भरवसा, विश्वास
Confident (adj∘) *viśhvasta* विश्वस्त
Confidential (adj∘) *gupta, khāsgī* गुप्त, खासगी
Confirmation (f∘) *puṣhṭī, mañjurī,* (n∘) *samarthan* पुष्टि, मंजुरी, समर्थन
Confiscate (v∘) *kabjā karṇe* कब्जा क∘*
Conflict (m∘) *saṅgharṣha, matabhed* संघर्ष, मतभेद
Conform (v∘) *pālan karṇe* पालन क∘*
Confound (v∘) *gaḍbaḍṇe* गडबणे
Confront (v∘) *sāmanā karṇe* सामना करना
Confuse (v∘) *gaḍbaḍaṇe, gāṅgarṇe, bichakṇe* गडबडणे, गांगरणे, बिचकणे
Confusion (f∘) *gaḍbaḍa* गडबड
Congestion (f∘) *bhīḍ, gardī* भीड, गर्दी
Congratulation (n∘) *abhinandan* अभिनंदन
Congress (n∘) *sammelan* संम्मेलन
Conjunction (m∘) *joḍ* जोड
Connect (v∘) *joḍṇe* जोडणे*
Connection (m∘) *sambandha* संबंध
Conquer (v∘) *jinkṇe* जिंकणे*
Conquest (f∘) *jīt,* (m∘) *vijay* जीत, विजय
Conscious (adj∘) *satark* सतर्क
Consciousness (f∘) *chetnā* चेतना
Consecutive (adj∘) *lagopāṭh* लागोपाठ
Consensus (f∘) *sarvānumati* सर्वानुमति
Consent (f∘) *anumati* अनुमति
Consequence (m∘) *pariṇām* परिणाम
Conservative (adj∘) *rūḍhivādī* रूढीवादी
Consider (v∘) *vichār karṇe* विचार क∘*
Considerable (adj∘) *yodnya* योग्य
Consideration (m∘) *mobadlā* मोबदला
Consign (v∘) *sopavaṇe* सोपवणे*
Consistent (adj∘) *niyamit* नियमित
Consolation (n∘) *samādhān* समाधान
Consolidation (n∘) *druḍhikaraṇ* दृढीकरण
Consonant (n∘) *vyañjan* व्यंजन
Conspiracy (n∘) *ṣhaḍyantra* षड्यंत्र
Constable (m∘) *śhipāī* शिपाई
Constant (adj∘) *sthir, aṭal* स्थिर, अटल
Constantly (adv∘) *nitya, nirantar* नित्य, निरंतर
Constipation (m∘) *baddhakoṣhṭha* बद्धकोष्ठ
Constituent (m∘) *ghaṭak, avayav* घटक, अवयव
Constitution (n∘) *saṁvidhān* संविधान
Consul (m∘) *dūt* दूत
Consulate (n∘) *dūtāvās* दूतावास
Consumer (m∘) *upa-bhoktā* उपभोक्ता
Consumption (m∘) *upabhog* उपभोग
Contact (m∘) *sparśha, sampark* स्पर्श, संपर्क
Container (n∘) *pātra* पात्र
Contamination (n∘) *dūṣhaṇ* दूषण
Contemporary (adj∘) *samakālīn* समकालीन
Contempt (m∘) *apamān* अपमान
Contension (m∘) *saṅgharṣha* संघर्ष
Content (adj∘) *santuṣhṭa* संतुष्ट
Contest (f∘) *spardhā* स्पर्धा
Context (m∘) *sandarbha* संदर्भ
Continent (m∘) *khaṇḍa* खंड
Contingent (adj∘) *sambhāvit* संभावित
Continue (v∘) *surū ṭhevṇe* सुरू ठेवणे*
Continuity (f∘) *akhaṇḍtā* अखंडता
Continuous (adj∘) *akhaṇḍ* अखंड
Contract (m∘) *karār* करार
Contractor (m∘) *ṭhekedār* ठेकेदार
Contrary (adj∘) *viparīt* विपरीत
Contrast (n∘) *vaiṣhamya* वैषम्य
Contribution (n∘) *yogdān* योगदान
Control (n∘) *niyantraṇ* नियंत्रण
Controversy (m∘) *vād* वाद
Convenience (f∘) *sukhsoy* सुखसोय
Convenient (adj∘) *upayukta* उपयुक्त
Convention (m∘) *sammelan,* (f∘) *sabhā* सम्मेलन, सभा
Conversation (m∘) *vārtālāp* वार्तालाप
Conversion (n∘) *parivartan* परिवर्तन
Convert (v∘) *badalṇe** बदलणे*
Convict (m∘) *aparādhī, doṣhī* अपराधी, दोषी
Cook (v∘) *shijvaṇe* शिजवणे*
Cool (adj∘) *thaṇḍā* थंड
Cooperation (m∘) *sahayog* सहयोग
Copper (n∘) *tāmbe* ताबे
Copy (f∘) mimic *nakkal* नक्कल; (f∘) notebook *vahī* वही; (v∘) *nakkal karṇe* नकल क∘*
Cord (m∘) *tār,* (f∘) *dorī* तार, दोरी
Coriander (m∘) *sāmbār* सांबार
Corn (m∘) *makā* मका
Corner (m∘) *koprā* कोपरा
Corporation (n∘) *nigam* निगम
Corpse (n∘) *pret, śhav* प्रेत, शव
Correct (adj∘) *ṭhīk karṇe, barobar karṇe* ठीक क∘, बरोबर क∘; (adj∘) *ṭhīk, barobar* ठीक, बरोबर
Correction (f∘) *śhuddhi* शुद्धि
Corrupt (adj∘) *bhraṣṭa* भ्रष्ट
Corruption (m∘) *bhrāṣhṭāchār* भ्रष्टाचार
Cosmatics (n∘) *saundarya prasādhan* सौंदर्य प्रसाधन
Cosmos (n∘) *brahmāṇḍ* ब्रह्मांड
Cost (m∘) *kharcha,* (f∘) *kimmat* खर्च, किम्मत

adj∘ = Adjective, adv∘ = Adverb; *conj.* = Conjunction, f∘ = Feminine gender, *ind.* = Indeclinable, m∘ = Masculine gender, n∘ = Neuter gender, pl∘ = Plural

Costly (adj∘) *mahāg* महाग

Costume (m∘) *pos̓hāk* पोशाक

Cot (f∘) *khāṭ, bāj* खाट, बाज

Cottage (f∘) *jhopaḍī, kuṭi* झोपडी, कुटि

Cotton (f∘) *ruī,* (m∘) *kāpus* रुई, कापुस

Couch (m∘) *palaṅg* पलंग

Could (v∘) *s̓hakṇe* शकणे

Council (f∘) *parishad* परिषद्

Counsel (f∘) *sallā* सल्ला; (v∘) *samjāvṇe* समजावणे*

Count (v∘) *mojṇe* मोजणे*

Country (m∘) *des̓h* देश

Couple (n∘) *yugma, joḍpe* युग्म, जोडपे

Courage (n∘) *sāhas* साहस

Court (f∘) *kacherī,* (n∘) *nyāyālay* कचेरी, न्यायालय

Courtious (adj∘) *bhadra* भद्र

Courtsy (n∘) *saujanya,* (m∘) *s̓hishṭāchār* सौजन्य, शिष्टाचार

Cousult (v∘) *sallā gheṇe* सल्ला घेणे*

Cousultation (f∘) *sallā* सल्ला

Cover (n∘) *jhākaṇ, āvaraṇ* झाकण, आवरण

Cover (v∘) *jhākaṇe* झाकणे*

Covert (adj∘) *gupta* गुप्त

Covet (v∘) *lalachāvṇe* ललचावणे

Cow (f∘) *gāy* गाय

Coward (adj∘) *bhyāḍ* भ्याड

Crab (m∘) *khekḍā* खेकडा

Crack (f∘) *bheg, chīr* (m∘) *taḍā* भेग, चीर, तडा

Cradle (m∘) *palṇā* पाळणा

Craft (f∘) *kalā* कला

Cram (v∘) *ṭhūsṇe* ठूसणे*

Cramp (f∘) *vaḷ* वळ

Crane (m∘) *baglā, sāras* बगळा, सारस

Crash (f∘) *ṭakkar* टक्कर

Crave (f∘) *hāv* हाव

Crease (f∘) *ghaḍī* घडी

Creation (f∘) *utpatti, sṛshṭi* उत्पत्ति; सृष्टि

Creative (adj∘) *utpādak* उत्पादक

Creativity (n∘) *utpādan* उत्पादन

Creator (m∘) *kartā* कर्ता

Creature (m∘) *prāṇī, jīv* प्राणी, जीव

Credible (adj∘) *vis̓hvasanīya* विश्वसनीय

Credit (f∘) *pratīti* प्रतीति

Creditor (m∘) *ruṇadātā* ऋणदाता

Credulity (n∘) *bhoḷēpaṇ* भोळेपण

Creduluous (adj∘) *bhoḷā* भोळा

Creed (m∘) *pantha, dharma* पंथ, धर्म

Creek (m∘) *nālā* नाला

Creep (v∘) *reṅgṇe* रेंगणे

Creeper (f∘) *latā, vel* लता, वेल

Cremation (n∘) *dahan* दहन

Crime (m∘) *aprādh* अपराध

Criminal (m∘) *aparādhī* अपराधी

Crimson (adj∘) *kirmijī* किरमिजी

Crinkle (f∘) *vaḷī* वळी

Cripple (m∘) *apaṅg* अपंग

Crippled (adj∘) *lūlā* लूला

Crisis (n∘) *saṅkaṭ* संकट

Crisp (adj∘) *kurkurā* कुरकुरा

Critic (m∘) *ṭīkākār, nindak* टीकाकार, निंदक

Criticism (f∘) *nindā, ālochanā* निंदा, आलोचना

Crocodile (m∘) *magar* मगर

Crook (m∘) *dhūrta* धूर्त

Crooked (adj∘) *kapaṭī, beīmān* कपटी, बेईमान

Crop (n∘) *pīk* पीक

Cross (v∘) *pār karṇe* पार क∘*

Crow (m∘) *kāvḷā* कावळा

Crowd (f∘) *bhīḍ, gardī* भीड, गर्दी

Cruel (adj∘) *krūr, nirday* क्रूर, निर्दय

Cruelty (f∘) *krūratā* क्रुरता

Crush (v∘) *kuchalṇe* कुचलणे*

Cry (n∘) *raḍṇe* रडणे; (v∘) *raḍṇe* रडणे

Crystal (m∘) *sphaṭik* स्फटिक

Cube (m∘) *ghana* घन

Cubic (adj∘) *ghanākār* घनाकार

Cuckoo (f∘) *kokiḷā* कोकिळा

Cucumber (f∘) *kakḍī* काकडी

Cue (m∘) *saṅket, is̓hārā* संकेत, इशारा

Culmination (f∘) *parākashṭhā* पराकाष्ठा

Culprit (m∘) *doshī, aprādhī* दोषी, अपराधी

Cultivation (f∘) *s̓hetī* शेती

Cultural (adj∘) *sānskrutik* सांस्कृतिक

Culture (f∘) *sanskruti* संस्कृति

Culvert (m∘) *nālā* नाला

Cumbersome (adj∘) *kaṭhiṇ, bhārī* कठिण, भारी

Cumbustible (adj∘) *jwālāgrahī* ज्वालाग्रही

Cumulative (adj∘) *sañchit* संचित

Cunning (adj∘) *dhūrta, chatur* धूर्त, चतुर

Cup (m∘) *pyālā* प्याला

Curable (adj∘) *sādhya* साध्य

Curd (m∘) *dahī* दही

Cure (m∘) *upchār* उपचार

Curiosity (n∘) *kutuhal* कुतुहल

Curious (adj∘) *utsuk* उत्सुक

Curl (n∘) *vaḷaṇ,* (f∘) *mod* वळण, मोड

Curly (adj∘) *vaḷaṇdār* वळणदार

Currency (f∘) *mudrā* मुद्रा

Current (adj∘) *vartamān, prachalit* वर्तमान, प्रचलित; (m∘) *pravāha* प्रवाह

Curriculum (m∘) *pāṭhyakram* पाठ्यक्रम

Curry (f∘) *bhājī* भाजी

Curse (m∘) *s̓hāp* शाप

Curtail (v∘) *ghaṭavaṇe* घटवणे*

Curtain (m∘) *paḍadā* पडदा

Curve (m∘) *vāk, moḍ* वाक, मोड

Curved (adj∘) *vakra* वक्र

Cushion (f∘) *gādī* गादी

Custard apple (m∘) *sītāfaḷ* सीताफळ

Custodian (m∘) *rakshak* रक्षक

Custody (m∘) *tābā,* (f∘) *kaid* ताबा, कैद

Customer (m∘) *girhāhik, grāhak* गिऱ्हाइक, ग्राहक

Cut, bite, cut (v∘) *chavṇe, kāpṇe* चावणे, कापणे*

Cute (adj∘) *sundar* सुंदर

Cycle (m∘) *kram* क्रम

Cyclone (m∘) *chakravāt* चक्रवात

D

Dad, Daddy (m∘) *vaḍīl, bābā* वडील, बाबा

Daggar (f∘) *surī* सुरी

Daily (adj∘) *dainik* दैनिक; (adv∘) *pratidin,*

adj∘ = Adjective, adv∘ = Adverb; *conj.* = Conjunction, f∘ = Feminine gender, *ind.* = Indeclinable, m∘ = Masculine gender, n∘ = Neuter gender, pl∘ = Plural

nitya, roj प्रतिदिन, नित्य, रोज

Dairy (n∘) *dugdhālay* दुग्धालय

Dall (f∘) *bāhulī* बाहुली

Dam (m∘) *bāndh* बांध

Damage (n∘) *nuksān,* (f∘) *hāni* नुक्सान, हानि

Damnation (f∘) *kharābī* खराबी

Damp (adj∘) *damaṭ, olsar* दमट, ओलसर

Dampness (m∘) *olāvā* ओलावा

Dance (m∘) *nāch,* (n∘) *nrutya* नाच, नृत्य; (v∘) *nāchaṇe* नाचणे

Dancer (f∘) *nartakī* नर्तकी

Danger (m∘) *dhokā,* (n∘) *saṅkaṭ* धोका, संकट

Dangerous (adj∘) *bhayankar* भयंकर

Dangle (v∘) *laṭakṇe* लटकणे

Dare (v∘) *dhajṇe* धजणे

Daring (adj∘) *sāhasī, niḍar* साहसी, निडर

Dark (adj∘) *gard; kāḷā* गर्द; काळा

Dark (m∘) *āndhār* आंधार

Darling (adj∘) *priya* प्रिय

Dash (v∘) *jhapaṭṇe* झपटणे

Date (f∘) *tithi, tārīkh* तिथि, तारीख

Daughter (f∘) *mulgī* मुलगी

Daughter-in-law (f∘) *sūn* सून

Dawn (f∘) *prabhāt, sakāḷ* प्रभात, सकाळ

Day (m∘) *vār, divas* वार, दिवस

Day after tomorrow(adv∘) *paravā* परवा

Day before yesterday (adv∘) *paravā* परवा

Dead (adj∘) *mrut, melelē* मृत, मेलेला

Deadly (adj∘) *ghātak* घातक

Deaf (adj∘) *bahrā, badhir* बहरा, बधिर

Deal (m∘) *samjhautā* समझौता

Deal (v∘) *nipaṭṇe* निपटणे*

Dealing (m∘) *vyavahār* व्यवहार

Dear (adj∘) *pyāra, laḍkā* प्रिय, लाडका

Dearth (f∘) *kamī* कमी

Death (m∘) *mrutyu* (n∘) *maraṇ* मृत्यु, मरण

Debacle (f∘) *hār* हार

Debanture (n∘) *ruṇapatra* ऋणपत्र

Debate (m∘) *vādvivād* वाद-विवाद

Debris (m∘) *kacharā* कचरा

Debt (n∘) *ruṇ, udhār, karj* ऋण, उधार, कर्ज

Decade (n∘) *daśhak* दशक

Decay (m∘) hrās, (f∘) *avanati* ह्रास, अवनति

Decay (v∘) *saḍṇe* सडणे

Deceased (adj∘) *mrut, melelā* मृत, मेलेला

Deceit (m∘) *dhokā,* (f∘) *beīmāmī* धोका, बेईमानी

Deceive (v∘) *dhokā deṇe* धोका देणे*

Decency (m∘) *śhiśhṭāchār* शिष्टाचार

Decent (adj∘) *śhiśhṭa, uchit* शिष्ट, उचित

Deception (f∘) *dhokebājī* धोकेबाजी

Deceptive (adj∘) *dhokebāj* धोकेबाज

Decide (n∘) *inaśhchit karṇe* निश्चिय क∘

Decimal (adj∘) *daśhāmśha* दशांश

Decision (m∘) *nirṇay* निर्णय

Decisive (adj∘) *nirṇayātmak* निर्णयात्मक

Declaration (f∘) *ghoṣhaṇā* घोषणा

Declare (v∘) *ghoṣhit karṇe* घोषित क∘*

Decline (f∘) *avanati,* (m∘) *kṣhaya* अवनति, क्षय; v∘) decrease *ghaṭṇe* घटणे

Decompose (v∘) *saḍṇe* सडणे

Decor (f∘) *sajāvaṭ* सजावट

Decorate (v∘) *sajavṇe* सजवणे

Decoration (f∘) *sajāvaṭ* सजावट

Decorative (adj∘) *sajāvaṭī* सजावटी

Decoy (m∘) *fāsā* फासा

Decrease (v∘) *ghaṭṇe* घटणे

Dedication (n∘) *samarpaṇ* समर्पण

Deduct (v∘) *kamī karṇe* कमी क∘

Deduction (f∘) *kamī, kapāt* कमी, कपात

Deed (n∘) *kārya, kām* कार्य, काम

Deep (adj∘) *khol, gahan* खोल, गहन

Deer (m∘) *hariṇ* हरिण

Defamation (f∘) *badnāmī* बदनामी

Defeat (v∘) *hārṇe, jinkṇe* हारणे; जिंकणे*

Defect (m∘) *doṣh* (f∘) *kharābī* दोष, खराबी

Defence (f∘) *rakṣhā* रक्षा

Defend (v∘) *rakṣha karṇe* रक्षा क∘*

Defer (v∘) *sthagit larṇe* स्थगित क∘*

Defiance (m∘) *virodh, iṅkār* विरोध, इनकार

Deficiency (f∘) *kamī,* (m∘) *abhāv* कमी, अभाव

Deficit (f∘) *kamī,* (m∘) *ghāṭā* कमी, घाटा

Definite (adj∘) *pakkā, nischit* पक्का, निश्चित

Definition (f∘) *vyākhyā* व्याख्या

Deformation (m∘) *bighāḍ,* (f∘) *vikṛti* बिघाड, विकृति

Defraud (v∘) *ṭhagṇe* ठगणे*

Defunct (adj∘) *anupayukta* अनुपयुक्त

Deity (f∘) *devtā* देवता

Dejected (adj∘) *nirāśh* निराश

Dejection (f∘) *nirāśhā* निराशा

Delay (m∘) *uśhīr* उशीर

Delhi (f∘) *dillī* दिल्ली

Delicate (adj∘) *nājuk* नाजुक

Delicious (adj∘) *svādiṣṭa* स्वादिष्ट

Delight (f∘) *prasannatā* प्रसन्नता

Deluge (f∘) *pūr* पूर

Delusion (f∘) *bhrānti,* (m∘) *bhram* भ्रांति, भ्रम

Demand (f∘) *māgaṇī* मागणी; (v∘) *māgṇe* मागणे*

Demeanour (n∘) *ācharaṇ* आचरण

Demise (m∘) *mrutyu,* (n∘) *maraṇ* मृत्यु, मरण

Democracy (n∘) *loktantra* लोकतंत्र

Demolish (v∘) *pāḍṇe* पाडणे*

Demon (m∘) *rākṣhas* राक्षस

Demonstrate (v∘) *dākhavṇe* दाखवणे*

Demonstration (n∘) *pradarśhan* प्रदर्शन

Demotion (f∘) *padāvnati* पदावनति

Den (f∘) *guhā* गुहा

Dense (adj∘) *dāṭ, ghana* दाट, घन

Density (n∘) *ghanatva* घनत्व

Dent (m∘) *pochā* पोचा

Dentist (m∘) *dant-vaidya* दंत-वैद्य

Deny (v∘) *nākārṇe* नाकारणे*

Depart (v∘) *prasthān karṇe, jāṇe* प्रस्थान क∘, जाणे

Department (m∘) *vibhāg* विभाग

Departure (m∘) *prasthān* प्रस्थान

Depend (v∘) *bharavsā karṇe* भरवसा क∘*

Dependent (adj∘) *āśhrit* आश्रित

Deplorable (adj∘) *nindanīya* निंदनीय

Deplore (v∘) *nindā karṇe* निंदा क∘*

Deposit (f∘) *jamā rakkam* जमा रक्कम

Deposit (v∘) *jamā karṇe* जमा क∘*

adj∘ = Adjective, adv∘ = Adverb; *conj.* = Conjunction, f∘ = Feminine gender, *ind.* = Indeclinable, m∘ = Masculine gender, n∘ = Neuter gender, pl∘ = Plural

Depot (n∘) *godām* गोदाम

Depression (f∘) *udāsī;* (m∘ dent) *khalgā* उदासी; खळगा

Depth (f∘) *kholī* खोली

Descend (v∘) *utarṇe* उतरणे

Describe (v∘) *varṇan karṇe* वर्णन क∘*

Description (n∘) *varṇan* वर्णन

Desert (n∘) *vaḷvanṭ* वाळवंट

Deserve (v∘) *lāyak hoṇe* लायक हो∘

Design (f∘) *rūpreṣhā* रूपरेषा

Designation (n∘) *pad* पद

Desirable (adj∘) *iṣhṭa* इष्ट

Desire, want (f∘) *ichhā* इच्छा; to want (v∘) *chāhaṇe* चाहणे*

Desk, table (m∘) *mej* मेज

Despair (f∘) *inarāśhā* निराशा

Desperate (adj∘) *nirāśh* निराश

Despise (v∘) *tiraskār karṇe* तिरस्कार क∘*

Despite (prep∘) *śhivāy* शिवाय

Despondent (adj∘) *udās* उदास

Destination (n∘) *lakṣhya* लक्ष्य

Destiny (f∘) *niyati,* (n∘) *bhāgya* नियति, भाग्य

Destroy (v∘) *naṣṭa karṇe* नष्ट क∘*

Destruction (m∘) *vināśh* विनाश

Destructive (adj∘) *nāśhkārī* नाशकारी

Detach (v∘) *alag karṇe* अलग क∘*

Detail (f∘) *tapshil* तपशिल

Detariorate (v∘) *kṣhaya hoṇe* क्षय हो∘

Detarioration (m∘) *kṣhaya* क्षय

Detect (v∘) *pattā lāvṇe* पत्ता लावणे*

Detective (m∘) *jāsūs, her* जासूस, हेर

Detention (f∘) *kaid* कैद

Determination (m∘) *saṅkalpa* संकल्प

Determine (v∘) *ṭharavṇe* ठरवणे*

Deterrent (adj∘) *nivārak* निवारक

Detest (v∘) *ghruṇā karṇe* घृणा क∘*

Detestation (f∘) *ghruṇa* घृणा

Detonation (m∘) *visphoṭ* विस्फोट

Detriment (f∘) *hāni* हानि

Devastation (f∘) *nāsāḍī* नासाडी

Development (m∘) *vikās* विकास

Deviate (v∘) *vaḷṇe* वळणे

Device (f∘) *yukti,* (n∘) *sādhan* युक्ति, साधन

Devil (m∘) *duṣhṭātmā* दुष्टात्मा

Devious (adj∘) *beīmān* बेईमान

Devoid (adj∘) *rahit* रहित

Devote (v∘) *arpit karṇe* अर्पित क∘*

Devotee (m∘) *bhakta* भक्त

Devotion (f∘) *bhakti* भक्ति

Devour (v∘) *giṭakṇe* गिटकणे*

Devout (adj∘) *śhraddhāḷu* श्रद्धाळु

Dew (n∘) *dav* दव

Dexterity (f∘) *nipuṇatā* निपुणता

Dexterous (adj∘) *nipuṇ* निपुण

Diabetes (m∘) *madhumeh* मधुमेह

Diagram (f∘) *ākruti* आकृति

Dialogue (n∘) *sambhāṣhaṇ,* (m∘) *vārtālāp* संभाषण, वार्तालाप

Diameter (m∘) *vyās* व्यास

Diamond, gem (m∘) *hīrā* हीरा

Diarrhoea (f∘) *hagvaṇ* हगवण

Diary (f∘) *rojniśhī* रोजनिशी

Dice (m∘) *fāsā* फासा

Dictator (m∘) *mukhtyār* मुखत्यार

Dictionary (m∘) *śhabda kośh* शब्दकोश

Die (v∘) *maraṇe* मरणे

Diet (f∘) *pathya* पथ्य

Difference (m∘) *antar,* (f∘) *bhinnatā* अंतर, भिन्नता

Different (adj∘) *bhinna, alag* भिन्न, अलग

Difficult (adj∘) *kaṭhiṇ* कठिण

Difficulty (f∘) *kaṭhiṇtā* कठिणता

Dig (v∘) *khodṇe* खोदणे*

Digest (v∘) *pachavṇe* पचवणे*; summary (m∘) *sārāṁśha* सारांश

Digestion (n∘) *pachan* पचन

Digit (m∘) *aṅk, ākḍā* अंक, आकडा

Dignity (f∘) *pratiṣhṭhā,* (m∘) *mān* प्रतिष्ठा, मान

Dilemma (f∘) *kachāṭī,* (m∘) *pech* कचाटी, पेच

Diligent (adj∘) *sāvadhān* सावधान

Dilute (adj∘) *patlā* पतला

Dim (adj∘) *andhuk* अंधुक

Dimension (m∘) *vistār* विस्तार

Diminish (v∘) *ghaṭṇe, kamī hoṇe* घटणे, कमी हो∘

Dine (v∘) *bhojan karṇe* भोजन क∘*

Dinghy (f∘) *hoḍī* होडी

Dinner (n∘) *bhojan* भोजन

Dip (v∘) *buḍavṇe* बुडवणे*

Diploma (n∘) *pramāṇ-patra* प्रमाण-पत्र

Diplomacy (f∘) *kūṭnīti* कूटनीति

Dire (adj∘) *bhayaṅkar* भयंकर

Direct (adj∘) *saraḷ* सरळ

Direction (f∘) *diśhā* दिशा

Director (m∘) *nirdeśhak, digdarśhak* निर्देशक, दिग्दर्शक

Directory (f∘) *sūchī* सूची

Disappear (v∘) *gāyab hoṇe, adruśhya hoṇe* गायब हो∘, अदृश्य हो∘

Disappointment (f∘) *nirāśhā* निराशा

Disapprove (v∘) *nākārṇe* नाकारणे*

Disarmed (adj∘) *nihśhastra* नि:शस्त्र

Disassociation (f∘) *asahamati* असहमति

Disaster (f∘) *durghaṭnā, āfat* दुर्घटना, आफत

Disbelief (m∘) *aviśhvās* अविश्वास

Discard (v∘) *tyāgṇe* त्यागणे*

Discern (v∘) *jāṇaṇe* जाणणे*

Disciple (m∘) *anuyāyī* अनुयायी

Discipline (n∘) *anuśhāsan* अनुशासन

Disclose (v∘) *prakaṭ karṇe* प्रकट क∘*

Discomfort (f∘) *asvasthatā* अस्वस्थता

Disconcert (f∘) *gaḍbaḍ* गडबड

Disconnected (adj∘) *alag, pruthak* अलग, पृथक्

Discord (f∘) *asahamati* असहमति

Discount (f∘) *sūṭ, kapāt* सूट, कपात

Discouraged (adj∘) *hatotsāhit* हतोत्साहित

Discourse (n∘) *pravachan* प्रवचन

Discourteous (adj∘) *abhadra, aśhiṣhṭa* अभद्र, अशिष्ट

Discover (v∘) *śhodhṇe* शोधणे*

Discovery (m∘) *śhodh* शोध

Discreet (adj∘) *satark, sāvadhān* सतर्क, सावधान

Discrepancy (n∘) *antar* अंतर

adj∘ = Adjective, adv∘ = Adverb; *conj.* = Conjunction, f∘ = Feminine gender, *ind.* = Indeclinable, m∘ = Masculine gender, n∘ = Neuter gender, pl∘ = Plural

Discretion (m∘) *vivek* विवेक

Discrimanation (m∘) *bhedbhāva* भेदभाव

Discriminate (v∘) *bhed karṇe* भेद क∘*

Discus (m∘) *vichār-ivamars'ha* विचार-विमर्श

Disease (m∘) *rog,* (f∘) *bīmārī* रोग, बीमारी

Disgrace (f∘) *badnāmī* बदनामी

Disgruntled (adj∘) *nārāj* नाराज

Disguise (n∘) *soṅg* सोंग

Disgust (m∘) *khed,* (f∘) *jugupsā* खेद, जुगुप्सा

Dish (f∘) *bas'hī* बशी

Dishonest (adj∘) *beīmān, dhokebāj* बेईमान, धोकेबाज

Dishonour (m∘) *badnāmī* बदनामी

Disillusion (m∘) *bhram* भ्रम

Dislike (f∘) *nāpasantī* नापसंती

Disloyal (adj∘) *nimakharām* निमकहराम

Dismay (m∘) *udveg* उद्वेग

Dismiss (v∘) *barkhāst karṇe, badtarf karṇe* बरखास्त क∘, बडतर्फ क∘*

Disobey (v∘) *ādnyā bhaṅg karṇe* आज्ञा भंग क∘*

Disorder (f∘) *gaḍbaḍī* गडबडी

Disparity (f∘) *asamānatā* असमानता

Dispatch (v∘) *pāthavṇe* पाठवणे*

Dispensary (m∘) *davākhānā* दवाखाना

Dispersion (n∘) *vitaraṇ* वितरण

Display (n∘) *pradars'han* प्रदर्शन; (v∘) *dākhavna* दाखवणे*

Displeasure (f∘) *nārājagī,* (m∘) *asantoṣh* नाराजगी, असंतोष

Disposition (f∘) *chitta-vrutti* चित्त-वृत्ति

Dispute (m∘) *mata-bhed* मत-भेद

Disregard (f∘) *upekṣhā* उपेक्षा

Disrepute (f∘) *badnāmī* बदनामी

Disrespect (m∘) *anādar* अनादर

Disrupt (v∘) *bhaṅg karṇe* भंग क∘*

Dissatisfaction (f∘) *nārājagī,* (m∘) *asantoṣh* नाराजगी, असंतोष

Disseration (m∘) *prabandh* प्रबंध

Dissimilar (adj∘) *asamān* असमान

Dissolve (v∘) *virghaḷṇe* विरघळणे

Dissuade (v∘) *parāvrutta karṇe* परावृत्त क∘*

Distance (n∘) *antar* अंतर

Distant (adj∘) *dūrchā* दूरचा

Distinct (adj∘) *spaṣhṭa* स्पष्ट

Distortion (f∘) *vikruti* विकृति

Distraction (n∘) *vighna* विघ्न

Distress (f∘) *pīḍā* पीडा

Distribution (n∘) *vitaraṇ* वितरण

District (m∘) *jilhā* जिल्हा

Distrust (f∘) *s'haṅkā* शंका

Disturbance (f∘) *as'hānti, dhumākuḷ* अशांति, धुमाकुळ

Dive (f∘) *buḍī* बुडी

Diverse (adj∘) *vividh* विविध

Diversity (f∘) *vividhatā* विविधता

Divesion (n∘) *vibhājan* विभाजन

Divide (v∘) *vibhājan karṇe* विभाजन क∘*

Divine (adj∘) *daivī* दैवी

Divinity (f∘) *devatā* देवता

Divisive (adj∘) *vibhājak* विभाजक

Divorce (m∘) *ghaṭasphoṭ* घटस्फोट

Dizzyness (f∘) *bhovaḷ, gherī* भोवळ, घेरी

Do (v∘) *karaṇe* क∘*

Doctor (m∘) *vaidya* वैद्य

Document (m∘) *dastaivaj* दस्तऐवज

Doe (f∘) *hariṇī* हरिणी

Dog (m∘) *kutrā* कुत्रा

Dogmā (m∘) *dharmādesh* धर्मादेश

Dominion (n∘) *svāmitva* स्वामित्व

Donate (v∘) *dān karṇe* दान क∘*

Donation (n∘) *dān* दान

Donkey (n∘) *gādhav* गाढव

Donor (m∘) *dātā* दाता

Door (m∘) *darawājā* दरवाजा

Dot (f∘) *bindī,* (m∘) *bindu* बिंदी, बिंदु

Double (adj∘) *duherī* दुहेरी

Doubt (m∘) *sandeha* संदेह

Doubtful (adj∘) *sandigdha* संदिग्ध

Doubtless (adj∘) *asandigdha* असंदिग्ध

Dove (n∘) *kabūtar* कबूतर

Down (adv∘) *khālī* खाली

Doze (v∘) *ḍulkī ghenā* डुलकी घेणे*

Dozen (adj∘) *dazan* डझन

Drab (adj∘) *niras* निरस

Drag (v∘) *ghasīṭṇe* घसीटणे*

Drain (f∘) *nālī* नाली

Drama (n∘) *nāṭak* नाटक

Draw (v∘) *kāḍhṇe* काढणे*

Dream (n∘) *swapna* स्वप्न

Dreñch (v∘) *bhijavṇe* भिजवणे*

Dress (m∘) *pos'hākh* पोशाख

Drink (n∘) *peya* पेय; (v∘) *piṇe* पिणे*

Drip (v∘) *ṭapkaṇe* टपकणे

Drive (v∘) *chalavaṇe* चालवणे*

Driver (m∘) *hchālak* चालक

Drizzle (f∘) *zirmir* झिरमिर

Droop (v∘) *jhukṇe* झुकणे

Drop (m∘) *themb* थेंब

Drug (n∘) *auṣhadh* औषध

Drum (m∘) *tablā* तबला

Drunk (adj∘) *madhos'h* मदहोश

Dry (adj∘) *sūklelā* सुकलेला; (v∘) *sūkṇe, sukavṇ** सुकणे, सुकवणे*

Duck (n∘) *badak* बदक

Due (adj∘) *deya* देय

Duel (n∘) *dvandva* द्वंद्व

Dull (adj∘) *mand, sust* मंद, सुस्त

Dumb (adj∘) *mukā* मुका

Dung (m∘) *s'heṇ* शेण

Duplicate (f∘) *pratikruti* प्रतिकृति

Duplicity (m∘) *chhaḷ* छळ

Dust (f∘) *dhūḷ* धूळ

Duty (m∘) *kartavya, kārya* कर्तव्य, कार्य

Dye, paint (v∘) *raṅgavṇe* रंगवणे*

Dynasty (m∘) *rājvams'ha* राजवंश

Dysentry (m∘) *hagvaṇ* हगवण

E

Each (adj∘) *pratyek, harek* प्रत्येक, हरेक

Eager (adj∘) *utsuk, ātur* उत्सुक, आतुर

Eagle (f∘) *ghār* घार

Ear (m∘) *kān* कान

Early (adv∘) *lavakar, agodar, ādhī* लवकर, अगोदर, आधी

Earn (v∘) *kamāvṇe* कमावणे*

Earnest (adj∘) *gambhīr* गंभीर

adj∘ = Adjective, adv∘ = Adverb; *conj.* = Conjunction, f∘ = Feminine gender, *ind.* = Indeclinable, m∘ = Masculine gender, n∘ = Neuter gender, pl∘ = Plural

Earning (f∘) *kamāī, miḷkat* कमाई, मिळकत
Earth (f∘) *jamīn, pruthvī* जमीन, पृथ्वी
Earthquake (m∘) *bhūkamp* भूकंप
Ease (n∘) *saukhya* सौख्य
East (f∘) *pūrva* पूर्व
Easy (adj∘) *sopā* सोपा
Eat (v∘) *khāṇe* खाणे*
Eccentric (adj∘) *laharī* लहरी
Economic (adj∘) *ārthik* आर्थिक
Economics (n∘) *arthaśhastra* अर्थशास्त्र
Economy (f∘) *kāṭkasar* काटकसर
Eczema (m∘) *charma rog* चर्म रोग
Edge (m∘) *kāṭh, kinārā* काठ, किनारा
Edible (adj∘) *khādya* खाद्य
Edifice (m∘) *prāsād,* (n∘) *bhavan* प्रासाद, भवन
Edit (v∘) *sampādan karṇe* संपादन क∘*
Edition (n∘) *sanskaraṇ* संस्करण
Editor (m∘) *sampādak* संपादक
Editorial (n∘) *sampādakīya* संपादकीय
Education (n∘) *ṣhikṣhaṇ* शिक्षण
Eecology (n∘) *paryāvaraṇ* पर्यावरण
Eemerge (v∘) *uday hoṇe* उदय हो∘
Effect (m∘) *prabhāv, pariṇām* प्रभाव, परिणाम
Effective (adj∘) *prabhāvī* प्रभावी
Efficiency (f∘) *kṣhamatā* क्षमता
Efficient (m∘) *sakṣham* सक्षम
Effort (m∘) *prayās, prayatna* प्रयास, प्रयत्न
Egg (n∘) *aṇḍe* अंडे
Eggplant (n∘) *vānge* वांगे
Ego (m∘) *ahamkār* अहंकार
Egocentric (adj∘) *ahamkārī* अहंकारी
Eight (adj∘) *āṭh* आठ
Eighteen (adj∘) *aṭharā* अठरा
Eighty (adj∘) *anśhī* अंशी
Either (pron∘) *pratyek* प्रत्येक
Elaboration (m∘) *vistār* विस्तार
Elapse (v∘) *gujarṇe* गुजरणे
Elastic (adj∘) *lavachīk* लवचीक
Elbow (n∘) *dhopar* ढोपर
Elder (adj∘) *jyeṣhtha* ज्येष्ठ
Elderly (adj∘) *vaḍīl* वडील
Eldest (adj∘) *agraj* अग्रज
Elect (v∘) *nivaḍṇe* निवडणे*
Election (m∘) *nivaḍṇūk* निवडणूक
Electricity (f∘) *vīj vidyut* वीज, विद्युत
Elegant (adj∘) *lalit* ललित
Elegible (m∘) *yodnya* योग्य
Element (n∘) *tattva* तत्त्व
Elementary (adj∘) *prārambhik* प्रारंभिक
Elemiante (v∘) *haṭavṇe* हटवणे*
Elephant (m∘) *hatthī* हत्ती
Eleven (adj∘) *akrā* अकरा
Elimination (m∘) *lop* लोप
Ellipse (m∘) *aṇḍākār* अंडाकार
Elocution (n∘) *vaktrutva* वक्तृत्व
Elongate (v∘) *vāḍhṇe, vāḍhavṇe** वाढणे, वाढवणे*
Elongation (f∘) *vāḍh, vruddhi* वाढ, वृद्धि
Eloquent (adj∘) *vākpaṭu* वाक्पटु
Else (adv∘) *anyathā* अन्यथा
Elsewhere (adv∘) *anyatra* अन्यत्र
Emanate (v∘) *nighaṇe* निघणे
Emancipation (f∘) *mukti* मुक्ति
Embargo (f∘) *aṭkāv* अटकाव
Embark (v∘) *savār honāī* सवार हो∘*
Embassy (n∘) *dūtāvās* दूतावास
Embelish (v∘) *sajavṇe* सजवणे*
Emblem (n∘) *pratīk, chihna* प्रतीक, चिह्न
Embrace (v∘) *kavaṭāḷṇe* कवटाळणे*
Embracement (f∘) *lāj* लाज
Embryo (m∘) *bhrūṇa* भ्रूण
Emergency (m∘) *āṇībāṇī, āpatkāḷ* आणीबाणी, आपतकाळ
Emigrant (adj∘) *āvāsī* आवासी
Emigration (m∘) *āvās* आवास
Emission (n∘) *nissaraṇ* निस्सरण
Emotion (m∘) *manobhāv* मनोभाव
Empathy (f∘) *sahānubhūti* सहानुभूति
Emperor (m∘) *mahārājā* महाराजा
Emphasis (n∘) *mahattva* महत्त्व
Empire (n∘) *sāmrājya* साम्राज्य
Employment (f∘) *naukarī,* (n∘) *kām* नौकरी, काम
Empty (adj∘) *rikāmā* रिकामा
Encircle (v∘) *gherṇe* घेरणे*
Encore (int∘) *punhā* पुन्हा
Encounter (m∘) *sāmanā* सामना
Encouragement (n∘) *protsāhan* प्रोत्साहन
Encyclopedia (m∘) *viśhvakośh* विश्वकोश
End (m∘) *ant, śhevaṭ* अंत, शेवट; (v∘) *samāpta karṇe* समाप्त क∘*
Endavour (m∘) *prayās* प्रयास
Endless (adj∘) *anthīn* अंतहीन
Endorsement (n∘) *samarthan* समर्थन
Endurance (f∘) *sahanśhakti* सहनशक्ति
Endure (v∘) *sahaṇe* सहणे*
Enemy (m∘) *śhatru* शत्रु
Energetic (adj∘) *utsāhī* उत्साही
Enfold (v∘) *lapeṭṇe* लपेटणे*
Enforce (v∘) *lāgū karṇe* लागू क∘*
Engage (v∘) *guntaṇe* गुंतणे*
Engagement (m∘) *karār, vāydā* करार, वायदा
Engine (m∘) *yantra, iñjan* यंत्र, इंजन
Engineer (m∘) *abhiyantā* अभियंता
English (adj∘) *ingrajī* इंग्रजी
Engrave (v∘) *korṇe* कोरणे*
Engrossed (adj∘) *tallīn* तल्लीन
Engrossment (f∘) *tallinatā* तल्लीनता
Enhance (v∘) *vāḍhaṇe, vāḍhavṇe** वाढणे, वाढवणे*
Enjoin (v∘) *lāgū karṇe* लागू क∘*
Enjoy (v∘) *upabhogṇe* उपभोगणे*
Enlarge (v∘) *vāḍhaṇe, vadhavaṇe** वाढणे, वाढवणे*
Enlighten (v∘) *prabuddha karṇe* प्रबुद्ध क∘*
Enlist (v∘) *bhartī karṇe* भरती क∘*
Enlistment (f∘) *bhartī* भरती
Enmity (n∘) *vair* वैर
Enormous (adj∘) *viśhāl* विशाल
Enough (adv∘) *bas, pure* बस, पुरे
Enrichment (f∘) *samruddhī* समृद्धि
Ensure (v∘) *niśhchit karṇe* निश्चित क∘*
Enter (v∘) *praveśh karaṇe* प्रवेश क∘*
Enterprise (m∘) *udyam, udyog* उद्यम, उद्योग

adj∘ = Adjective, adv∘ = Adverb; *conj.* = Conjunction, f∘ = Feminine gender, *ind.* = Indeclinable, m∘ = Masculine gender, n∘ = Neuter gender, pl∘ = Plural

Entertainment (n∘) *manorañjan* मनोरंजन
Enthusiasm (m∘) *utsāha* उत्साह
Entice (v∘) *fuslāvṇe* फुसलावणे*
Entire (adj∘) *sampurṇa* संपूर्ण
Entrance, door (n∘) *dvār,* (m∘) *darvājā* द्वार, दरवाजा
Entry (m∘) *pravesh* प्रवेश
Enumerate (v∘) *gaṇaṇe* गणणे*
Envelop (m∘) *lifāfā* लिफाफा
Environment (n∘) *vātāvaraṇ* वातावरण
Envoy (m∘) *dūt* दूत
Envy (f∘) *īrṣhā* ईर्ष्या
Epic (n∘) *mahākāvya* महाकाव्य
Epidemic (f∘) *mahāmārī* महामारी
Epigram (n∘) *subhāṣhit,* (f∘) *sūkti* सुभाषित, सूक्ति
Epilogue (m∘) *upasaṁhār* उपसंहार
Episode (m∘) *vruttānt* वृत्तांत
Epithet (f∘) *upādhi* उपाधि
Epoch (n∘) *yug,* (m∘) *kāḷ* युग, काळ
Equal (adj∘) *barobar, samān* बरोबर, समान
Equality (f∘) *samānatā* समानता
Equanimity (f∘) *samabuddhi* समबुद्धि
Equation (n∘) *samīkaraṇ, sūtra* समीकरण, सूत्र
Equator (f∘) *bhūmadhya rekhā* भूमध्य रेखा
Equidistant (adj∘) *samadūrastha* समदूरस्थ
Equilateral (m∘) *sama-bhuja* समभुज
Equilibrium (n∘) *santulan* संतुलन
Equipment (n∘) *upkaraṇ, sāmān* उपकरण, सामान
Equipped (adj∘) *sajja* सज्ज
Equitable (adj∘) *uchit* उचित
Equivalent (adj∘) *barobar, samatulya* बरोबर, समतुल्य
Era (n∘) *saṁvat, yug* संवत्, युग
Erase (v∘) *miṭavṇe* मिटवणे*
Erratic (adj∘) *laharī* लहरी
Erroneous (adj∘) *chūk* चूक
Error (f∘) *chukī, bhūl* चुकी, भूल
Erudite (adj∘) *paṇḍit* पंडित
Escalate (v∘) *vāḍhaṇe, vāḍhavṇe** वाढणे, वाढवणे*
Escalator (m∘) *jinā* जिना
Escape (v∘) *nisaṭṇe* निसटणे
Especial (adj∘) *vishiṣhṭa* विशिष्ट
Espionage (f∘) *hergirī* हेरगिरी
Essay (m∘) *nibandh* निबंध
Essence (n∘) *sār, tattva* सार, तत्त्व
Establish (v∘) *sthāpan karṇe* स्थापन क∘*
Estate (f∘) *mālmattā* मालमत्ता
Estimate (m∘) *anumān, andāj* अनुमान, अंदाज
Eternal (adj∘) *nitya* नित्य
Eternally (adv∘) *nitya, sadā, nirantar* नित्य, सदा, निरंतर
Ethics (n∘) *nītishastra* नीतिशास्त्र
Ethnic (adj∘) *jātīy* जातीय
Etiquate (m∘) *ṣhiṣhṭāchār* शिष्टाचार
Evade (v∘) *ṭāḷṇe* टाळणे*
Evaluation (n∘) *mūlyāṅkan* मूल्यांकन
Evaporation (n∘) *bāṣhpibhavan* बाष्पीभवन
Eve (f∘) *pūrvasandhyā* पूर्वसंध्या
Even (adj∘) *sama, ekrūp* सम, एकरूप; (adv∘) *jarī* जरी
Even if, even though (adv∘) *yadyapi* यद्यपि
Evening (f∘) *sandhyākāḷ* संध्याकाळ
Event (f∘) *ghaṭṇā* घटणा
Ever (adv∘) *sarvadā* सर्वदा
Every (adv∘) *pratyek* प्रत्येक
Everyday (adv∘) *pratidin, roj* प्रतिदिन, रोज
Everytime (adv∘) *nehamī, hameshā* नेहमी, हमेशा
Everywhere (adv∘) *sarvatr* सर्वत्र
Evidence (n∘) *pramāṇ,* (f∘) *gavāhī* प्रमाण, गवाही
Evil (adj∘) *pāpī, duṣhṭa* पापी, दुष्ट
Evolution (m∘) *vikās* विकास
Evolve (v∘) *vikasit hoṇe* विकसित हो∘
Exact (adj∘) *tantotant* तंतोतंत
Exaggeration (f∘) *atishayokti* अतिशयोक्ति
Examination (f∘) *parīkṣhā* परीक्षा
Examine (v∘) *parakhṇe, jāchṇe* परखणे, जाचणे*
Example (m∘) *namūnā,* (n∘) *udāharaṇ* नमूना, उदाहरण
Excavation (n∘) *khodṇe* खोदणे
Exceed (v∘) *adhik hoṇe* अधिक हो∘
Excellence (f∘) *shreṣhṭhatā* श्रेष्ठता
Excellent (adj∘) *uttam* उत्तम
Except (adv∘) *atirikta, shivāy* अतिरिक्त, शिवाय
Exception (m∘) *apvād* अपवाद
Excess (f∘) *adhiktā* अधिकता
Exchange (v∘) *badalṇe* बदलणे*
Excitement (n∘) *uttejan* उत्तेजन
Exclamation (m∘) *udgār* उद्गार
Excrement (f∘) *viṣhṭhā,* (m∘) *maḷ* विष्ठा, मळ
Excuse (m∘) *bahāṇā,* (f∘) *māfī* बहाणा, माफ़ी
Execution (f∘) 1. *fāshī* (by noose) फाशी
Executive (m∘) *prabandhak* प्रबंधक
Exemption (f∘) *sūṭ, māfī* सूट, माफी
Exercise (m∘) *vyāyām,* (f∘) *kasrat* व्यायाम, कसरत
Exist (v∘) *rāhṇe, asṇe* राहणे, असणे
Expedient (adj∘) *hitkar* हितकर
Expedition (n∘) *abhiyān* अभियान
Expel (v∘) *kāḍhṇe* काढणे*
Expenditure (m∘) *kharcha* खर्च
Experience (m∘) *anubhav* अनुभव
Experient (m∘) *prayog* प्रयोग
Expert (adj∘) *nipuṇ* निपुण
Expire (v∘) *samāpta hoṇe, marṇe* समाप्त हो∘, मरणे
Explain (v∘) *samajāvṇe* समजावणे*
Explicit (adj∘) *spaṣhṭa* स्पष्ट
Exploration (m∘) *shodh* शोध
Explosion (m∘) *sphoṭ* स्फोट
Explosive (adj∘) *sphoṭak* स्फोटक
Export (f∘) *niryāt* निर्यात
Expose (v∘) *dākhavṇe* दाखवणे*
Exposure (n∘) *pradarshan* प्रदर्शन
Expression (f∘) *abhivyakti* अभिव्यक्ति
Extend (v∘) *failāṇe, pasarṇe* फैलणे, पसरणे
Extension (m∘) *vistār* विस्तार
Extensive (adj∘) *vistīrṇa* विस्तीर्ण
Extensively (adv∘) *vistrut* विस्तृत

adj∘ = Adjective, adv∘ = Adverb; *conj.* = Conjunction, f∘ = Feminine gender, *ind.* = Indeclinable, m∘ = Masculine gender, n∘ = Neuter gender, pl∘ = Plural

Extent (f◦) *sīmā* सीमा

Exterior (adj◦) *bāherī* बाहेरी

External (adj◦) *bāhya* बाह्य

Extince (adj◦) *lupta* लुप्त

Extinguish (v◦) *vizṇe, vizavṇe** विझणे, विझवणे*

Extra (adj◦) *adhik* अधिक

Extract (n◦) *sār* सार

Extraordinary (adj◦) *asādhāraṇ* असाधारण

Extravagent (adj◦) *fizūlkharchī* फिजूलखर्ची

Extreme (adj◦) *param, charam* परम, चरम

Extremist (m◦) *ugravādī* उग्रवादी

Eye (m◦) *ḍoḷā* डोळा

Eyeball (f◦) *putaḷī* पुतळी

Eyebrow (f◦) *bhuvaī* भुवई

Eyeglasses (m◦) *chaśhmā* चश्मा

Eyelid (f◦) *pāpṇī* पापणी

F

Fable (f◦) *laghukathā, nītikathā* लघुकथा, नीतिकथा

Fabric (n◦) *kāpaḍ,* (m◦) *tantu* कापड, तंतु

Fabricate (v◦) *tayār karṇe* तयार क◦*

Fabulous (adj◦) *kālpanik* काल्पनिक

Face (m◦) *cheharā* चेहरा

Facet (m◦) *pailū* पैलू

Facial (adj◦) *maukhik* मौखिक

Facility (f◦) *soy* सोय

Facinating (adj◦) *ākarṣhak* आकर्षक

Facination (n◦) *ākarṣhaṇ* आकर्षण

Fact (n◦) *tathya* तथ्य

Faction (n◦) *daḷ* दळ

Factor (m◦) *ghaṭak* घटक

Factory (m◦) *kārkhānā* कारखाना

Faculty (m◦) *vibhāg* विभाग

Fad (m◦) *nād,* (f◦) *lahar* नाद, लहर

Fade (v◦) *komejṇe* कोमेजणे

Failure (f◦) *asafalatā* असफलता

Faint (adj◦) *aspaṣhṭa* अस्पष्ट

Fair (adj◦) *surekh* सुरेख; (m◦) *meḷā* मेळा

Fairy (f◦) *parī* परी

Faith (f◦) *śhraddhā, niṣhṭhā* श्रद्धा, निष्ठा

Fake (adj◦) *naklī* नकली

Falcon (m◦) *sasāṇā* ससाणा

Fall (v◦) *paḍṇe* पडणे

Fallacy (f◦) *bhrānti* भ्रान्ति

False (adj◦) *khoṭā* खोटा

Falter (v◦) *aḍkhaḷṇe* अडखळणे

Fame (f◦) *prasiddhi, kīrti* प्रसिद्धि, कीर्ति

Famed (adj◦) *prasiddha* प्रसिद्ध

Familiar (adj◦) *parichit* परिचित

Family (m◦) *pariwār* परिवार

Famine (m◦) *akāḷ* अकाळ

Famous (adj◦) *prasiddha* प्रसिद्ध

Fan (m◦) *paṅkhā* पंखा

Fanatic (adj◦) *kaṭṭar* कट्टर

Fantastic (adj◦) *ajab, vilakṣhaṇ, asāmānya* अजब, विलक्षण, असामान्य

Fantasy (f◦) *kalpanā* कल्पना

Far (adv◦) *dūr* दूर

Farce (n◦) *soṅg, nāṭak* सोंग, नाटक

Fare (m◦) *kirāyā,* (n◦)*bhāḍe* किराया, भाडे

Farewell (m◦) *nirop* निरोप

Farm (n◦) *śhet* शेत

Farmer (m◦) *śhetkarī* शेतकरी

Fashion (f◦) *śhailī* शैली

Fast (adj◦) *jalad* जलद; (m◦) *upvās,* उपवास

Fasten (v◦) *bāndhaṇe* बांधणे*

Fat (adj◦) *laṭṭha* लट्ठ; (f◦) *charbī* चरबी

Father (m◦) *pitā, vaḍīl* पिता, वडील

Father-in-law (m◦) *sāsrā* सासरा

Fault (m◦) *doṣh, aparādh* दोष, अपराध

Faulty (adj◦) *doṣhī, aparādhī* दोषी, अपराधी

Favour (m◦) *upkār* उपकार

Favourable (adj◦) *anukūl* अनुकूल

Favoutite (adj◦) *priya, pasant* प्रिय, पसंत

Fear (f◦) *bhīti,* (n◦)*bhay* भीति, भय; (v◦) *bhiṇe* भिणे

Feast (f◦) *mejvānī* मेजवानी

Feat (f◦) *kamāl* कमाल

Feather (n◦) *paṅkh* पंख

Feature (n◦) *lakṣhaṇ* लक्षण

Federation (n◦) *saṅghaṭan* संघटन

Fee (n◦) *śhulk* शुल्क

Feed (n◦) *khādya,* (m◦) *chārā* खाद्य, चारा; (v◦) *chārṇe* चारणे*

Feel (m◦) *anubhav* अनुभव; (v◦) *bhāsṇe* भासणे

Feeling (f◦) *bhāvaṇe* भावना

Fellow (m◦) *sobtī* सोबती

Female (f◦) *mādī, nārī* मादी, नारी

Ferocious (adj◦) *krūr* क्रूर

Fertile (adj◦) *upajāū* उपजाऊ

Fertilizer (m◦) *khat* खत

Fervent (adj◦) *jośhīlā* जोशीला

Fervour (m◦) *jośh* जोश

Festival (m◦) *utsav, saṇ* उत्सव, सण

Fever (m◦) *tāp, jwar* ताप, ज्वर

Few (adj◦) *thoḍā* थोडा

Fez (f◦) *ṭopī* टोपी

Fiance (f◦) *maṅgetar* मंगेतर

Fib (n◦) *khoṭe* खोटे

Fibre (m◦) *tantu* तंतु

Fickle (adj◦) *asthir* अस्थिर

Fiction (f◦) *kādambarī* कादंबरी

Fictitious (adj◦) *kālpanik* काल्पनिक

Fiddle (f◦) *sārangī* सारंगी

Fidelity (f◦) *īmāndārī* ईमानदारी

Field (n◦) *śhet, maidān* शेत, मैदान

Fierce (adj◦) *ugra, tīvra* उग्र, तीव्र

Fifteen (adj◦) *pandrā* पंधरा

Fifth (adj◦) *pāchavā* पाचवा

Fig (n◦) *añjīr* अंजीर

Fight (f◦) *laḍhāī* लढाई; (v◦) *laḍhaṇe* लढणे

Figure (f◦) *ākruti,* (m◦) *aṅka* आकृति, अंक

Fill (v◦) *bharṇe* भरणे

Filling (f◦) *bharaṇī* भरणी

Filth (f◦) *ghāṇ,* (m◦)*maḷ* घाण, मळ

Final (adj◦) *antim* अंतिम

Finale (n◦) *samāpan* समापन

Finance (m◦) *bhāṇḍval* भांडवल

Find (v◦) *dhūndaṇe* धूंडणे*

Fine (adj◦) *talam, chhāndār* तलम, छानदार; (m◦) *daṇḍ* दंड;

Finger (n◦) *boṭ* बोट

Fire (f◦) *āg,* (m◦) *agni* आग, अग्नि

Firefly (m◦) *kājvā* काजवा

adj◦ = Adjective, adv◦ = Adverb; *conj.* = Conjunction, f◦ = Feminine gender, *ind.* = Indeclinable, m◦ = Masculine gender, n◦ = Neuter gender, pl◦ = Plural

Firework (n∘) *dārūkām* दारूकाम

Firm (adj∘) *pakkā, majbūt* पक्का, मजबूत

First (adj∘) *pratham, pahilā* प्रथम, पहिला

Fish (m∘) *māsā* मासा

Fisherman (m∘) *koḷī* कोळी

Fissure (f∘) *bheg* भेग

Fist (f∘) *mūṭh* मूठ

Fit (adj∘) *lāyak, upayukta, uchit, yodnya, anukūl* लायक, उपयुक्त, उचित, योग्य, अनुकूल; (f∘) *mūrchhā,* मूर्छा

Fitness (f∘) *yodnyatā* योग्यता

Five (adj∘) *pāch* पाच

Fix (v∘) *ṭhīk karaṇe* ठीक क∘*

Fixation (f∘) *sthirtā* स्थिरता

Flabbergasted (adj∘) *niruttar* निरुत्तर

Flag (m∘) *jheṇḍā* झेंडा

Flagrant (adj∘) *lajjājanak* लज्जाजनक

Flair (f∘) *śhailī* शैली

Flake (f∘) *pāpḍī, pātaḍī* पापडी, पातडी

Flamboyant (adj∘) *ākarṣhak* आकर्षक

Flame (f∘) *jwālā* ज्वाला

Flamingo (m∘) *marāl* मराल

Flammable (adj∘) *jwālāgrahī* ज्वालाग्रही

Flap (f∘) *faḍfaḍ* फडफड; (v∘) *faḍfaḍṇe* फडफडणे

Flash (f∘) *chamak* चमक

Flat (adj∘) 1. *sapāṭ* (flat surface) सपाट; 2. (flat drink) *niras, fikkā* निरस, फिक्का; 3. *besurā* (flat voice) बेसुरा

Flattering (f∘) *khuśhāmat* खुशामत

Flavour (m∘) *svād,* (f∘) *ruchi* स्वाद, रुचि

Flaw (m∘) *doṣh,* (f∘) *truṭi* दोष, तृटि

Flee (v∘) *palṇe* पळणे

Fleece (f∘) *lokar* लोकर

Fleet (f∘) *nau-seṇe* नौ-सेना

Flesh (n∘) *mās* मास

Flexible (adj∘) *lauchik, parivartanśhīl* लौचिक, परिवर्तनशील

Flicker(v∘) *ṭimṭimṇe* टिमटिमणे

Flight (f∘) *uḍḍāṇ* उड्डाण

Flimsy (adj∘) *kamzor* कमजोर

Flip (v∘) *palaṭṇe, palaṭvaṇe** पलटणे, पलटवणे*

Flirt (f∘) *praṇaycheṣhṭā* प्रणयचेष्टा

Float (v∘) *tarangṇe* तरंगणे

Flock (f∘) *jhuṇḍ* झुंड

Flood (f∘) *pūr* पूर

Floor (f∘) 1. *jamīn, farśhī* जमीन, फर्शी; 2. (m∘) story *majlā* मजला

Flour (m∘) *kaṇīk* कणीक

Flow (f∘) *dhār,* (m∘) *pravāh* धार, प्रवाह; (v∘) *vāhaṇe* वाहणे

Flower (n∘) *fūl* फूल

Fluctuation (m∘) *chaḍhāv-utār* चढाव-उतार

Fluid (m∘) *drava* द्रव

Flute (f∘) *bāsarī, murlī* बासरी, मुरली

Flutter (v∘) *ghuṭmaḷṇe* घुटमळणे

Fly (f∘) *māśhī* माशी; (v∘) *uḍaṇe, uḍavṇe** उडणे, उडवणे*

Foam (m∘) *fes* फेस

Focus (m∘) *kendra-bindu* केन्द्रबिंदु

Fodder (m∘) *chārā* चारा

Foe (m∘) *śhatru* शत्रु

Foetus (n∘) *bhrūṇa,* (m∘) *garbha* भ्रूण, गर्भ

Fog (n∘) *dhuke* धुके

Fold (f∘) *ghaḍī* घडी

Folk (n∘) *lok* लोक

Follow (f∘) 1. *anusaraṇe* (a mentor) अनुसरणे 2. *māge jāṇe* (go behind) मागे जाणे 3. *samajṇe* (understand) समजणे

Following (adj∘) 1. *puḍhachā* (next) पुढचा; 2. *khālīl* (given below) खालील

Folly (f∘) *mūrkhatā* मूर्खता

Fond (adj∘) *priya* प्रिय

Fondle (v∘) *dulārṇe* दुलारणे*

Food (m∘) *ahār,* (n∘)*bhojan* आहार, भोजन

Fool (m∘) *bekūb, mūrkha* बेकूब, मूर्ख

Foolish (adj∘) *mūrkha* मूर्ख

Foot (n∘) *charaṇ* चरण

Foot (m∘) *pāy* पाय

Footnote (f∘) *pād-ṭipaṇī* पाद-टिपणी

For (prep∘) *karitā* करिता

Forbid (v∘) *manā karṇe* मना क∘*

Force (f∘) *śhakti* (n∘) *baḷ* शक्ति, बळ

Forceps (m∘) *chimṭā* चिमटा

Forcibly (adv∘) *baḷpūrvak* बळपूर्वक

Fore (adj∘) *puḍhachā* पुढचा

Forecast (f∘) *pūrva-sūchaṇe* पूर्वसूचना

Forefather (m∘) *pūrvaj* पूर्वज

Forefinger (f∘) *tarjanī* तर्जनी

Forehead (n∘) *lalāṭ, kapāḷ* ललाट, कपाळ

Foreign (m∘) *videśh* विदेश

Foremost (adj∘) *agresar* अग्रेसर

Foresight (f∘) *dūr-dṛṣhṭi* दूरदृष्टि

Forest (n∘) *jaṅgal, van* जंगल, वन

Forever (adv∘) *sadā, sarvadā* सदा, सर्वदा

Forge (v∘) *nakkal karṇe* नक्कल क∘*

Forgery (f∘) *nakkal* नक्कल

Forget (v∘) *visarṇe* विसरणे*

Forgive (v∘) *māf karṇe* माफ क∘*

Fork (m∘) *kāṭā* (knife & fork) काटा

Form (n∘) *rūp* रूप; (v∘) *rūp deṇe* रूप देणे*

Formal (adj∘) *aupachārik* औपचारिक

Formality (m∘) *śhiṣhṭāchār* शिष्टाचार

Format (f∘) *rūpreśhā* रूपरेशा

Formation (n∘) *nirmāṇ* निर्माण

Former (adj∘) *pahilā, pūrva* पहिला, पूर्व

Formerly (adv∘) *pahile* पहिले

Formidable (adj∘) *ajeya* अजेय

Formula (n∘) *sūtra, samīkaraṇ* सूत्र, समीकरण

Forsake (v∘) *tyāgṇe* त्यागणे*

Fort (m∘) *killā, gaḍ* किल्ला, गड

Forthcoming (adj∘) *āgāmī* आगामी

Forthright (adj∘) *kharā, spaṣhṭa* खरा, स्पष्ट

Forthwith (adv∘) *jalad, jhaṭ* जलद, झट

Fortniht (m∘) *pandharvāḍā* पंधरवाडा

Fortress (m∘) *gaḍhī* गढी

Fortunately (adv∘) *daivayogāne* देवयोगाने

Fortune (n∘) *bhāgya* भाग्य

Fortutide (n∘) *sāhas* साहस

Forty (adj∘) *chāḷīs* चाळीस

Forward (adv∘) *puḍhe* पुढे

Foul (adj∘) *ongaḷ; bhraṣhṭa* ओंगळ, भ्रष्ट

Foundation (m∘) *pāyavā* पायवा

Founder (m∘) *sansthāpak* संस्थापक

adj∘ = Adjective, adv∘ = Adverb; *conj.* = Conjunction, f∘ = Feminine gender, *ind.* = Indeclinable, m∘ = Masculine gender, n∘ = Neuter gender, pl∘ = Plural

Fountain (m∘) *favārā,* (n∘) *kāranj* फवारा, कारंज

Four (adj∘) *four* चार

Fourteen (adj∘) *chavdā* चवदा

Fowl (m∘) *kombḍā* (f∘) *kombḍī* कोंबडा, कोंबडी

Fox (m∘) *kolhā* कोल्हा

Fraction (m∘) *aṁśha, hissā* अंश, हिस्सा

Free (v∘) *soḍṇe* सोडणे

Frequency (f∘) *āvrutti* आवृत्ति

Frequently (adv∘) *punaḥ-punaḥ, vāramvār* पुनः पुनः, वारंवार

Friction (n∘) *gharṣhaṇ* घर्षण

Friday (m∘) *śhukravār* शुक्रवार

Friend (m∘) *mitra, dost* मित्र, दोस्त

Friendship (f∘) *maitrī, dosti* मैत्री, दोस्ती

Frightful (adj∘) *bhatankar* भयंकर

Frog (n∘) *beḍuk* बेडुक

From (prep∘) *pāsūn* पासून

Front (f∘) *āghāḍī* आघाडी

Frsh (adj∘) *tājā, navā* ताजा, नवा

Fruit (n∘) *faḷ* फळ

Fruitful (adj∘) *safal* सफल

Frustration (m∘) *nirutsāh* निरुत्साह

Fry (v∘) *taḷṇe, bhājṇe* तळणे, भाजणे*

Frying-pan (f∘) *kaḍhaī* कढई

Fuel (n∘) *indhan* इंधन

Fully (adv∘) *bilkul, purṇa* बिलकुल, पूर्ण

Fumes (m∘) *dhūr* (f∘) *vāf* धूर; वाफ

Fun (m∘) *ānand; changaḷ* आनंद; चंगळ

Function (m∘) 1. (event) *samārambha;* समारंभ, 2. (n∘) (duty) *kārya* कार्य

Fund (f∘) *dhanrāśhi* धनराशि

Fundamental (adj∘) *mūlbhūt* मूलभूत

Fundamentalism (m∘) *rūḍhivād* रूढिवाद

Funds (m∘) *nidhi, koṣh* निधि, कोष

Funnel (f∘) *chāḍī* चाडी

Funny (adj∘) *hāsya-janak* हास्यजनक

Furious (adj∘) *krodhit* क्रोधित

Furnace (f∘) *bhaṭṭī* भट्टी

Further (adv∘) *puḍhe* पुढे

Fury (m∘) *unmād* उन्माद

Fuss (f∘) *dhāndal* धांदल

Futile (adj∘) *vyartha* व्यर्थ

Fuzzy (aj) *aspaṣhṭa* अस्पष्ट

G

Gadget (f∘) *kaḷ,* (n∘) *avajār* कळ, अवजार

Gain (v∘) *miḷavṇe* मिळवणे*; (f∘) *miḷkat,* (m∘)*nafā, lābh* मिळकत, नफा, लाभ

Gallant (adj∘) *bahādur, vīr* बहादुर, वीर

Gallows (f∘) *suḷī* सुळी

Gambit (f∘) *pahilī chāl* पहिली चाल

Garden (m∘) *bagīchā* बगीचा

Garland (m∘) *hār,* (f∘) *māḷ* हार, माळ

Garlic (m∘) *lasūṇ* लसूण

Garment (n∘) *vastra, kapḍe* वस्त्र, कपडे

Gas (m∘) *vāyu,* (n∘) *peṭrol* वायु, पेट्रोल

Gash (m∘) *ghāv* घाव

Gate (n∘) *fāṭak, dvār* फाटक, द्वार

Gather (v∘) *ekatra hoṇe, ekatra karṇē** एकत्र हो०, एकत्र क०*

Gathering (m∘) *jamāv,* (n∘) *sammelan* जमाव, संमेलन

Gauge (n∘) *māp* माप

Gear (m∘) 1. *dātedār chakra* (machine) दातेदार चक्र 2. *sāmān* (sport) सामान

Gem (m∘) *maṇi,* (n∘) *ratna* मणि, रत्न

Gemini (f∘) *mithun rāśhi* मिथुन राशि

Geneology (f∘) *vaṁśhāvaḷ* वंशावळ

General (adj∘) *sāmānya* सामान्य

Generality (f∘) *sāmānyatā* सामान्यता

Generation (f∘) *utpatti* (production) उत्पत्ति; 2. *piḍhī* (age group) पिढी

Generosity (f∘) *udārtā* उदारता

Genesis (m∘) *prārambha* प्रारंभ

Genius (f∘) *pratibhā* प्रतिभा

Genocide (m∘) *jātisaṁhār* जातिसंहार

Gentle (adj∘) *saumya, śhānt* सौम्य, शांत

Gentleman (m∘) *sajjan* सज्जन

Geography (m∘) *bhūgol* भूगोल

Geology (n∘) *bhūmiśhāstra* भूमिशास्त्र

Geometry (f∘) *bhūmiti* भूमिति

Geophysics (f∘) *bhautikī* भौतिकी

Germ (m∘) *jīvāṇu* जीवाणु

Germinate (v∘) *ugaṇe* उगणे

Gesture (m∘) *bhāv* भाव

Get (v∘) *miḷṇe* मिळणे

Ghost (n∘) *bhūt* भूत

Giant (adj∘) *viśhāl* विशाल

Gift (f∘) *bheṭ* (m∘) *upahār* भेट, उपहार

Gigantic (adj∘) *bhīmakāy* भीमकाय

Ginger (n∘) *āle* आले

Girl (f∘) *mulgī* मुलगी

Give (v∘) *deṇe* देणे*

Glad (adj∘) *khuśh* खुश

Gladly (adv∘) *khuśhīne* खुशीने

Glance (f∘) *jhaḷak* झळक

Gland (f∘) *granthi, gāṭh* ग्रंथि, गाठ

Glass, (m∘) 1. *kāch* काच; 2. (tumbler) *pyālā* प्याला

Glasses (m∘) *chaṣhmā* चष्मा

Glide (v∘) *ghasarṇe* घसरणे

Glimpse (f∘) *jhaḷak* झळक

Glitter (f∘) *chamak* चमक; (v∘) *chamakṇe* चमकणे

Global (adj∘) *jāgatik* जागतिक

Gloom (f∘) *udāsī* उदासी

Glorification (f∘) *stuti* स्तुति

Glory (f∘) *kīrti* कीर्ति

Glossary (f∘) *artha sūchī* अर्थ सूची

Glossy (adj∘) *chopḍā* चोपडा

Glove (m∘) *hātmojā* हातमोजा

Glow (f∘) *chamak* चमक; (v∘) *chamakṇe* चमकणे

Glue (m∘) *gond* गोंद

Glue (v∘) *chikṭvaṇe* चिकटवणे*

Gnat (m∘) *ḍās* डास

Go (v∘) *jāṇe* जाणे

Goad (m∘) *aṅkuśh* अंकुश

Goal (n) *dhyeya, lakṣhya* ध्येय, लक्ष्य

Goat (f∘) *bakarī, (m∘) bakrā* बकरी, बकरा

God (m∘) *dev* देव

Goddess (f∘) *devī* देवी

Gold (n) *soṇe* सोने

Goldsmith (m∘) *sonār* सोनार

Good (adj∘) *chhān* छान

adj∘ = Adjective, adv∘ = Adverb; *conj.* = Conjunction, f∘ = Feminine gender, *ind.* = Indeclinable, m∘ = Masculine gender, n∘ = Neuter gender, pl∘ = Plural

Goodbye (m◦) *namaskār, rāmrām* नमस्कार, रामराम

Goodness (m◦) *chānglepaṇā* चांगलेपणा

Goose (f◦) *varaṭī* वरटी

Gorgeous (adj◦) *śhāndār* शानदार

Gossip (f◦) *gappā* गप्पा

Gourd (n◦) *kohḷe* कोहळे

Government (n◦) *sarkār* सरकार

Governor (m◦) *rājyapāl* राज्यपाल

Gown (m◦) *Jagā* झगा

Grab (v◦) *pakaḍṇe* पकडणे*

Grace (f◦) *krupā, krupādruṣhṭi* कृपा, कृपादृष्टि

Graceful (adj◦) *manoram* मनोरम

Gracious (adj◦) *udār* उदार

Grade (f◦) *śhreṇī* श्रेणी

Gradual (adj◦) *kramik* क्रमिक

Graduate (m◦) *snātak* स्नातक

Graft (f◦) *kalam* कलम

Grain (m◦) *dāṇā, kaṇ, ravā* दाणा, कण, रवा

Gram, chickpea (m◦) *chaṇā* चणा

Grammar (m◦) *vyākaraṇ* व्याकरण

Grand (adj◦) *bhavya, śhāndār* भव्य, शानदार

Granddaughter (f◦) *nāt* नात

Grandeur (n◦) *vaibhav* (f◦) *śhān* वैभव, शान

Grandfather (m◦) *ājobā* आजोबा

Grandmother (f◦) *ājī* आजी

Grandson (m◦) *nātu* नातु

Grant (v◦) *anumati deṇe* अनुमति देणे

Grape (n◦) *drākṣha* द्राक्ष

Grass (n◦) *gavat* गवत

Grasshopper (m◦) *nāktoḍā* नाकतोडा,

Grating (f◦) *jāḷī* जाळी

Gratitude (f◦) *krutadnyatā* कृतज्ञता

Gratuity (m◦) *ināṁ* इनाम

Grave (adj◦) *gambhīr* गंभीर

Grave (f◦) *kabar* कबर

Gravel (f◦) *bajrī* बजरी

Gravity (n◦) *gurutvākarṣhaṇ* गुरुत्वाकर्षण

Gravy (m◦) *rasā* रसा

Graze (v◦) *charṇe* चरणे

Grease (f◦) *charbī* चरबी

Greasy (adj◦) *telkaṭ* तेलकट

Great (adj◦) *mahān* महान

Greed (f◦) *lāluch* लालुच

Green (adj◦) *hirvā* हिरवा

Greeting (m◦) *abhinandan* अभिनंदन

Grey (adj◦) *karḍā* करडा

Grid (n◦) *jāḷe* जाळे

Grief (m◦) *śhok, santāp* शोक, संताप

Grievance (n◦) *gārhāṇe* गाऱ्हाणे

Grind (v◦) *daḷṇe* दळणे*

Grip (f◦) *pakaḍ* पकड

Grocery *kirāṇā* किराणा

Groom (m◦) *var* वर

Groove (f◦) *kor, khāch* कोर, खाच

Grotesque (adj◦) *vidrūp* विद्रूप

Ground (n◦) *maidān* (f◦) *jamīn* मैदान, जमीन

Group (m◦) *samūha, sangha* समूह, संघ

Grow (v◦) *ugṇe, vāḍhṇe;, vāḍhavṇe** उगणे, वाढणे, वाढवणे*

Growth (m◦) *vikās,* (f◦) *vruddhi* विकास, वृद्धि

Grumble (v◦) *kurkurṇe* कुरकुरणे*

Grumpy (adj◦) *chiḍkhor* चिडखोर

Gtuesome (adj◦) *bībhatsa* बीभत्स

Guarantee (f◦) *jamānat* जमानत

Guarantor (m◦) *jāmin* जामिन

Guard (m◦) *pahredār, santrī* पहरेदार, संतरी; (v◦) *pahrā deṇe* पहरा देणे*

Guardian (m◦) *rakṣhak* रक्षक

Guava (m◦) *jāmb, peru* जांब, पेरु

Guess (m◦) *anumān, andāj* अनुमान, अंदाज

Guest (m◦) *pāhuṇā, atithi* पाहुणा, अतिथि

Guidance (m◦) *upadeśh* उपदेश

Guide (m◦) *mārga-darśhak* मार्गदर्शक

Guilt (m◦) *doṣh, aparādh* दोष, अपराध

Guilty (adj◦) *doṣhī, aparādhī* दोषी, अपराधी

Gulp (v◦) *giṭakṇe* गिटकणे*

Gum (m◦) glue: *ḍink, gond* डिंक, गोंद

Gun (f◦) *bandūk, tof* बंदूक, तोफ

Gust (m◦) *jhokā* झोका

Gut (n◦) *ātaḍe* आतडे

Gutter (f◦) *nālī* नाली

Gymnasium (f◦) *vyāyāma-śhāḷā* व्यायामशाळा

Gymnastics (f◦) *kasrat* कसरत

H

Habit (f◦) *savay* सवय

Habitat (m◦) *āvās* आवास

Habitual (adj◦) *niyamit* नियमित

Had (v◦) *hotā, hotī, hote* होता, होती, होते

Hag (f◦) *jakhīṇ* जखीण

Haggard (adj◦) *martukḍā* मरतुकडा

Hair (m◦) *kes* केस

Half (adj◦) *ardha* अर्ध

Hall (m◦) *narak* नरक

Halt (v◦) *thāmbṇe* थांबणे

Handle (m◦) *mūṭh* मूठ; (v◦) *hatāḷṇe* हाताळणे

Hammer (f◦) *hatoḍī* हतोडी

Hand (m◦) *hāt* हात

Handcuff (f◦) *hātkaḍī* हातकडी

Handicap (f◦) *vikalāngtā* विकलांगता

Handicapped (adj◦) *vikalāng* विकलांग

Handkerchief (m◦) *rumāl* रुमाल

Handy (adj◦) *soīskar* सोईसकर

Hang (v◦) *laṭakṇe, laṭakavṇe** लटकणे, लटकवणे*

Hanker (v◦) *lalachāvṇe* ललचावणे

Haphazzard (adj◦) *avyavasthit* अव्यवस्थित

Happen (v◦) *hoṇe* हो◦

Happily (adv◦) *khuśhīne* खुशीने

Happy (adj◦) *khuśh, prasanna* खुश, प्रसन्न

Harass (v◦) *satāvṇe* सतावणे

Harbinger (m◦) *agradūt* अग्रदूत

Harbour (n◦) *bandar* बंदर

Hard (adj◦) *kaḍak, kaṭhiṇ* कडक, कठिन

Hare (m◦) *sasā* ससा

Harsh (adj◦) *kaṭhor* कठोर

Harvest (f◦) *pīk* पीक

Has (v◦) *āhe, asṇe* आहे, असणे

Hashish (m◦) *gānjā* गांजा

Hassle (f◦) *tvarā* त्वरा

Hat (f◦ m◦) *ṭopī, ṭop* टोपी, टोप

Hatchet (f◦) *kurhāḍ* कुऱ्हाड

Hatred (f◦) *ghruṇā* घृणा

adj◦ = Adjective, adv◦ = Adverb; *conj.* = Conjunction, f◦ = Feminine gender, *ind.* = Indeclinable, m◦ = Masculine gender, n◦ = Neuter gender, pl◦ = Plural

Have (v∘) *āsṇe, āhe* असणे, आहे

Head (n∘) *ḍoke* डोके

Health (n∘) *svāsthya* स्वास्थ्य

Healthy (adj∘) *svastha* स्वस्थ

Heap (f∘) *rāśhi, ḍher* राशि, ढेर

Hear (v∘) *aikṇe* ऐकणे*

Heart (m∘) *hruday* हृदय

Hearty (adj∘) *hārdik* हार्दिक

Heat (f∘) *garamī* गरमी

Heaven (m∘) *svarg* स्वर्ग

Heavy (adj∘) *bhārī* भारी

Hedge (m∘) *kumpaṇ* कुंपण

Heed (v∘) *dhyān deṇe* ध्यान देणे*

Heel (f∘) *ṭāch* टाच

Hefty (adj∘) *bhārī* भारी

Height (f∘) *uñchī* उंची

Heighten (v∘) *vāḍhaṇe* वाढणे

Heir (m∘) *vāras* वारस

Help (f∘) *madat* मदत

Hemisphere (m∘) *ardhavrutta* अर्धवृत्त

Hen (f∘) *kombaḍī* कोंबडी

Hence (adv∘) *Atha, ātā* अथ, आता

Her (prep∘) *tichā, tichī, tiche* तिचा, तिची, तिचे

Here (adv∘) *ithe* इथे

Here and there (adv∘) *ithe-tithe* इथे–तिथे

Hereafter (adv∘) *ātāpāsūn* आतापासून

Hermit (m∘) *yati, ruṣhi* यति, ऋषि

Hero (m∘) *nāyak* नायक

Hero (m∘) *vīr, bahādur* वीर, बहादुर

Heroin (f∘) *nāyikā* नायिका

Hesitate (v∘) *hichakichaṇe* हिचकिचणे

Hexagon (m∘) *shaṭkoṇa* षट्कोण

Hide (n∘) *chāmḍe* चामडे; (v∘) *lapṇe, lapavṇe** लपणे, लपवणे*

Hierarchy (m∘) *padānukram* पदानुक्रम

High (adj∘) *uccha, uñcha* उच्च, उंच

Hill (f∘) *ṭekḍī* टेकडी

Hinge (m∘) *kabjā* कब्जा

Hint (m∘) *iṣhārā, saṅket* इषारा, संकेत

Hippo (m∘) *pāṇghoḍā* पाणघोडा

His (pro∘) *tyāchā, tyāchī, tyāche* त्याचा, त्याची, त्याचे

History (m∘) *itihās* इतिहास

Hit (v∘) *māraṇe* मारणे*

Hive (n∘) *poḷe* पोळे

Hobby (m∘) *chhanda, nād* छंद, नाद

Hoe (f∘) *kudaḷī* कुदळी

Hog (n∘) *ḍukkar* डुक्कर

Hold, catch (v∘) *pakaḍaṇe* पकडणे

Hole (n∘) *chhidra* छिद्र

Holiday (f∘) *suṭṭī* सुट्टी

Hollow (adj∘) *pokaḷ* पोकळ

Holy (adj∘) *pavitra* पवित्र

Homage (f∘) *śhraddhāñjali* श्रद्धांजलि

Home, house (n∘) *ghar* घर

Homely (adj∘) *gharelu* घरेलु

Homicide (f∘) *nar-hatyā* नरहत्या

Homogeneous (adj∘) *ek-rūp* एकरूप

Honest (adj∘) *prāmāṇik* प्रामाणिक

Honesty (f∘) *imānadārī* इमानदारी

Honey (n∘) *sahad, madh* सहद, मध

Honour (m∘) *sanmān, ādar* सन्मान, आदर

Honourable (adj∘) *ādarṇīya* आदरणीय

Hoof (n∘) *khur* खुर

Hooligan (m∘) *guṇḍā* गुंडा

Hope (f∘) *āśhā* आशा

Horizon (m∘) *kṣhitij* क्षितिज

Horizontal (adj∘) *sapāṭ* सपाट

Horn (n∘) *śhiṅg* शिंग

Horoscope (f∘) *janmakuṇḍalī* जन्मकुंडली

Horrendous (adj∘) *bhayānak* भयानक

Horrible (adj∘) *bhayānak* भयानक

Horrific (adj∘) *bhayānak* भयानक

Horror (f∘) *śhisārī* शिसारी

Horse (m∘) *ghoḍā* घोडा

Horsepower (f∘) *aśhvaśhakti* अश्वशक्ति

Hospital (m∘) *davākhānā* दवाखाना

Hospitality (m∘) *atithi-satkār* अतिथि–सत्कार

Host (m∘) *yajmān* यजमान

Hostel (n∘) *chhātrāvās* छात्रावास

Hot (adj∘) *garam* गरम

Hothead (adj∘) *utāvaḷā* उतावळा

Hour (m∘) *tās, ghaṇṭā* तास, घंटा

House (n∘) *ghar* घर

How (adv∘) *kase* कसे?

However (adv∘) *tarī, paṇ* तरी, पण

Hug (v∘) *kavaṭāḷṇe* कवटाळणे*

Huge (adj∘) *viśhāl* विशाल

Hum (v∘) *guṇguṇaṇe* गुणगुणणे

Human (m∘) *mānava* मानव

Humane (adj∘) *dyāmaya* दयामय

Humanity (f∘) *mānav jāti* मानव जाति

Humble (adj∘) *namra* नम्र

Humidity (m∘) *olāvā* ओलावा

Humility (f∘) *namratā* नम्रता

Humour (m∘) *vinod* विनोद

Hump (m∘) *kubaḍ* कुबड

Hundred (adj∘) *śhambhar* शंभर

Hunger (f∘) *bhūk* भूक

Hungry (adj∘) *bhūkelā* भुकेला

Hunt (v∘) *śhikār karṇe* शिकार क∘*

Hunter (m∘) *śhikārī* शिकारी

Hurdle (f∘) *bādhā* बाधा

Hurry (f∘) *jaldī* जल्दी

Hurt (adj∘) *duhkhī* दुःखी; (v∘) *dukhavṇe* दुखवणे*

Husband (m∘) *pati* पति

Husk (m∘) *bhusā* भुसा

Hut (f∘) *jhopaḍī* झोपडी

Hybrid (adj∘) *saṅkar* संकर

Hyena (m∘) *taras* तरस

Hygine (n∘) *ārodnya* आरोग्य

Hymn (m∘) *śhlok* श्लोक

Hypocrisy (n∘) *pākhaṇḍ, ḍhong* पाखंड, ढोंग

Hysteria (m∘) *unmād* उन्माद

I

I (pron∘) *mī* मी

Ice (m∘) *barfa* बर्फ

Idea (f∘) *kalpanā* कल्पना

Ideal (adj∘) *ādarśha* आदर्श

Identical (adj∘) *samān* समान

Identity (f∘) *oḷakh* ओळख

Ideology (f∘) *vichārdhārā* विचारधारा

Idiom (m∘) *vākprachār* वाक्प्रचार

adj∘ = Adjective, adv∘ = Adverb; *conj.* = Conjunction, f∘ = Feminine gender, *ind.* = Indeclinable, m∘ = Masculine gender, n∘ = Neuter gender, pl∘ = Plural

Idiot (adj∘) *mūrkha* मूर्ख

Idle (adj∘) *bekār* बेकार

Idly (adv∘) *vruthā* वृथा

Idol (f∘) *mūrti* मूर्ति

If (adv∘) *jar, yadi* जर, यदि

If not (adv∘) *nāhī tar, anyathā* नाही तर अन्यथा

Ignite (v∘) *sulgavṇe* सुलगवणे*

Ignomity (f∘) *badnāmī* बदनामी

Ignorance (n∘) *adnyān* अज्ञान

Ignorant (adj∘) *adnyānī* अज्ञानी

Ignore (v∘) *upekṣhā karṇe* उपेक्षा क∘*

Iiem (f∘) *vastu* वस्तु

Iindefinite (adj∘) *aniśhchit* अनिश्चित

Iinteresting (adj∘) *manoram* मनोरम

Iivasion (n∘) *ākramaṇ*, (m∘) *dhāvā* आक्रमण, धावा

Ilcit (adj∘) *avaidh* अवैध

Ill (adj∘) *ājārī* आजारी

Illegal (adj∘) *avaidh* अवैध

Illegitimate (adj∘) *avaidh* अवैध

Illiterate (adj∘) *anpaḍh, nirakṣhar* अनपढ, निरक्षर

Illness (m∘) *ājār* आजार

Illuminate (v∘) *prakāśhit larṇe* प्रकाशित क∘*

Illusion (f∘) *māyā, bhrānti* माया, भ्रांति

Illustration (n∘) *udāharaṇ* उदाहरण

Illustrious (adj∘) *prasiddha* प्रसिद्ध

Image (f∘) *pratimā, mūrti* प्रतिमा, मूर्ति

Imagination (f∘) *kalpanā* कल्पना

Imagine (v∘) *kalpanā karṇe* कल्पना क∘*

Imbecile (adj∘) *mūrkha* मूर्ख

Imitate (v∘) *nakkal karṇe* नक्कल क∘*

Imitattion (f∘) *nakkal* नक्कल

Immaculate (adj∘) *truṭīhīn* त्रुटीहीन

Immature (adj∘) *kacchā* कच्चा

Immediately (adv∘) *tatkāḷ, jalad* तत्काल, जलद

Immense (adj∘) *viśhāl* विशाल

Immerse (v∘) *buḍavṇe* बुडवणे*

Immigrant (m∘) *āpravāsī* आप्रवासी

Immigration (m∘) *āpravās* आप्रवास

Immobile (adj∘) *achal, sthir* अचल, स्थिर

Immoral (adj∘) *anaitik* अनैतीक

Immortal (adj∘) *amar* अमर

Immune (adj∘) *mukta* मुक्त

Immunity (f∘) *mukti* मुक्ति

Impact (m∘) *prabhāv* प्रभाव

Impaired (adj∘) *durbaḷ* दुर्बळ

Impartial (adj∘) *taṭastha* तटस्थ

Impatient (adj∘) *ātur, utāvḷā* आतुर, उतावळा

Impediment (f∘) *aḍchaṇ* अडचण

Imperfect (adj∘) *adhūrā* अधुरा

Imperialism (m∘) *sāmrājya-vād* साम्राज्यवाद

Impervious (m∘) *abhedya* अभेद्य

Impetus (f∘) *preraṇā* प्रेरणा

Implement (m∘) *avajār, upakaraṇ* अवजार, उपकरण

Implement (v∘) *lagū karṇe* लागू क∘

Implication (m∘) *āśhay* आशय

Implore (v∘) *prārthaṇe karṇe* प्रार्थना क∘*

Import (f∘) *āyāt* आयात

Important (adj∘) *mahattvapūrṇa* महत्त्वपूर्ण

Imposter (m∘) *ḍhongī, pākhaṇḍī* ढोंगी, पाखंडी

Impotent (adj∘) *napunsak* नपुंसक

Impregnable (adj∘) *abhedya* अभेद्य

Impression (f∘) *chhāp* छाप

Impressive (adj∘) *prabhāvī* प्रभावी

Improper (adj∘) *anuchit* अनुचित

Improve (v∘) *sudhārṇe* सुधारणे*

Impulse (m∘) *āveg*, (f∘) *prerṇā* आवेग, प्रेरणा

Impure (adj∘) *aśhuddha* अशुद्ध

In (prep∘) *madhye* मध्ये

In a short time (adv∘) *lagech* लगेच

In front of (adv∘) *samor* समोर

In the morning (adv∘) *sakāḷī* सकाळी

Inability (f∘) *aśhakti* अशक्ति

Inaccessible (adj∘) *agamya* अगम्य

Inaccurate (adj∘) *chūk* चूक

Inadequate (adj∘) *aparyāpta* अपर्याप्त

Inadvertantly (adv∘) *chukūn* चुकून

Inappropriate (adj∘) *anuchit* अनुचित

Inauguration (n∘) *udghāṭan* उद्घाटन

Incapable (adj∘) *asamartha* असमर्थ

Incarnation (m∘) *avatār* अवतार

Incentive (n∘) *protsāhan* प्रोत्साहन

Inception (f∘) *survāt* सुरवात

Incessant (adj∘) *nirantar* निरंतर

Incessantly (adv∘) *nirantar* निरंतर

Incident (f∘) *ghaṭnā* घटणा

Incite (v∘) *bhaḍkāvṇe* भडकावणे*

Inclination (m∘) *jhukāv* झुकाव

Incline (v∘) *jhukaṇe* झुकणे

Include (v∘) *sāth miḷavṇe* साथ मिळवणे*

Inclusion (m∘) *samāveśh* समावेश

Inclusive (adj∘) *sammilit* संमिलित

Income (f∘) *miḷkat* मिळकत

Incompetent (adj∘) *akṣham* अक्षम

Incomplete (adj∘) *adhurā* अधुरा

Incongruous (adj∘) *visangat* विसंगत

Inconsistent (adj∘) *visangat* विसंगत

Inconspicuous (adj∘) *nagaṇya* नगण्य

Incorrect (adj∘) *chūk* चूक

Increase (f∘) *vṛddhi, vāḍh* वृद्धि, वाढ; (v∘) *vāḍhṇe, vāḍhavnā** वाढणे, वाढवणे*

Incredible (adj∘) *aviśhvasanīya* अविश्वसनीय

Incursion (n∘) *ākramaṇ* आक्रमण

Indebted (adj∘) *ābhārī, ruṇī* आभारी, ऋणी

Indecision (m∘) *anirṇay* अनिर्णय

Indecisive (adj∘) *aniśhchit* अनिश्चित

Indeed (adv∘) *vastutaḥ* वस्तुत:

Indefinitely (adv∘) *satat* सतत

Independent (adj∘) *svatantra* स्वतंत्र

Index (m∘) *suchak* (f∘) *suchī* सूचक, सूची

India (m∘) *bhārat, hindustān* भारत, हिंदुस्थान

Indian (m∘) *bhāratīya* भारतीय

Indicate (v∘) *dākhavaṇe* दाखवणे*

Indicator (m∘) *sanket*, (n∘) *lakṣhaṇ* संकेत, लक्षण

Indifferent (adj∘) *taṭastha* तटस्थ

Indigenous (m∘) *deśhī* देशी

Indigestion (n∘) *apachan* अपचन

Indirect (adj∘) *apratyakṣha* अप्रत्यक्ष

Inference (n∘) *anumān* अनुमान

Infertile (adj∘) *nāpīk* नापीक

adj∘ = Adjective, adv∘ = Adverb; *conj.* = Conjunction, f∘ = Feminine gender, *ind.* = Indeclinable, m∘ = Masculine gender, n∘ = Neuter gender, pl∘ = Plural

Infiltrate (v◦) *ghusṇe* घुसणे
Infinite (adj◦) *anant* अनंत
Inflame (v◦) *bhaḍkāvṇe* भडकावणे*
Inflammable (adj◦) *dāhya* दाह्य
Inflammation (f◦) *sūj* सूज
Inflexible (adj◦) *kaḍak, kaṭhor* कडक, कठोर
Infliction (f◦) *pīḍā* पीडा
Influence (m◦) *prabhāv* प्रभाव
Influencial (adj◦) *prabhāvī* प्रभावी
Information (f◦) *sūchaṇā* सूचना
Infrastructure (m◦) *ḍhāchā* ढाचा
Infringement (n◦) *ākramaṇ* आक्रमण
Ingenuity (f◦) *kuśhaltā* कुशलता
Ingredient (m◦) *ghaṭak* घटक
Input (n◦) *yogdān* योगदान
Inquiry (f◦) *vichārpūs, chaukaśhī* विचारपूस, चौकशी
Insane (adj◦) *pāgal, veḍā* पागल, वेडा
Insect (m◦) *kīḍā* कीडा
Insecure (adj◦) *asurakṣhit* असुरक्षित
Insert (v◦) *ghusavṇe* घुसवणे*
Inside (adv◦) *ā̐t* आंत
Insignificant (adj◦) *nagaṇya* नगण्य
Insipid (adj◦) *fikkā* फिक्का
Insist (v◦) *āgraha karṇe* आग्रह क◦*
Insolent (adj◦) *uddhaṭ* उद्धट
Inspect (v◦) *parakhaṇe* परखणे*
Inspection (n◦) *parīkṣhaṇ* परीक्षण
Inspector (m◦) *parīkṣhak* परीक्षक
Inspiration (f◦) *preraṇā* प्रेरणा
Inspire (v◦) *prerit karṇe* प्रेरित क◦*
Integration (n◦) *ekīkaraṇ* एकीकरण
Integrity (f◦) *ektā* एकता
Intellect (f◦) *buddhi* बुद्धि
Intelligence (f◦) *buddhi* बुद्धि
Intense (adj◦) *tīvra* तीव्र
Intent (m◦) *hetu* हेतु
Intention (m◦) *hetu, irādā* हेतु, इरादा
Intercourse (m◦) *samāgam* समागम
Interest (m◦) *ruchi* रुचि
Interim (adj◦) *antarim* अंतरिम
Interior (adj◦) *antastha* अंतस्थ
Interlock (v◦) *sāndhaṇe* सांधणे*
Intermediate (adj◦) *mādhyamik* माध्यमिक
Intermission (n◦) *madhyāntar* मध्यांतर
Intermittent (adj◦) *savirām* सविराम
Internal (adj◦) *āntarik* आंतरिक
International (adj◦) *antar-rāṣhṭrīya* अंतर्राष्ट्रीय
Interpretation (f◦) *vyākhyā* व्याख्या
Interrogate (v◦) *praśhna krṇe* प्रश्न क◦*
Interrupt (v◦) *bādhā ṭākṇe* बाधा टाकणे*
Interruption (f◦) *bādhā* बाधा
Intersection (m◦) *chaurastā* चौरस्ता
Interval (m◦) *madhyāntar* मध्यांतर
Interview (f◦) *bheṭ* भेट
Intestine (f◦) *ātaḍe* आतडे
Intimate (adj◦) *ghaniṣhtha* घनिष्ट
Intimidate (v◦) *dhamkāvṇe* धमकावणे*
Intimidation (f◦) *dhamkī* धमकी
Into (prep◦) *ā̐t* आंत
Intolerable (adj◦) *asahanīya* असहनीय
Intoxication (m◦) *naśhā* नशा
Intrepid (adj◦) *sāhasī* साहसी
Intricate (adj◦) *avaghaḍ* अवघड
Intrigue (m◦) *ṣhaḍyantra* षड्यंत्र
Intrinsic (adj◦) *āntarik* आंतरिक
Introduce (v◦) *kprastut karṇe* प्रस्तुत क◦*
Introduction (m◦) *parichay* (f◦) *prastāvanā* परिचय, प्रस्तावना
Introductory (adj◦) *prārambhik* प्रारंभिक
Intrusion (n◦) *ākramaṇ* आक्रमण
Intuition (f◦) *sahajbuddhi* सहजबुद्धि
Invalid (adj◦) *agrāhya* अग्राह्य
Invariable (adj◦) *sthir* स्थिर
Invencible (adj◦) *ajay, ajeya* अजय, अजेय
Invention (m◦) *āviṣhkār* आविष्कार
Inverse (adj◦) *ulaṭā* उलटा
Investigate (v◦) *khoj karṇe* खोज क◦*
Investigation (f◦) *khoj,* (m◦) *śhodh* खोज, शोध
Investment (n◦) *bhāṇḍval* भांडवल
Invisible (adj◦) *agochar* अगोचर
Involve (v◦) *sāmil hoṇe* सामिल हो◦
Invonvenience (f◦) *asuvidhā* असुविधा
Ire (n◦) *krodh* क्रोध
Iron (f◦) *istarī;* (m◦) *lokhaṇḍ* इस्तरी; लोखंड
Irony (f◦) *viḍambanā* विडंबना
Irrational (adj◦) *tarkhīn* तर्कहीन
Irregular (adj◦) *aniyamit* अनियमित
Irrelevant (adj◦) *asaṅgat* असंगत
Irrigate (v◦) *bhijavṇe* भिजवणे
Is (v◦) *āhe* आहे
Island (m◦) *dvīp* द्वीप
Isolate (v◦) *alag karṇe* अलग क◦*
Issue (m◦) 1. *viṣhay* (subject) विषय; 2. (n◦) (publication) *prachālan* प्रचालन 3. (n◦) (child) (f◦) *mūl* मूल
It (pron◦) *he* हे
Itch (f◦) *khāj* खाज
Itself (pron◦) *svayam* स्वयं
Ivitation (n◦) *āmantraṇ* आमंत्रण

J

Jab (m◦) *dhakkā* धक्का
Jackel (m◦) *kolhā* कोल्हा
Jacket (n◦) *āvaraṇ* आवरण
Jackfruit (m◦) *kaṭhal* कटहल
Jaelousy (f◦) *īrṣhā, ḍāh* ईर्ष्या, डाह
Jagged (adj◦) *dātedār, dantur* दातेदार, दंतुर
Jail (n◦) *kārāgār,* (f◦) *kaid* कारागार, कैद
January (m◦) *jānevārī* जानेवारी
Jar (n◦) *bhāṇḍe* भांडे
Jasmine (f◦) *chamelī* चमेली
Jaundice (m◦) *kāvīḷ* कावीळ
Javelin (m◦) *bhālā* भाला
Jaw (m◦) *jabḍā* जबडा
Jay bird (f◦) *bulbul* बुलबुल
Jeopardy (n◦) *saṅkaṭ* संकट
Jerk (adj◦) *mūrkha* मूर्ख; (m◦) *jhaṭkā* झटका
Jet (f◦) *dhār* धार
Jew (m◦) *yahūdī* यहूदी
Jewel (n◦) *ratna* रत्न
Jingle (f◦) *ruṇjhuṇ* रुणझुण
Jinx (m◦) *abhiśhāp* अभिशाप
Job (f◦) *anukarī* (n◦) *kām* नौकरी, काम

adj◦ = Adjective, adv◦ = Adverb; *conj.* = Conjunction, f◦ = Feminine gender, *ind.* = Indeclinable, m◦ = Masculine gender, n◦ = Neuter gender, pl◦ = Plural

Join (v∘) *judṇe, jodṇe** जुडणे, जोडणे*
Joint (m∘) *joḍ* जोड
Joke (m∘) *vinod* विनोद
Joker (m∘) *vidushak* विदुषक
Jolly (adj∘) *ānandit* आनंदित
Jolt (m∘) *jhaṭkā, dhakkā* झटका, धक्का
Journey (f∘) *yātrā,* (m∘) *safar* यात्रा, सफर
Joy (m∘) *ānaand,* (f∘) *khuśhī* आनंद, खुशी
Jubilant (adj∘) *ullāsit* उल्लासित
Jubilation (m∘) *ullās* उल्लास
Judge (m∘) *nyāyādhīśh* न्यायाधीश
Judgement (m∘) *nyāy* न्याय
Judisdiction (f∘) *sīmā* सीमा
Jug (f∘) *suraī,* (m∘) *ghaḍā* सुरई, घडा
Juggler (m∘) *gāruḍī* गारुडी
Juice (m∘) *ras* रस
Juicy (adj∘) *rasdār* रसदार
Jumble (m∘) *gaḍbaḍ* गडबड
Jumbo (adj∘) *viśhal* विशाल
Jump (v∘) *kudṇe* कुदणे
Junction (n∘) *sandhi-sthān* संधि-स्थान
Juncture (n∘) *ghaṭnāchakra* घटनाचक्र
Junior (adj∘) *chhoṭa, lahān* छोटा, लहान
Junk (f∘) *aḍgaḷ* अडगळ
Jupitor (m∘) *bruhaspati* बृहस्पति
Jury (m∘) *pañch* पंच
Just (adv∘) 1. (now) *nuktāch* नुकताच 2. (only) *kevaḷ* केवळ 3. (fair) *vaidh, uchit* वैध, उचित
Justice (m∘) *nyāy* न्याय
Justification (n∘) *samarthan* समर्थन
Juvenile (adj∘) *kiśhor, taruṇ* किशोर, तरुण
Juxtapose (v∘) *lāvaṇe* लावणे*

K

Keen (adj∘) *utkaṭ* उत्कट
Keep (v∘) *ṭhevṇe* ठेवणे*
Keeper (m∘) *rākhaṇḍār* राखणदार
Kernel (m∘) *gar, magaj* गर, मगज
Kettle (f∘) *keṭlī* केटली
Key (f∘) *killī* किल्ली
Kick (f∘) *ṭhokar* ठोकर; (v∘) *tuḍaṇe* तुडवणे*
Kid (m∘) *bacchā, bālak* बच्चा, बालक
Kidnap (n∘) *apaharaṇ* अपहरण
Kidney (m∘) *gurdā* गुरदा
Kill (v∘) *māraṇe* मारणे*
Kiln (f∘) *bhaṭṭī* भट्टी
Kin (m∘) *nātedār* नातेदार
Kind (adj∘) *dayāḷu* दयाळु; (m∘) *prakār* (f∘) *jāti* प्रकार, जाति
Kindle (v∘) *peṭavṇe* पेटवणे*
Kindness (f∘) *dayā* दया
King (m∘) *rājā* राजा
Kingdom (n∘) *rājya* राज्य
Kink (f∘) *vaḷī* वळी
Kinship (n∘) *nāte* नाते
Kiss (m∘) *mukā* मुका
Kitchen (f∘) *svayampākghar* स्वयंपाकघर
Kite (f∘) 1. *patang* पतंग, 2. (bird) *ghār* घार
Knack (f∘) *kalā* कला
Knapsack (f∘) *pishvī* पिशवी
Knead (v∘) *maḷṇe* मळणे*
Knee (m∘) *guḍaghā* गुडघा
Kneel (v∘) *guḍghe ṭekṇe* गुडघे टेकणे*
Knife (f∘) *surī* सुरी, (m∘) *chāku* चाकु
Knit (v∘) *viṇaṇe* विणणे*
Knob (m∘) *muṭh* मुठ
Knock (v∘) *āpaṭṇe, ādḷṇe* आपटणे, आदळणे
Knot (f∘) *gāṭh* गाठ
Know (v∘) *jāṇaṇe* जाणणे*
Knowledge (n∘) *dnyān,* (m∘) *bodh* ज्ञान, बोध

L

Label (f∘) *chiṭhī, chiṭṭhī* चिठी, चिी
Laboratory (f∘) *prayogśhāḷā* प्रयोगशाळा
Labour (f∘) *mehnat,* (m∘) *śhram,* (n∘) *kashṭa* मेहनत, श्रम, कष्ट
Labourer (m∘) *majūr* मजूर
Lace (f∘) *fīt, jāḷī* फीत, जाळी
Lack (f∘) *kamī* कमी
Lad (m∘) *bālak* बालक
Ladder (f∘) *śhīḍī, niśhāṇī* शीडी, निशाणी
Ladle (f∘) *paḷī,* (m∘) *ḍāv* पळी, डाव
Lady (f∘) *strī, mahilā* स्त्री, महिला
Lagoon (n∘) *sarovar* सरोवर
Lake (n∘) *sarovar* (m∘) *talāv* सरोवर, तलाव
Lamb (n∘) *kokrū* कोकरू
Lame (adj∘) *langḍā* लंगडा
Lamp (m∘) *divā* दिवा
Language (f∘) *bhāshā* भाषा
Lap (f∘) *oṭī, mānḍī* ओटी, मांडी
Lapse (f∘) *chūk* चूक
Lard (f∘) *charbī* चरबी
Large (adj∘) *moṭhā, viśhāl* मोठा, विशाल
Last (adj∘) *antim* अंतिम; (v∘) *ṭikṇe* टिकणे
Latch (f∘) *kḍī, khiṭī* कडी, खिटी
Late (adj∘) 1. (time) *uśhīr* 2. (passed away) *mṛt* मृत
Lately (adv∘) *ājakāl* आजकाल
Later (adv∘) *mag* मग
Laugh (n∘) *hansū* हंसू; (v∘) *hasaṇe* हंसणे
Law (m∘) *kāyadā* कायदा
Lawyer (m∘) *vakīl* वकील
Lazy (adj∘) *āḷaśhī* आळशी
Lead (n∘) *śhīse* शिसे; (v∘) *puḍhākārṇe* पुढाकारणे
Leader (m∘) *netā* नेता
Leading (adj∘) *mukhya* मुख्य
Leaf (n∘) *pān* पान
League (m∘) *sangh* संघ
Lean (adj∘) *dubḷā, patlā* दुबळा, पतला
Leap (v∘) *kudṇe* कुदणे
Learn (v∘) *śhikṇe* शिकणे*
Lease (m∘) *ijārā* इजारा
Least (pron∘) *kamītkamī* कमीतकमी
Leave (f∘) *suṭī* सुटी; (v∘) *soḍṇe, vagaḷṇe* सोडणे*, वगळणे*
Lecture (n∘) *bhāshaṇ* भाषण
Left (adj∘) *ḍavā* डावा
Leg (f∘) *tāngaḍī* तंगडी; (m∘) *pāy* पाय
Legal (adj∘) *vaidh, kāyadeśhīr* वैध, कायदेशीर
Legend (f∘) *dantakathā* दंतकथा
Legible (adj∘) *suvācchya* सुवाच्य
Legislature (f∘) *vidhansabhā* विधानसभा
Legitimate (adj∘) *vaidh, kāyadeśhīr* वैध,

adj∘ = Adjective, adv∘ = Adverb; *conj.* = Conjunction, f∘ = Feminine gender, *ind.* = Indeclinable, m∘ = Masculine gender, n∘ = Neuter gender, pl∘ = Plural

कायदेशीर

Leisure (f∘) *fursat* फुरसत

Lemon (n∘) *limbū* लिंबू

Lend (v∘) *udhār deṇe* उधार देणे*

Length (f∘) *lāmb* लांब

Lengthy (adj∘) *lambā* लंबा

Leniecy (f∘) *udārtā* उदारता

Lenient (adj∘) *udār, saumya* उदार, सौम्य

Lentil (n∘) *masūr* मसूर

Leopard (m∘) *chittā* चित्ता

Less (adj∘) *kamī* कमी

Lesson (m∘) *pāṭh, dhaḍā* पाठ, धडा

Lethargy (m∘) *āḷas* आळस

Letter 1. (n∘ alphabet) *akṣhar* अक्षर 2. (n∘ mail) *patra* पत्र

Level (adj∘) *samtaḷ, sapāṭ* समतळ, सपाट

Level (m∘) *star* स्तर

Levy (m∘) *kar* कर

Liability (n∘) *uttardāyītva* उत्तरदायीत्व

Liable (adj∘) *uttardāyī* उत्तरदायी

Liar (adj∘) *khoṭāḍā* खोटाडा

Liberal (adj∘) *udār* उदार

Liberate (v∘) *mukta karṇe* मुक्त क∘*

Liberation (f∘) *mukti* मुक्ति

Liberty (f∘) *mukti,* (n∘) *svātantrya* मुक्ति, स्वातंत्र्य

Libra (f∘) *tulā raśhi* तुला राशि

Library (n∘) *pustakālay* पुस्तकालय

Licence (f∘) *anumati* अनुमति

Lick (v∘) *chāṭṇe* चाटणे*

Lid (n∘) *jhākaṇ* झाकण

Lie (v∘) 1. (speaking) *khoṭe bolṇe* खोटे बोलणे* 2. (rest) *loṭṇe* लोटणे

Life (m∘) *prāṇ, jīvan* प्राण, जीवन

Lift (v∘) *uchalṇe* उचलणे*

Ligament (m∘) *snāyu* स्नायु

Light (adj∘) 1. (weight) *halkā* हलका 2. (colour) *fikkā* फिक्का; (m∘) *prakāśh,* प्रकाश

Lightning (f∘) *vīj* वीज

Like (adj∘) *samān, sārkhā* समान, सारखा; (v∘) *āvaḍṇe* आवडणे*

Like that (adv∘) *tasā* तसा

Like this (adv∘) *asā* असा

Like what (adv∘) *kasā* कसा?

Likely (adj∘) *sambhāvya* संभाव्य

Likelyhood (f∘) *sambhāvaṇe* संभावना

Likewise (adv∘) *tyāchpramāṇe* त्याचप्रमाणे

Lily (f∘) *kumudinī* कुमुदिनी

Lime (n∘) 1. (fruit) *limbū* लिंबू 2. (chemical) (m∘) *chunā* चुना

Limit (f∘) *sīmā* सीमा

Limited (adj∘) *sīmit* सीमित

Limp (v∘) *laṅgḍṇe* लंगडणे

Line (f∘) *rekhā, reśhā* रेखा, रेशा

Lining (n∘) *astar* अस्तर

Link (f∘) *kaḍī* कडी

Lion (m∘) *siṁha* सिंह

Lioness (f∘) *siṁhīṇ* सिंहीण

Lip (m∘) *oṭh* ओठ

Liquid (m∘) *drav* द्रव

Liquidation (n∘) *diwāḷe* दिवाळे

Liquor (n∘) *madya* मद्य

List (f∘) *sūchī, tālikā* सूची, तालिका

Listen (v∘) *aikṇe* ऐकणे*

Literacy (f∘) *sākṣhartā* साक्षरता

Literal (adj∘) *śhābdik* शाब्दिक

Little (adj∘) *chhoṭā, lahān* छोटा, लहान; (adv∘) *kiñchit, jarā* किंचित्, जरा

Little finger (f∘) *kanīkā* कनीका

Live (adj∘) *jīvit, jivant* जीवित, जिवंत

Live (v∘) *jagṇe* जगणे

Lively (adj∘) *uṭhāvdār* उठावदार

Livelyhood (f∘) *jīvikā* जीविका

Liver (n∘) *yakrut* यकृत्

Living (adj∘) *jīvit, jivant* जीवित, जिवंत

Living (f∘) *jīvikā* जीविका

Lizard (f∘) *pāl* पाल

Load (m∘) *bhār* भार

Loan (n∘) *karj, ruṇ* कर्ज, ऋण

Local (adj∘) *sthānik* स्थानिक

Locality (m∘) *mohallā,* (f∘) *jāgā* मोहल्ला, जागा

Locate (v∘) *śhodhṇe* शोधणे*

Location (n∘) *sthān,* (f∘) *jāgā* स्थान, जागा

Lock (n∘) *kulup* कुलुप

Locust (m∘) *ṭoḷ* टोळ

Loft (n∘) *āḍe, āḍhe* आड, आढे

Lofty (adj∘) *bhavya* भव्य

Logic (m∘) *tark* तर्क

Logo (n∘) *pratīk-chihna* प्रतीक-चिह्न

Loitering (f∘) *reṅgāḷṇe* रेंगाळणे

Lone (adj∘) *ekṭā* एकटा

Lonely (adj∘) *ekṭā, eklā* एकटा, एकला

Lonesome (adj∘) *ekṭā, eklā* एकटा, एकला

Long (adj∘) *lāmb* लांब

Look (v∘) *pāhaṇe* पाहणे*

Loom (m∘) *māg* माग

Loose (adj∘) *ḍhīlā* ढीला

Lopsided (adj∘) *ektarfī* एकतरफी

Lord (m∘) *mālak, swāmī* मालक, स्वामी

Lose (v∘) *haravṇe* हरवणे*

Loss (n∘) *nuksān,* (m∘) *toṭā* नुकसान, तोटा

Lot (adj∘) *puṣhkaḷ* पुष्कळ

Lotus (n∘) *kamaḷ* कमळ

Loud (adj∘) *moṭhā* मोठा

Louse (f∘) *ū* ऊ

Lovable (adj∘) *priya* प्रिय

Love (n∘) *prem,* (m∘) *sneha* प्रेम, स्नेह; **Love** (v∘) *prem karṇe* प्रेम क∘*

Lovely (adj∘) *sundar* सुंदर

Lover (m∘ f∘) *premī, premikā* प्रेमी, प्रेमिका

Low (adj∘) *khālchā, kṣhudra* खालचा, क्षुद्र

Loyal (adj∘) *imāndār* इमानदार

Lucid (adj∘) *subodh* सुबोध

Lucious (adj∘) *sumadhur* सुमधुर

Luck (n∘) *bhāgya* भाग्य

Luckily (adv∘) *bhāgyavaśha* भाग्यवश

Lucky (adj∘) *bhāgyaśhālī* भाग्यशाली

Lucrative (adj∘) *fāyademand* फायदेमंद

Lump (m∘) *gaḍā* गडा

Lunatic (adj∘) *pāgal* पागल

Lung (n∘) *fuffus* फुफ्फुस

Lure (n∘) *pralobhan* प्रलोभन

Lust (f∘) *lālsā* लालसा

Luxuriant (adj∘) *prachur* प्रचुर

adj∘ = Adjective, adv∘ = Adverb; *conj.* = Conjunction, f∘ = Feminine gender, *ind.* = Indeclinable, m∘ = Masculine gender, n∘ = Neuter gender, pl∘ = Plural

Luxury (m∘) *vilās* विलास

Lyric (f∘) *kavitā* कविता

M

Machine (n∘) *yantra* यंत्र

Mad (adj∘) *pāgal* पागल

Madam (f∘) *mahilā* महिला

Madium (adj∘) *madhyam* मध्यम; (m∘) *mādhyam* माध्यम

Magazine (f∘) *patrikā* पत्रिका

Magic (f∘) *jādū* जादू

Magician (m∘) *jādūgār* जादूगार

Magnet (m∘) *chumbak* चुंबक

Magnificient (adj∘) *śhāndār* शानदार

Magnify (v∘) *vākhāṇaṇe* वाखाणणे*

Magnitude (f∘) *mahattā* महत्ता

Maid (f∘) *dāsī* दासी

Mail (f∘) *ḍāk* डाक

Mailman (m∘) *ṭapāl* टपाल

Main (adj∘) *mukhya* मुख्य

Maize, corn (m∘) *makā* मका

Major (adj∘) *mukhya* मुख्य

Majority (m∘) *bahumat* बहुमत

Make (v∘) *banavṇe* बनवणे*

Maker (m∘) *kartā* कर्ता

Male (adj∘) *nar* नर

Malice (m∘) *dveṣh* द्वेष

Malign (v∘) *nindā karṇe* निंदा क∘*

Mammoth (adj∘) *viśhāl* विशाल

Man (m∘) *manuṣhya* मनुष्य

Management (f∘) *vyavasthā* व्यवस्था

Manager (m∘) *vyavasthāpak* व्यवस्थापक

Mane (n∘) *āyāḷ, kesar* आयाळ, केसर

Mango (m∘) *āmbā* आंबा

Mania (f∘) *lahar* लहर

Mankind (f∘) *mānava jāti* मानव जाति

Manner (f∘) *rīti, ḍhaṅg* रीति, ढंग

Mansion (f∘) *havelī, koṭhī* हवेली, कोठी

Manslaughter (f∘) *narhatyā* नरहत्या

Manufacture (n∘) *utpādan* उत्पादन

Manure (n∘) *khat* खत

Many (pron∘) *anek* अनेक

Map (m∘) *nakśhā* नकाशा

Marble (m∘) *saṅgamaravar* संगमरवर

Margin (m∘) *kinārā* किनारा

Maritime (adj∘) *daryāvardī* दर्यावर्दी

Mark (n∘) *niśhāṇ, chinha* निशाण, चिन्ह

Market (m∘) *bāzār* बाजार

Marriage (m∘) *vivāha,* (n∘) *lagna* विवाह, लग्न

Marrow (f∘) *majjā* मज्जा

Marry (v∘) *vivāh karṇe* विवाह क∘*

Mars (m∘) *maṅgaḷ* मंगळ

Martyr (m∘) *śhahīd* शहीद

Marvel (m∘) *chamatkār* चमत्कार

Marvelous (adj∘) *chamatkārik* चमत्कारिक

Mascara (n∘) *añjan* अंजन

Mask (m∘) *mukhavṭā* मुखवटा

Massacre (f∘) *kattal* कत्तल

Massage (f∘) *māliśh* मालिश

Massive (adj∘) *mahākāy* महाकाय

Master (m∘) *swāmī* स्वामी

Mat (f∘) *chaṭaī* चटई

Match (f∘) *spardhā* स्पर्धा

Matchbox (f∘) *āgpeṭī* आगपेटी

Mate (m∘ f∘) *sobtī* सोबती

Material (n∘) *sāmān* सामान

Materialism (m∘) *bhautikvād* भौतिकवाद

Maternal uncle (m∘) *māmā* मामा

Mathematics (n∘) *gaṇit* गणित

Matter (m∘) *viṣhay,* (f∘) *goṣhṭa* विषय, गोष्ट

Mattress (f∘) *gādī* गादी

Mature (adj∘) *pakva, prauḍh* पक्व, प्रौढ

Maximum (m∘) *adhiktam* अधिकतम

Maybe (adv∘) *kadāchit* कदाचित्

Maze (f∘) *cakravyūha* चक्रव्यूह

Me (pron∘) *malā* मला

Meal (n∘) *bhojan* भोजन

Mean (adj∘) *halkā* हलका

Meaning (m∘) *arth* अर्थ

Means (m∘) *upāy* उपाय

Meanwhile (adv∘) *darmyān* दरम्यान

Measles (n∘) *govar* गोवर

Measure (m∘) *upāy* उपाय

Measure (v∘) *nāpaṇe* नापणे*

Measurement (n∘) *māp* माप

Meat (n∘) *mās* मास

Medal (n∘) *padak* पदक

Meddling (m∘) *hastakṣhep* हस्तक्षेप

Media (n∘) *mādhyam* माध्यम

Medication (n∘) *auṣhadh* औषध

Medicine (n∘) *auṣhadh* औषध

Medoicre (adj∘) *māmulī* मामुली

Meet (v∘) *milaṇe* मिळणे

Meeting (f∘) *sabhā* सभा

Melañcholy (f∘) *udāsī* उदासी

Melody (f∘) *dhun* धुन

Melon (n∘) *kharbūj* खरबूज

Melt (v∘) *pighaḷaṇe* पिघळणे

Member (m∘) *sadsya* सदस्य

Memento (f∘) *āṭhavaṇ* आठवण

Memorable (adj∘) *smaranīya* स्मरणीय

Memorandum (f∘) *dnyāpikā* ज्ञापिका

Memorial (n∘) *smārak* स्मारक

Memory (f∘) *smruti* स्मृति

Menace (n∘) *saṅkaṭ* संकट

Mend (v∘) *ṭhīk karṇe* ठीक क∘*

Mental (adj∘) *mānasik* मानसिक

Mentality (f∘) *manovrutti* मनोवृत्ति

Merchandise (m∘) *māl,* (n∘) *sāmān* माल, सामान

Merchant (m∘) *vyāpārī* व्यापारी

Merciful (adj∘) *dayāvān* दयावान

Mercury, metal (m∘) *pārā* पारा; planet (m∘) *budh* बुध

Mercy (f∘) *dayā* दया

Mere (adj∘) *keval, mātra* केवळ, मात्र

Merely (adv∘) *kevaḷ* केवळ

Merge (v∘) *ek hoṇe, milṇe* एक हो∘, मिळणे

Merit (m∘) *guṇ* गुण

Meritorious (adj∘) *stutya* स्तुत्य

Merry (adj∘) *ānandit* आनंदित

Mesh (f∘) *jāḷī* जाळी

Message (m∘) *sandeśh* संदेश

Metal (f∘) *dhātu* धातु

Metaphor (m∘) *rūpak* रूपक

adj∘ = Adjective, adv∘ = Adverb; *conj.* = Conjunction, f∘ = Feminine gender, *ind.* = Indeclinable, m∘ = Masculine gender, n∘ = Neuter gender, pl∘ = Plural

Meteor (f∘) *ulkā* उल्का

Method (m∘) *paddhati, rīti* पद्धति, रीति

Meticulous (adj∘) *dhyānpūrvak* ध्यानपूर्वक

Microbe (m∘) *jīvāṇu* जीवाणु

Midday (f∘) *dupār* दुपार

Middle (m∘) *madhya* मध्य

Middle finger (f∘) *madhyamā* मध्यमा

Middleman (m∘) *dalāl* दलाल

Midst (adv∘) *madhye* मध्ये

Might (n∘) *bal,* (f∘) *śhakti* बळ, शक्ति

Mild (adj∘) *saumya* सौम्य

Mile (m∘) *mail* मैल

Militant (adj∘) *yoddhā* योद्धा

Military (f∘) *seṇā* सेना

Milk (n) *dūdh* दूध

Milkmaid (f∘) *gavaḷīṇ* गवळीण

Milkman (m∘) *gavaḷī* गवळी

Mill (m∘) *kārkhāṇā* कारखाना; (v∘) *daḷṇe* दळणे*

Millionaire (m∘) *lakhpati* लखपति

Mimic (v∘) *nakkal utārṇe* नक्कल उतारणे*

Mind (n∘) *man* मन

Mindful (adj∘) *sāvadhān* सावधान

Mine (f∘) *khāṇ* खाण; (pron∘ m∘ f∘) *mājhā* माझा, माझी, माझे

Mineral (adj∘) *khanij* खनिज

Minimum (adj∘) *laghutam* लघुतम

Minister (m∘) *mantri* मंत्री

Ministry (n∘) *mantrālay* मंत्रालय

Minor (adj∘) *gauṇ* गौण

Mint (f∘ money) *ṭāksāḷ* टाकसाळ; (m∘ plant) *padīṇe* पदीना

Minute (adj∘) *sūkṣhma* सूक्ष्म

Miracle (m∘) *chamatkār* चमत्कार

Mire (m∘) *chikhal* चिखल

Mirror (m∘) *ārsā* आरसा

Miscellaneous (adj∘) *saṅkīrṇa* संकीर्ण

Mischief (f∘) *khoḍ* खोड

Mischievous (adj∘) *khoḍkar* खोडकर

Miscreant (m∘) *badmāśh* बदमाश

Miser (adj∘) *kañjūs, chikkū* कंजूस, चिक्कू

Miserable (adj∘) *dayanīya* दयनीय

Misery (f∘) *durdaśhā* दुर्दशा

Misfortune (n∘) *durbhāgya* दुर्भाग्य

Misgiving (m∘) *sandeha* संदेह

Mishap (f∘) *durghaṭṇe* दुर्घटना

Miss (v∘) *chukṇe* चुकणे*

Mist (n∘) *dhuke* धुके

Mistake (f∘) *chūk* चूक

Mistrust (m∘) *aviśhvās* अविश्वास

Misuse (m∘) *durupayog* दुरुपयोग

Mix (v∘) *miḷṇe, miḷavṇe** मिळणे, मिळवणे*

Mixture (n∘) *miśhraṇ* मिश्रण

Moan (v∘) *kaṇhaṇe* कण्हणे

Mob (f∘) *gardī* गर्दी

Mockery (m∘) *upahās* उपहास

Mode (f∘) *rīti* रीति. (m∘) *ḍhaṅg* ढंग

Modern (adj∘) *ādhunik* आधुनिक

Modest (adj∘) *sādhāraṇ* साधारण

Modification (n∘) *parivartan,* (m∘) *badal* परिवर्तन, बदल

Moist (adj∘) *olsar* ओलसर

Moisture (f∘) *ol* ओल

Molar (f∘) *dāḍh* दाढ

Mole (m∘) *tīḷ* तीळ

Molecule (m∘) *aṇu* अणु

Molestaion (m∘) *balātkār* बलात्कार

Moment (m∘) *kṣhaṇ* क्षण

Momentary (adj∘) *kṣhaṇik* क्षणिक

Momentum (m∘) *saṁveg* संवेग

Monarch (m∘) *rājā* राजा

Monday (m∘) *somwār* सोमवार

Money (m∘) *paise* पैसे

Monitor (m∘) *nirīkṣhak* निरीक्षक

Monk (m∘) *bhikṣhu* भिक्षु

Monkey (n∘) *vānar* वानर

Monopoly (m∘) *ekādhikār* एकाधिकार

Monotonous (adj∘) *eksurā* एकसुरा

Monster (m∘) *rākṣhas* राक्षस

Month (m∘) *mahinā* महिना

Monument (n∘) *smārak* स्मारक

Mood (f∘) *manaḥsthiti* मन:स्थिति

Moon (m∘) *chandra* चंद्र

Moral (adj∘) *naitik* नैतिक

Morality (f∘) *naitiktā* नैतिकता

More (adj∘) *adhik* अधिक

Moreover (adv∘) *śhivāy* शिवाय

Morning (f∘) *sakāḷ* सकाळ

Mortal (adj∘) *naśhvar* नश्वर

Mortgage (m∘) *dhanko* धनको

Mosquito (m∘) *ḍās* डास

Most (pron∘) *bahutek* बहुतेक

Mostly (adv∘) *bahutek* बहुतेक

Moth (m∘) *pataṅg* पतंग

Mother (f∘) *āī* आई

Mother-in-law (f∘) *sāsū* सासू

Motion (f∘) *gati, chāl* गति, चाल

Mountain (m∘) *pahāḍ* पहाड, *parvat* पर्वत

Mouse (m∘) *undir* उंदिर

Mouth (n∘) *toṇḍ* तोंड

Move (v∘) *hālṇe, hālavṇe** हालणे, हालवणे*

Movement (f∘) *gati-vidhi* गतिविधि

Movie (n∘) *chitrapaṭ* चित्रपट

Much (adv∘) *puṣhkaḷ* पुष्कळ

Mule (n∘) *gāḍhav* गाढव

Multiplication (m∘) *guṇākār* गुणाकार

Mumble (v∘) *budbudaṇe* बुदबुदणे

Murder (m∘) *khūn,* (f∘) *hatyā* खून, हत्या

Murmer (v∘) *fusfusaṇe* फुसफुसणे

Muscle (f∘) *peśhī* पेशी

Museum (n∘) *saṅgrahālay* संग्रहालय

Music (n∘) *saṅgīt* संगीत

Musician (m∘) *saṅgītakār* संगीतकार

Must (adv∘) *avaśhya* अवश्य

Mustache (f∘) *miśhī* मिशी

Mute (adj∘) *mukā* मुका

Mutually (adv∘) *paraspar* परस्पर

Myself (pron∘) *svatah* स्वत:

Mysterious (adj∘) *rahasyamay* रहस्यमय

Mystery (n∘) *rahasya* रहस्य

Mythology (n∘) *purāṇaśhāstra* पुराणशास्त्र

N

Nab (v∘) *paṭkāvṇe* पटकावणे*

Nail, 1. on finger (n∘) *nakh* नख 2. to hammer (f∘) *khiḷā* खिळा

adj∘ = Adjective, adv∘ = Adverb; *conj.* = Conjunction, f∘ = Feminine gender, *ind.* = Indeclinable, m∘ = Masculine gender, n∘ = Neuter gender, pl∘ = Plural

Naive (adj∘) *bhoḷā* भोळा

Naked (adj∘) *nagna, nāgaḍā* नग्न, नागडा

Name (m∘) *nāँv* नांव

Namely (adv∘) *arthāt* अर्थात्

Nap (f∘) *dulkī* डुलकी

Narration (n∘) *vivaraṇ, varṇan* विवरण, वर्णन

Narrow (adj∘) *arund* अरुंद

Nasty (adj∘) *ongaḷ* ओंगळ

Nation (m∘) *deśh,* (n∘) *rāṣhtra* देश, राष्ट्र

National (adj∘) *rāṣhtrīya* राष्ट्रीय

Nationality (f∘) *nāgrīktā* नागरीकता

Nationalization (n∘) *rāṣhtrīyīkaraṇ* राष्ट्रीयीकरण

Native (adj∘) 1. *deśhī* देशी; 2, *nivāsī* निवासी

Natural (adj∘) *naisargik* नैसर्गिक

Nature (f∘) *prakruti, sruṣhṭi* प्रकृति, सृष्टि

Naughty (adj∘) *khoḍkar* खोडकर

Navel (f∘) *nābhi, bembī* नाभि, बेंबी

Navigation (n∘) *sañchālan* संचालन

Navy (f∘) *nau-senā* नौसेना

Near (adj∘) *nikaṭ, samīp, javaḷ* निकट, समीप, जवळ

Nearly (adv∘) *ljavaḷjavaḷ* जवळजवळ

Neat (adj∘) *sāf* साफ

Necessary (adj∘) *jarūrī, āvaśhyak* जरूरी, आवश्यक

Neck (f∘) *mān* मान

Necklace (m∘) *hār* हार

Nectar(n∘) *sahad* सहद

Need (f∘) *jarūrat, garaj, āvaśhyaktā* जरूरत, गरज, आवश्यकता

Needle (f∘) *suī* सुई

Needy (adj∘) *garajvant* गरजवंत

Negative (adj∘) *nakārātmak* नकारात्मक

Neglect (f∘) *upekṣhā, haygay* उपेक्षा, हयगय; (v∘) *haygay karṇe* हयगय क∘*

Negligence (f∘) *haygay* हयगय

Negotiation (m∘) *vinimay* विनिमय

Neigh (v∘) *khinkāḷṇe* खिंकाळणे

Neighbor (m∘) *śhejārī* शेजारी

Nephew (m∘) *putaṇyā; bhāchā* पुतण्या; भाचा

Nepotism (m∘) *pakṣhapāt* पक्षपात

Neptune (m∘) *varuṇ* वरुण

Nerve (f∘) *nas, snāyu* नस, स्नायु

Nervous (adj∘) *bhitrā* भित्रा

Nest (n∘) *gharṭe* घरटे

Net (n∘) *jāḷe* जाळे

Neutral (adj∘) *taṭastha* तटस्थ

Never (adv∘) *kadhī nāhī* कधी नाही

Nevertheless (adv∘) *tathāpi* तथापि

News (m∘) *samāchār* समाचार

Newspaper (n∘) *vartamanpatra* वर्तमानपत्र

Next (adj∘) *puḍhīl* पुढील

Nibble (v∘) *kurtuḍṇe* कुरतुडणे*

Nice (adj∘) *manohar* मनोहर

Nickname (n∘) *upnāँva* उपनांव

Niece (f∘) *putaṇī; bhāchī* पुतणी; भाची

Night (f∘) *rātra* रात्र

Nightfall (f∘) *sandhyā* संध्या

Nightingale (f∘) *bulbul* बुलबुल

Nil (n∘) *śhūnya* शून्य

Nimble (adj∘) *chapaḷ, chalākh* चपळ, चलाख

Nine (adj∘) *naū* नऊ

Nineteen (adj∘) *ekoṇvīs* एकोणवीस

Ninety (adj∘) *navvad* नव्वद

Ninth (adj∘) *navavā* नववा

Nipple (n∘) *stanāgra* स्तनाग्र

Nitwit (m∘) *mūrkha, buddū* मूर्ख, बुद्दू

No (adv∘) *na, nāhī* न, नाही

Nobility (f∘) *kulīnatā* कुलीनता

Noble (adj∘) *kulīn* कुलीन

Nobody (pron∘) *koṇīhī nāhī* कोणीही नाहीं

Nocturnal (adj∘) *niśhāchar* निशाचर

Noise (m∘) *kalloḷ* कल्लोळ

Nomad (adj∘) *āwārā* आवारा

Nominal (adj∘) *nāmamātra* नाममात्र

Nomination (n∘) *nāmāṅkan* नामांकन

None (pron∘) *koṇīhī nāhī* कोणीही नाही

Nose (n∘) *nāk* नाक

Not (adv∘) *nāhī, na* नाही, न

Not at all (adv∘) *bilkul nāhī* बिलकुल नाही

Notice (f∘) *sūchaṇe* सूचना

Notification (f∘) *sūchaṇe* सूचना

Notify (v∘) *sūchaṇe deṇe* सूचना देणे*

Novel (m∘) *kādambarī* कादंबरी

Now (adv∘) *ātā* आता

Now a days (adv∘) *ājakāl* आजकाल

Now and then (adv∘) *kadhī-kadhī* कधी कधी

Nowhere (adv∘) *koṭhehī nāhī* कोठेही नाही

Nurse (f∘) *parichārikā* परिचारिका

Nutmeg (n∘) *jāyfaḷ* जायफळ

Nutrition (m∘) *āhār* आहार

Nymph (f∘) *apsarā* अप्सरा

O

O' Clock (adv∘) *vājtā* वाजता

Oasis (n∘) *marudyān* मरुद्यान

Oath (f∘) *śhapath* शपथ

Obese (adj∘) *laṭhṭha* लठ्ठ

Obey (v∘) *ādnyā pāḷṇe* आज्ञा पाळणे*

Object (f∘) *vastu* वस्तु

Objection (f∘) *harkat* हरकत

Objective (m∘) *hetu,* (n∘) *dhyeya,* (m∘) *uddeśha* हेतु, ध्येय, उद्देश

Obligation (n∘) *dāyitva* दायित्व

Oblique (adj∘) *vākḍā* वाकडा

Obliterate (v∘) *miṭavṇe* मिटवणे*

Oblong (m∘) *āyat* आयत

Obscene (adj∘) *aśhlīl* अश्लील

Obscure (adj∘) *aprasiddha* अप्रसिद्ध

Observation (n∘) *nirīkṣhaṇ* निरीक्षण

Observatory (f∘) *vedhaśhālā* वेधशाला

Observe (v∘) *inirīkṣhaṇ karṇe* निरीक्षण क∘*

Obsession (n∘) *pachhāḍṇe* पछाडणे

Obsolete (adj∘) *aprachalit* अप्रचलित

Obstacle (f∘) *bādhā* बाधा

Obstinate (adj∘) *jiddī* जिद्दी

Obstruct (v∘) *bādhā ṭākṇe* बाधा टाकणे*

Obstruction (f∘) *bādhā,* (n∘) *vighna* बाधा, विघ्न

Obtain (v∘) *sampādṇe* संपादणे*

Obvious (adj∘) *suspaṣhṭ, prakaṭ* सुस्पष्ट, प्रकट

Occasion (m∘) *avsar* अवसर

Occupation (m∘) *dhandā* धंदा

adj∘ = Adjective, adv∘ = Adverb; *conj.* = Conjunction, f∘ = Feminine gender, *ind.* = Indeclinable, m∘ = Masculine gender, n∘ = Neuter gender, pl∘ = Plural

Occupy (v◦) *rāhṇe* राहणे

Occur (v◦) *hoṇe* हो◦

Occurence (f◦) *ghaṭaṇā* घटणा

Ocean (m◦) *samudra, sāgar* समुद्र, सागर

Octagon (m◦) *ashṭabhuj* अष्टभुज

Octave (n◦) *ashṭak* अष्टक

Odd (adj◦) *visham, vichitra* विषम, विचित्र

Odor (m◦) *gandh, vās* गंध, वास

Of (pron◦) *chā, chī, che; jhā, jhī, jhe,* चा, ची च, झा, झी, झे

Off (adj◦) *band* बंद

Offence (m◦) *aparādh* अपराध

Offensive (adj◦) *ghātak* घातक

Offensive (m◦) *hallā* हल्ला

Offer (m◦) *prastāv* प्रस्ताव; (v◦) *arpaṇ karṇe* अर्पण क◦*

Office (n◦) *kāryālay, daptar* कार्यालय, दप्तर

Officer (m◦) *adhikārī* अधिकारी

Official (adj◦) *sarkārī* सरकारी

Offspring (f◦) *santati* संतति

Often (adv◦) *vāraṁvār* वारंवार

Oil (n◦) *tel* तेल

Ok (adj◦ adv◦) *ṭhīk, ṭhīk āhe* ठीक, ठीक आहे

Okra (f◦) *bhenḍī* भेंडी

Old (adj◦) *purāṇa, būḍḍhā* पुराणा, बुड्ढा

Old lady (f◦) *buḍḍhī* बुड्ढी

Old man (m◦) *vṛddha* वृद्ध

Omen (m◦) *śhakun* सकुन

Omission (f◦) *vagaḷṇe* वगळणे

Omit (v◦) *soḍṇe* सोडणे*, *vagaḷṇe* वगळणे*

Omnipotent (adj◦) *sarvaśhaktimān* सर्वशक्तिमान

Omniscient (adj◦) *sarvadnya* सर्वज्ञ

On (m◦) *-var* वर

On both sides (adv◦) *dutarfā* दुतर्फा

Once (adv◦) *ek veḷ* एक वेळ

One (adj◦) *ek* एक

Oneself (pron◦) *svayam, svatah* स्वयं, स्वत:

Onion (m◦) *kāndā* कांदा

Only (adv◦) *kewaḷ, fakta* केवळ, फक्त

Onset (m◦) *ārambha* आरंभ

Onslaught (m◦) *hallā, chaḍhāī* हल्ला, चढाई

Onto (prep◦) *-var* –वर

Onus (m◦) *dāyitva* दायित्व

Onward (adv◦) *puḍhe* पुढे

Obdient (adj◦) *ādnyākārī* आज्ञाकारी

Ooze (v◦) *pāzarṇe, zirapṇe, gaḷṇe* पाझरणे, झिरपणे, गळणे

Opaque (adj◦) *apārdarśhak* अपारदर्शक

Open (adj◦) *ughaḍā* उघडा; (v◦) *ugdaḍṇe* उघडणे*

Opening 1. (aparture) (n◦) *chhidra* छिद्र; 2. (opportunity) (m◦) *avsar* अवसर; 3. (way out) *mārga* मार्ग; 4. (unveiling) *ārambha* आरंभ

Openly (adv◦) *ughaḍughaḍ* उघडउघड

Operate (v◦) *chālvaṇe* चालवणे*

Operation (f◦) *kaiyā, kruti* क्रिया, कृति

Operational (adj◦) *chālū, lāgū* चालू, लागू

Operator (m◦) *chālak* चालक

Opinion (n◦) *mat* मत

Opium (f◦) *afū* अफू

Opponent (m◦) *pratispardhī* प्रतिस्पर्धी

Opportune (adj◦) *upayukta* उपयुक्त

Opportunity (f◦) *sandhī* संधी

Oppose (v◦) *virodh karṇe* विरोध क◦*

Opposite (adj◦) *viruddha* विरुद्ध

Opposition (m◦) *virodh* विरोध

Oppress (v◦) *satāvṇe* सतावणे*

Oppression (m◦) *atyāchār* अत्याचार

Oppulent (adj◦) *samruddha* समृद्ध

Optimist (m◦) *āśhāvādī* आशावादी

Option (m◦) *vikalp* विकल्प

Or (adv◦) *athawā, kimvā* अथवा, किंवा

Oral (adj◦) *tonḍī* तोंडी

Orange fruit (n◦) & color *nārangī* नारंगी

Orator (m◦) *vaktā* वक्ता

Orchard (n◦) *upvan* उपवन

Order (m◦) *ādeśh* (f◦) *ādnyā* आदेश, आज्ञा; (v◦) *ādnyā deṇe* आज्ञा देणे*

Ordinary (adj◦) *sādhā, sādhāraṇ* साधा, साधारण

Ore (n◦) *khanij* खनिज

Organ (m◦) *avayav,* (n◦) *aṅg* अवयव, अंग

Organism (m◦) *jīv* जीव

Organization (f◦) *sansthā* संस्था

Origin (m◦) *ugam* उगम

Original (adj◦) *mūḷ* मूळ

Ornament (n◦) *ābhūṣhaṇ,* (m◦) *alaṅkār* आभूषण, अलंकार

Orphan (adj◦) *anāth* अनाथ

Orthodox (adj◦) *rūḍhivādī* रूढिवादी

Ostination (n◦) *pākhanḍ* पाखंड

Ostrich (n◦) *śhahāmrug* शहामृग

Other (pron◦) *dusrā* दुसरा

Otherwise (adv◦) *athvā, anyathā* अथवा, अन्यथा

Oulandish (adj◦) *ajab* अजब

Our (pron◦) *āplā* आपला

Ourselves (pron◦) *āmhī svatah* आम्ही स्वत:

Out (adv◦) *bāher* बाहेर

Outbreak (m◦) *prakop* प्रकोप

Outcome (m◦) *pariṇām,* परिणाम

Outdated (adj◦) *aprachalit* अप्रचलित

Outer (adj◦) *bāhya* बाह्य

Outfit (m◦) *pośhāk* पोशाक

Outlaw (adj◦) *bahiṣhkrut* बहिष्कृत

Outlay (m◦) *kharcha, vyay* खर्च, व्यय

Outlet (n◦) *dvār* द्वार

Outline (f◦) *rūpreṣhā* रूपरेषा

Outlook (m◦) *druṣhṭikoṇ* दृष्टिकोण

Out-of-date (adj◦) *aprachalit* अप्रचलित

Outpost (m◦) *nākā* नाका

Outrage (m◦) *julūm* जुलूम

Outrageous (adj◦) *nindanīya* निंदनीय

Outset (m◦) *prārambha* प्रारंभ

Outside (adj◦) *bāher* बाहेर

Outsider (adj◦) *bāhya* बाह्य

Oval (f◦) *anḍḍākrutī* अंडाकृति

Oven (f◦) *bhaṭṭī* भट्टी

Over (adv◦) *var* वर

Overall (adj◦) *ekūṇ* एकूण

Overbaring (adj◦) *uddhaṭ* उद्धट

Overcome (v◦) *jīnkṇe* जिकणे*

Overnight (adv◦) *rātre-bhar* रात्रभर

adj◦ = Adjective, adv◦ = Adverb; *conj.* = Conjunction, f◦ = Feminine gender, *ind.* = Indeclinable, m◦ = Masculine gender, n◦ = Neuter gender, pl◦ = Plural

Overpower (v◦) *jinkṇe* जिंकणे*

Overt (adj◦) *gupta* गुप्त

Overturn (v◦) *ulaṭṇe* उलटणे

Owe (v◦) *ruṇī hoṇe* ऋणी हो◦

Owl (n◦) *ghubaḍ* घुबड

Own (pron◦) *aplā, nijī* आपला, निजी

Owner (m◦) *swāmī, mālak* स्वामी, मालक

Ox (m◦) *bail* बैल

Oxygen (m◦) *prāṇvāyu* प्राणवायु

P

Pace (f◦) *gatī* (motion) गति

Pacify (v◦) *śhānt karṇe* शांत क◦*

Pack (f◦) 1. (bundle) *poṭlī* पोटली, 2. (group) *jhuṇḍ*, (m◦) *samūh* झुंड, समूह

Package, box (m◦) *ḍabbā*, bundle *gaṭṭhā* डब्बा, गट्ठा

Packet (f◦) *poṭlī* पोटली

Pact (m◦) *samjhautā, karār* (f◦) *sandhi* समझौता, करार, संधि

Pad (f◦) *gādī* गादी

Paddy (m◦) *dhān* धान

Page (v◦) *bolāvṇe* बोलावणे*

Page, book (m◦) *prushṭha* पृष्ठ

Paint (m◦) *raṅg* रंग

Painter (m◦) *raṅgwālā* रंगवाला

Pair (m◦ f◦) *joḍā, joḍī* जोडा, जोडी

Pal (m◦) *sobtī, joḍīdār* सोबती, जोडीदार

Palace (m◦) *rajmahāl* राजमहाल

Palatable (adj◦) *svādishṭa* स्वादिष्ट

Palate (f◦) *ṭāḷu* टाळु

Pale (adj◦) *fīkKā, nistej* फिक्का, निस्तेज

Palm, hand (m◦) *taḷhāt* तळहात; tree (n◦) *tāḍ* ताड

Palpitation (f◦) *ḍhukḍhukī* धुकधुकी

Pamper (v◦) *laḍ karṇe* लाड क◦*

Pan (n◦) *bhāṇḍe* भांडे

Pandemonium (m◦) *hullaḍ* हुल्लड

Panic (f◦) *dhaḍkī*, (n◦) *dhassa* धडकी, धस्स

Panther (m◦) *chittā* चित्ता

Pants (f◦) *vijār* विजार

Papaya (f◦) *papaī* पपई

Paper (m◦) *kāgad* कागद; news (n◦) *vartamānpatra* वर्तमानपत्र

Parable (f◦) *nītikathā* नीतिकथा

Parade (f◦) *miravṇūk* मिरवणूक

Paradise (m◦) *svarg* स्वर्ग

Paradox (m◦) *virodhābhās* विरोधाभास

Paragraph (m◦) *anucchhed* अनुच्छेद

Parallel (adj◦) *ksamānāntar* समानांतर

Paralyse (v◦) *balahīn karṇe* बलहीन क◦*

Paralysis (m◦) *lakhvā* लखवा

Paramount (adj◦) *sarvocchya* सर्वोच्च

Paranoid (adj◦) *aviśhvāsu* अविश्वासु

Paraphernalia (f◦) *sāmagrī* सामग्री

Parch (v◦) *bhājṇe, vāḷvaṇe* भाजणे, वाळवणे

Pardon (f◦) *kṣhamā, māfī* क्षमा, माफी; (v) *kṣhmā karṇe, māf karṇe* क्षमा क◦, माफ क◦

Parent (m◦) *mātā-pitā* माता-पिता

Pariah (adj◦) *achhūt* अछूत

Parity (f◦) *samānatā* समानता

Park (n◦) *udyān* उद्यान

Parliament (f◦) *saṅsad* संसद

Parody (f◦) *nakkal* नक्कल

Parrot (m◦) *miṭṭhū, popaṭ* मिट्ठु, पोपट

Part (m◦) *bhāg, hissā* भाग, हिस्सा

Part (v◦) *alag hoṇe* अलग हो◦

Participate (v◦) *bhāg gheṇe* भाग घेणे*

Partner (m◦) *sāthī, joḍīdār* साथी, जेडीदार

Partridge (n◦) *titar*, (m◦) *kavḍā* तितर, कवडा

Pass (v◦) 1. (go) *gujarṇe* गुजरणे; 2. (success) *uttirṇa hoṇe* उत्तीर्ण हो◦; 3. (time) *bītaṇe* बीतणे; 4. (give) *deṇe* देणे*; 5. (law) *anumodit karṇe* अनुमोदित क◦*; 6. (excrete) *visarjit karṇe* विसर्जित क◦*; 7. (bill) accep *manjaūr karṇe* मंजूर क◦

Passage (m◦) *rastā, mārg* रस्ता, मार्ग

Passenger (m◦) *yātrī* यात्री

Passion (m◦) *manobhāv* मनोभाव

Past (adj◦) *vyatalta, atīt* व्यतीत, अतीत

Past (m◦) *bhūtkāḷ* भूतकाळ

Paste (v◦) *chikṭavṇe* चिकटवणे*

Pasture (n◦) *kuraṇ* कुरण

Pat (v◦) *thapthapṇe* थपथपणे*

Patch (n◦) *thigaḷ* ठिगळ

Paternal uncle (m◦) *kākā* काका

Path (m◦) *rastā* रस्ता

Pathetic (adj◦) *dayanīya* दयनीय

Pathology (n◦) *rog vidnyān* रोग विज्ञान

Patience (f◦) *sahanśhakti* सहनशक्ति

Patient (m◦) *rogī* रोगी

Patriot (m◦) *deśhbhakta* देशभक्त

Patriotism (f◦) *deśhbhakti* देशभक्ति

Patrol (f◦) *gasta* गस्त

Patron (m◦) *āśhrayadātā* आश्रयदाता

Patronage (m◦) *āsgray* आश्रय

Pattern (m◦) *ḍhaṅg*, (f◦) *tarhā* ढंग, तऱ्हा

Paucity (m◦) *abhāv* अभाव

Pauper (adj◦) *kaṅgāl* कंगाल

Pause (m◦) *virām* विराम

Pavillion (m◦) *maṇḍap* मंडप

Paw (m◦) *pañjā* पंजा

Pea (m◦) *vāṭāṇā* वाटाणा

Peace (f◦) *śhānti* शांति

Peaceful (adj◦) *śhānt* शांत

Peach (m◦) *āḷū* आळू

Peacock (m◦) *mor* मोर

Peahen (f◦) *morṇī* मोरणी

Peak (n◦) *śhikhar* शिखर

Peanut (m◦) *bhuīmūg* भुईमुग

Pear (n◦) *safarchand* सफरचंद

Pearl (m◦) *motī* मोती

Peasant (m◦) *śhetkarī* शेतकरी

Peciliar (adj◦) *viśheṣha* विशेष

Peculiarity (f◦) *viśheṣhatā* विशेषता

Peek (v◦) *ḍokāvṇe* डोकावणे*

Peel (f◦) *sāl* साल; (v◦) *chhlṇe* छिलणे*

Peer (m◦) *sobtī* सोबती

Peg (f◦) *khuṇṭī* खुंटी

Pen (m◦) *ṭāk* टाक

Penalty (m◦) *daṇḍ*, (f◦) *sajā* दंड, सजा

Penance (f◦) *tapasyā* तपस्या

Pencil (f◦) *lekhaṇī* लेखणी

Pendulum (m◦) *lambak* लंबक

Penetrate (v◦) *śhirṇe* शिरणे

Penitentiary (n◦) *kārāgruha* कारागृह

adj◦ = Adjective, adv◦ = Adverb; *conj.* = Conjunction, f◦ = Feminine gender, *ind.* = Indeclinable, m◦ = Masculine gender, n◦ = Neuter gender, pl◦ = Plural

Penitration (m∘) *praveśh* प्रवेश

Penniless (adj∘) *kangāl* कंगाल

Pension (f∘) *sevāvrutti* सेवावृत्ति

Pentagon (m∘) *pañchabhuj* पंचभुज

Penultimate (adj∘) *upāntya* उपान्त्य

Penury (f∘) *garībī* गरीबी

People (n∘) *lok* लोक

Perceive (v∘) *jāṇaṇe* जाणणे*

Percent (adj∘) *pratiśhat* प्रतिशत

Perceptible (adj∘) *gochar* गोचर

Perception (m∘) *bodh* बोध

Perfect (adj∘) *paripūrṇa* परिपूर्ण

Perfection (f∘) *paripūrṇatā* परिपूर्णता

Perform (v∘) *krṇe* क∘*

Performance (n∘) *kārya* कार्य

Perfume (n∘) *attar* अत्तर

Perhaps (adv∘) *kadāchit* कदाचित्

Peril (m∘) *dhokā* धोका

Perimeter (m∘) *parīgh* परीघ

Period (m∘) *kāl, avadhi* काळ, अवधि

Periodic (adj∘) *āvartī* आवर्ती

Periphery (m∘) *kinārā* किनारा

Perish (v∘) *naṣhṭa hoṇe* नष्ट हाणे

Permanent (adj∘) *sthir, sthāyī* स्थिर, स्थायी

Permission (f∘) *parvānagī* परवानगी

Permit (f∘) *anumati* अनुमति; (v∘) *anumati deṇe* अनुमति देणे*

Perpendicular (adj∘) *lamb* लंब

Perpetual (adj∘) *anant* अनंत

Perplexed (adj∘) *ghoṭāḷlā* घोटाळला

Persecute (v∘) *chhaḷṇe* छळणे*

Persecution (m∘) *chhaḷ, atyāchār* छळ, अत्याचार

Person (f∘) *vyakti* व्यक्ति

Personality (n∘) *vyaktitva* व्यक्तित्व

Perspiration (m∘) *ghām* घाम

Persuade (v∘) *rājī karṇe* राजी क∘*

Perturb (v∘) *ghābraṇe* घाबरणे

Pervade (v∘) *pasarṇe* पसरणे

Pessimism (m∘) *nirāśhā-vād* निराशावाद

Pessimist (adj∘) *nirāśhā-vādī* निराशावादी

Pest (m∘) *vināśhī* विनाशी

Pester (v∘) *satāvṇe* सतावणे*

Pestilence (f∘) *mahamārī* महामारी

Petal (f∘) *pākḷī* पाकळी

Pharmacy (n∘) *auṣhadhālay* औषधालय

Phase (f∘) *avasthā, sthiti* अवस्था, स्थिति

Pheasant bird (m∘) *titar,* (m∘) *kavḍā* तितर, कवडा

Phenomenal (adj∘) *asādhāraṇ* असाधारण

Philosopher (m∘) *tattvadnya* तत्त्वज्ञ

Philosophy (n∘) *darśhan-śhāstra* दर्शन शास्त्र

Phone (m∘) *dūrabhāṣh* दूरभाष

Phoney (adj∘) *naklī* नकली

Photograoh (n∘) *chhāyāchitra* छायाचित्र

Phrase (m∘) *vākprachār* वाक्प्रचार

Physics (n∘) *bhautik-śhastra* भौतिक शास्त्र

Physical (adj∘) *bhautik* भौतिक

Pick (v∘) *uchalṇe, nivaḍṇe* उचलणे*, निवडणे*

Pickle (n∘) *loṇche* लोणचे

Pictorial (adj∘) *sachitra* सचित्र

Picture (n∘) *chitra* चित्र

Piece (m∘) *tukḍā* तुकडा

Pierce (v∘) *bhedṇe* भेदणे*

Pig (c∘) *ḍukkar* डुक्कर

Pigeon (n∘) *kapot* कपोत

Pigment (m∘) *rang* रंग

Pile (f∘) *ḍherī, rāśhi* ढेरी, राशि

Pilgrim (m∘) *tīrthyātrī* तीर्थयात्री

Pill (f∘) *goḷī* गोळी

Pillage (f∘) *lūṭmār* लूटमार

Pillar (m∘) *khambā* खंबा

Pillow (f∘) *uśhī* उशी

Pimple (f∘) *fuṭkuḷī* फुटकुळी

Pin (f∘) *ṭāchaṇī* टाचणी

Pine (n∘) *devadār* देवदार

Pineapple (n∘) *ananas* अननस

Pink (adj∘) *gulābī* गुलाबी

Pinnacle (n∘) *śhikhar* शिखर

Pioneer (adj∘) *ādi* आदि

Pious (adj∘) *pavitra* पवित्र

Pipe (m∘) *naḷ,* (f∘) *naḷī* नळ, नळी

Pit (m∘) *gaḍḍā* गड्डा

Pitch (m∘) *sur* सुर

Pitcher (f∘) *suraī* सुरई

Pity (f∘) *dayā* दया

Pivot (f∘) *kāṭā* काटा

Place (n∘) *sthān,* (f∘) *jāgā* स्थान, जागा; (v∘) *ṭhevṇe* ठेवणे*

Plague (f∘) *mahāmārī* महामारी

Plain (adj∘) *sādhā, saraḷ* साधा, सरळ

Plan (f∘) *yojṇā* योजना

Plane (n∘) *vimān* विमान

Planet (m∘) *graha* ग्रह

Plank (f∘) *pāṭī, faḷī,* (m∘) *taktā* पाटी, फळी; तक्ता

Plant (n) *jhāḍ* झाड

Plantation (f) *bāg,* (m∘) *maḷā* बाग, मळा

Plate, dish (f∘) *baśhī,* (n∘) *tāṭ* बशी, ताट

Platform (n∘) *vyāspīṭh* व्यासपीठ

Play (m∘) 1. (game) *kheḷ,* (f∘) *krīḍā* खेळ, क्रीडा; 2. (n∘) (drama) *nāṭak* नाटक

Play (v∘) *kheḷṇe* खेळणे

Playback Singer (m∘) *pārshva-gāyak* पार्श्वगायक

Player (m∘) *kheḷādu* खेळाडु

Pleasant (adj∘) *ramaṇīya* रमणीय

Please (v∘) *khuśh karṇe* खुश क∘*

Pleasure (n∘) *sukh,* (m∘) *ānand* सुख, आनंद

Pledge (f∘) *partidnyā* प्रतिज्ञा

Plenty (adj∘) *prachur, puṣhkaḷ* प्रचुर, पुष्कळ

Pliars (m∘) *vhimṭā,* (f∘) *pakaḍ* चिमटा, पकड

Plot (m∘) 1. (land) *bhūmi-khanḍ* भूमिखंड; 2. (scheme) (n∘) *ṣhaḍyantra* षडयंत्र; 2. (story) (f∘) *kathā-vastu* कथावस्तु

Plough (m∘) *haḷ,* (n∘) *nāngar* हळ, नांगर

Pluck (v∘) *khuḍṇe* खुडणे*

Plum (n∘) *bor* बोर

Plumet (v∘) *paḍṇe, ghasarṇe* पडणे, घसरणे

Plump (adj∘) *gol-maṭol, fugīr* गोल-मटोल, फुगीर

Plunder (v∘) *luṭṇe* लुटणे*

Plunge (v∘) 1. (sink) *būḍṇe* बुडणे* 2. (pierce) *ghusavṇe* घुसवणे*

Plural (n∘) *bahuvachan* बहुवचन

adj∘ = Adjective, adv∘ = Adverb; *conj.* = Conjunction, f∘ = Feminine gender, *ind.* = Indeclinable, m∘ = Masculine gender, n∘ = Neuter gender, pl∘ = Plural

Plus (prep∘) *adhik* अधिक

Plush (f∘) *makhamal* मखमल

Pocket (m∘) *khisā* खिसा

Pod (f∘) *śheng* शेंग

Podium (m∘) *mañch* मंच

Poem (f∘) *kavitā* कविता

Poet (m∘) *kavi* कवि

Poetry (n∘) *kāvya* काव्य

Point (n∘) 1. (tip: *nok* टोक; 2. (dot) (m∘) *bindu* बिंदु; 3. (place) (n∘) *sthān* स्थान; 4. (moment) (m∘) *kṣhaṇa* क्षण; 5 (item) (n∘) *pad* पद

Pointless (adj∘) *vyartha* व्यर्थ

Poison (n∘) *viṣh* विष

Poke (v∘) *ḍhos* ढोसणे*

Pole (m∘) 1. (North or South) *dhruva* ध्रुव 2. (a post) *khambā* खंबा

Police (m∘) *polīs, śhipāī* पोलीस, शिपाई

Police Station (m∘) *ṭhāṇā* ठाणा

Polish (f∘) *chamak* चमक; (v∘) *chamkavṇe* चमकवणे*

Polite (adj∘) *namra, śhiṣhṭa* नम्र, शिष्ट

Politics (f∘) *rājnīti* राजनीति

Poll (f∘) *nivaḍṇūk* निवडणूक

Pollen (m∘) *parāg* पराग

Pollution (n∘) *pradūṣhaṇ* प्रदूषण

Pomegranate (n∘) *ḍāḷimba* डाळिंब

Pomp (m∘) *thāṭ* थाट

Pond (n∘) *taḷe* तळे

Ponytail (f∘) *veṇī* वेणी

Pool (n∘) *ṭāke* टाके

Poor (adj∘) *garīb* गरीब

Poppy (f∘) *khaskhas* खसखस

Popular (adj∘) *lokpriya* लोकप्रिय

Population (f∘) *loksankhyā* लोकसंख्या

Porcupine (f∘) *sāḷū* साळू

Pore (n∘) *chhidra* छिद्र

Porridge (f∘) *lāpśhī* लापशी

Port (n∘) *bandar* बंदर

Portion (m∘) *bhāg, hissā* भाग, हिस्सा

Portray (v∘) *dākhavṇe* दाखवणे*

Position (f∘) *sthiti* स्थिति

Possess (v∘) *bāḷgaṇe* बाळगणे

Possession (f∘) *mālkī* मालकी

Possibility (f∘) *sambhāvaṇā* संभावना

Possible (adj∘) *sambhav* संभव

Possibly (adv∘) *kadāchit*, sambhavataḥ कदाचित्, संभवत:

Post 1. (mail) (f∘) *ḍāk*, (n∘) *ṭapāl* डाक, टपाल; 2. (pole) (m∘) *khambā* खंबा 3. (designation) (n∘) *pad* पद

Post office (n∘) *ḍākghar* डाकघर

Postman (n∘) *ṭapāl* टपाल;

Post-mortem (f∘) *śhav-parīkṣhā* शव-परीक्षा

Postpone (v∘) *sthagit karṇe* स्थगित क∘*

Posture (f∘) *mudrā* मुद्रा

Pot (n∘) *bhāṇḍe* भांडे

Potato (m∘) *baṭāṭā* बटाटा

Potential (adj∘) *sambhāvya* संभाव्य

Potter (m∘) *kumhār* कुम्भार

Pouch (f∘) *thailī* थैली

Pour (v∘) *otaṇe* ओतणे*

Poverty (f∘) *garībī* गरीबी

Powder (n∘) *chūrṇa* चूर्ण

Power (f∘) *śhakti* शक्ति

Powerful (adj∘) *śhaktiśhālī* शक्तिशाली

Powerless (adj∘) *śhaktihīn* शक्तिहीन

Practice (m∘) 1. (experience) *abhyās* अभ्यास, 2. (work) *vyavahār* व्यवसाय

Praise (f∘) *stuti* स्तुति (v∘) *stuti karṇe* स्तुति क∘*

Prank (f∘) *cheṣhṭā* चेष्टा

Prawn (m∘) *jhingā* झिंगा

Prayer (f∘) *prārthaṇ* प्रार्थना

Precarious (adj∘) *khatarnāk* खतरनाक

Precaution (f∘) *sāvadhānī* सावधानी

Precious (adj∘) *kimtī* किंमती

Precise (adj∘) *tantotant* तंतोतंत

Predicate (m∘) *vidheya* विधेय

Prediction (f∘) *bhaviṣhya-vāṇī* भविष्यवाणी

Predominant (adj∘) *prabaḷ* प्रबळ

Preface (f∘) *prastāvaṇe* प्रस्तावना

Preference (f∘) *pasant* पसंत

Prefix (m∘) *upasarg* उपसर्ग

Pregnant (adj∘) *garbhavati* गर्भवति

Prejudice (m∘) *pakṣhapāt* पक्षपात

Preliminary (adj∘) *prārambhik* प्रारंभिक

Premises (n∘) *āvār* आवार

Preparation (f∘) *tayārī* तयारी

Prepare (v∘) *banavṇe* बनव्णे*

Prescription (m∘) *vidhi* विधि

Presence (f∘) *upasthiti* उपस्थिति

Present (adj∘) *upasthit, vartamān, vidyamān* उपस्थित, वर्तमान, विद्यमान

Present (f∘) *bheṭ*, (m∘) *upahār* भेट, उपहार; (v∘) *prastut karṇe* प्रस्तुत क∘*

Preserve (v∘) *surakṣhit rākhṇe* सुरक्षित राखणे*

President (m∘) *sabhāpati, rāṣhṭrapati* सभापति, राष्ट्रपति

Press (m∘) *chhāpkhāṇe* छापखाना; (v∘) *dābaṇe* दाबणे*

Pressure (m∘) *dabāv* दबाव

Prestige (f∘) *pratiṣhṭhā* प्रतिष्ठा

Presumption (f∘) *parikalpaṇe* परिकल्पना

Pretence (f∘) *bahāṇebājī* बहाणेबाजी

Pretend (v∘) *ḍhoṅg rachṇe* ढोंग रचणे*

Pretension (n∘) *soṅg* सोंग

Pretext (m∘) *bahāṇā* बहाणा

Pretty (adj∘) *manoram* मनोरम; (adv∘) *puṣhkaḷ* पुष्कळ

Prevelent (adj∘) *prachalit* प्रचलित

Prevent (v∘) *rokṇe* रोकणे*

Prevention (f∘) *rok*, (n∘) *nivāraṇ* रोक, निवारण

Preview (n∘) *pūrvadarśhan* पूर्वदर्शन

Previous (adj∘) *pūrva* पूर्व

Prey (f∘) *śhikār* शिकार

Price (f∘) kīmmat किंमत

Prickle (m∘) *kāṭā* काटा

Pricy (adj∘) *kimatī* किमती

Pride (m∘) *abhimān;* (f∘) *ghameṇḍ* अभिमान, घमेंड

Priest (m∘) *pujārī, purohit* पुजारी, पुरोहित

Primary (adj∘) *prāthamik* प्राथमिक

Prime (adj∘) *mukhya* मुख्य

Primitive (adj∘) *ādim* आदिम

adj∘ = Adjective, adv∘ = Adverb; *conj.* = Conjunction, f∘ = Feminine gender, *ind.* = Indeclinable, m∘ = Masculine gender, n∘ = Neuter gender, pl∘ = Plural

Prince (m∘) *rājkumār* राजकुमार

Princess (f∘) *rājkumārī* राजकुमारी

Principal (m∘) *pradhān, mukhya* प्रधान, मुख्य

Principle (n∘) *tattva* तत्त्व

Print (n∘) *mudraṇ* मुद्रण

Print (v∘) *chhāpṇe* छापणे*

Prior (adj∘) *pūrva* पूर्व

Priority (f∘) *agratā* अग्रता

Prison (f∘) *kaid* कैद

Prisoner (m∘) *kaidī* कैदी

Privacy (f∘) *ekāntatā* एकांतता

Private (adj∘) *nijī, vyaktigat* निजी, व्यक्तिगत

Privilage (f∘) *suvidhā* सुविधा

Prize (m∘) *inām, puraskār* इनाम, पुरस्कार

Pro (adj∘) *peśhevar* पेशेवर

Probability (f∘) *sambhāvaṇe* संभावना

Probably (adv∘) *kadāchit* कदाचित्

Probihition (m∘) *niṣhedh,* (f∘) *rok* निषेध, रोक

Problem (f∘) *samasyā* समस्या

Procedure (f∘) *rīti, paddhati* रीति, पद्धति

Proceed (v∘) *puḍhe jāṇe,* पुढे जाण

Process (f∘) *prakriyā, vidhi* प्रक्रिया, विधि

Procession (m∘) *miravṇūk* मिरवणूक

Proclamation (f∘) *ghoṣhaṇā* घोषणा

Procrastinate (v∘) *ṭāḷṇe* टाळणे*

Procrastination (f∘) *ṭāl-maṭol* टाल-मटोल

Procrastinator (m∘) *dīrghasūtrī* दीर्घसूत्री

Produce (n∘) *utpādan,* (f∘) *nirmiti* उत्पादन, निर्मिति

Produce (v∘) *utpanna karṇe* उत्पन्न क∘*

Producer (m∘) *nirmātā* निर्माता

Product (n∘) *utpādan,* (f∘) *upaj* उत्पादन, उपज

Production (n∘) *nirmāṇ* (f∘) *nirmiti, upaj* निर्माण, निर्मिति, उपज

Productivity (f∘) *utpādaktā* उत्पादकता

Profess (v∘) *dāvā karṇe* दावा क∘*

Profession (m∘) *dhandā,* (f∘) *jīvikā* धंदा, जीविका

Professional (adj∘) *vyavasāyik, nipuṇ* व्यवसायिक, निपुण

Professor(m∘) *adhyāpak* अध्यापक

Proficient (adj∘) *nipuṇ. kuśhal* निपुण, कुशल

Profit (m∘) *lābh, fāyadā* लाभ, फायदा

Profitable (adj∘) *lābhdāyak* लाभदायक

Profound (adj∘) *gahrā, gahan* गहरा, गहन

Profuse (adj∘) *prachur* प्रचुर

Progeny (f∘) *santati* संतति

Program (m∘) *kāryakram* कार्यक्रम

Progress (f∘) *pragati* प्रगति

Prohibit (v∘) *rokṇe* रोकणे

Project (f∘) *yojṇe* योजना

Prolong (v∘) *vāḍhavṇe* वाढवणे*

Prominent (adj∘) *prasiddha* प्रसिद्ध

Promise (f∘) *pratidnyā,* (n∘) *vachan* प्रतिज्ञा, वचन

Promise (v∘) *pratidnyā karṇe, vachan deṇe* प्रतिज्ञा क∘, वचन देणे*

Promote (v∘) *pragati karṇe, prachār karṇe* प्रगति क∘, प्रचार क∘*

Promoter (m∘) *prachārak* प्रचारक

Promotion (f∘) *pragati,* (m∘) *prachār* प्रगति, प्रचार

Prone (adj∘) *grahaṇśhīl* ग्रहणशील

Prong (m∘) *kāṭā* काटा

Pronoun (n∘) *sarvanām* सर्वनाम

Pronounce (v∘) *uchchārṇe* उच्चारणे*

Pronunciation (m∘) *ucchār* उच्चार

Proof (n∘) *pramāṇ,* (m∘) *purāvā, dākhalā* प्रमाण, पुरावा, दाखला

Propagate (v∘) *prasār karṇe* प्रसार क∘*

Propagation (m∘) *prasār* प्रसार

Propel (v∘) *ḍhakalṇe* ढकलणे*

Proper (adj∘) *yathārtha, uchit* यथार्थ, उचित

Properly (adv∘) *vyavasthit* व्यवस्थित

Property (f∘) *sampatti* संपत्ति

Prophesy (f∘) *bhaviṣhyavāṇī* भविष्यवाणी

Proponent (adj∘) *samarthak* समर्थक

Proportion (n∘) *pramāṇ,* (m∘) *anupāt* प्रमाण, अनुपात

Proportional (adj∘) *pramāṇbaddha* प्रमाणबद्ध

Proposal (m∘) *prastāv* प्रस्ताव

Propose (v∘) *prastut karṇe* प्रस्तुत क∘*

Proposition (m∘) *prastāv* प्रस्ताव

Proprietor (m∘) *mālak* मालक

Prosaic (adj∘) *bechav, nīras* बेचव, नीरस

Prose (n∘) *gadya* गद्य

Prosecute (v∘) *kārvāī karṇe* कारवाई क∘*

Prosecution (f∘) *kārvāī* कारवाई

Prospect (f∘) *sambhāvaṇe* संभावना

Prosper (v∘) *samruddha hoṇe* समृद्ध हो∘

Prosperity (f∘) *samruddhi* समृद्धि

Prosperous (adj∘) *samruddha* समृद्ध

Prostitute (f∘) *veśhyā* वेश्या

Protect (v∘) *rakṣhā karaṇe* रक्षा क∘*

Protection (n∘) *saṁrakṣhaṇ, rakṣhaṇ* संरक्षण, रक्षण

Protector (adj∘) *rakṣhak* रक्षक

Protest (m∘) *virodh* विरोध

Protest (v∘) *virodh karṇe* विरोध क∘*

Proud (adj∘) *abhimānī; ghameṇḍī* अभिमानी; घमेंडी

Prove (n∘) *siddha karṇe* सिद्ध क∘

Proven (adj∘) *siddha* सिद्ध

Proverb (f∘) *mhṇ* म्हण

Provide (n∘) *pradān karṇe, upalabdha karṇe* प्रदान क∘, उपलब्ध क∘

Providence (m∘) *vidhātā, īśhvar* विधाता, ईश्वर

Province (m∘) *pradeśh, prānt* प्रदेश, प्रांत

Provincial (adj∘) *prādeśhik* प्रादेशिक

Provision (m∘) *prabandh* प्रबंध

Provisional (adj∘) *kām-chalāū* काम-चलाऊ

Proviso (f∘) *śhart* शर्त

Provocate (v∘) *uksavṇe, bhaḍkāvṇe* उकसवणे, भडकावणे*

Provocation (m∘) *uksāvā, bhaḍkāvā* उकसावा, भडकावा

Prowess (m∘) *parākram* पराक्रम

Prpaganda (m∘) *duṣhprachār* दुष्प्रचार

Psalm (n∘) *stotra* स्तोत्र

Pseudo (adj∘) *chhadma* छद्म

Pseudomym (n∘) *upanam* उपनाम

Psychic (adj∘) *mānasik* मानसिक

Psychology (n∘) *manovidnyān* मनोविज्ञान

Psychopath (m∘) *manovikārī* मनोविकारी

Pub (f∘) *madhuśhāḷā* मधुशाळा

adj∘ = Adjective, adv∘ = Adverb; *conj.* = Conjunction, f∘ = Feminine gender, *ind.* = Indeclinable, m∘ = Masculine gender, n∘ = Neuter gender, pl∘ = Plural

Public (adj∘) *sārvajanik* सार्वजनिक

Publication (n∘) *prakāśhan* प्रकाशन

Publicity (f∘) *prasiddhi* प्रसिद्धि

Publish (m∘) *prakāśhit karṇe* प्रकाशित क∘

Published (adj∘) *prakāśhit* प्रकाशित

Publisher (m∘) *prakāśhak* प्रकाशक

Pudding (m∘) *śhirā* शिरा

Puddle (n∘) *ḍabke* डबके

Puff (m∘) *funkārā* फुंकारा

Puff (v∘) *fugṇe* फुगणे

Puke (f∘) *okārī* ओकारी

Pull (v) *oḍhṇe* ओढणे

Pully (n∘) *chāk* चाक

Pulp (f∘) *lugdī* लुगदी

Pulsate (m∘) *dhaḍdhaḍṇe* धडधडणे

Pulsation (f∘) *dhaḍdhaḍ* धडधड

Pulse (f∘) 1. (vein) *nāḍī* नाडी 2. (cereal) *ḍāḷ* डाळ

Pump (f∘) *pichkārī* पिचकारी

Pumpkin (n∘) *kohḷe* कोहळे

Punch (c∘) *mukkā mārṇe* मुक्का मारणे

Punch (m∘) *mukkā,* (f∘) *bukkī* मुक्का, बुक्की

Punctual (adj∘) *niyamit* नियमित

Puncture (n∘) *chhidra* छिद्र

Pungent (adj∘) *tikhaṭ* तिखट

Punish (v∘) *daṇḍa deṇe* दंड देणे*; *sajā deṇe* सजा देणे*

Punishment (f∘) *sajā,* (m∘) *daṇḍ* सजा, दंड

Punitive (adj∘) *kaṭhor* कठोर

Puny (m∘) *chhoṭā, nikrushṭa* छोटा, निकृष्ट

Pupil (m∘) *vidyārthī, chhatra, śhishya* विद्यार्थी, छात्र, शिष्य

Puppet (f∘) *kaṭhputḷī* कठपुतळी

Puppy, pup (adj∘) *pillu* पिल्लु

Purchase (f∘) *kharedī* खरेदी; (v∘) *kharīdṇe* खरीदणे*

Pure (m∘) *śhuddha* शुद्ध

Purification (f∘) *śhuddhi* शुद्धि

Purify (v∘) *śhuddha karṇe* शुद्ध क∘*

Purple (adj∘) *jāmbhaḷā* जांभळा

Purpose (m∘) *irādā, hetu* इरादा, हेतु

Purr (v∘) *gurgurāṇe* गुरगुरणे

Purse (m∘) *baṭvā* बटवा

Pursue (v∘) *anusarṇe* अनुसरणे

Pursuit (m∘) 1. (going after) *pāṭhlāg* पाठलाग 2. (activity) *dhandā, lakshya* धंदा, लक्ष्य; 3. (to follow) (n∘) *anusaraṇ* अनुसरण.

Pus (m∘) *pū, rand* पू, रंद

Push (m∘) *dhakkā* धक्का; (v∘) *ḍhakalṇe* ढकलणे*

Put, keep (v∘) *ṭhevṇe* ठेवणे*

Putrify (v∘) *saḍṇe* सडणे

Puzzle (n∘) *koḍe;* (m∘) *ukhāṇā* कोडे, उखाणा

Pyre (f∘) *chitā* चिता

Python (m∘) *ajgar* अजगर

Q

Quadrilateral (m∘) *chaturbhuj* चतुर्भुज

Quagmire (f∘) *daldal* दलदल

Quail bird (f∘) *lāvī* लावी

Quake (m∘) *kamp* कंप

Qualification (f∘) *yogyatā* योग्यता

Qualified (adj∘) *yogya* योग्य

Quality (f∘) *yogyatā,* (m∘) *guṇ* योग्यता, गुण

Qualm (f∘) *śhaṅkā* शंका

Quandary (f∘) *pañchāīt* पंचाईत

Quantity (m∘) *pramāṇ,* (f∘) *mātrā* प्रमाण, मात्रा

Quarrel (n∘) *bhāṇḍan* भांडन; (v∘) *bhāṇḍaṇe* भांडणे

Quarry (f∘) mine *khāṇ* खाण

Quarter 1/4 (adj∘) *chauth* चौथ

Quarterly (adj∘) *timāhī* तिमाही

Queen (f∘) *rāṇī* राणी

Queer (adj∘) *asādhāraṇ* असाधारण

Query (m∘) *raśhṇa* प्रश्न

Quest (m∘) *śhodh, tapās* शोध, तपास

Question (m∘) *praśhna* प्रश्न

Questionaire (f∘) *praśhnāvalī* प्रश्नावली

Queue (m∘) *oḷ, paṅkti* ओळ, पंक्ति

Quick (adj∘) *chañchal* चंचल

Quickly (adv∘) *jalad, jalad* जलद, जलद

Quiet (adj∘) *śhānt* शांत

Quietly (adv∘) *śhāntīne* शांतीने

Quietness (f∘) *śhānti* शांति

Quilt (f∘) *rajaī* रजई

Quit (v∘) *tyāgṇe, soḍṇe* त्यागणे, सोडणे*

Quiver (m∘) *bhātā* भाता

Quiver (v∘) *tharthaṛṇe* थरथरणे

Quotation (n∘) *avataraṇ* अवतरण

R

Rabbit (m∘) *sasā* ससा

Race (f∘) 1. (sport) *pratiyogitā* प्रतियोगिता, 2. (class) *jāti* जाति

Racial (adj∘) *jātīya* जातीय

Racism (m∘) *jativād* जातिवाद

Racket, noise (m∘) *hallā* हल्ला; (f∘) *ghoṭāḷā* घोटाळा

Radiant (adj∘) *chamakdār* चमकदार

Radical, basic (adj∘) *mūlbhūt* मूलभूत; view (m∘) *ugravādī* उग्रवादी

Radio (f∘) *ākāśhavāṇī* आकाशवाणी

Radish (m∘) *muḷā* मुळा

Radius (f∘) *trijyā* त्रिज्या

Rag (f∘) *chindhī* चिंधी; (v∘) *satāvṇe* सतावणे*

Rage (f∘) *hiṁsā* हिंसा

Raid (m∘) *chhāpā* छापा

Rail (f∘) train *āg-gāḍī* आगगाडी

Railing (m∘) *kaṭhaḍā* कठडा

Rain (m∘) *pa!ūs,* (f∘) *varshā* पाऊस, वर्षा

Rainbow (n∘) *indra-dhanushya* इंद्रधनुष्य

Raise (f∘) *vāḍh* वाढ; (v∘) *var karṇe* वर क∘*

Raisin (m∘) *kismis* किसमिस

Ram (m∘) *meṇḍhā* मेंढा

Ramp (m∘) *utār* उतार

Rampage (f∘) *khaḷbaḷ* खळबळ

Range (m∘) *ṭappā* टप्पा

Rank (m∘) *star, darjā* स्तर, दर्जा

Ransom (f∘) *khaṇḍaṇī* खंडणी

Rant (v∘) *baḍbaḍṇe* बडबडणे

Rap (f∘) *thāp* थाप

Rape (m∘) *balātkār* बलात्कार

Rapid (adj∘) *śhīghra* शीघ्र

Raply (n∘) *uttar* उत्तर

adj∘ = Adjective, adv∘ = Adverb; *conj.* = Conjunction, f∘ = Feminine gender, *ind.* = Indeclinable, m∘ = Masculine gender, n∘ = Neuter gender, pl∘ = Plural

Rare (adj∘) *viraḷ* विरळ

Rarely (adv∘) *kvachit* क्वचित्

Rat (f∘) *ghūs* घूस

Rate (m∘) *dar* दर; speed (f∘) *gati* गति

Rather (adv∘) *khachit* खचित

Ratio (n∘) *pramāṇ* प्रमाण

Rational (adj∘) *samajdār* समजदार

Rattle (m∘) *khaḍkhaḍṇe* खडखडणे

Ravage (v∘) *ujāḍṇe* उजाडणे*

Ravine (f∘) *darī* दरी

Raw (adj∘) *kacchā* कच्चा

Ray (n∘) *kiraṇ* किरण

Raze (v∘) *miṭavṇe* मिटवणे*

Razor (m∘) *vastarā* वस्तरा

Re (pref∘) *punhā* पुन्हा

Reach (v∘) *pahuchṇe* पहुचणे

Reaction (f∘) *pratikriyā* प्रतिक्रिया

Read (v∘) *vāchaṇe* वाचणे*

Reader (m∘) *vāchak* वाचक

Ready (adj∘) *tayār* तयार

Real (adj∘) *aslī, kharā* असली, खरा

Reality (n∘) *tathya* तथ्य

Realization (f∘) *anubhūti* अनुभूति

Really (adv∘) *vastutaḥ* वस्तुत:

Reap (v∘) *pīk kāpṇe* पीक कापणे*

Rear (f∘) *pichhāḍī* पिछाडी; (v∘) *poshaṇ karṇe* पोषण क∘*

Reason (n∘) *kāraṇ*, (m∘) *hetu* कारण, हेतु; (v∘) *tark karṇe* तर्क क∘*

Reasonable (adj∘) *yathochit* यथोचित

Reassurance (n∘) *āśhvāsan* आश्वासन

Rebate (f∘) *sūṭ* सूट

Rebel (m∘) *vidrohī* विद्रोही

Rebellion (f∘) *vidroha* विद्रोह

Rebound (v∘) *ulaṭṇe* उलटणे

Rebuke (v∘) *dhamkāvṇe* धमकावणे*

Recede (v∘) *ghaṭṇe* घटणे

Receipt (f∘) *rasīd, pāvtī* रसीद, पावती

Receive (v∘) *pāvṇe* पावणे

Recent (adj∘) *navīn* नवीन

Recess (m∘) *madhyāvakāśh* मध्यावकाश

Recession (f∘) *avanati* अवनति

Reciprocal (adj∘) *pārasparik* पारस्परिक

Recital (m∘) *pāṭh* पाठ

Reckless (adj∘) *beparvā* बेपरवा

Recline (v∘) *loṭṇe* लोटणे

Reclusion (m∘) *ekānt* एकांत

Recognition (f∘) *mānyatā* मान्यता

Recognize (v∘) *oḷakhṇe* ओळखणे*

Recollect (v∘) *smarṇe* स्मरणे*

Recollection (f∘) *smruti* स्मृति

Recommendation (f∘) *śhifāras* शिफारस

Record (m∘) *lekh* लेख; (v∘) *lihīṇe* लिहीणे*

Recorded (adj∘) *likhit* लिखित

Recreation (n∘) *manorañjan* मानोरंजन

Recruit (m∘) *raṅgrūṭ* रंगरूट

Rectangle (f∘) *āyat* आयत

Rectum (n∘) *malāśhay* मलाशय

Recycling (f∘) *punarnirmiti* पुनर्निर्मिति

Red (adj∘) *lāl* लाल

Redemption (m∘) *uddhār* उद्धार

Reduce (v∘) *ghaṭṇe, ghaṭavṇe** घटणे, घटवणे*

Refliction (n∘) *parāvartan* परावर्तन

Reform (v∘) *sudhārṇe* सुधारणे*

Reformation (m∘) *sudhār* सुधार

Refrain (v∘) *dūr rāhṇe* दूर राहणे

Refresh (v∘) *tājā karṇe* ताजा क∘*

Refreshed (adj∘) *tājātawānā* ताजातवाना

Refreshment (n∘) *jal-pān* जलपान; (m∘) *nāstā* नास्ता

Refuge (f∘) *śharaṇ* शरण

Refugee (m∘) *śharaṇārthī* शरणार्थी

Refusal (m∘) *nakār* नकार

Refuse (m∘) *kachrā* कचरा; (v∘) *nakārṇe* नकारणे*

Region (n∘) *kṣhetra*, (m∘) *vibhāg* क्षेत्र, विभाग

Register (f∘) *pañjikā* पंजिका; (v∘) *bhartī karṇe, lihīṇe* भरती क∘, लिहीणे*

Registration (n∘) *pañjīkaraṇ* पंजीकरण

Regret (m∘) *khed*, (n∘) *duhkh* खेद, दु:ख

Regret (v∘) *dukhī hoṇe* दुखी हो∘

Regulation (n∘) *niyantraṇ* नियंत्रण

Rein (f∘) *lagām* लगाम

Reject (v∘) *nakārṇe* नकारणे*

Rejection (m∘) *nakār*, (f∘) *asvīkruti* नकार, अस्वीकृति

Relation (m∘) *sambandh* संबंध

Relationship (n∘) *nāte* नाते

Relative (m∘) *nātedār* नातेदार

Relax (v∘) *viśhrām karṇe* विश्राम क∘*

Release (v∘) *soḍṇe* सोडणे

Relevant (adj∘) *sambaddh, saṅgat* संबद्ध, संगत

Reliable (adj∘) *viśhvāsu* विश्वासु

Reliance (m∘) *bharosā* भरोसा

Relief (m∘) *ārām* आराम

Religion (m∘) *dharma* धर्म

Religious (adj∘) *dhārmik* धार्मिक

Relinquish (v∘) *tyāgṇe, soḍṇe* त्यागणे, सोडणे*

Reluctance (f∘) *anichhā* अनिच्छा

Reluctant (adj∘) *anichhuk* अनिच्छुक

Remain (v∘) *urṇe* उरणे

Remainder (f∘) *bāķī*, (m∘) *śheṣh* बाक़ी, शेष

Remedy (m∘) *ilāj, upāy* इलाज, उपाय

Remember (v∘) *āṭhavṇe* आठवणे*

Remembrance (f∘) *āṭhavaṇ*, (n∘) *smaraṇ* आठवण, स्मरण

Remind (v∘) *suchavṇe* सुचवणे*

Remorse (m∘) *paschātāp* पश्चाताप

Remote (adj∘) *dūrchā* दूरचा

Remove (v∘) *haṭavṇe* हटवणे*

Renounce (v∘) *tyāgṇe, soḍṇe* त्यागणे, सोडणे*

Renovation (m∘) *punaruddhār* पुनरुद्धार

Repair (v∘) *ṭhīk karṇe* ठीक क∘*

Repeat (v∘) *punhā karṇe* पुन्हा क∘

Repeatedly (adv∘) *vāramvār, punaḥ-punaḥ* वारंवार, पुन: पुन:

Repeatedly (adv∘) *vārmvār* वारंवार

Repeatition (f∘) *punarāvrutti* पुनरावृत्ति

Repel (v∘) *radda karṇe* रद्द क∘*

Repent (v∘) *prastāvṇe* प्रस्तावणे

Repentance (m∘) *prastavā* प्रस्तावा

Repercusision (m∘) *pratighāt* प्रतिघात

adj∘ = Adjective, adv∘ = Adverb; *conj.* = Conjunction, f∘ = Feminine gender, *ind.* = Indeclinable, m∘ = Masculine gender, n∘ = Neuter gender, pl∘ = Plural

Replacement (m◦) *badlā* बदला
Replete (adj◦) *paripūrṇa* परिपूर्ण
Report (m◦) *vruttānt,* (n◦) *vivaraṇ* वृत्तांत, विवरण; (v◦) *vruttānt deṇe* वृत्तांत देणे*
Representative (m◦) *pratinidhi* प्रतिनिधि
Reproach (m◦) *dhikkār* धिक्कार
Reproduce (v◦) *punhā karṇe* पुन्हा क◦
Republic (n◦) *gaṇatantra* गणतंत्र
Repulsion (f◦) *aruchi, ghruṇā* अरुचि, घृणा
Reputable (adj◦) *pratiṣhṭhit* प्रतिष्ठित
Reputation (f◦) *pratiṣhṭhā* प्रतिष्ठा
Request (m◦) *vinanti, prārthanā* विनंति, प्रार्थना; (v◦) *prārthaṇe karṇe* प्रार्थना क◦*
Require (v◦) *garaj asṇe* गरज असणे*
Requirement (f◦) *āvaśhyaktā* आवश्यकता
Requisite (adj◦) *jarūrī* जरूरी
Research (n◦) *anusandhān* अनुसंधान
Resemblance (f◦) *samānatā* समानता
Resent (v◦) *nārāj hoṇe* नाराज हो◦
Resentment (f◦) *nārājī* नाराजी
Reservation (n◦) *ārakṣhaṇ* आरक्षण
Reserved (adj◦) *ārakṣhit* आरक्षित
Reside (v◦) *rāhaṇe* राहणे
Residence (n◦) *nivās-sthān* निवास-स्थान
Resident (m◦) *nivāsī* निवासी
Residue (m◦) *avaśhesh* अवशेष
Resignation (m◦) *pad-tyāg* पदत्याग
Resist (v◦) *virodh karṇe* विरोध क◦*
Resistance (m◦) *virodh* विरोध
Resolution (m◦) *saṅkalp* संकल्प
Resourse (m◦) *upāy,* (n◦) *sādhan* उपाय, साधन
Respect (m◦) *ādar, sanmān* आदर, सन्मान; (v◦) *ādar karṇe* आदर क◦*
Respite (m◦) *ārām* आराम
Respond (m◦) *uttar deṇe* उत्तर देणे
Responsibility (f◦) *jabābdārī* जबाबदारी
Responsible (adj◦) *jabābdār* जबाबदार
Rest (m◦) *ārām* आराम
Rest (v◦) *ārāma karṇe* आराम क◦*
Restless (adj◦) *bechain* बेचैन
Restlessness (f◦) *bechainī* बेचैनी
Restoration (f◦) *jīrṇoddhār* जीर्णोद्धार
Restrain (v◦) *rokṇe* रोकणे*
Restraint (n◦) *niyantraṇ* नियंत्रण
Restricted (adj◦) *sīmiy* सीमित
Restriction (m◦) *pratibandh* प्रतिबंध
Retail (m◦) *chillar* चिल्लर
Retaliate (v◦) *badlā gheṇe* बदला घेणे*
Retarded (adj◦) *mandbuddhi* मंदबुद्धि
Retirement (f◦) *nivrutti* निवृत्ति
Retreat (v◦) *māge haṭṇe* मागे हटणे
Retribution (m◦) *daṇḍ* दंड
Return (v◦) *paratṇe* परतणे
Reveal (v◦) *prakaṭ karṇe* प्रकट क◦*
Revenge (m◦) *badlā* बदला
Revere (v◦) *ādar karṇe* आदर क◦*
Reverence (m◦) *ādar* आदर
Reverse (adj◦) *ulṭā* उलटा
Review (n◦) *punar-parīkṣhaṇ* पुनर्परीक्षण
Revile (v◦) *śhivī deṇe* शिवी देणे*
Revision (f◦) *ujaḷṇī* उजळणी
Revival (n◦) *punar-jīvan* पुनर्जीवन
Revoke (v◦) *radda karṇe* रद्द क◦*
Revolt (m◦) *vidroha* विद्रोह; (v◦) *vidroha karṇe* विद्रोह क◦*
Revolution (f◦) *krānti* क्रांति
Revolve (v◦) *gol firṇe* गोल फिरणे
Revolver (m◦) *tamañchā* तमंचा
Reward (n◦) *bakṣhis,* (m◦) *ināṃ* बक्षिस, इनाम
Rhino (m◦) *geṇḍā* गेंडा
Rhyme (n◦) *yamak* यमक
Rhythm (m◦) *lay* लय
Rib (f◦) *fāṅsḷī* फांसळी
Ribbon (f◦) *fīt* फीत
Rice seeds(n◦) *tānduḷ* तांदुळ, cooked (m◦) भात
Rich (adj◦) *dhanī, amīr* धनी, अमीर
Riddle (n◦) *koḍe* कोडे
Ride, drive (v◦) *chālavṇe* चालवणे*
Ridicule (m◦) *uphās* उपहास
Rift (m◦) *taḍā* तडा
Right, direction (adj◦) *ujvā* उजवा; proper (adj◦) *uchit* उचित
Rightly (adv◦) *yathā -tathā, samyak* यथातथा, सम्यक्
Rigor (m◦) *saṃyam* संयम
Rind (f◦) *sāl* साल
Ring (f◦) *āṅgṭhī* आंगठी
Ring finger (f◦) *anāmikā* अनामिका
Riot (m◦) *daṅgā* दंगा
Rip (v◦) *chīrṇe* चीरणे*
Ripe (adj◦) *pakva* पक्व
Ripen (v◦) *pikṇe* पिकणे
Ripple (f◦) *lahar* लहर
Rise (m◦) *chaḍhāv* चढाव; (v◦) *uṭhṇe, uṭhavṇe** उठणे, उठवणे*
Risk (m◦) *jokhīm* जोखीम
Ritual (m◦) *karma-kāṇḍ* कर्मकांड
River (f◦) *nadī* नदी
Road (m◦) *rastā, mārg* रस्ता, मार्ग
Roam (v◦) *firṇe* फिरणे
Roar (f◦) *garajnā* गर्जना; (v◦) *garajṇe* गरजणे
Roast (v◦) *bhajṇe* भाजणे*
Rob (v◦) *luṭṇe* लुटणे*
Robust (adj◦) *mazbūt* मजबूत
Rock (m◦) *khaḍak* खडक
Rod (m◦) *daṇḍā* दंडा
Role (f◦) *bhūmikā* भूमिका
Roll (v◦) *luḍhakṇe* लुढकणे*
Rolling pin (n◦) *lāṭṇe* लाटणे
Romantic (adj◦) *romāñchak* रोमांचक
Roof (n◦) *chhappar, āḍhe* छप्पर, आढे
Room (f◦) *kholī* खोली
Rooster (m◦) *kombḍā* कोंबडा
Root (n◦) *mūḷ* मूळ
Rope (f◦) *dorī* दोरी
Rose (m◦) *gulāb* गुलाब
Rot (v◦) *saḍaṇe* सडणे
Rotate (v◦) *gol firṇe* गोल फिरणे
Rotation (m◦) *chakkar* चक्कर
Rough (adj◦) 1. (not smooth) *khaḍbaḍīt* खडबडीत, 2. (not final) *kacchā* कच्चा
Roughly (adv◦) *admāse* अदमासे

adj◦ = Adjective, adv◦ = Adverb; *conj.* = Conjunction, f◦ = Feminine gender, *ind.* = Indeclinable, m◦ = Masculine gender, n◦ = Neuter gender, pl◦ = Plural

Round (adj∘) *gol* गोल

Row (f∘) *oḷ, pankti* ओळ, पंक्ति

Rowdy (adj∘) *puṇḍ* पुंड

Rub (v∘) *ragaḍṇe* रगडणे*

Rubbish (m∘) *kachrā* कचरा

Rude (adj∘) *kaṭhor* कठोर

Ruffian (m∘) *guṇḍā, badmāśh* गुंडा, बदमाश

Rug (m∘) *gālīchā* गालीचा

Rugged (adj∘) *mazbūt* मजबूत

Ruin (m∘) *nāśh* नाश; (v∘) *naṣhṭa karṇe* नष्ट क∘*

Rule (m∘) *niyam, kāydā* नियम, कायदा

Ruler king (m∘) *śhāsak* शासक

Rumble (m∘) *gaḍgaḍṇe* गडगडणे

Rumour (f∘) *afavā* अफवा

Run (v∘) *bpaḷṇe, dauḍṇe* पळणे, दौडणे

Rupee (m∘) *rupayā* रुपया

Rural (adj∘) *grāmīṇ* ग्रामीण

Rush (f∘) *ghāī* घाई

Rust (m∘) *jang* जंग

Ruthless (adj∘) *krūr, nirday* क्रूर, निर्दय

S

Sack (n∘) *pote* पोते

Sacred (adj∘) *pavitra* पवित्र

Sacrifice (m∘) *tyāga* त्याग

Sad (adj∘) *duhkhī, udās* दु:खी, उदास

Saddle (n∘) *khogīr* खोगीर

Safe (adj∘) *surakṣhit* सुरक्षित

Safeguard (f∘) *surakṣhā* सुरक्षा

Safety (f∘) *surakṣhā* सुरक्षा

Saffron (adj∘) *keśhrī* केशरी; (n∘) *keśhar* केशर

Sage (m∘) *muni* मुनि

Sagittariua (f∘) *dhanu rāśhi* धनु राशि

Sailor (m∘) *nāvik* नाविक

Saint (m∘) *sādhu* साधु

Sale (f∘) *vikrī* विक्री

Salivā (f∘) *thunk* थुंक

Salt (n∘) *mīṭh* मीठ

Salute (n∘) *naman* नमन

Salvation (m∘) *mokṣha,* (f∘) *mukti* मोक्ष, मुक्ति

Same (adj∘) *samān* समान

Sample (m∘) *namūṇe* नमूना

Sancity (f∘) *pavitratā* पवित्रता

Sanction (f∘) *anumati* अनुमति; (v∘) *anumati deṇe* अनुमति देणे*

Sand (f∘) *ret, vāḷū* रेत, वाळू

Sane (adj∘) *samajdār* समजदार

Sanitation (f∘) *safāī* सफाई

Sanity (f∘) *sanajdārī* समजदारी

Saphire (m∘) *nīlam* नीलम

Sarcasm (m∘) *ṭomṇā* टोमणा

Satisfaction (m∘) *santoṣh* संतोष

Satisfactory (adj∘) *santoṣh janak* संतोष जनक

Satisfy (v∘) *santuṣhṭa karṇe* संतुष्ट क∘*

Saturday (m∘) *śhanivār* शनिवार

Saturn (m∘) *śhani* शनि

Sauce (f∘) *chaṭṇī* चटणी

Savage (adj∘) *janglī* जंगली

Save (v∘) *vāchavṇe* वाचवणे

Saving (f∘) *bachat* बचत

Savour (m∘) *svād* स्वाद

Savoury (adj∘) *svādiṣhṭa* स्वादिष्ट

Saw (f∘) *ārī* आरी

Say (v∘) *bolṇe* बोलणे*

Saying (n∘) *vachan, kathan* वचन, कथन

Scab (f∘) *khaplī* खपली

Scale (n∘) 1. (measure) *māp* माप; 2. (balance) (m∘) *tarājū* तराजू; 2. (coat) (n∘) *kavach* कवच

Scam (m∘) *ghoṭāḷā* घोटाळा

Scandal (f∘) *badnāmī* बदनामी

Scanty (adj∘) *alp* अल्प

Scar (n∘) *vraṇ, dāg, niśhaṇ* व्रण, दाग, निशाण

Scarce (adj∘) *durlabh* दुर्लभ

Scare (n∘) *āntak* आंतक

Scarf (m∘) *dupaṭṭā* दुपट्टा

Scarlet (adj∘) *śhendrī* शेंदरी

Scary (adj∘) *bhayānak* भयानक

Scathing (adj∘) *kaṭhor* कठोर

Scatter (v∘) *failaṇe, failāvṇe* फैलणे, फैलावणे*

Scenario (n∘) *druṣhya,* (f∘) *paṭkathā* दृश्य, पटकथा

Scene (n∘) *druṣhya* दृश्य

Scenic (adj∘) *ramya* रम्य

Scent (m∘) *sugandh* सुगंध

Sceptical (adj∘) *śhankāyukta* शंकायुक्त

Schedule (f∘) *kārya-sūchī* कार्यसूची

Scheme (f∘) *yojṇe* योजना

Scholar (m∘) *paṇḍit, vidvān* पंडित, विद्वान

Scholarship (f∘) 1. (aid) *chhātravrutti* छात्रवृत्ति; 2. (erudition) (n∘) *pāṇḍitya,* (f∘) *vidvattā* पांडित्य, विद्वत्ता

School (n∘) *vidyālaya,* (f∘) *pāṭhaśhāḷā* विद्यालय, पाठशाळा

Science (n∘) *śhāstra, vidnyān* शास्त्र, विज्ञान

Scientific (adj∘) *śhāstrīya, vaidnyānik* शास्त्रीय, वैज्ञानिक

Scientist (m∘) *vaidnyānik* वैज्ञानिक

Scissors (f∘) *kaichī* कैची

Scold (v∘) *jhāḍṇe, dāṭṇe* झाडणे, दाटणे*

Scoop (m∘) *chamchā* चमचा

Scope (f∘) 1. (possibility) *vāv* वाव 2. (range) (m∘) *vistār* विस्तार

Scorch (v∘) *horpaḷṇe* होरपळणे*

Score (m∘) *hiśhob* हिशोब

Scorn (m∘) *apamān* अपमान

Scorpio (f∘) *vruschic rāśhi* वृश्चिक राशि

Scorpion (m∘) *vinchū* विंचू

Scoundrel (adj∘) *badmāśh* बदमाश

Scramble (v∘) (to mix up) *milavṇe* मिळवणे*

Scrap (m∘) *kachrā* कचरा

Scrape (v∘) *kharvaḍṇe* खरवडणे*; (f∘) *khāj* खाज

Screen (m∘) *chitrapaṭ* चित्रपट

Screw (m∘) *pech* पेच

Screwdriver (m∘) *pechkas* पेचकस

Scribble (v∘) *ghasīṭṇe* घसीटणे*

Script (f∘) *paṭa-kathā* पटकथा

Scripture (m∘) *dharma-granth* धर्मग्रंथ

Scruple (m∘) *naitik sankoch* नैतिक संकोच

Scrupulous (adj∘) *imāndār* इमानदार

Scrutinize (v∘) *jāch karṇe* जाच क∘*

adj∘ = Adjective, adv∘ = Adverb; *conj.* = Conjunction, f∘ = Feminine gender, *ind.* = Indeclinable, m∘ = Masculine gender, n∘ = Neuter gender, pl∘ = Plural

Scrutiny (f∘) *jāch* जाच
Scuffle (f∘) *dhakkābukkī* धक्काबुक्की
Sculptor (m∘) *mūrtikār* मूर्तिकार
Sculpture (f∘) *mūrtī* मूर्ति
Scum (m∘) *fes* फेस
Scurry (v∘) *paḷṇe* पळणे
Sea (m∘) *samudra, sāgar* समुद्र, सागर
Seal (f∘) *mohor* मोहोर
Seam (f∘) *śhivaṇ* शिवण
Search (f∘) *khoj, talāśhī* खोज, तलाशी
Search (v∘) *khojṇe, ḍhunḍaṇe* खोजणे, धुंडणे*
Season (m∘) *rutu, mausam* ऋतु, मौसम
Seasonal (adj∘) *mausamī* मौसमी
Seasoned (adj∘) *anubhavī* अनुभवी
Seat (n∘) *āsan, sthān* आसन, स्थान
Second (adj∘) *dusrā* दुसरा
Secondary (adj∘) *duyyam, gauṇ* दुय्यम, गौण
Secret (adj∘) *gopanīya, gupt* गोपनीय, गुप्त; (n∘) *rahasya,* (m∘) *bhed* रहस्य, भेद
Secretary (m∘) *sachiv* सचिव
Sect (m∘) *sampradāy* संप्रदाय
Section (m∘) *vibhāg, khanḍ* विभाग, खंड
Sector (n∘) *kṣhetra* क्षेत्र
Secular (adj∘) *dharma-nirapekṣha* धर्म-निरपेक्ष
Secure (adj∘) *surakṣhit* सुरक्षित
Secure (v∘) *miḷavṇe* मिळवणे*
Security (f∘) *surakṣha* सुरक्षा
See (v∘) *pāhṇe* पाहणे*
Seed (f∘) *bī* बी
Seek (v∘) *khojṇe, dhunḍṇe* खोजणे, धुंडणे*
Segment (m∘) *hissā, khanḍ* हिस्सा, खंड
Segregation (n∘) *pruthakkaraṇ* पृथक्करण
Seige (f∘) *gherābandī* घेराबंदी
Seize (v∘) *haḍapṇe* हडपणे*
Seldom (adj∘) *kadāchit* कदाचित्
Select (v∘) *nivaḍṇe* निवडणे*
Selection (f∘) *nivaḍnūk* निवडणूक
Self (pref∘) *asvatah, ātma, svayam* स्वत:, आत्म, स्वयं
Self-centered (adj∘) *āp-matalabī* आप-मतलबी
Self-control (m∘) *ātma-saṁyam* आत्मसंयम
Self-defence (f∘) *ātma-rakṣhā* आत्मरक्षा
Self-inspired (adj∘) *svayam-sfurta* स्वयं-स्फूर्त
Selfless (adj∘) *niḥsvārtha* नि:स्वार्थ
Self-respect (m∘) *ātma-gaurav* आत्मगौरव
Self-sufficient (adj∘) *ātma-nirbhar* आत्म-निर्भर
Sell (v∘) *vikṇe* विकणे*
Seller (m∘) *vikretā* विक्रेता
Semi (pref∘) *ardh-* अर्ध-
Semicolon (m∘) *ardha-virām* अर्धविराम
Seminar (f∘) *sabhā* सभा
Senate (f∘) *sanad* सनद
Send (v∘) *pāṭhavṇe* पाठवणे*
Senior (adj∘) *jyeṣhṭha* ज्येष्ठ
Senriment (f∘) *bhāvuktā* भावुकता
Sense (n∘) *bhān,* (f∘) *saṁvednā* भान, संवेदना
Senselass (adj∘) *behośh, beśhuddha* बेहोश, बेशुद्ध
Sensible (adj∘) *samajdār* समजदार
Sensitive (adj∘) *bhāvuk* भावुक
Sentence (n∘) *vākya* वाक्य
Sentry (m∘) *pahāredār* पहारेदार
Separate (adj∘) *alag* अलग
Separately (adv∘) *alag* अलग
Separation (n∘) *pruthakkaraṇ* पृथक्करण
Separete (v∘) *alag hoṇe, alag karṇe** अलग हो∘, अलग क∘*
Sepulture (f∘) *samādhi* समाधि
Sequence (m∘) *kram* क्रम
Serial (adj∘) *kramik* क्रमिक
Series (f∘) *śhruṅkhalā* शृंखला
Serinity (f∘) *śhāntatā* शांतता
Serious (adj∘) *gambhīr* गंभीर
Seriousness (n∘) *gāmbhīrya* गांभीर्य
Sermon (n∘) *pravachan* प्रवचन
Serpent (m∘) *sāp* साप
Serrated (adj∘) *dantur* दंतुर
Servant (m∘) *naukar* नौकर
Serve (v∘) *sevā karaṇe* सेवा क∘*
Service (f∘) *naukarī,* (n∘) *kām* नौकरी, काम
Sesame (m∘) *tīḷ* तीळ
Set (m∘) *samucchay* समुच्चय; (v∘) *rachṇe* रचणे*
Settle, compromise (v∘) *nipaṭṇe* निपटणे
Settlement (m∘) *samjhautā, niptārā* समझौता, निपटारा
Seven (adj∘) *sāt* सात
Seventeen (adj∘) *satarā* सतरा
Seventy (adj∘) *sattar* सत्तर
Sever (v∘) *kāpṇe* कापणे*
Several (adj∘) *anek* अनेक
Severe (adj∘) *kaṭhor* कठोर
Sew (v∘) *śhivṇe* शिवणे*
Sewer (m∘) *nālā* नाला
Sex (n∘) *liṅg* लिंग
Sexual (adj∘) *laiṅgik* लैंगिक
Shack (f∘) *kuṭi, jhopaḍī* कुटि, झोपडी
Shackle (f∘) *beḍī* बेडी
Shade (f∘) *sāvlī, chhāyā* सावली, छाया
Shadow (f∘) *sāvlī* सवली
Shaft (m∘) *danḍā* दंडा
Shake (v∘) *hālavṇe* हालवणे*
Shaky (adj∘) *kamzor* कमजोर
Shallow (adj∘) *uthḷ* उथळ
Shame (f∘) *lajjā* लज्जा
Shape (m∘) *ākār,* (f∘) *ākrutī* आकार, आकृति; (v∘) *ākār deṇe* आकार देणे*
Share (m∘) *bhāg, hissā* भाग, हिस्सा; (v∘) *vāṭṇe* वाटणे*
Sharp (adj∘) *tīkṣhṇa* तीक्ष्ण
Shave (v∘) *hajāmat karṇe* हजामत क∘*
She (pron∘) *tī* ती
Shear (v∘) *kāpṇe* कापणे*
Shears (f∘) *kaichī* कैची
Sheep (f∘) *menḍhī* मेंढी
Sheet, bed sheet (f∘) *chādar* चादर
Shelf (f∘) *kapāṭ* कपाट
Shell (f∘) *śhimp* शिंप
Shelter (m∘) *āśhray* आश्रय
Shepherd (m∘) *dhangar* धनगर
Shield (m∘) *kavach,* (f∘) *ḍhāl* कवच, ढाल
Shift (m∘) *badal* बदल; (v∘) *badalṇe*

adj∘ = Adjective, adv∘ = Adverb; *conj.* = Conjunction, f∘ = Feminine gender, *ind.* = Indeclinable, m∘ = Masculine gender, n∘ = Neuter gender, pl∘ = Plural

बदलणे*

Shimmer (v∘) *luklukṇe* लुकलुकणे

Shine (v∘) *chamakṇe, chamkavṇe** चमकणे, चमकवणे*; (f∘) *chamak* चमक

Ship (n∘) *jahāj* जहाज

Shirt (f∘) *kamīj* कमीज

Shock (m∘) *dhakkā* धक्का

Shoe, boot (m∘) *joḍā* जोडा

Shoot (v∘) *goḷī mārṇe* गोळी मारणे*

Shop (f∘) *dukān* दुकान

Shore (m∘) *taṭ, kinārā* तट, किनारा

Short (adj∘) *chhoṭā, laghu* छोटा, लघु

Shortage (m∘) *abhāv* अभाव

Shortly (adv∘) *jalad* जलद

Shoulder (m∘) *khāndā* खांदा

Shout (f∘) *ārolī* आरोळी; (v∘) *oraḍṇe* ओरडणे

Shovel (n∘) *pāvḍe* पावडे

Show (n∘) *pradarśhan* प्रदर्शन; (v∘) *dākhavṇe* दाखवणे*

Shower (m∘) *varṣhāv* वर्षाव

Shred (f∘) *chindhī* चिंधी

Shrewd (adj∘) *samajdār* समजदार

Shrimp (m∘) *hjiṅgā* झिंगा

Shrine (f∘) *samādhi* समाधि

Shrink (v∘) *āṭṇe, ākrasṇe* आटणे, आक्रसणे

Shroud (n∘) *kafan, āvaraṇ* कफन, आवरण

Shrub (f∘) *jhāḍī* झाडी

Shudder (v∘) *thartharṇe* थरथरणे

Shuffle (v∘) *pisṇe* पिसणे

Shun (v∘) *ṭāḷṇe* टाळणे

Shut (v∘) *band karṇe* बंद क∘*

Shutter (f∘) *jhaḍap* झडप

Shy (adj∘) *lajjāyukta* लज्जायुक्त; (v∘) *lājṇe,* लाजणे

Sick (adj∘) *ājārī, asvastha* आजारी, अस्वस्थ

Sickness (m∘) *ājār* आजार

Side (f∘) *bāju* बाजु

Sieve (f∘) *chāḷṇī* चाळणी

Sift (v∘) *chāḷṇe* चाळणे*

Sigh (m∘) *usāsā* उसासा

Sight (f∘) *druṣhṭi* दृष्टि

Sign (n∘) *pratik, chihna* प्रतिक, चिह्

Signal (m∘) *saṅket* संकेत

Signature (n∘) *hastākṣhar* हस्ताक्षर

Significance (n∘) *mahattva* महत्त्व

Silence (n∘) *maun* मौन

Silent (adj∘) *chup* चुप

Silently (adv∘) *chupachāp* चुपचाप

Silk (n∘) *reśhim* रेशिम

Silky (adj∘) *reśhmī* रेशमी

Silly (adj∘) *vātraṭ* वात्रट

Silver (f∘) *chāndī* चांदी

Similar (adj∘) *samān* समान

Similarly (adv∘) *tasech* तसेच

Simile (f∘) *upamā* उपमा

Simmer (v∘) *ukaḷṇe* उकळणे

Simple (adj∘) *sādhā, sādhāraṇ, saraḷ* साधा, साधारण, सरळ

Simplicity (f∘) *saraḷtā* सरळता

Simplify (v∘) *sope karṇe* सोपे क∘*

Simultaneous (adj∘) *ek-kālik* एककालिक

Simultaneously (adv∘) *barobar* बरोबर

Sin (n∘) *pāp* पाप

Since (m∘) 1. (from) *pāsūn* पासून 2. (because) *kāraṇ kī* कारण की

Sing (v∘) *gāṇe* गाणे*

Singer (f∘) *gāyikā,* (m∘) *gāyak* गायिका, गायक

Single (adj∘) *akelā* अकेला

Singular (n∘) *ek-vachan* एक वचन

Sinister (adj∘) *kuṭil* कुटिल

Sink (v∘) *buḍṇe, buḍavṇe** बुडणे, बुडवणे*

Sip (v∘) *chuskī gheṇe* चुस्की घेणे*

Sir (m∘) *mahoday, śhrimān* महोदय, श्रीमान

Siren (m∘) *bhongā* भोंगा

Sister (f∘) *bahiṇ* बहिण

Sister-in-law (f∘) *sālī, vahinī* साळी, वहीनी

Sit (v∘) *basṇe* बसणे

Site (n∘) *sthān,* (f∘) *jāgā* स्थान, जागा

Situation (f∘) *sthiti, hālat* स्थिति, हालत

Six (adj∘) *sahā* सहा

Sixteen (adj∘) *soḷā* सोळा

Sixty (adj∘) *sāṭh* साठ

Size (m∘) *ākār* आकार

Skeleton (m∘) *sāpḷā* सापळा

Sketch (f∘) *rūp-reśhā* रूपरेशा

Skid (v∘) *ghasarṇe* घसरणे

Skin (n∘) *chamḍe,* (f∘) *tvachā* चमडे, त्वचा

Skip (v∘) *vagaḷṇe* वगळणे*

Skirmish (f∘) *chakmak* चकमक

Skirt (m∘) *jhagā* झगा

Skull (f∘) *kavṭī* कवटी

Sky (n∘) *ākāśh* आकाश

Slab (m∘) *lāfā* लाफा

Slack (f∘) *ḍhīl* ढील

Slam (v∘) *paṭakṇe* पटकणे*

Slander (f∘) *khoṭī nindā* खोटी निंदा

Slant (adj∘) *tirpā* तिरपा

Slap (f∘) *thāpaḍ* थापड; (v∘) *thāpaḍ mārṇe* थापड मारणे*

Slash (v∘) *kāpṇe* कापणे*

Slaughter (f∘) *hatyā* हत्या

Slave (m∘) *dās, gulām* दास, गुलाम

Slay (v∘) *hatyā karṇe* हत्या क∘*

Sleek (adj∘) *chopḍā* चोपडा

Sleep (f∘) *zop* झोप; (v∘) zope झोपणे

Sleeve (f∘) *bāhī* बाही

Slender (adj∘) *patlā* पतला

Slice (f∘) *phā̃k* फांक

Slide (v∘) *ghasarṇe, fisalṇe* घसरणे, फिसलणे

Slight (adj∘) *kiñchit* किंचित

Slightly (adv∘) *jarā* जरा

Slip (v∘) *fisalṇe* फिसलणे

Slit (f∘) *chīr* चीर

Slogan (m∘) *nārā* नारा

Slope (m∘) *utār* उतार

Slot (m∘) *khā̃ch* खांच

Slow (adj∘) *mand* मंद

Slowly (adv∘) *haḷū* हळू

Sluggish (adj∘) *sust* सुस्त

Slumber (f∘) *zop* झोप

Slump (f∘) *mandī* मंदी

Smack (f∘) *thāpaḍ,* (m∘) *tamāchā* थापड, तमाचा

Small (adj∘) *chhoṭā, lahān* छोटा, लहान

Smallpox (m∘) *chechak* चेचक

adj∘ = Adjective, adv∘ = Adverb; *conj.* = Conjunction, f∘ = Feminine gender, *ind.* = Indeclinable, m∘ = Masculine gender, n∘ = Neuter gender, pl∘ = Plural

Smart (adj∘) *hus̀hār* हुशार

Smash (f∘) *ṭakkar* टक्कर

Smell (f∘) *gandh, vās* गंध, वास; (v∘) *suṅghaṇe* सुंघणे*

Smelt (v∘) *pighaḷavṇe* पिघळवणे*

Smile (n∘) *hāsya* हास्य

Smoke (m∘) *dhūr* धूर; (v∘) *bīḍī piṇe* बीडी पिणे*

Smooth (adj∘) *chopḍā* चोपडा

Smoulder (v∘) *sulagṇe* सुलगणे

Smudge (m∘) *dhabbā, dāg* धब्बा, डाग

Snack (m∘) *nāstā* नास्ता

Snail (f∘) *gogalgāy* गोगलगाय

Snake (m∘) *sāp* साप

Snap (v∘) *tuṭṇe* तुटणे

Snare (n∘) *jāḷe* जाळे

Snatch (v∘) *hisakṇe* हिसकणे*

Sneeze (f∘) *s̀hink* शिंक; (v∘) *s̀hinkṇe* शिंकणे

Sniff (v∘) *sūnghaṇe* सुंघणे*

Snip (v∘) *kāpṇe* कापणे*

Snooze (f∘) *jhapkī, ḍulkī* झपकी, डुलकी; (v∘) *jhapkī gheṇe* झपकी घेणे*

Snore (v∘) *ghorṇe* घोरणे

Snout (f∘) *soṇḍ* सोंड

Snow (m∘) *barf* बर्फ

So (adv∘) *tathā* तथा; (adj∘) *itkā* इतका; (conj∘) *mhaṇūn* म्हणून

Soak (v∘) *bhijavṇe* भिजवणे*

Soap (f∘) *sābaṇ* साबण

Sob (m∘) *hundkā* हुंदका

Sober (adj∘) *saumya* सौम्य

Sociable (adj∘) *milansār* मिलनसार

Social (adj∘) *sāmājik* सामाजिक

Socialism (m∘) *samājvād* समाजवाद

Society (m∘) *samāj* समाज

Sociology (n) *samāj-s̀hāstra* समाजशास्त्र

Sock (m∘) *mojā* मोजा

Soft (adj∘) *komal, naram, mulāyam* कोमल, नरम, मुलायम

Soggy (adj∘) *dpāṇthaḷ* पाणथळ

Soil (f∘) *māṭī* माती

Soldier (m∘) *s̀hipāī* शिपाई, *sainik* (in army) सैनिक

Sole (adj∘) *akelā, ekmātra* अकेला, एकमात्र; (m∘) *taḷavā* तळवा

Solicit (v∘) *māgṇe* मागणे*

Solid (adj∘) *ghana* घन

Solidarity (f∘) *ektā* एकता

Solitary (adj∘) *akelā* अकेला

Solution (n∘) 1. (liquid) *dravaṇ* द्रावण 2. (answer) *samādhān* समाधान

Somber (adj∘) *khinna, udās* खिन्न, उदास

Some (pron∘) *kāhī* काही

Somersault (f∘) *kolaṇṭī* कोलांटी

Sometimes (adv∘) *kadhī kadhī* कधी कधी

Somewhat (adv∘) *jarā* जरा

Somewhere (adv∘) *kuṭhe tarī* कुठे तरी

Son (m∘) *putra* पुत्र

Song (n∘) *gāṇe* गाणे

Son-in-law (m∘) *jāvāī* जावाई

Soon (adv∘) *tatkāḷ* तत्काळ

Soot (n∘) *kājaḷ* काजळ

Soothe (v∘) *s̀hānt karṇe* शांत क∘*

Sophisticated (adj∘) *krutrum* कृत्रिम

Sorcery (f∘) *tāntrikī* तांत्रिकी

Sore (adj∘) *duhkhī* दुःखी

Sorry (adj∘) *duhkhī* दुःखी

Sort (m∘) *prakār* प्रकार

Sort (v∘) *nivaḍṇe* निवडणे*

Soul (m∘) *ātmā* आत्मा

Sound (m∘) *āwāj, dhvani* आवाज, ध्वनि

Sour (adj∘) *ambaṭ* आंबट

Source (n∘) *ugam sthān* उगम स्थान

South (f∘) *dakṣhiṇ* दक्षिण

Souvenir (f∘) *smārikā* स्मारिका

Sow (v∘) *perṇe* पेरणे*

Spacious (adj∘) *vistīrṇa* विस्तीर्ण

Spactator (m∘) *dars̀hak* दर्शक

Spade (n∘) *pāvaḍe* पावडे

Span (m∘) *failāv, vistār* फैलाव, विस्तार

Spanner (m∘) *pānā* पाना

Spare (adj∘) *fāltū* फालतू; (v∘) *vāchavṇe* वाचवणे*

Spark (f∘) *ṭhiṇgī* ठिणगी

Sparkle (v∘) *chamakṇe* चमकणे

Sparrow (f∘) *chimṇī* चिमणी

Spate (f∘) *pūr* पूर

Spatter (v∘) *s̀himpaḍṇe* शिंपडणे*

Speak (v∘) *bolaṇe* बोलणे

Speaker (m∘) *vaktā* वक्ता

Spear (m∘) *bhālā* भाला

Special (adj∘) *vis̀heṣh, khās* विशेष, खास

Speciality (f∘) *vis̀heṣhtā* विशेषता

Species (f∘) *jāti* जाति

Specific (adj∘) *vis̀hiṣhṭa* विशिष्ट

Specimen (m∘) *namūṇe* नमूना

Spectacle (m∘) *tamās̀hā* तमाशा

Spectacles (m∘) *chaṣhmā,* चष्मा

Spectacular (adj∘) *s̀hāndār* शानदार

Speculate (v∘) *aṭkaḷ lāvṇe* अटकळ लावणे*

Speculation (f∘) *aṭkaḷ* अटकळ

Speech (n∘) *bhāṣhaṇ* भाषण

Speed (f∘) *gati* गति

Speedily (adv∘) *jalad* जलद

Spellbound (adj∘) *mantramugdha* मंत्रमुग्ध

Spice (m∘) *masālā* मसाला

Spider (f∘) *koḷī* कोळी

Spike (m∘) *kāṭā, khiḷā* काटा, खिळा

Spill (v∘) *jhaḷakṇe* झळकणे

Spin (v∘) *gol firṇe* गोल फिरणे

Spinach (f∘) *pālak* पालक

Spindle (m∘) *akṣha, dhurā* अक्ष, धुरा

Spine (m∘) *kaṇā* कणा

Spiral (adj∘) *golākār, kuṇḍlākār* गोलाकार, कुंडलाकार

Spire (n∘) *shikhar* शिखर

Spirit (m∘) 1. (soul) *ātmā* आत्मा, 2. (liquor) (f∘) *dārū* दारू

Spiritual (adj∘) *adhyātmik, dhārmik* अध्यात्मिक, धार्मिक

Splendid (adj∘) *s̀hāndār* शानदार

Splendorous (adj∘) *s̀hāndār* शानदार

Splendour (f∘) *s̀hān* शान

Splinter (m∘) *s̀hiḷak* शिळक

Split (v∘) *chirṇe, vibhāgṇe* चिरणे, विभागणे*

adj∘ = Adjective, adv∘ = Adverb; *conj.* = Conjunction, f∘ = Feminine gender, *ind.* = Indeclinable, m∘ = Masculine gender, n∘ = Neuter gender, pl∘ = Plural

Spoil (v◦) *bighaḍṇe, nāsṇe, saḍṇe* बिघडणे, नासणे, सडणे

Spoke (m◦) *ārā* आरा

Spokesman (m◦) *pravaktā* प्रवक्ता

Spontaneous (adj◦) *svābhāvik* स्वाभाविक

Spontaneously (adv◦) *svayam, svatah* स्वयं, स्वत:

Spool (f◦) *firkī,* (n◦) *riḷ* फिरकी, रीळ

Spoon (m◦) *camchā* चमचा

Sport (f◦) *kheḷ-kūd* खेळ-कूद

Spot (m◦) 1. (mark) *dhabbā, ḍāg* धब्बा, डाग; 2. (place) (n◦) *sthān, ṭhikāṇ* स्थान, ठिकाण

Spring (f◦) 1. (coil) *kamānī* कमान, (m◦) 2. (flow) *jharā* झरा, 3. (m◦) (season) *vasant* वसंत; (v◦) *usaḷe* उसळणे

Sprinkle (v◦) *śhimpaḍṇe* शिंपडणे*

Sprout (m◦) *aṅkur,* (n◦) *komb* अंकुर, कोंब

Spurious (adj◦) *naklī* नकली

Spurn (v◦) *ṭhukrāvṇe* ठुकरावणे*

Spurt (m◦) *fawārā* फवारा

Spy (m◦) *her* हेर

Squabble (n◦) *tū-tū mī-mī* तू-तू मी-मी

Squad (f◦) *tukḍī* तुकडी

Squalor (f◦) *ghāṇ* घाण

Square (m◦) *vargākār, chauras* वर्गाकार, चौरस; *chaturbhuj* चतुर्भुज

Squash (v◦) *kuchalṇe* कुचलणे*

Squat (adj◦) *thengṇā* ठेंगणा

Squawk (m◦) *kal-rav* कलरव

Squeak (v◦) *karkarṇe* करक◦

Squeal (f◦) *karkar* करकर

Squeeze (v◦) *piḷṇe, chepṇe* पिळणे, चेपणे*

Squirrel (f◦) *khirāḍī* खिराडी

Squirt (m◦) *fawārā* फवारा

Stick (v◦) *chikaṭṇe, chikṭavṇe** चिकटणे, चिकटवणे*

Superintendent (m◦) *sañchālak* संचालक

Stable (adj◦) *sthir* स्थिर; (n◦) *tabele* तबेले

Stack (f◦) *ḍher* ढेर

Stag (n◦) *hariṇ* हरिण

Stage, condition (f◦) *avasthā* अवस्था; podium (m◦) *mañch* मंच

Stagger (v◦) *laḍkhaḍṇe* लडखडणे

Stagnet (v◦) *ṭhāmbṇe* थांबणे

Stain (m◦) *dhabbā, ḍāg* धब्बा, डाग

Stair (m◦) *jīnā* जीना

Stake, peg (m◦) *khunṭā* खुंटा

Stale (adj◦) *śhiḷā* शिळा

Stallion (m◦) *ghoḍā* घोडा

Stalwart (adj◦) *pakkā* पक्का

Stamina (m◦) *dam* दम

Stammer (v◦) *totare bolṇe* तोतरे बोलणे

Stamp (f◦) *tikiṭ* तिकिट; (m◦) *chhāpā* छापा; (v◦) *chhāpā mārṇe* छापा मारणे*

Stampede (f◦) *bhāgdauḍ* भागदौड

Stance (m◦) *drushṭikoṇ* दृष्टिकोण

Stand (v◦) 1. withstand *tagṇe;* 2. stand up *ubhe hoṇe* 1. तगणे, 2. उभे हो◦

Standard (adj◦) *sāmānya* सामान्य

Star (m◦) *tārā* तारा

Starch (m◦) *kalaf* कलफ

Stare (v◦) *vaṭārṇe* वटारणे

Start (m◦) *ārambha* आरंभ; (v◦) *ārambha karṇe* आरंभ क◦*

Starvation (f◦) *upāsmār* उपासमार

Starve (v◦) *khaṅgṇe* खंगणे

State 1. (m◦ province) *prānt* प्रांत; 2. (condition) (f◦) *avasthā* अवस्था

Statement (n◦) *kathan* कथन

Static (adj◦) *thir* स्थिर

Station (m◦) *aḍḍā,* (f◦) *chaukī* अड्डा, चौकी

Stationary (adj◦) *sthir* स्थिर

Statue (f◦) *mūrtī,* (m◦) *putaḷā* मूर्ति, पुतळा

Stature (f◦) *yashṭi* यष्टि

Status (m◦) *darjā,* (n◦) *pad* दर्जा, पद

Stauñch (adj◦) *pakkā* पक्का

Stay (v◦) *rāhṇe, ṭhāmbṇe* राहणे, थांबणे

Steadfast (adj◦) *pakkā, aṭaḷ* पक्का, अटळ

Steady (adj◦) *sthir* स्थिर

Steal (v◦) *chorṇe* चोरणे*

Stealth (adj◦) *gupt* गुप्त

Steam (f◦) *vāf* वाफ

Steel (n◦) *polād, ispāt* पोलाद, इस्पात

Steep (adj◦) *chaḍh* चढ

Steeple (m◦) *mināra* मिनार

Stem (n◦) *khoḍ* खोड

Steñch (m◦) *durgandh* दुर्गंध

Step (m◦) *pāūl* पाऊल; (v◦) *pāūi ṭhevṇe* पाऊल ठेवणे*

Sterile (adj◦) *bajnar* बंजर

Stern (adj◦) *gambhīr* गंभीर

Stick (f◦) *chhaḍī* छडी

Sticky (adj◦) *chikaṭ* चिकट

Stiff (adj◦) *kaḍak* कडक

Stigmā (m◦) *kalaṅk,* (n◦) *lāñchhan* कलंक, लांछन

Still (adj◦) *sthir* स्थिर; (adv◦) *tarī* तरी

Stimulant (adj◦) *prerak, uttejak* प्रेरक, उत्तेजक

Stimulate (v◦) *uksavṇe* उकसवणे*

Stimulus (n◦) *uttejan* (f◦) *prerṇā* उत्तेजन, प्रेरणा

Sting (m◦) *ḍaṅk* डंक; (v◦) *ḍaṅk mārṇe* डंक मारणे*

Stingy (adj◦) *kañjūs* कंजूस

Stink (m◦) *durgandh* दुर्गंध

Stir (v◦) *misaḷṇe* मिसळणे*

Stitch (m◦) *ṭākā* टाका; (v◦) *sivṇe* शिवणे*

Stock (m◦) *māl* माल

Stolid (adj◦) *bhāva-śhūnya* भावशून्य

Stomach (n◦) *poṭ* पोट

Stomp (v◦) *rendṇe* रेंदणे*

Stone (m◦) *goṭā, khaḍak* गोटा, खडक

Stony (adj◦) *khaḍkāḷ* खडकाळ

Stool (f◦) *chārpaī, tipāī* चारपाई, तिपाई

Stoop (v◦) *jhukṇe* झुकणे

Stop (v◦) *thāmbṇe* थांबणे

Storage (n◦) *godām* गोदाम

Store (n◦) *dukān, bhāṇḍār* दुकान, भांडार; (v◦) *jamā karṇe* जमा क◦*

Stork (m◦) *sāras* सारस

Storm (n◦) *vādaḷ* वादळ

Story (f◦) *kathā, kahāṇī* कथा, कहाणी

Stout (adj◦) *pakkā, majbūt* पक्का, मजबूत

Stove (f◦) *chūl* चूल

Straight (adj◦) *saraḷ* सरळ

Straightforward (adj◦) *sīdhā, saraḷ* सीधा,

adj◦ = Adjective, adv◦ = Adverb; *conj.* = Conjunction, f◦ = Feminine gender, *ind.* = Indeclinable, m◦ = Masculine gender, n◦ = Neuter gender, pl◦ = Plural

सरळ

Strain (m∘) *tanāv, dabāv* तनाव, दबाव

Stress (m∘) *tanāv, dabāv* तनाव, दबाव; (v∘) *jor lāvṇe* जोर लावणे*

Stretch (m∘) *tanāv* तनाव; (v∘) *tāṇaṇe. oḍhṇe* ताणणे, ओढणे*

Strict (adj∘) *kaḍak* कडक

Strife (m∘) *saṅgharṣh* संघर्ष; (m∘) *hartāḷ* हरताळ

String (f∘) *dorī* दोरी

Stringent (adj∘) *kaḍak* कडक

Strip (f∘) *paṭṭī* पट्टी

Stripe (m∘) *paṭṭā* पट्टा

Strive (v∘) *prayās karṇe* प्रयास क∘*

Stroke (m∘) *āghāt* आघात

Stroll (v∘) *ṭahalṇe, firṇe* टहलणे, फिरणे

Strong (adj∘) *balavān* बलवान्

Structure (f∘) 1. (makeup) *banāvaṭ* बनावट; 2. (building) (n∘) *bhavan* भवन

Struggle (m∘) *saṅgharṣh* संघर्ष

Stubborn (m∘) *haṭṭī, jiddī* हट्टी, जिद्दी

Student (m∘) *chhātra* छात्र

Studious (adj∘) *mehnatī* मेहनती

Study (m∘) *abhyās* अभ्यास; (v∘) *shikṇe* शिकणे*

Stuff (n∘) *sāmān,* (f∘) *sāmagrī* सामान, सामग्री

Stumble (v∘) *aḍkhalṇe* अडखळणे

Stun (v∘) *awāk hoṇe* अवाक हो∘

Stunt (n∘) *dhāḍas* धाडस

Stupendous (adj∘) *mahān* महान

Stupid (adj∘) *mūrkh* मूर्ख

Sturdy (adj∘) *mazbūt* मजबूत

Stutter (v∘) *totaḍe bolṇe* तोतडे बोलणे

Style (f∘) *śhailī, banāvaṭ* शैली, बनावट

Subdue (m∘) *kābū karṇe* काबू क∘

Subject (m∘) *viṣhay* विषय

Sublime (adj∘) *udātta* उदात्त

Submarine (f∘) *pāṇḍubbī* पाणडुब्बी

Submission (n∘) *samarpaṇ* समर्पण

Subsequent (adj∘) *anugāmī* अनुगामी

Subside (v∘) *ghaṭṇe* घटणे

Substance (m∘) *padārtha* पदार्थ

Subtle (adj∘) *sūkṣhma* सूक्ष्म

Suburb (n∘) *upnagar* उपनगर

Subway (m∘) *suraṅg-path* सुरंग–पथ

Succed (v∘) *uttarādhikārī hoṇe* उत्तराधिकारी हो∘

Succeptible (adj∘) *grahanśhīl* ग्रहणशील

Success (n∘) *yaśha* यश

Succession (m∘) *uttarādhikār* उत्तराधिकार

Successive (adj∘) *kramik* क्रमिक

Successor (m∘) *uttarādhikārī* उत्तराधिकारी

Such (adj∘) *asā* असा

Suck (v∘) *chokhṇe* चोखणे*

Sudden (adj∘) *achānak* अचानक

Suddenly (adv∘) *ekdam* एकदम

Sue (v∘) *mukadmā karṇe* मुकदमा क∘*

Suffer (v∘) *bhogṇe* भोगणे

Suffering (f∘) *pīḍā* पीडा

Suffice (v∘) *putr hoṇe* पुरे हो∘

Sufficient (adj∘) *pure* पुरे

Sufficiently (adv∘) *paryāpta* पर्याप्त

Suffix (m∘) *pratyay* प्रत्यय

Suffocate (v∘) *dam ghuṭṇe* दम घुटणे

Sugar (f∘) *sākhar* साखर

Sugarcane (m∘) *ūs* ऊस

Suggest (v∘) *sallā deṇe* सल्ला देणे*

Suggestion (m∘) *sallā* सल्ला

Suicide (f∘) *ātmahtyā* आत्महत्या

Suit (m∘) *mukadmā* मुकदमा

Suitable (adj∘) *ṭhīk, uchit* ठीक, उचित

Sulk (v∘) *kuḍhṇe* कुढणे

Sullen (adj∘) *chiḍchiḍā* चिडचिडा

Sulphur (n∘) *gandhak* गंधक

Sum (m∘) *yog* योग; (f∘) *berīj* बेरीज

Summary (m∘) *sārāmśh* सारांश

Summer (m∘) *grīṣhma* ग्रीष्म

Summit (n∘) *śhikhar* शिखर

Summon (n∘) *bolāvṇe* बोलावणे*

Sun (m∘) *sūrya* सूर्य

Sunday (m∘) *ravivār* रविवार

Sundry (adj∘) *kirkoḷ* किरकोळ

Sunflower (n∘) *sūryamukhī* सूर्यमुखी

Super- (pref∘) *atyadhik, asāmānya, asādhāraṇ* अत्यधिक, असामान्य, असाधारण

Superb (adj∘) *śhreṣhtha* श्रेष्ठ

Supercilious (adj∘) *dambhī* दंभी

Superficial (adj∘) *bāhya* बाह्य

Superfluous (adj∘) *fāltu* फालतू

Superior (adj∘) *śhreṣhṭha, uccha* श्रेष्ठ, उच्च

Superiority (f∘) *śhreṣhṭhatā, ucchatā* श्रेष्ठता, उच्चता

Superlative (adj∘) *sarvaśhreṣhṭha, ucchatama* सर्वश्रेष्ठ, उच्चतम

Supernatural (adj∘) *alaukik* अलौकिक

Superstition (m∘) *andhaviśhvās* अंधविश्वास

Supervise (v∘) *dekhrekh karṇe* देखरेख क∘*

Supervision (f∘) *nigrāṇī* निगराणी

Supervisor (m∘) *nirīkṣhak* निरीक्षक

Supplement (m∘) *pūrak,* (f∘) *pūrti* पूरक, पूर्ति; (v∘) *pūrti karṇe* पूर्ति क∘*

Supplementary (adj∘) *pūrak, pariśhiṣhṭ* पूरक, परिशिष्ट

Supply (f∘) *pūrti,* (m∘) *puravṭhā* पूर्ति, पुरवठा (v∘) *pūrti karṇe* पूर्ति क∘*

Support (f∘) *sahāyatā, madat* सहायता, मदत

Supporting Actor (m∘) *upanāyak* उपनायक

Supportive (adj∘) *sahayak* सहायक

Suppose (v∘) *mānaṇe* मानणे*

Supreme (adj∘) *sarvaśhreṣhṭha, ucchatam* सर्वश्रेष्ठ, उच्चतम

Supress (v∘) *dābāṇe* दाबणे*

Supression (m∘) *dabāv* दबाव

Sure (adj∘) *nischit, pakkā* निश्चित, पक्का

Surely (adv∘) *niśhchit, avaśhya* निश्चित्, अवश्य

Surface (f∘) *pruṣhtha* पृष्ठ

Surge (m∘) *baḍhāvā,* (f∘) *baḍhatī* बढावा, बढती

Surge (v∘) *vāḍhṇe* वाढणे

Surgeon (m∘) *śhalya chikitsak* शल्य चिकित्सक

Surgery (f∘) *śhalya chikitsā* शल्य चिकित्सा

Surmise (m∘) *andāj, anumān* अंदाज, अनुमान

Surmount (v∘) *pār karṇe* पार क∘*

Surname (n∘) *kulanā̐v* कुलनांव

adj∘ = Adjective, adv∘ = Adverb; *conj.* = Conjunction, f∘ = Feminine gender, *ind.* = Indeclinable, m∘ = Masculine gender, n∘ = Neuter gender, pl∘ = Plural

Surplus (f∘) *bachat* बचत

Surprise (m∘) *āscharya, achambā* आश्चर्य, अचंबा

Surrender (n∘) *ātmasamarpaṇ,* (f∘) *s̒haraṇ* आत्मसमर्पण, शरण

Surreptitious (adj∘) *pracchhanna* प्रच्छन्न

Surround (v∘) *gherṇe* घेरणे*

Surveillance (f∘) *nigrāṇī* निगराणी

Survey (f∘) *jāch,* (n∘) *nirīkṣhaṇ,* जाच, निरीक्षण; (v∘) *jāchṇe* जाचणे*

Survival (m∘) *vāchṇe* वाचणे; (v∘) *bachāvṇe* बचावणे

Survivor (adj∘) *vāchalelā* वाचलेला

Suspect (v∘) *sandeha karṇe* संदेह क∘*

Suspend (v∘) *laṭkṇe, laṭkavṇe,* ṭāṅgṇe* लटकणे, लटकवणे*, टांगणे*

Suspense (m∘) *saṁs̒hay* संशय

Suspension (v∘) *laṭakṇe* लटकणे

Suspicion (m∘) *sandeha* संदेह

Suspicious (adj∘) *s̒haṅkāyukta* शंकायुक्त

Sustain (v∘) *sahan karṇe* सहन क∘*

Sustenance (m∘) *sahārā* सहारा

Suzerain (m∘) *adhipati, rājā* अधिपति, राजा

Svelte (adj∘) *komal* कोमल

Swab (m∘) *kūchlā* कूंचला

Swainish (adj∘) *kheḍvaḷ* खेडवळ

Swallow (v∘) *giḷṇe* गिळणे*

Swamp (f∘) *daldal* दलदल

Swan (m∘) *haṁsa* हंस

Swap (f∘) *adal-badal* अदल-बदल; (v∘) *adal-badal karṇe* अदल-बदल क∘*

Swash (m∘) *kolāhal* कोलाहल

Sway (m∘) *jhukṇe, jhukavṇe** झुकणे, झुकवणे*

Swear (f∘) 1. (vow) *s̒hapath, kasam* शपथ, कसम 2. (rebuke) *s̒hivī* शिवी

Sweat (m∘) *ghām* घाम

Sweep (v∘) *jhāḍṇe* झाडणे*

Sweeper, broom (m∘) *faḍā,* (f∘) *zāḍṇī* फडा, झाडणी

Sweet (adj∘) *goḍ* गोड

Sweets (f∘) *miṭhāī* मिठाई

Swell (n∘) *fugṇe, sujṇe* फुगणे, सुजणे

Swelling (f∘) *sūja* सूज

Swerve (v∘) *bhaṭakṇe* भटकणे

Swift (adj∘) *chañchal* चंचल

Swim (v∘) *pohṇe* पोहणे

Swindle (v∘) *ṭhagṇe* ठगणे*

Swindler (adj∘) *ṭhag* ठग

Swine (n∘) *ḍukkar* डुक्कर

Swing (m∘) *pāḷṇā* पाळणा

Swing (v∘) *jhūlṇe* झूलणे

Swipe (m∘) *āghāt* आघात

Swirl (m∘) *chakkar* चक्कर

Switch (v∘) *badalṇe* बदलणे*

Swivel (v∘) *chakrākār firṇe* चक्राकार फिरणे

Swoon (f∘) *mūrchhā* मूर्छा; (v∘) *mūrchhit hoṇe* मूर्छित हो∘

Swoop (f∘) *jhaḍap* झडप

Sword (f∘) *talvār* तलवार

Sycophant (adj∘) *chāplūs, khus̒hāmatī* चापलूस, खुशामती

Syllabus (m∘) *pāṭhyakram* पाठ्यक्रम

Symbol (n∘) *chihna, pratīk* चिह्न, प्रतीक

Symmetrical (adj∘) *bāndhesūd* बांधेसूद

Symmetry (f∘) *samānatā* समानता

Sympathetic (adj∘) *kanvālū* कनवाळू

Sympathy (f∘) *sahānubhūti* सहानुभूति

Symphony (n∘) *svarsaṅgīt* स्वरसंगीत

Symposium (n∘) *sammelan* सम्मेलन

Symptom (n∘) *lakṣhaṇ* लक्षण

Syndicate (m∘) *jvyāpār saṅgh* व्यापार संघ

Synonym (m∘) *paryāyvāchī s̒habd* पर्यायवाची शब्द

Synopsis (m∘) *sārāṁs̒h* सारांश

Syntax (f∘) *vākya rachaṇe* वाक्य रचना

Synthesis (m∘) *saṁyog* संयोग

Synthetic (adj∘) *krutrim* कृत्रिम

Syring (f∘) *pichkārī* पिचकारी

Syrup (f∘) *chāchṇī* चाचणी

System (m∘) *tantra,* (f∘) *vyavasthā* तंत्र, व्यवस्था

Systematic (adj∘) *vyavasthit* व्यवस्थित

T

Table, chart (f∘) *tālikā, sāraṇī* तालिका, सारणी; desk (m∘) *mej* मेज

Tablet (f∘) *goḷī* गोळी

Tack (f∘) *birañjī* बिरंजी

Tact (n∘) *kaus̒halya* कौशल्य

Tactic (f∘) *chāl* चाल

Tadpole (f∘) *beḍuklī* बेडुकली

Tag (n∘) *patrak* पत्रक

Tail (f∘) *s̒hepaṭī* शेपटी

Tailor (m∘) *s̒himpī* शिंपी

Take (v∘) *gheṇe* घेणे*

Tale (f∘) *kathā, kahāṇī* कथा, कहाणी

Talent (f∘) *pratibhā* (m∘) *guṇ* प्रतिभा, गुण

Talisman (n∘) *tāvij* ताविज

Talk (v∘) *bolaṇe* बोलणे

Tall (adj∘) *uñcha* उंच

Tallow (f∘) *charbī* चरबी

Tally (m∘) *meḷ, his̒heb* मेळ, हिशेब

Talon (m∘) *pañjā* पंजा

Tamarind (f∘) *chiñcha* चिंच

Tamper (v∘) *chheḍṇe* छेडणे*

Tangible (adj∘) *spars̒hanīya* स्पर्शनीय

Tangle (m∘) *guṇḍāḷā, ghoṭāḷā* गुंडाळा, घोटाळा

Tank, container (n∘) *ṭāke* टाके; reservoir (m∘) *talāv* तलाव

Tanslation (n∘) *bhāṣhāntar,* (m∘) *anuvād* भाषांतर, अनुवाद

Tantalize (v∘) *lalchāvṇe* तरसणे, ललचावणे

Tantamount (adj∘) *barobar* बरोबर

Tap, faucet (m∘) *naḷ, toṭī* नळ, तोटी

Tap, knock (v∘) *khaṭkhaṭaṇe* खटखटणे*

Tap, pat (f∘) *thapkī* थपकी

Tar (n∘) *ḍāmbar* डांबर

Tarantulā (m∘) *koḷī* कोळी

Tardiness (f∘) *susti* सुस्ति

Tardy (adj∘) *sust, dīrghasūtrī* सुस्त, दीर्घसूत्री

Target (n∘) *dhyeya, lakṣhya,* (m∘) *nis̒hāṇā* ध्येय, लक्ष्य, निशाणा

Tarnish (v∘) *kalaṅk lāvṇe* कलंक लावणे*

Task (n∘) *kārya* कार्य

Taste (m∘) *svād* स्वाद; (v∘) *chākhaṇe* चाखणे*

adj∘ = Adjective, adv∘ = Adverb; *conj.* = Conjunction, f∘ = Feminine gender, *ind.* = Indeclinable, m∘ = Masculine gender, n∘ = Neuter gender, pl∘ = Plural

Tattoo (v∘) *gondṇe* गोंदणे*

Taunt (m∘) *ṭomṇā* टोमणा

Taurus (f∘) *vruṣhabh rāśhi* वृषभ राशि

Tax (m∘) *kar* कर

Tea (m∘) *chahā* चहा

Teacher (m∘) *guru, śhikṣhak* (f∘) *śhikṣhikā* गुरु, शिक्षक, शिक्षिका

Teak, wood (n∘) *sāgvan* सागवन

Team (n∘) *daḷ* दळ

Tear (m∘) *aṣhuū* अश्रु

Tear (v∘) *fāḍṇe* फाडणे*

Tease (v∘) *chiḍavṇe* चिडवणे*

Technical (adj∘) *tāntrīk* तांत्रिक

Technique (n∘) *tantra* तंत्र

Tedious (adj∘) *thakāū* थकाऊ

Teenage (f∘) *kiśhorāvasthā* किशोरावस्था

Teenager (m∘) *kiśhor* किशोर

Teeth (m∘) *dāt* दात

Telegram (f∘) *tār* तार

Telepathy (m∘) *dūrbodh* दूरबोध

Telephone (m∘) *dūrbhāṣh* दूरभाष

Telescopr (f∘) *dūrbīṇ* दुर्बीण

Television (n∘) *dūrdarśhan* दूरदर्शन

Tell (v∘) *sāngṇe* सांगणे*

Temper (f∘) *marjī* मर्जी

Temperamental (adj∘) *saṅkī* सनकी

Temperance (m∘) *saṁyam* संयम

Temperature (n∘) *tāpmān* तापमान

Temple (n∘) *mandir* मंदिर

Tempo (f∘) *gati* गति

Temporal (adj∘) *saṅsārik* सांसारिक

Temporary (adj∘) *asthāyī* अस्थायी

Tempt (v∘) *bahkavṇe* बहकवणे*

Temptation (n∘) *pralobhan* प्रलोभन

Ten (adj∘) *dahā* दहा

Tenacious (adj∘) *pakkā, haṭṭī* पक्का, हट्टी

Tenant (m∘) *kirāyedār* किरायेदार

Tender, bid (m∘) *ṭhekā* ठेका; (adj∘) delicate *najuk* नाजुक

Tenet (n∘) *mat* मत

Tenous (adj∘) *nājuk* नाजुक

Tense (adj∘) *bechain, tāṭh* बेचैन; ताठ

Tension (m∘) *tanāv, dabāv* तनाव, दबाव

Tent (m∘) *tambū* तंबू

Tenure (m∘) *avadhi* अवधि

Term 1. period (m∘) *avadhi* अवधि; 2. expression (f∘) *abhivyakti* अभिव्यक्ति; 3. (relationship) *sambandha* संबंध

Terminate (v∘) *samāpta karṇe* समाप्त क∘*

Termination (f∘) *samāpti* समाप्ति

Terminology (f∘) *paribhāṣhā* परिभाषा

Terminus (m∘) *aḍḍā* अड्डा

Termite (f∘) *udhaī* उधई

Terresterial (adj∘) *bhū-jīvī* भूजीवी

Terrible (adj∘) *bhayānak* भयानक

Terrific (adj∘) *mahān* महान

Territory (n∘) *kṣhetra* क्षेत्र

Terror (n∘) *bhay* भय

Terrorism (m∘) *ātaṅkvād* आतंकवाद

Terrorist (m∘) *ātaṅkvādī* आतंकवादी

Tertiary (adj∘) *tisrā* तिसरा

Test (f∘) *parīkṣhā* परीक्षा

Test (v∘) *jāchaṇe* जाचणे*

Testify (v∘) *gavāhī deṇe, bayān deṇe* गवाही देणे, बयान देणे*

Testimonial (n∘) *pramāṇpatra* प्रमाणपत्र

Testimony (m∘) *bayān*, (f∘) *gavāhī* बयान, गवाही

Text (m∘) *lekhā* लेखा

Textbook (n∘) *pāṭhya-pustak* पाठ्यपुस्तक

Textile (n∘) *vastra* वस्त्र

Texture (f∘) *banāvaṭ* बनावट

Than (adv∘) *pekṣhā* पेक्षा

Thank (v∘) *dhanyavād deṇe* धन्यवाद देणे*

Thankful (adj∘) *krutadnya* कृतज्ञ

Thanks (m∘) *dhanyavād* धन्यवाद

That (pron∘) *to* तो

Thaw (v∘) *pighaḷṇe* पिघळणे

Theatre (f∘) *raṅgśhāḷā* रंगशाळा

Theft (f∘) *chorī* चोरी

Their (pron∘) *tyāñchā* त्यांचा

Them (pron∘) *tyānā* त्याना

Theme (m∘) *viṣhay* विषय

Then (adv∘) *mag* मग

Thence (adv∘) *mhaṇūn* म्हणून

Thenceforward (adv∘) *nantar* नंतर

Theology (m∘) *āstikvād* आस्तिकवाद

Theorem (m∘) *siddhānt* सिद्धांत

Theoritical (adj∘) *saiddhāntik* सैद्धांतिक

Theory (m∘) *siddhānt* सिद्धांत

Therby (adv∘) *tyāmuḷe* त्यामुळे

There (adv∘) *tithe* तिथे

Thereafter (adv∘) *mag, tyānantar* मग, त्यानंतर

Therefore (adv∘) *mhaṇūn, atah* म्हणून, अत:

Thermal (adj∘) *garma* गरम

Thermometer (n∘) *tāpmāpak* तापमापक

Thesaurus (m∘) *paryāy-kośh* पर्यायकोश

These (pron∘) *he* हे

Thesis (m∘) *prabandh* प्रबंध

Thick (adj∘) *jāḍā* जाडा

Thicket (f∘) *jhāḍī* झाडी

Thickness (f∘) *jāḍī* जाडी

Thief (m∘) *chor* चोर

Thigh (f∘) *jāṅg* जांग

Thin (adj∘) *pātaḷ, bārīk* पातळ, बारीक

Thing (f∘) *vastu* वस्तु

Think (v∘) *āṭhavṇe* आठवणे*

Third (adj∘) *tisrā* तिसरा

Thirteen (adj∘) *terā* तेरा

Thirty (adj∘) *tīs* तीस

This (pron∘) *he* हे

Thorax (m∘) *chhātī* छाती

Thorn (m∘) *kāṭā* काटा

Thorney (adj∘) *kāṭedār* काटेदार

Thorough (adj∘) *pakkā, parioūrṇa* पक्का, परिपूर्ण

Those (pron∘) *te* ते

Though (adv∘) *jarī, adyapi* जरी, यद्यपि

Thought (m∘) *vichār* विचार

Thousand (m∘) *hajār, sahasra* हजार, सहस्त्र

Thrash (v∘) *pīṭṇe* पीटणे*

Thrashing (f∘) *piṭāī* पिटाई

Thread (m∘) *dorā* दोरा

Threat (m∘) 1. (danger) *saṅkaṭ, khatrā* संकट, खतरा 2. (challenge) *dhamkī* धमकी

adj∘ = Adjective, adv∘ = Adverb; *conj.* = Conjunction, f∘ = Feminine gender, *ind.* = Indeclinable, m∘ = Masculine gender, n∘ = Neuter gender, pl∘ = Plural

Threaten (v∘) *dhamkāvṇe* धमकावणे*

Three (adj∘) *tīn* तीन

Thresh (v∘) *kuṭṇe, pīṭṇe* कुटणे, पीटणे*

Threshold (m∘) *umbarṭhā* उंबरठा

Thrice (adv∘) *tīn veḷa* तीन वेळा

Thrill (n∘) *romāñch* रोमांच

Thrilling (adj∘) *romāñchkārī* रोमांचकारी

Throat (m∘) *gaḷā, kaṇṭh* गळा, कंठ

Throb (n∘) *spandan* स्पंदन; (v∘) *dhaḍakṇe* धडकणे

Throne (n∘) *siṁhāsan* सिंहासन

Throng (f∘) *bhīḍ* भीड

Throttle (v∘) *gaḷā ghoṭṇe* गळा घोटणे*

Through (prep∘) *ār-pār* आरपार

Throughfare (m∘) *ām rastā* आम रस्ता

Throught (adv∘) *sarvatra* सर्वत्र

Throw (v∘) *fekṇe* फेकणे*

Throw up (v∘) *okaṇe* ओकणे*

Thrust (m∘) *prahār* प्रहार

Thug (m∘) *ṭhag* ठग

Thumb (m∘) *āṅgṭhā* आंगठा

Thump (m∘) *āghāt* आघात; (v∘) *ṭhokṇe* ठोकणे*

Thunder (f∘) *garjaṇā* गर्जना

Thunderstruck (adj∘) *hakkā-bakkā, awāk* हक्काबक्का, अवाक्

Thursday (m∘) *guruvār* गुरुवार

Thus (adv∘) *ase* असे

Tide (f∘) *bhartī* भरती

Tidy (adj∘) *ṭhik-ṭhāk* ठीक-ठाक

Tie (m∘) *fitā* फिता; (v∘) *bāndhaṇe* बाँधणे*

Tiger (m∘) *wāgh* वाघ

Tight (adj∘) *tāṭh, taṅg* ताठ, तंग

Tighten (v∘) *kasṇe, jakaḍṇe* कसणे, जकडणे*

Tigress (f∘) *wāghiṇ* वाघिण

Till, farming (v∘) *nāṅgarṇe* नांगरणे*

Tilt (m∘) *jhukāv* झुकाव; (v∘) *jhukṇe, jhukavnā** झुकणे, झुकवणे*

Timber (f∘) *imārtī lākūḍ* इमारती लाकूड

Time (m∘) *samay, kāḷ* समय, काळ

Timely (adj∘) *samayovhit* समयोचित

Timid (adj∘) *bhyāḍ, bujaṭ* भ्याड, बुजट

Tin, can (m∘) *ḍabba* डब्बा

Tingle (f∘) *jhaṇjhaṇ* झणझण

Tinkle (f∘) *ruṇjhuṇ* रुणझुण

Tint (f∘) *jhaḷak* झळक

Tiny (adj∘) *sūkṣhma* सूक्ष्म

Tip (f∘) *nok* नोक; (v∘) *ulṭaṇe* उलटणे

Tire (v∘) *thakṇe* थकणे

Tit (m∘) *stanāgra* स्तनाग्र

Title (m∘) *śhīrśhak, upādhi, padvī* शीर्शक, उपाधि, पदवी

To (suff∘) *lā* ला

Toad (m∘) *beḍuk* बेडुक

Toadstool (f∘) *chhatrī* छत्री

Toast (v∘) *śhekṇe, bhājṇe* शेकणे, भाजणे*

Tobacco (m∘) *tambākhū* तंबाखू

Today (adv∘) *āj* आज

Together (adv∘) *ekatra* एकत्र

Token (adj∘) *pratīk* प्रतीक

Tolerate (v∘) *sahaṇe* सहणे

Toll (m∘) *mahasūl, kar* महसूल, कर

Tomato (n∘) *bhedur* भेदुर

Tomb (f∘) *makbarā* समाधि

Tomorrow (adv∘) *udyā* उद्या

Tone (m∘) *svar* स्वर

Tongs (m∘) *chimṭā* चिमटा

Tongue (f∘) *jībh* जीभ

Tonight (f∘) *āj rātrī* आज रात्री

Tool (m∘) *avjār* अवजार

Tooth (m∘) *dāt* दात

Top (n∘) 1. (tip) *śhikhar* शिखर, 2. (lid) *jhakaṇ* झाकण; 3. (toy) (m∘) *bhavrā* भवरा

Topaz (m∘) *pukhrāj* पुखराज

Topic (m∘) *viṣhay* विषय

Topple (v∘) *luḍhakṇe* लुढकणे

Topsy-turvey (adj∘) *ulṭā-pulṭā* उलटा-पुलटा

Torch (f∘) *maśhāl* मशाल; (v∘) *jāḷṇe, āg lāvṇe* जाळणे, आग लावणे*

Torential (adj∘) *musḷdhār* मुसळधार

Torment (v∘) *satāvṇe* सतावणे*

Torn (adj∘) *fāṭkā* फाटका

Tornado (m∘) *vādaḷ* वादळ

Torso (n∘) *dhaḍ* धड

Tortoise (n∘) *kāsav* कासव

Torture (f∘) *pīḍā* पीडा; (v∘) *pīḍā deṇe* पीडा देणे*

Toss (v∘) *bhirkāvṇe* भिरकावणे

Total (adj∘) *pūrṇa* पूर्ण

Totalitarian (adj∘) *ekādhikārī* एकाधिकारी

Totter (v∘) *laḍkhaḍṇe* लडखडणे

Touch (m∘) *sparśha* स्पर्श

Tough (adj∘) *kaḍak* कडक

Tour (m∘) *davrā*, (f∘) *yātrā* दवरा, यात्रा

Tourism (n∘) *paryaṭan* पर्यटन

Tourist (m∘) *yātrī* यात्री

Tournament (f∘) *pratiyogitā* प्रतियोग्िता

Tow (v∘) *khīchṇe, oḍhṇe* खिचण, ओढणे*

Towards (adv∘) *kaḍe, javaḷ* कडे, जवळ

Towel (m∘) *rumāl* रुमाल

Tower (m∘) *minār* मिनार

Town (m∘) *gāv* गाव

Toxic (adj∘) *jaharī* जहरी

Toxin (n∘) *jahar, viṣh* जहर, विष

Toy (n∘) *kheḷṇe* खेळणे

Trace (m∘) *avaśheṣh* अवशेष; (v∘) *ckhojṇe* खोजणे*

Track (f∘) *vahivāṭ* वहिवाट

Tract (m∘) *ilākhā, bhūbhāg* इलाखा, भूभाग

Trade (m∘) *vyāpār, dhandā* व्यापार, धंदा

Trade (v∘) *vyāpār karṇe* व्यापार क∘*

Trader (m∘) *vyāpārī* व्यापारी

Tradition (f∘) *paramparā* परंपरा

Traffic (m∘) *yātāyāt* यातायात

Tragedy (f∘) *durghaṭnī* दुर्घटना

Trail (n∘) *niśhāṇ, chihna* निशाण, चिह्न

Train (f∘) *gāḍī* गाडी

Trait (f∘) *viśheṣhtā* विशेषता

Traitor (m∘) *dorhī, ghātak* द्रोही, घातक

Traitorous (adj∘) *ghātakī* घातकी

Tramp (adj∘) *āvārā* आवारा

Trample (v∘) *kuchalṇe* कुचलणे*

Trance (f∘) *behośhī, supti* बेहोशी, सुप्ति

Tranquil (adj∘) *stabdha, śhānt* स्तब्ध, शांत

Transaction (m∘) *kārbhār, saudā* कारभार, सौदा

adj∘ = Adjective, adv∘ = Adverb; *conj.* = Conjunction, f∘ = Feminine gender, *ind.* = Indeclinable, m∘ = Masculine gender, n∘ = Neuter gender, pl∘ = Plural

Transcend (v∘) *pār jāṇe* पार जाणे
Transcribe (v∘) *lihīṇe* लिहीणे*
Transcript (m∘) *pratilekh* प्रतिलेख
Transfer (f∘) *badlī* बदली
Transform (v∘) *badalṇe* बदलणे
Transformation (m∘) *badal* बदल
Transgression (n∘) *ullanghan* उल्लंघन
Transient (adj∘) *kṣhaṇik* क्षणिक
Transition (n∘) *sankramaṇ* संक्रमण
Transitive (adj∘) *sakarmak* सकर्मक
Transmission (n∘) *sañcharaṇ, vahan* संचारण, वहन
Transmit (v∘) *pāṭhavṇe* पाठवणे*
Transperant (adj∘) *pārdarśhak* पारदर्शक
Transplant (n∘) *pratiropaṇ* प्रतिरोपण
Transport (n∘) *vahna, parivahan* वहन, परिवहन
Transport (v∘) *vāhaṇe* वाहणे*
Transverse (adj∘) *āḍvā, tirpā* आडवा, तिरपा
Trap (m∘) *faesā* फासा; (v∘) *pakaḍṇe* पकडणे*
Trash (m∘) *kachrā* कचरा
Traumā (m∘) *āghāt* आघात
Travel (f∘) *yātrā* यात्रा
Traveler (m∘) *yātrī* यात्री
Traversity (m∘) *tamāśhā* तमाशा
Tray (f∘) *thāḷī*, (n∘) *tabak* थाळी, तबक
Treacherous (adj∘) *viśhvāsghātakī* विश्वासघातकी
Treason (m∘) *deśh-droha* देशद्रोह
Treasure (m∘) *khajinā* खजिना
Treasurer (m∘) *khajāñchī* खजांची
Treasury (m∘) *khajinā, kośh* खजिना, कोष
Treatment (m∘) (remedy) *upchār* उपचार
Treaty (f∘) *sandhi* संधि
Treble (adj∘) *tippaṭ* तिप्पट
Trechery (m∘) *droha, ghāt, dhokā* द्रोह, घात, धोका
Tree (n∘) *jhāḍ* झाड
Tremble (v∘) *laḍkhaḍṇe, thartharṇe* लडखडणे, थरथरणे
Tremendous (adj∘) *prachaṇḍ* प्रचंड
Tremor (m∘) *kamp* कंप
Treñch (f∘) *khāī* खाई
Trend (f∘) *pravrutti* प्रवृत्ति
Trespass (n∘) *atikramaṇ* अतिक्रमण
Tresses, hair (f∘) *laṭ* लट
Trial, court (m∘) *mukadmā* मुक्दमा; test (n∘) *oarīkṣhaṇ* परीक्षण
Triamphant (adj∘) *vijayī, safal* विजयी, सफल
Triangle (m∘) *trikoṇ* त्रिकोण
Tribe (f∘) *jāti* जाति
Tributary (adj∘) *sahāyak* सहायक
Tribute (m∘) *upahār*, (f∘) *bheṭ* उपहार, भेट
Trick (f∘) *chāl*, (m∘) *ḍāv* चाल, डाव
Trickle (v∘) *ṭapakṇe* टपकणे
Tricky (adj∘) *kapṭī* कपटी
Trident (m∘) *triśhūḷ* त्रिशूळ
Trifle (adj∘) *nagaṇya, tucchha* नगण्य, तुच्छ
Trigger (m∘) *ghoḍā* घोडा
Trigonometry (f∘) *trikoṇamiti* त्रिकोणमिती
Trillion (adj∘) *ek lākh karoḍ* एक लाख करोड
Trim (f∘) *sajāvaṭ* सजावट
Trim (v∘) *kutarṇe* कुतरणे*
Trinity (f∘) *trimūrti* त्रिमूर्ति
Trio (m∘) *tighāḍā* तिघाडा
Trip (f∘) *khep, ferī* खेप, फेरी
Trip (v∘) *laḍkhaḍaṇe* लडखडणे
Tripod (f∘) *tipāī* तिपाई
Tripple (adj∘) *tiherī, tīnpaṭ, tippaṭ* तिहेरी, तीनपट, तिप्पट
Triumph (f∘) *vijay*, (f∘) *safaltā* विजय, सफलता
Trivial (adj∘) *nagaṇya* नगण्य
Trophy (n∘) *padak* पदक
Trouble (n∘) *kaṣhṭa* कष्ट
Trowel (f∘) *khurpī* खुरपी
Truce (m∘) *virām* विराम
Truck (m∘) *ṭhelā* ठेला
True (adj∘) *kharā* खरा
Truly (adv∘) *kharech* खरेच
Trumpet (f∘) *tutārī* तुतारी
Truth (n∘) *satya* सत्य
Try (m∘) *prayatna, prayās* प्रयत्न, प्रयास; (v∘) (make effort) *prayatna karṇe* प्रयत्न क∘*
Tube (f∘) *naḷī* नळी
Tuber (m∘) *kand* कंद
Tuberculosis (m∘) *kṣhay* क्षय
Tuck (f∘) *dumaḍ* दुमड
Tuck (v∘) *dumaḍṇe* दुमडणे*
Tuesday (m∘) *mangaḷvār* मंगळवार
Tuft (m∘) *guchhā* गुच्छा
Tune (f∘) *sūr* सूर
Tunnel (m∘) *surang* सुरंग
Turban (f∘) *pagaḍī*, (n∘) *pāgoṭe* पगडी, पागोटे
Turbulence (f∘) *gaḍbaḍ* गडबड
Turbulent (adj∘) *ugra* उग्र
Turmoil (f∘) *khaḷbaḷ* खळबळ
Turn (f∘) *vaḷaṇ* वळण; (v∘) *vaḷṇe* वळणे
Turnip (n∘) *salgam* सलगम
Turquoise (adj∘) *firosā* फिरोसा
Turret (m∘) *kanhorā* कँगोरा
Turtle (n∘) *kāsav* कासव
Tusk, elephant (m∘) *dāt* दात
Tussel (m∘) *jhagaḍā* झगडा
Tutor (m∘) *śhikṣhak* शिक्षक
TV (n∘) *dūradarśhan* दूरदर्शन
Tweak (v∘) *hisakṇe* हिसकणे*
Tweezers (m∘) *chimṭā* चिमटा
Twelve (adj∘) *bārā* बारा
Twenty (adj∘) *vīs* वीस
Twice (adv∘) *dondā* दोनदा
Twiddle (f∘) *girkī* गिरकी
Twig (f∘) *ḍahāḷī, fāndī* डहाळी, फांदी
Twilight (m∘) *sandhiprakāsh*, (f∘) *sandhyā* संधिप्रकाश, संध्या
Twin (adj∘) *juḷā* जुळा
Twine (f∘) *dorī, sutaḷī* दोरी, सुतळी
Twinkle (v∘) *ṭimṭimṇe* टिमटिमणे
Twirl (v∘) *girkī gheṇe* गिरकी घेणे
Twist (f∘) *pīḷ* पीळ; (v∘) *piḷṇe, lapeṭṇe* पिळणे, लपेटणे*
Twitch (f∘) *faḍfaḍ* फडफड
Twitter (f∘) *kilbilṇe* किलबिलणे
Two (adj∘) *don* दोन

adj∘ = Adjective, adv∘ = Adverb; *conj.* = Conjunction, f∘ = Feminine gender, *ind.* = Indeclinable, m∘ = Masculine gender, n∘ = Neuter gender, pl∘ = Plural

Tycoon (m∘) *punjīpati* पुंजीपति

Type, kind (m∘) *prakār*, (f∘) *jāti* प्रकार, जाति

Type, printing (n∘) *mudraṇ* मुद्रण

Typhoon (n∘) *vādaḷ* वादळ

Typical (adj∘) *lākṣhaṇik* लाक्षणिक

Tyranny (f∘) *tānāśhāhī*, (m∘) *atyāchār* तानाशाही, अत्याचार

Tyrant (m∘) *atyāchārī* अत्याचारी

U

Ugly (adj∘) *kurūp* कुरूप

Ulcer (m∘) *foḍa* फोड

Ultimate (adj∘) *antim* अंतिम

Ultimatum (f∘) *dhamkī* धमकी

Umbrella (f∘) *chhatrī* छत्री

Unable (adj∘) *asamartha* असमर्थ

Unacceptable (adj∘) *agrāhya* अग्राह्य

Unanimity (n∘) *ekmat, mataikya* एकमत, मतैक्य

Unanimous (adj∘) *ekmat* एकमत

Unarmed (adj∘) *nihshastra* नि:शस्त्र

Unauthorised (adj∘) *avaidh* अवैध

Unaware (adj∘) *ajāṇ* अजाण

Unbalanced (adj∘) *asantulit* असंतुलित

Unbearable (adj∘) *asahnīya* असहनीय

Unbelievable (adj∘) *aviśhvasanīya* अविश्वसनीय

Unborn (adj∘) *ajanmā* अजन्मा

Unbroken (adj∘) *atūṭ* अतूट

Uncertain (adj∘) *anischit* अनिश्चित

Uncle (m∘) *kākā, māmā* काका, मामा

Unclear (adj∘) *aspaṣhṭa* अस्पष्ट

Uncomfortable (adj∘) *bechain* बेचैन

Uncommon (adj∘) *asāmānyā* असामान्य

Uncompromising (adj∘) *haṭṭī* हट्टी

Unconcerned (adj∘) *chintāhīn* चिंताहीन

Unconscious (adj∘) *behośh* बेहोश

Uncountable (adj∘) *asaṅkhya* असंख्य

Uncouth (adj∘) *asabhya* असभ्य

Uncover (v∘) *ughaḍṇe* उघडणे*

Under (prep∘) *khālī* खाली

Undercover (adj∘) *jāsūsī* जासूसी

Underdone (adj∘) *ardhpakvā* अर्धपक्व

Undergo (v∘) *bhogṇe* भोगणे

Underground (adj∘) *bhūmigat* भूमिगत

Underhanced (adj∘) *beīmān* बेईमान

Underneath (prep∘) *Khālī* खाली

Understand (v∘) *samajaṇe* समजणे*

Unemployed (adj∘) *bekār* बेकार

Unending (adj∘) *anant* अनंत

Unequal (adj∘) *asamāna* असमान

Unequivocal (adj∘) *sāf-sāf* साफ–साफ

Unerring (adj∘) *achūk* अचूक

Unethical (adj∘) *anaitik* अनैतिक

Uneven (adj∘) (level) *asapāṭ* असपाट

Unexpected (adj∘) *apratyāśhit* अप्रत्याशित

Unexplained (adj∘) *aspaṣhṭa* अस्पष्ट

Unfair (adj∘) *anyāypūrṇa* अन्यायपूर्ण

Unfaithful (adj∘) *beīmān* बेईमान

Unfamiliar (adj∘) *aparichit* अपरिचित

Unfashionable (adj∘) *aprachalit* अप्रचलित

Unfasten (v∘) *kholṇe* खोलणे*

Unfavourable (adj∘) *apratikūl* अप्रतिकूल

Unfit (adj∘) *ayodnya, bekār* अयोग्य, बेकार

Unfold (v∘) *khulṇe, kholnā** खुलणे, खोलणे*

Unforeseen (adj∘) *apratyāśhit* अप्रत्याशित

Unforgettable (adj∘) *avismaraṇīya* अविस्मरणीय

Unfortunate (adj∘) *abhāgā* अभागा

Unfounded (adj∘) *nirādhār* निराधार

Ungrateful (adj∘) *krutaghna* कृतघ्न

Unhappy (adj∘) *duhkhī* दु:खी

Unhealthy (adj∘) *asvastha* अस्वस्थ

Unheard (adj∘) *abhūtapūrva* अभूतपूर्व

Unification (n∘) *ekīkaraṇ* एकीकरण

Uniform (adj∘) *sama, ekrūp* सम, एकरूप

Uniform, dress (m∘) *pośhakh*, (f∘) *vardī* पोशाख, वर्दी

Unify (v∘) *joḍṇe* जोडणे*

Unike (adj∘) *asamān, bhinna* असमान, भिन्न

Union (f∘) *sandhi*, (m∘) *saṅgha* संधि, संघ

Unique (adj∘) *ananya, advitīya* अनन्य, अद्वितीय

Unit (adj∘) *ekank* एकांक

Unite (v∘) *joḍṇe* जोडणे*

Unity (f∘) *ektā* एकता

Universal (adj∘) *sārvabhaumaik* सार्वभौमिक

Universally (adv∘) *viśhvataḥ* विश्वत:

Universe (adj∘) *brahmāṇḍ* ब्रह्मांड

Unjust (adj∘) *anyāyī* अन्यायी

Unkind (adj∘) *krūr, nirdayī* क्रुर, निर्दयी

Unknown (adj∘) *adnyāt* अज्ञात

Unlawful (adj∘) *avaidh* अवैध

Unlikely (adj∘) *asambhavanīya* असंभवनीय

Unlimited (adj∘) *asīmit* असीमित

Unlucky (adj∘) *abhāgā* अभागा

Unmarried (adj∘) *avivāhit* अविवाहित

Unmistakable (adj∘) *sāf, spaṣhṭa* साफ, स्पष्ट

Unnecessary (adj∘) *anāvaśhyak* अनावश्यक

Unnoticed (adj∘) *alakṣhit* अलक्षित

Unpleasant (adj∘) *apriya* अप्रिय

Unpopular (adj∘) *apriya* अप्रिय

Unprecedented (adj∘) *abhūtpūrva* अभूतपूर्व

Unpreparedness (f∘) *gaflat* गफलत

Unpretentious (adj∘) *vinit* विनित

Unqualified (adj∘) *ayogya* अयोग्य

Unquestionable (adj∘) *nischit* निश्चित

Unreal (adj∘) *naklī, banāvaṭī* नकली, बनावटी

Unreasonable (adj∘) *anuchit* अनुचित

Unreliable (adj∘) *aviśhavsanīya* अविश्वसनीय

Unrest (adj∘) *aśhānti* अशांति

Unrivalled (adj∘) *niṣhkaṇṭak* निष्कंटक

Unsafe (adj∘) *asurakṣhit* असुरक्षित

Unsavory (adj∘) *apriya* अप्रिय

Unscrupulous (adj∘) *kapṭī* कपटी

Unsightly (adj∘) *kurūp* कुरूप

Unspeakable (adj∘) *akathanīya* अकथनीय

Unstable (adj∘) *asthir* अस्थिर

Unsteady (adj∘) *asthir* अस्थिर

Unsuccessful (adj∘) *asafal* असफल

Unsuitable (adj∘) *anupayukta* अनुपयुक्त

Unsure (adj∘) *sandigdha* संदिग्ध

Untamed (adj∘) *jaṅglī* जंगली

Untangle (v∘) *ukalṇe* उकलणे*

Unthinkable (adj∘) *lakpanātīt* कल्पनातीत

adj∘ = Adjective, adv∘ = Adverb; *conj.* = Conjunction, f∘ = Feminine gender, *ind.* = Indeclinable, m∘ = Masculine gender, n∘ = Neuter gender, pl∘ = Plural

Untidy (adj∘) *avyavasthit* अव्यवस्थित
Untie (v∘) *kholṇe* खोलणे*
Until (prep∘) *paryant* पर्यंत
Untimely (adj∘) *asāmayik* असामयिक
Unto (prep∘) *to pāveto* तो पावेतो
Untold (adj∘) *asaṅkhya* असंख्य
Untouchable (adj∘) *achhūt* अछूत
Untrue (adj∘) *khoṭā, asatya* खोटा, असत्य
Untruth (m∘) *khoṭe* खोटे
Unuguarded (adj∘) *arakṣhit* अरक्षित
Unuruly (adj∘) *bekābū* बेकाबू
Unused (adj∘) *korā* कोरा
Unusual (adj∘) *vichitra* विचित्र
Unveil (v∘) *dākhavṇe* दाखवणे*
Unwanted (adj∘) *anāvas̒hyak* अनावश्यक
Unwell (adj∘) *bīmār, ājārī* बीमार, आजारी
Unwilling (adj∘) *anicchhuk* अनिच्छुक
Unwitting (adj∘) *anabhidnya* अनभिज्ञ
Unwrap (v∘) *kholṇe* खोलणे*
Uproar (m∘) *haṅgāmā* हंगामा
Up (adv∘) *var* वर
Upheaval (f∘) *ulath-pulath* उलथ-पुलथ
Uphil (adj∘) *kaṭhiṇ* कठिण
Uphold (v∘) *samarthan karṇe* समर्थन क∘*
Upper (adj∘) *ūparī, varchā* ऊपरी, वरचा
Uppermost (adj∘) *sarvoccha* सर्वोच्च
Upright (adj∘) *sīdhā* सीधा
Uprising (m∘) *vidroha* विद्रोह
Uproot (v∘) *ukhāḍṇe* उखाडणे*
Upset (v∘) *gaḍbaḍaṇe* गडबडणे
Upshot (m∘) *pariṇām* परिणाम
Upside-down (adj∘) *ulṭā-pulṭā* उल्टा-पुल्टा
Uptight (adj∘) *bhay-bhīt* भयभीत
Upward (adv∘) *var* वर
Urban (adj∘) *s̒aharī* शहरी
Urbane (adj∘) *sabhya* सभ्य
Urge (f∘) *sanak* सनक
Urgency (m∘) *s̒hīghratā* शीघ्रता
Urgent (adj∘) *s̒hīghra* शीघ्र
Urine (n∘) *mūtra,* (f∘) *laghvī* मूत्र, लघवी
Urn (m∘) *asthikalas̒h* अस्थिकलश
Use (m∘) *prayog* प्रयोग; (v∘) *upayog karaṇe* उपयोग क∘*
Useful (adj∘) *upayogī* उपयोगी
Useless (adj∘) *bekār, nirupayogī* बेकार, निरुपयोगी
Uselessly (adv∘) *vruthā, vyartha* वृथा, व्यर्थ
User (m∘) *upabhoktā* उपभोक्ता
Usual (adj∘) *sāmānya* सामान्य
Utensil (n∘) *bhāṇḍe* भांडे
Utility (f∘) *upayogitā* उपयोगिता
Utilization (m∘) *upayog* उपयोग

V

Vacant (adj∘) *rikāmā* रिकामा
Vacate (v∘) *khālī karṇe* खाली क∘*
Vacation (f∘) *suṭṭī* सुट्टी
Vaccination (m∘) *ṭikā* टिका
Vacuum (m∘) *nirvāt* निर्वात
Vagabond (adj∘) *āvārā* आवारा
Vague (adj∘) *aspaṣhṭa* अस्पष्ट
Vainly (adv∘) *bekār, fāltū* बेकार, फालतू
Valiant (adj∘) *s̒hūr, vīr* शूर, वीर
Valid (adj∘) *vaidh* वैध
Valour (adj∘) *bahādurī* बहादुरी
Valuable (adj∘) *kimmtī* किंमती
Valuation (n∘) *mūlyāṅkan* मूल्यांकन
Value (f∘) *kimmat* किंमत
Vanished (adj∘) *farār* फरार
Vanity (m∘) *dambh* दंभ
Variety (f∘) *bhinnatā* भिन्नता
Various (adj∘) *vividh* विविध
Variously (adv∘) *nānāvidh* नानाविध
Vassal (m∘) *jāgīrdār* जागीरदार
Vast (adj∘) *vis̒hal* विशाल
Vegetable (f∘) *bhājī* भाजी
Vegetarian (adj∘) *s̒hākāhārī* शाकाहारी
Vegetation (f∘) *vanaspati* वनस्पति
Vehicle (n∘) *vāhan* वाहन
Veil (m∘) *paḍdā* पडदा
Vein (f∘) *nas* नस
Velocity (f∘) *gati,* (m∘) *veg* गति, वेग
Velvel (f∘) *makhmal* मखमल
Vendetta (n∘) *vair* वैर
Venerable (adj∘) *pūjya* पूज्य
Vengeance (m∘) *badlā* बदला
Venom (n∘) *jahar, viṣh* जहर, विष
Vent (m∘) *nikās* निकास
Venturesome (adj∘) *niḍar, sāhsī* निडर, साहसी
Venus (m∘) *s̒hukra* शुक्र
Veracity (f∘) *sacchāī* सच्चाई
Veranda (m∘) *varāṇḍā* व्हरांडा
Verb (n∘) *kriyāpad* क्रियापद
Verbal (adj∘) *s̒hābdik* शाब्दिक
Verdict (m∘) *nirṇay* निर्णय
Verification (f∘) *jāch* जाच
Verily (adv∘) *sachmuch* सचमुच
Vermilion (adj∘) *s̒hendrī* शेंदरी
Vermilion (m∘) *s̒hendūr* शेंदूर
Verse (n∘) *padya* पद्य
Versed (adj∘) *anubhavī* अनुभवी
Versus (prep∘) *viruddha* विरुद्ध
Vertical (adj∘) *sīdhā, saraḷ* सीधा, सरळ
Very (adv∘) *ati, fār* अति, फार
Vessel, 1. boat (n∘) *jahāj* जहाज; 2. pot (n∘) *pātra* पात्र
Vestige (m∘) *avas̒heṣh* अवशेष
Vet (m∘) *pas̒huchikitsak* पशुचिकित्सक
Vex (v∘) *chiḍavṇe* चिडवणे*
Vibrant (adj∘) *chamkīlā* चमकीला
Vibrate (v∘) *kāpṇē* कापणे
Vice (n∘) *vyasan* व्यसन; clamp (f∘) *pakaḍ* पकड
Vicinity (f∘) *samīptā* समीपता
Vicious (adj∘) *kaṭu* कटु
Victim (f∘) *s̒hikār* शिकार
Victor (adj∘) *vijetā* विजेता
Victory (m∘) *vijay* विजय
View (f∘) *najar, druṣhṭi* नजर, दृष्टि
Vigil (f∘) *nigrāṇī* निगराणी
Vigilant (adj∘) *satark* सतर्क
Vigor (m∘) *utsāh* उत्साह
Vile (adj∘) *nikruṣhta* निकृष्ट
Villa (m∘) *mahāl* महाल
Village (n∘) *gāv* गाव
Villian (m∘) *khalanāyak* खलनायक

adj∘ = Adjective, adv∘ = Adverb; *conj.* = Conjunction, f∘ = Feminine gender, *ind.* = Indeclinable, m∘ = Masculine gender, n∘ = Neuter gender, pl∘ = Plural

Vine (f∘) *latā, vel* लता, वेल

Vinegar (m∘) *śhirkā* शिरका

Violation (n∘) *ullaṅghan* उल्लंघन

Violence (f∘) *hiṁsā* हिंसा

Violent (adj∘) *ugra, jabardast* उग्र, जबरदस्त

Violet (adj∘) *baiṅgaṇī* बैंगणी

Violin (f∘) *sārangī* सारंगी

Virgin (adj∘) *kumārī* कुमारी

Virgo (f∘) *kanyā rāśhi* कन्या राशि

Virtue (m∘) *sadguṇ* सद्गुण

Virtuous (adj∘) *sadguṇī* सद्गुणी

Virulent (adj∘) *ugra* उग्र

Virus (m∘) *viṣhāṇu* विषाणु

Visible (adj∘) *druṣhṭi-gochar* दृष्टिगोचर

Vision (f∘) *druṣhṭi* दृष्टि, *najar* नजर

Visitor (m∘) *paryaṭak* पर्यटक

Vivid (adj∘) *bhaḍak* भडक

Vocabulary (f∘) *śhabdabhāṇḍār* शब्दभांडार

Vocal (adj∘) *maukhik* मौखिक

Vocation (m∘) *peśhā* पेशा

Voice (m∘) *āvāj,* (f∘) *vāṇī* आवाज, वाणी

Void (adj∘) *rikāmā* रिकामा

Volatile (adj∘) *chañchal* चंचल

Volcano (m∘) *jwālāmukhī* ज्वालामुखी

Volume (m∘) *āyātan, vyāp* आयातन, व्याप

Volunteer (m∘) *svayaṁsevak* स्वयंसेवक

Vomit (f∘) *ulṭī, okārī* उल्टी, ओकारी

Voracious (adj∘) *khāū* खाऊ

Vote (m∘) *mat* मत; (v∘) *mat deṇe* मत देणे*;

Vow (f∘) *pratidnyā, śhapath* प्रतिज्ञा, शपथ

Voyage (f∘) *yātrā,* (m∘) *safar* यात्रा, सफर

Vulgar (adj∘) *asabhya* असभ्य

Vulnarable (adj∘) *asurakṣhit* असुरक्षित

Vulture (n∘) *gidhāḍ* गिधाड

W

Wage (f∘) *majūrī* मजूरी

Wager (f∘) *śhart* शर्त

Waist (f∘) *kambar* कंबर

Wait (v∘) *vāṭ pāhṇe* वाट पाहणे*

Waiter (m∘) *vāḍhapī* वाढपी

Wake (v∘) *jāgṇe, jāgavṇe** जागणे, जागवणे*

Walk (m∘) *chālṇe* चालणे

Wall (f∘) *bhint* भिंत

Wallet (m∘) *baṭavā* बटवा

Walnut (m∘) *akroḍ* अक्रोड

Wander (v∘) *bhaṭakṇe* भटकणे

Want (f∘) need *garaj* गरज; (v∘) *garaj asṇe* गरज असणे*

Wanton (adj∘) *vilāsī* विलासी

War (n∘) *yuddha,* (f∘) *laḍhāī* युद्ध, लढाई

Warble (v∘) *kūjaṇe, kilbilṇe* कूजणे, किलबिलणे

Ward (m∘) *vibhāg* विभाग

Warm (adj∘) *garam* गरम; (v∘) *garam karṇe* गरम करना

Warn (v∘) *chetāvaṇī deṇe* चेतावणी देणे*

Warning (f∘) *chetāvaṇī, tākid* चेतावणी, ताकिद

Warrior (m∘) *yoddhā, sainik* योद्धा, सैनिक

Wary (adj∘) *sāvadhān* सावधान

Was (v∘) *hotā, hotī, hote* होता, होती, होते

Wash (v∘) *dhuṇe* धुणे*

Washerman (m∘) *dhobī, parīṭ* धोबी, परीट

Wasp (f∘) *gāndhīlmāśhī* गांधीलमाशी

Waste (f∘) *kharābī* खराबी; (v∘) *kharāb karaṇe* खराब क∘*

Watch, clock (n∘) *ghaḍyāḷ* घड्याळ

Water (n∘) *pāṇī, jal* पाणी, जल

Watermelon (n∘) *ṭarbūj, kaliṅgaḍa* टरबूज, कलिंगड

Watery (adj∘) *patlā, pāṇkaṭ* पतला, पाणकट

Wave (f∘) *lahar,* (n∘) *taraṅg* लहर, तरंग

Waver (v∘) *ḍagmagaṇe* डगमगणे

Wax (n∘) *meṇ* मेण

Way (m∘) *rastā, mārg* मार्ग, रस्ता

We (pron∘) *āmhī* आम्ही

Weak (adj∘) *kamjor, aśhakta* कमजोर, अशक्त

Wear (v∘) *nesṇe* नेसणे*

Weather (n∘) *havāmān* हवामान

Weave (f∘) *vīṇ* वीण; (v∘) *viṇaṇe* विणणे*

Weaver (m∘) *koṣhṭī* कोष्टी

Web (n∘) *jāḷe* जाळे

Wed (v∘) *lagna karṇe* लग्न क∘*

Wedding (m∘) *vivāh,* (n∘) *lagna* विवाह, लग्न

Wedge (f∘) *pāchar* पाचर

Wednesday (m∘) *budhvār* बुधवार

Week (m∘) *āṭhavaḍā, haptā* आठवडा, हप्ता

Weekly (adj∘) *sāptāhik* साप्ताहिक

Weep (v∘) *raḍṇe* रडणे

Weigh (v∘) *tolṇe* तोलणे*

Weight (n∘) *vajan,* (m∘) *bhār* वजन, भार

Weird (adj∘) *vilakṣhaṇ* विलक्षण

Welcome (n∘) *svāgat* स्वागत्

Welfare (n∘) *kalyāṇ* कल्याण

Well (adj∘) *chhān* छान; (f∘) *vihīr* विहीर

Were (pron∘) *hote, hotyā* होते, होत्या

West (f∘) *paśchim* पश्चिम

Western (adj∘) *pāśchātya* पाश्चात्य

Wet (adj∘) *olā* ओला

Wharf (m∘) *ghaṭ* घाट

What (pron∘) *kāy* काय?

What else (adv∘) *aṇkhī kāy?* आणखी काय?

Whatever (pron∘) *je kāhī* जे काही

Whatsoever (adj∘) *kāhī hī* काही ही

Wheat (m∘) *gahū* गहू

Wheel (n∘) *chāk* चाक

When (adv∘) *jevhā* जेव्हा

When? (adv∘) *kevā* केव्हा?

Whence (adv∘) *jithūn* जिथून

Whenever (adv∘) *kevhāhi* केव्हाहि

Where (adv∘) *jithe* जिथे

Where? (adv∘) *kuṭhe? koṭhe?* कुठे, कोठे?

Whereas (conj∘) *jyā arthī* ज्या अर्थी

Wherefore (adv∘) *kā̐? kā̐* कां

Wherever (adv∘) *jithe kuṭhe* जिथे कुठे

Whether (conj∘) *ki* कि

Which (pron∘) *koṇatā?* कोणता?

Whichever (pron∘) *koṇatā hī* कोणता ही

While (conj∘) *toparyant* तोपर्यंत

Whim (f∘) *sanak, lahar* सनक, लहर

Whimper (v∘) *ṭhuṇakṇe, kirkirṇe* ठुणकणे, किरकि∘

Whimsical (adj∘) *laharī* लहरी

Whip (m∘) *chābuk* चाबुक; (v∘) *chābuk mārṇe* चाबुक मारणे*

Whirl (m∘) *bhovarā* भोवरा

adj∘ = Adjective, adv∘ = Adverb; *conj.* = Conjunction, f∘ = Feminine gender, *ind.* = Indeclinable, m∘ = Masculine gender, n∘ = Neuter gender, pl∘ = Plural

Whisper (v∘) *kujbujṇe* कुजबुजणे

Whistle (f∘) *śhiṭṭī, śhiṭī* शिट्टी, शिटी; (v∘) *śhiṭī* शिटी मारणे*

White (adj∘) *pāṇḍharā* पांढरा

Who (pron∘) *koṇ* कोण?

Whoever (pron∘) *jo koṇī* जो कोणी

Whole (adj∘) *pūrā, pūrṇa* पूरा, पूर्ण

Wholesale (adj∘) *ṭhok* ठोक

Wholly (adv∘) *sarvaśhaḥ* सर्वश:

Why (adv∘) *kā̃* कां?

Wicked (adj∘) *duṣhṭa* दुष्ट

Wide (adj∘) *rund, viśhāl* रुंद, विशाल

Widow (f∘) *vidhvā* विधवा

Widower (m∘) *vidhur* विधुर

Width (adj∘) *rundī* रुंदी

Wife (f∘) *patnī* पत्नी

Wild (adj∘) *jaṅglī* जंगली

Will (f∘) *icchhā, khuśhī* इच्छा, खुशी

Willingly (adv∘) *khuśhīne* खुशीने

Willy (adj∘) *chalākh* चलाख

Wilt (v∘) *komejṇe* कोमेजणे

Win (v∘) *jinkṇe* जिंकणे

Wind (f∘) *havā,* (m∘) *vārā* हवा, वारा

Window (f∘) *khiḍakī* खिडकी

Windy (adj∘) *vādaḷī* वादळी

Wine (f∘) *madirā* मदिरा

Wing (n∘) *paṅkh* पंख

Wink (f∘) *palak, nimiṣh* पलक, निमिष

Winner (adj∘) *vijetā* विजेता

Winter (m∘) *hivāḷā* हिवाळा

Wipe (v∘) *pusṇe* पुसणे*

Wire (f∘) *tār* तार

Wisdom (n∘) *dnyān, śhāṇpaṇ* ज्ञान, शहाणपण

Wise (adj∘) *dnyānī, śhāhṇā* ज्ञानी, शहाणा

Wish (f∘) *icchhā* इच्छा; (v∘) *chāhaṇe* चाहणे*

Witch (f∘) *cheṭkī* चेटकी

With (prep∘) *ne, sah* ने, सह

Withdraw (v∘) *kāḍhṇe* काढणे*

Within (adv∘) *ā̃t* आंत

Withold (v∘) *rokṇe* रोकणे*

Without (adv∘) *viṇā śhivāy* विना, शिवाय

Withstand (v∘) *sahan karṇe* सहन क∘

Witness (f∘) *sākṣhī* साक्षी

Wizard (m∘) *cheṭkyā* चेटक्या

Wobble (v∘) *ḍulṇe* डुलणे

Woe (f∘) *pīḍā* पीडा

Wok (f∘) *kaḍhaī* कढई

Wolf (m∘) *lāṇḍgā* लांडगा

Woman (f∘) *strī, nārī* स्त्री, नारी

Womb (n∘) *garbhāśhay* गर्भाशय

Wonder (n∘) *āśhcharya* आश्चर्य

Wood (n∘) *lākūḍ* लाकूड

Woodpecker (m∘) *sutār* सुतार

Wool (f∘) *lokarn* लोकर;

Work (n∘) *kām* काम; (v∘) *kām karṇe* काम क∘*

Worker (m∘) *śhramik, majūr* श्रमिक, मजूर

World (n∘) *jag* जग

Worm (m∘) *kīḍā* कीडा

Worry (f∘) *chintā* चिंता; (v∘) *chintā karṇe* चिंता क∘*

Worse (adj∘) *vāīṭ* वाईट

Worship (f∘) *pūjā* पूजा; (v∘) *pūjā karaṇe* पूजा क∘*

Worst (adj∘) *fār vāīṭ* फार वाईट

Worthy (adj∘) *yodnya* योग्य

Wound (f∘) *jakhm,* (m∘) *ghāv* जखम, घाव

Wrangle (m∘) *jhagḍā* झगडा

Wrap (v∘) *lapeṭṇe* लपेटणे*

Wrath, anger (m∘) *roṣh* रोष

Wreath (m∘) *hār* हार

Wreñch (m∘) *pānā* पाना

Wrestle (v∘) *laḍhṇe* लढणे

Wrestler (m∘) *pahelwān* पहेलवान

Wrestling (f∘) *kustī* कुस्ती

Wretched (adj∘) *abhāgā* अभागा

Wriggle (v∘) *chhaṭpaṭṇe* छटपटणे

Wrinkle (f∘) *surkutī* सुरकुती

Wrist (n∘) *mangaṭ* मनगट

Write (v∘) *lihīṇe* लिहीणे*

Writer (m∘) *lekhak* लेखक

Writing (m∘) *lekh* लेख

Wrong (adj∘) *chūk* चूक

Wrongdoing (m∘) *anyāy* अन्याय

Wrought (adj∘) *krut, ghaṭit* कृत, घटित

Y

Yam (n∘) *kand* कन्द

Yard, 3ft. (m∘) *gaj* गज; court (n∘) *āṅgaṇ* आंगण

Yarn (m∘) *dhāgā, sūt* धागा, सूत

Yawn (f∘) *jāmbhāī* जांभाई

Year (n∘) *varṣh* वर्ष

Yeast (f∘) *āmb* आंब

Yellow (adj∘) *pivḷā* पिवळा

Yelp (v∘) *bhunkṇe* भुंकणे

Yesterday (m∘) *kāl* काल

Yet (adv∘) *adyāp* अद्याप

Yogurt (n∘) *dahī* दही

Yoke (n∘) *jū* जू

Yolk (n∘) *balak* बलक

Yonder (adv∘) *tikḍe* तिकडे

You (pron∘) *tū, tumhī, āpaṇ* तू, तुम्ही, आपण

Young (adj∘) *taruṇ* तरुण

Your (pron∘) *tujhā, tumchā, āpalā* तुझा, तुमचा, आपला

Your honour (m∘) *śhrīmān,* (f∘) *śhrīmatī* श्रीमान्, श्रीमती

Youth (m∘) *yuvak,* (f∘) *yuvatī* युवक, युवती

Z

Zebra (m∘) *gorkhar* गोरखर

Zero (adj∘) *śhūnya* शून्य

Zest (m∘) *ras* रस

Zigzag (adj∘) *teḍhā-meḍhā, nāgmoḍī* तेढा–मेढा, नागमोडी

Zink (n∘) *jasta* जस्त

Zone (m∘) *vibhāg* विभाग

Zoo (n∘) *praṇīsangrahālay* प्राणीसंग्रहालय

Zoology (n∘) *prāṇīśhāstra* प्राणीशास्त्र

Zucchini (n∘) *doḍke* दोडके

adj∘ = Adjective, adv∘ = Adverb; *conj.* = Conjunction, f∘ = Feminine gender, *ind.* = Indeclinable, m∘ = Masculine gender, n∘ = Neuter gender, pl∘ = Plural

www.ingramcontent.com/pod-product-compliance
Lightning Source LLC
Chambersburg PA
CBHW081002140626
46546CB00018B/2932
9781989416983